M000267553

Celebrations!

2,735 Holidays and Events
with
1,264 Activities to Remember Them!

by Marjorie Frank

Designed and Illustrated
by Kathleen Bullock

Incentive Publications, Inc.
Nashville, Tennessee

Illustrated by Kathleen Bullock
Cover by Geoffrey Brittingham
Edited by Jill Norris

ISBN 978-0-86530-032-3

Copyright ©2007 by Incentive Publications, Inc., Nashville, TN. All rights reserved. No part of this publication may be reproduced, stored in a retrieval system, or transmitted in any form or by any means (electronic, mechanical, photocopying, recording, or otherwise) without written permission from Incentive Publications, Inc.

1   2   3   4   5   6   7   8   9   10   10   09   08   07

PRINTED IN THE UNITED STATES OF AMERICA
www.incentivepublications.com

Contents

ALL KINDS OF HOLIDAYS TO CELEBRATE . . .

. . . ordinary and extraordinary, traditional and wacky, historical and hysterical!

You've probably celebrated the usual holidays, such as **Valentine's Day**, **Mother's Day**, **Halloween**, **Fourth of July**, **Thanksgiving**, and the major holidays of your country or religion.

Most likely, you've also paid some attention to other days for memory or celebration, such as **Veteran's Day**, **Earth Day**, **President's Day**, **Poetry Week**, **the first day of spring**, or **Columbus Day**.

But . . . when have you remembered **Vitamin C Discovery Day**, **Pet Peeve Week**, **Cheese Pizza Day**, **Bubble Wrap Appreciation Day**, **Keep Your Shoelaces Tied Month**, or **Bubblegum Week**?

Have you ever stopped to appreciate air conditioning on **Air Conditioning Appreciation Day**, or thought about cows on **Cow Appreciation Day**, or considered coral reefs during **Coral Reef Awareness Week**? Did you eat baked beans in **Baked Bean Month** or clean your closet during **Clean Your Closet Week**? Have you fought boredom during **Anti-Boredom Month**? Did you give any gifts during **Anonymous Giving Week**? Have you listened to jazz every day during **Jazz Month** or used **Moldy Cheese Day** to investigate why cheese molds?

There are hundreds of occasions that you can have fun celebrating . . . if you know about them! Besides having fun, you can learn things you didn't know before. Your knowledge about science and history are broadened when you commemorate the discovery of the X-ray or neon, the introduction of the Greyhound bus, the founding of the FBI, the debut of Mickey Mouse, the first parachute jump, or the invention of the shopping cart. In addition, when you have a list of important accomplishments and events, you can remember and honor the people who made history—people such as Albert Einstein, Elizabeth Blackwell, writers of your country's Constitution, victims of the Holocaust, cancer survivors, or the *Columbia* Space Shuttle astronauts.

Pickle Time Week Feb.

Bad Hair Day Dec. 6

This book presents several occasions worth remembering for every month, week, and day of the year.

Meow? Answer Your Cat's Questions Day Jan. 22

Freckle Pride Day Nov. 27

Cluck, Cluck! Dance Like a Chicken Day May 14

Good News! X-Ray discovered Nov. 8

It's Wrinkled Raincoat Day Sept. 16 splish, splash

Thank goodness for Parade Day Nov. 9

The Months' Names

January from *Janus*—the Roman god of doorways and beginnings

February from *Februa*—the Roman festival of purification

March from *Mars*—the Roman god of war

April from Latin *aperire* meaning "to open"

May from *Maia*—the goddess of spring

June from *Juno*—queen of the heavens and gods

July named for Julius Caesar

August named for Augustus Caesar

September from Latin *septum* meaning "seven"

October from Latin *octo* meaning "eight"

November from Latin *nove* meaning "nine"

December from Latin *decim* meaning "ten"

It must have been a dog that thought up **Get Out of The Doghouse Day** in July.

What you'll find in this book . . .

Celebrations! is the **ultimate calendar book** of official and unofficial holidays, remembrance days, historical events, inventions, discoveries, firsts and lasts, birthdays, and accomplishments.

The book has a chapter for each of the twelve months. Each chapter includes month-long celebrations, weeklong celebrations, and dates that vary—with great ideas for remembering special months, weeks, and days. Then, for each day, there is a list of the holidays, birthdays, and other events. There is not enough space to give an activity for each of the 2,735 different calendar events. So, one event is featured for each day. In addition, there are brief ideas for honoring other events.

Shiver me timbers . . .

Talk Like A Pirate Day (Sept. 19) was the creation of two friends who had a lot of fun talking like pirates!

These pages offer all kinds of activities. There are instructions for craft projects and art adventures. There are investigations to pursue, websites to examine, problems and brainteasers to solve, math challenges, and plenty of intriguing things to write or describe. Recipes are sprinkled throughout the book. You will be surprised by new and fascinating information. The activities and experiences will stretch your mind and spark your imagination—and keep you busy ALL YEAR LONG!

How does a holiday get to be a holiday?

- Some holidays are adopted and approved by legislation of a government *(Veterans Day, Presidents' Day, Thanksgiving)*.

- Other commemorative events are set by proclamation of the highest government official *(Mother's Day, American Heart Month)*.

- The United Nations or state governments also proclaim holidays *(UNICEF Day or Texas Wildflower Day)*.

- Organizations sponsor commemorative holidays *(Georgia Pecan Month or Deaf Awareness Week)*.

- Some "holidays" are actually the anniversaries of historical events such as wars, natural disasters, "firsts," inventions, openings or closings, discoveries, or birthdays.

- Different churches or religions set dates for religious observances.

- **And then** there are all those other holidays! There are no rules for these. Anybody can start a holiday. All you need is a way to describe the holiday and spread the news.

How to Use this Book . . .

Use it as you need it, depending on the setting, age group, and time you have. There are so many different ways . . .

- At the beginning of the month, review all the holidays and events listed for the month, weeks, dates that vary, and days. Plan for the events and special days that you wish to celebrate during the month.

- Grab the book on any day. Find today's date. Do ONE of the suggested activities for a month, week, or day.

- Do ALL of the suggested activities for a date.

- Look up ALL the events listed for a date. Find out something about each one of them.

- Choose a holiday that is NOT featured. Do some extensive research on it and think of ideas for celebrating.

- Start with an activity from the book or choose one holiday name. Brainstorm enough ideas to fill a whole class period, school day, Saturday, evening, or other time period.

On Lost Sock Memorial Day, you could . . .

- Make sock puppets.
- Make cut-out sock cookies.
- Write letters to missing socks.
- Design a home for lost socks.
- Write directions lost socks can follow to get home.
- Compare prices of socks at different stores.
- Fill socks with goodies to leave on doorsteps for gifts.
- Write a sock biography.
- Find out where and how socks are made.
- Do probability experiments with socks.
- Design special socks for different characters.

Those Tricky Dates

It's easy to pin down the dates for some events. There is no question about official holidays or birthdays. An event such the Pearl Harbor attack clearly happened on one specific day. But dates for some events vary. The date for Father's Day, for instance, changes. It is on the third Sunday in June.

Some dates are even harder to identify. There are several Chocolate Days. Different organizations, states, or regions celebrate the same thing at different times. There are many similar holidays. Ice Cream gets celebrated in numerous ways on numerous days. There are many Peace Days (some national, some international) and many Good Neighbor Days with slightly different names. There is a Donut Day (November 4) and there are Donut Days (in June). Patriots Day is April 19 and Patriot Day is September 11.

Blame Someone Else Day shows up somewhere in the world almost every month. No Homework Day is celebrated at least twice during the year. Some sources list August 4 as Chocolate Chip Day. Other sources give the date as May 15. There are sources that definitely place the first U.S. train robbery in Indiana on October 6, 1866. Other sources claim the first train robbery in the U.S. occurred in Ohio on May 5, 1865.

We have made every effort to verify dates. Be aware that an event date can change from year to year or can be celebrated on a different day in your area. Check the date for the current year, and don't worry if you can't pin it down. The idea is to enjoy holidays and remember events. If the date is not quite right, you can honor the occasion anyway. In some cases, where there is more than one date, we have even suggested celebrating both times!

There's a Rattlesnake Roundup Day in January and a Rattlesnake Derby in April.

Clashing Clothes Day is always the fourth Thursday in January.

And really, shouldn't every day be Save a Spider Day?

January

1
- Z Day*
- New Year's Day*
- Polar Bear Swim Day*
- Bonza Bottler Day
- New Year's Dishonor List*
- First "Baby Boomer" Born*
- Euro Introduced*
- Ellis Island Immigration Station Opened (1892)*
- Tournament of Roses Parade & Rose Bowl Game
  Birthdays: Paul Revere*, Betsy Ross*

2
- Kakizome Festival*
- Happy "Mew" Year for Cats Day*
- National Cream Puff Day
- Raising of 1st U.S. Flag
- Launch of *Luna I*
  Birthdays: Georgia

3
- Drinking Straw Patented*
- Congress Assembles*
- Festival of Sleep Day
- Chocolate-Covered Cherry Day
- Hobbit Day
- March of Dimes Formed
  Birthdays: Lucretia Coffin Mott, John R.R. Tolkien, Alaska*

4
- Trivia Day*
- First Successful Appendectomy*
- Earth at Perihelion*
- Dimpled Chad Day*
- National Spaghetti Day
- Great Fruitcake Toss
- First Pop Music Chart
  Birthdays: Sir Isaac Newton, Louis Braille, Elizabeth Seton, Utah

5
- National Whipped Cream Day*
- Twelfth Night
- First Woman Governor
- President Harry Truman's "Fair Deal"

6
- National Smith Day*
- Birthday of Sherlock Holmes*
- Organize Your Home Day*
- Bean Day
- National Shortbread Day*
- Epiphany Day or Twelfth Day*
- Three Kings' Day (Mexico)
- First Around-the-World Commercial Flight
  Birthdays: Joan of Arc, Jedediah Smith*, Captain John Smith*, Carl Sandburg, New Mexico

7
- Old Rock Day*
- Typewriter Day*
- I'm Not Going to Take It Anymore Day*
- First Transatlantic Phoning*
  Birthdays: Millard Fillmore

8
- Rock 'n' Roll Day*
- Earth's Rotation Proved*
- National English Toffee Day*
- National Bubble Bath Day*
- First Computer Patented
- Eat Something Raw Day
- National Show and Tell Day at Work
- Battle of New Orleans
  Birthdays: Elvis Presley*, Stephen Hawking

9
- Aviation in America Day*
- National Static Electricity Day*
- National Apricot Day
  Birthdays: Joan Baez, Richard Nixon, Connecticut

10
- Peculiar People Day*
- Women's Suffrage Amendment*
- "Where's the Beef?" Day*
- Volunteer Fireman's Day
- First Meeting of UN General Assembly
- Oil Discovered in Texas

11
- Secret Pal Day*
- International Thank You Day
- National Milk Day
- Cigarettes Declared Harmful
  Birthdays: Alexander Hamilton, John A. MacDonald, Jean Chretien

12
- Amelia Earhart's Pacific Flight
- First Museum in U.S.
- National Marzipan Day
- First Elected Woman Senator
  Birthdays: Charles Perrault*, John Hancock, Jack London

13
- Stephen Foster Memorial Day*
- Make Your Dreams Come True Day*
- Introduction of Frisbee
- National Clean Off Your Desk Day

14
- National Hot Pastrami Sandwich Day*
- Signing of the *Kremlin Accords*ate
- National Dress Up Your Pet Day
- Ratification Day*
- *Soyuz 4*

15
- National Humanitarian Day*
- National Strawberry Ice Cream Day*
- Elementary School Teacher Day*
- National Fresh-Squeezed Juice Day
- Pentagon Completed
- First Super Bowl
  Birthdays: Dr. Martin Luther King, Jr.

16
- International Hot & Spicy Food Day*
- National Nothing Day
- National Fig Newton Day
- National Religious Freedom Day
- 18th Amendment
- Persian Gulf War

17
- Pig Day
- Cable Car First Patented
- First Nuclear Submarine Voyage
- Major Earthquake in Southern California
- Major Earthquake in Japan
  Birthdays: Ben Franklin*, Muhammad Ali*

For each starred holiday, you will find one or more activities on pages 12–35.*

18
- Lewis & Clark Expedition Re-created*
- Pooh Day
- Maintenance Day
- Eagle Days (18–19)
  Birthdays: A. A. Milne

19
- Tin Can Patented*
- Archery Day*
- National Penguin Awareness Day
- Confederate Heroes Day
- Indira Gandhi Became India's Prime Minister
  Birthdays: Robert E. Lee, Edgar Allan Poe*, Paul Cézanne

20
- Cheese Day*
- U.S. Presidential Inauguration Day*
- Vanilla Milkshake Day
- National Buttercrunch Day
- U.S. Iran Hostages Freed
  Birthdays: George Burns, Buzz Aldrin

21
- Gimmicks Day*
- Squirrel Appreciation Day*
- Granola Bar Day*
- First Flight of *Concorde*
- National Hugging Day
  Birthdays: Thomas "Stonewall" Jackson

22
- Answer Your Cat's Questions Day*
- Celebration of Life Day
- Come in From the Cold Day
- National Blonde Brownie Day
- National Compliment Day

23
- Measure Your Feet Day*
- National Handwriting Day*
- National Pie Day
- 24th Amendment
- First Female M.D. in U.S.
  Birthdays: Edouard Manet

24
- National Peanut Butter Day*
- Just Do It Day*
- Eskimo Pie Patent Day*
- Gold Discovered in California

25
- Opposite Day*
- Weather Day
- A Room of One's Own Day
- Nelly Bly's Around-the-World Trip
- First Winter Olympics
- First Transcontinental Flight
- Apple Macintosh Computer Debut

26
- Dental Drill Patented *
- Australia Day*
- National Peanut Brittle Day
  Birthdays: Michigan

27
- Electric Light Bulb Patented*
- National Chocolate Cake Day
- Remembrance of Victims of Nazism
- *Apollo I* Fire
- Vietnam Peace Agreement
  Birthdays: Wolfgang Mozart, Lewis Carroll

28
- National Kazoo Day*
- Bubble Wrap Appreciation Day*
- U.S. Great Seal Approved*
- Christa McAuliffe Day
- *Challenger* Space Shuttle Explosion
- National Blueberry Pancake Day

29
- National Rattlesnake Roundup Day*
- National Puzzle Day*
- American League Baseball Organized*
- National Corn Chip Day
  Birthdays: John D. Rockefeller, Jr., William McKinley, Kansas

30
- Escape Day*
- National Croissant Day*
- National Inane Answering Message Day
  Birthdays: Franklin Delano Roosevelt, Barbara Tuchman

31
- National Popcorn Day*
- Inspire Your Heart with Art Day*
- National Backwards Day
- Tape It Day
- First Social Security Check
- *Explorer I*
- *Luna 9*
  Birthdays: Jackie Robinson

Month-long Celebrations
Bald Eagle Watch Month*
Bread Machine Baking Month*
Celebrate the Past Month*
Celebration of Life Month*
Clean Up Your Computer Month
Crime Stoppers' Month
Family Fit Lifestyle Month
Get Over It! Month*
Hot Tea Month*
International Creativity Month*
It's OK to Be Different Month*
Love Yourself Month*
March of Dimes Birth Defects Prevention Month
National Book Month*
National Eye Care Month*
National Hi-Tech Month
National Hobby Month*
National Letter-Writing Month*
National Mentoring Month
National Poverty in America Awareness Month*
National Soup Month*
National Staying Healthy Month
National Thank You Month*
Oatmeal Month*
Personal Self-Defense Month*
Prune Breakfast Month*
Reaching Your Potential Month
Volunteer Blood Donor Month*
Whale-Watching Month*

January was named in honor of the Roman god, Janus. Janus was the god of doorways, entrances, portals, and beginnings.
Janus has two faces, one looking to the future, the other looking at the past.
January Flower: carnation
January Birthstone: garnet

Weekly Celebrations

First Week: Braille Literacy Week*

Second Week: Universal Letter-Writing Week*, Someday We'll Laugh About This Week*, School Crossing Guard Week*, National Bowling Week*, National Pizza Week*, National Book Week

Third Week: National Creative Frugality Week*, National Fresh Squeezed Juice Days*

Fourth Week: Mozart Week*, National Meat Week*

Dates That Vary: Hat Day; Martin Luther King, Jr. Day; Clashing Clothes Day

11

January's Month-long Celebrations

International Creativity Month

Creativity is the ability to create or produce things—generally things that are original, imaginative, or in some other way beyond the ordinary. There are thousands of ways to stretch and express your creativity. For starters, try one of these challenges.

Creativity Challenges

On, off, on, off, on....

- Create (or describe) an invention that would allow you to turn the overhead light in your bedroom on and off without getting out of bed.
- Draw or trace 50 circles on drawing paper. Turn each circle into something different. (For example: a bicycle wheel, trash can lid, etc.)
- Think of 25 uses for a screwdriver other than driving screws. Write or illustrate these ideas.
- Make up 20 different names for a dentist or window washer.
- Write down the names of 20 foods. Tell how each of these foods is like a person you know.
- Start with the tune of a simple song, such as "Row, Row, Row Your Boat." Write new words to help you remember math facts.
- Explain one freedom from the Bill of Rights using only movements of your body (no words.)

Universal Letter-Writing Month

Letters are a great way to give opinions, ask questions, and express yourself. Think about something you'd like to know, something you want to get off your chest, something you'd like to change, or something you wish someone else would know or believe. Figure out who should get a letter that expresses or asks each of the above. (It can be anyone, anywhere in the world—not necessarily someone you know.) Find the address before you write the letter.

National Hobby Month

Everyone needs a hobby. If you don't have one—get one! Gather a list of some interesting and unusual hobbies. Track down some books of hobbies in your library, or visit a good hobby site on the Internet.

I need a hobby. Maybe I should start a collection.

Curious Collections

gum wrappers
buttons
license plates
light bulbs
postcards
hair
jet fighter planes
mousetraps
airsickness bags
bandages
antique parking
 meters
clover leafs
piggy banks

Get a Hobby!

astronomy	people watching	quilting
train spotting	woodcarving	bird-watching
dumpster diving	butterfly counting	junk sculpture
chemistry	news watching	computer programming
bus spotting	puzzles	weather forecasting
cooking	robots	hiking
kite flying	spelunking	dominoes
writing poetry	models	music

Whale-Watching Month

• Learn about good locations for whale-watching. Make a world map that shows where whales can be spotted.

• Make an illustrated "Guide to Whales" showing different kinds of whales. Include facts and statistics such as location, size, and weight.

• Create a life-sized whale to hang from your ceiling. Just draw the outline of your favorite whale on mural paper. Cut two identical shapes. Staple them together, leaving a large opening at the head and tail. Paint both sides of the whale. When it dries, staple the sides of the whale together, leaving the head and tail open. Stuff the whale with tissue paper. Staple the openings shut.

Bread Machine Baking Month

• Borrow a bread machine to make some bread in your home or classroom. Find a good recipe for the bread machine. Enjoy the fresh bread with your Stone Soup (below).

• Try this recipe for Chocolate Marble Bread.

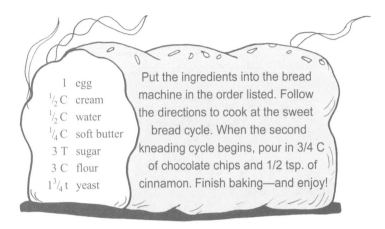

1 egg
$\frac{1}{2}$ C cream
$\frac{1}{2}$ C water
$\frac{1}{4}$ C soft butter
3 T sugar
3 C flour
$1\frac{3}{4}$ t yeast

Put the ingredients into the bread machine in the order listed. Follow the directions to cook at the sweet bread cycle. When the second kneading cycle begins, pour in 3/4 C of chocolate chips and 1/2 tsp. of cinnamon. Finish baking—and enjoy!

National Soup Month

• Read the folk tale *Stone Soup*. Find some smooth stones and clean them by boiling them. Get everyone in your group to contribute a vegetable. Clean them, place them in water with the clean stones, add broth is you wish, and cook up the soup for a tasty lunch.

• Gather favorite soup recipes into a "Good Soup Cookbook." Use your computer skills to create the book; then sell it as a fundraiser or give it away to friends, neighbors, or relatives.

• Gather several jokes that begin, "Waiter, there's a fly in my soup!" Find them in books or on the Internet. Write some of your own. Collect them into an illustrated joke book.

Hot Tea Month

- Learn about tea ceremonies around the world. Find out where and how tea is used for special events. Plan your own tea event. Gather as many different kinds of tea as you can find. Brew pots of different kinds, and get friends to sample the teas. Prepare a "Tea Rating Sheet" where they can compare, describe, and rate different teas.

- Replace the little paper tags on several teabags with brightly colored paper. On the tea-papers, write original tongue twisters (with T words), proverbs, alliterative phrases (with T), phrases of advice or wisdom, or bits of trivia about tea.

Oatmeal Month

- Get a box of dry oatmeal. Read the label to learn about its nutritional value.

- Make up a pan of oatmeal. Divide it into small dishes and try adding different things for flavor (for instance: brown sugar, maple syrup, yogurt, raisins, dried cranberries, strawberries, chunks of banana, pretzels, gumdrops, etc.). What is your favorite oatmeal concoction?

- Make oatmeal cookies. Enjoy a cookie with your favorite hot tea.

National Thank You Month

- Learn how to say "thank you" in ten different languages.

- Think of things you've been given that are not actual material "gifts." Write three different notes thanking the people who gave you these gifts.

- Think of many different ways that people say "thank you" in English. Make a list.

14

National Book Month

- Write a book this month. Start an alphabet book on January 1. Write and illustrate words or sentences that begin with the letter A. On January 2–26, write and illustrate another alphabet page each day. Use the last few days of the month to make covers, bind, and share the book.

- Choose a favorite book of fiction or poetry. Choose five lines, sentences, or short excerpts that you can read aloud to show-off the book.

- Choose a favorite nonfiction book. Write ten questions that will be answered when someone reads this book.

Bald Eagle Watch Month

- Learn about the history of the bald eagle. Find out why it became a symbol for the United States.

- Memorize the poem "The Eagle" by Alfred Lloyd Tennyson. Write your own eagle poem.

- Find some good pictures of bald eagles. Then use black paper to create a large silhouette of a bald eagle with its wings spread. Hang this on a wall, in a window, or from your ceiling.

Celebration of Life Month

- January marks a new beginning, a new year, a new phase of life, new possibilities, and new hopes. Make a "Possibility Poster" showing off positive things that can happen in the new year.

- Use a camera to capture photos that show meaningful moments in life. Combine the pictures with captions into a special celebratory collection. Title it "Got Life!"

Celebrate the Past Month

- Find pictures of yourself at different ages and in different situations. Add explanations or descriptions and arrange them into a photo-history of your own past.

- Get some large balloons. Think of past events worth celebrating. (Choose events concerning your family, yourself, your town, your school, your state, your country, and the world.) Write the names and dates of the events on balloons. Then blow up all the balloons and hang them around the room.

Get Over It! Month

- What do you need to get over? Make a list of ten things that bother you—things you'd be better off not stewing about. Choose one thing from your list. Get together with some friends and role-play a way to get over it.

- Create a comic-style cartoon strip showing a "story" about someone getting over something.

Prune Breakfast Month

- What, exactly, is a prune? Find out! Find out why prunes are good for you, too.

- Have a *Prune Party*. Track down some recipes that use prunes. Try one. Sample whole prunes, pureed prunes, chopped prunes, prune juice, prune smoothies, and prune cookies.

- After you've sampled some prunes, finish the prune similes, comparisons, and other observations. (See ideas in the box.)

A prune is as wrinkled as _____.

A prune in my mouth feels as _____ as _____.

Eating a prune is like _____.

The sound of someone chewing a prune reminds me of _____.

I'd rather eat prunes than _____.

_____ (a person) is like a prune because _____.

A bowlful of prunes is more valuable than _____.

The important thing about prunes is _____.

Never give a prune to _____.

Never eat a prune before _____.

Happy Prune Day!

Volunteer Blood Donor Month

- Track down information about blood types. Make a poster that explains what you learn about donating and receiving blood.

- Get some practice in gathering and displaying statistics. Try to find 100 people who know their blood types. Make a tally sheet of the numbers for each type. Then turn the data into a bar graph.

National Eye Care Month

- This is the month to pay special attention to your eyes. Learn about the structure of the eye and how it works to help you see.

- Visit an eye doctor's office or the Internet to learn some rules of eye care.

- Have fun with idioms that include the eye. Think of all the expressions and phrases you can. See if you can find enough to fill a "graffiti mural." Choose some of the expressions to illustrate.

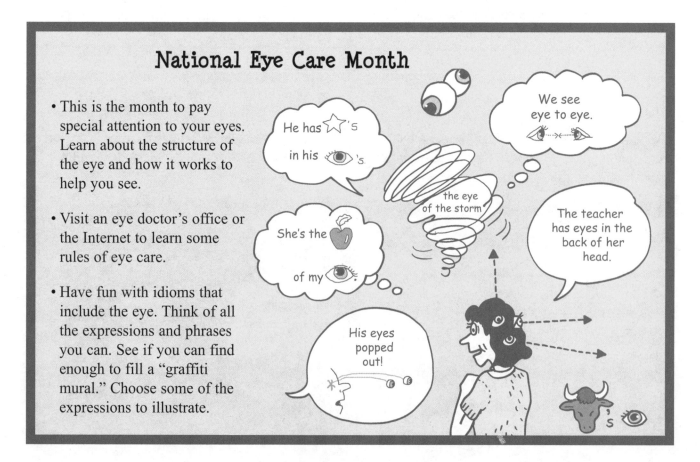

Personal Self-Defense Month

- Define and describe *martial arts*. Find some books or other sources that will help you learn the difference between *karate, tae kwando, judo,* and *aikido*.

- Find books, videos, or martial artists that will help you learn to demonstrate a pose or movement from each form of martial arts.

It's OK to Be Different Month

- Arrange a gathering of people. Plan ahead to come to the gathering prepared to highlight differences—in dress, appearance, hobbies, behaviors, ideas, and preferences. Celebrate differences in as many ways as you can.

- Get a large piece of mural paper. Make a giant poster on which you write as many differences as you can. Think of an advantage or gift represented by each difference.

National Poverty in America Awareness Month

- It is estimated that 33 million Americans live below the poverty level. Find out what the current poverty level is in America.

- Find three websites that give information about poverty. Discuss what citizens can do about this problem.

Love Yourself Month

- Write a love letter to yourself. Tell yourself how valuable and great you are. Be specific about some of the reasons you deserve love. Mail it to yourself!

- Show off your name with some kind of name art. Make a wild design with your signature, your initials, or any part of your name. Make a poster, banner, billboard, button, mobile, T-shirt, piece of jewelry, hat, mural, key chain, or bumper sticker.

See page 10 for other month-long holidays to celebrate.

Special Weeks in January

First Week

Translate this Braille sentence. What does it say?

Braille Literacy Week

• Research the life story of Louis Braille. Learn how Braille writing was developed.

• Find the Braille alphabet in a book or on the Internet. Learn to write your name and your favorite saying in Braille.

Second Week

Universal Letter-Writing Week

Try to write a letter every day during this week. Make each a different kind of letter. Think universally! Send the letters all over the universe. (Try for all seven continents, including Antarctica. Try to send a letter to the International Space Station.)

School Crossing Guard Week

• Surprise a crossing guard with a thank-you treat, note, gift certificate, flowers, special deed, or party.

• Design a uniform, hat, armband, or outfit for a school crossing guard.

National Bowling Week

• Learn the rules for the game of bowling. Find out how bowling is scored. Then figure out the score of each player whose game is described here. Who won the game? Create more bowling math problems.

Someday We'll Laugh About This Week

• Think of something that has happened that is not funny now, but which you might laugh about later. Prepare a skit about the event.

• Get in a circle and tell tales about the most embarrassing thing that has ever happened to you. Can you laugh about it now? When will you be able to laugh about it?

Ha ha!
Tee hee!
Ho ho!

• Design your own bowling ball. Use a cheap plastic or rubber ball and permanent markers to do the job!

National Pizza Week

• Do pizza geography! Make a pizza map in the shape of a state or continent. Use pepperoni and veggies to mark important spots. Then eat the pizza.

• Find out the nutritional makeup of different pizzas: the calories, carbohydrates, protein, fats, etc. Figure out how to make a healthy pizza.

Oh how I love the second week in January!

STAN

Frame	Pins
1	4, 4
2	0, 9
3	3, 7
4	5
5	5
6	2, 1
7	2, 8
8	9, 0
9	5
10	5, 1, 3

DAN

Frame	Pins
1	5
2	8, 2
3	6, 3
4	5
5	1, 4
6	9, 0
7	6, 4
8	8, 2
9	5
10	7, 3, 5

National Fresh-Squeezed Juice Day

• Gather oranges, lemons, grapefruits, and other juicy fruits or vegetables. Borrow a juicer or squeezer, and mix up your own fresh juice concoctions. Write original recipes for juice mixtures or smoothies.

• Take a survey around your school or neighborhood to find out what percentage of the people prefer pulp to no-pulp in their orange juice. Make a graph to show the results.

• Use some of your fruits and vegetables to make "flavorful" prints. Use the printed paper or cloth to decorate walls, cover books, or wrap presents!

Cut slices of fruits or vegetables and dry them with a paper towel. Dip the slices in ink or paint. Press them lightly onto paper or cloth to make interesting prints.

National Creative Frugality Week

Get creative about ways to save money. Make your own list of ways you can be frugal. Put your creative frugality ideas together with those of other people and publish an illustrated *Manual for Creative Frugality*. Practice using the ideas. Report back to your class on how well you succeeded at being frugal.

Mozart Week

• Find out about the life of Wolfgang Amadeus Mozart, one of the world's great musicians. Where did he live? When did he begin performing? What did he accomplish?

• Listen to some of Mozart's music. Let the music inspire your hands to move across drawing paper with ink, colored chalk, charcoal, or paints. Title your art creation with the same title that names the piece of music.

Get your fresh cooked meat!
Meat's taste can't be beat.
You can shred it, slice it,
Fry it, dice it,
Grill it over heat.

It warms your tummy
Tastes real yummy
It's not too sweet.
Don't wait to eat!

HOT DOGS

National Meat Week

• Create a dictionary of meats (and cuts of meat). Include many kinds. Write a description of each kind.

• Write and present an argument for the position that people should eat meat and the position that people should avoid eating meat. Have audience members "vote" for one or the other argument, based on the strength of the points made.

• Write and perform a rap about eating meat (or NOT eating meat).

See page 11 for other weeklong holidays to celebrate.

The Days of January

Martin Luther King, Jr. Day *(third Monday in January)*

• Find out what law made this a federal holiday. How long has this holiday been celebrated?

• Visit the Martin Luther King Day and the King Center websites for celebration ideas: www.mlkday.com and www.thekingcenter.com.

• Track down some of Dr. King's speeches. You can even hear him speaking on some Internet sites.

• Be able to define *civil disobedience*. Role-play situations of civil disobedience.

• Make a timeline of civil rights activities, laws, and key events in U.S. or world history.

• Read or listen to the "I Have a Dream" speech. Then write a speech, essay, or poem to communicate your own "I Have a Dream" ideas.

Clashing Clothes Day *(fourth Thursday in January)*

• Plan ahead for this day! Choose the most awful, glaring, eye-bothering combination of clothing items you can find in your closet! Wear the outfit to school or some other public place today.

• Get out some drawing paper and become a clothing designer. Sketch and color the most outlandish clashing outfits you can imagine—for people or pets.

Hat Day *(third Friday in January)*

• What else is better to do on this day than to design and make a hat? Don't just stop at one hat! Think of hats for different people (or other creatures) and different occasions.

• Design a hat and then write a character description of the person who would wear the hat.

• Make a list of all the places and occasions for which people wear hats. Turn the list into a *Hat Directory, Hat Encyclopedia,* or *Story of Hats*.

In Honor of Z

Z Day is a chance to celebrate everything **Z**! It's the one chance in a year for **Z** to come first. Let anyone with a **Z** name be first in line. Give a party for **Z** people! Make a list of **Z** words (any words that include **Z**). Use them to write **Z** poems, **Z** advertisements, **Z** books, **Z** recipes, **Z** bumper stickers, **Z** job descriptions, **Z** songs, or dialogues with **Z**. Find some famous **Z**s in world history. Do **Z** art with **Z** designs. Do a **Z** dance. Create a **Z** drama, a **Z** menu, or a **Z** garage sale.

- Z Day*
- New Year's Day*
- Polar Bear Swim Day*
- Bonza Bottler Day*
- New Year's Dishonor List*
- First "Baby Boomer" Born (1946)*
- Euro Introduced for Use (1999)*
- Ellis Island Immigration Station Opened (1892)*
- Tournament of Roses Parade & Rose Bowl Game

Birthdays

1735　Paul Revere*
1752　Betsy Ross*

More Ideas

- Create a polar bear dance, write a tribute to polar bears, and learn how to care for and feed a polar bear.

- Bonza Bottler Day was created by Elaine Fremont in 1985 when she realized there were no special occasions to celebrate one month. Find out what this day is all about. Look for a Bonza Bottler Day each month!

- What is a *baby boomer?* Who was the first one? Find five *baby boomers;* ask them each ten questions.

- Go to a store; find the prices of 20 favorite items. Figure out how much those items would cost in Euros.

- Learn about the *Dishonor List*. Decide on 20 words or phrases to add to the list! Make a *Diary of Dishonorable Phrases*.

- Memorize the poem "The Midnight Ride of Paul Revere" by Henry Wadsworth Longfellow.

- Draw and color all the official versions of the U.S. flag that have existed.

- Interview people to gather a list of New Year's Resolutions they didn't keep.

For each starred* holiday on pages 21–35, you will find at least one celebration activity.

21

- Kakizome Festival in Japan*
- Happy "Mew" Year for Cats Day*
- National Cream Puff Day
- Raising of 1st U.S. Flag by Continental Army *(1776)*
- Launch of *Luna I*—First Spacecraft to Orbit the Sun *(1959, USSR)*

Birthdays

1788   Georgia, 4th state

One More Idea

Write ten "Mew" Year's resolutions for your cat. Write the resolutions as the cat might choose to express them.

Kakizome Creations

Kakizome is the first writing done in the new year. It is a Japanese custom to write haiku and other poems of happiness during the Kakizome Festival. On this day, write at least one poem of happiness or try some Japanese calligraphy. Show off your writing on a Japanese-style fan.

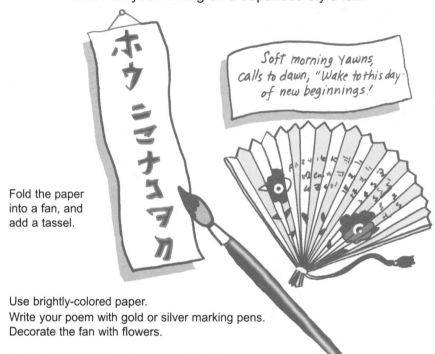

Soft morning yawns, calls to dawn, "Wake to this day of new beginnings!"

Fold the paper into a fan, and add a tassel.

Use brightly-colored paper.
Write your poem with gold or silver marking pens.
Decorate the fan with flowers.

- Drinking Straw Patented *(1888)*
- Congress Assembles*
- Chocolate-Covered Cherry Day
- Hobbit Day
- Festival of Sleep Day
- March of Dimes Formed *(1938)*

Birthdays

1793   Lucretia Coffin Mott
1892   John R.R. Tolkien
1959   Alaska, 49th state*

More Ideas

- Write a job description for a senator and a representative.
- Learn to make "Baked Alaska."

The Versatile Drinking Straw

Use drinking straws in as many ways as you can today. Count them, use them to show fractions, form geometric figures, give a speech describing how they are manufactured, find (and conduct) a science experiment that uses straws, create sculptures with straws and clay, write a mystery about straws, or design a tool that can be made with straws.

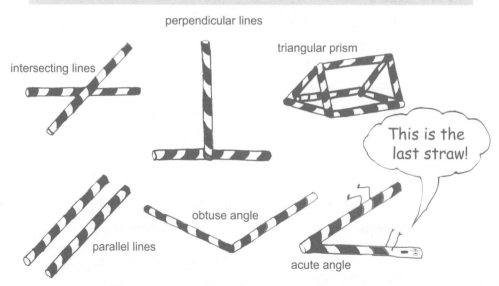

perpendicular lines

triangular prism

intersecting lines

This is the last straw!

obtuse angle

parallel lines

acute angle

Trivia Trail

Spend some time tracking down the most interesting or instructive trivia you can find. Find at least five good trivia books or websites. Then share your favorite bits of trivia by making a trivia trail. Write trivia on sticky notes and "stick" each one to an appropriate place.

Ants don't sleep.

The last U.S. $500 bill was printed in 1969.

A cow gives 200,000 glasses of milk during her lifetime.

In Marshalltown, Iowa, it is against the law for a horse to eat a fire hydrant.

Fingernails grow faster than toenails.

Rats cannot throw up.

Jan. 4th is National Spaghetti Day!

January 4th

- Trivia Day*
- First Successful Appendectomy (1885)*
- Earth at Perihelion*
- Dimpled Chad Day*
- National Spaghetti Day
- Great Fruitcake Toss
- First Pop Music Chart (1936)

Birthdays

1642   Sir Isaac Newton
1809   Louis Braille
1821   Elizabeth Seton
1896   Utah, 45th state

More Ideas

- Find out what kind of training a person must have in order to perform an appendectomy.
- Find out what *perihelion* means. Draw a diagram of Earth at its perihelion.
- Learn about dimpled chads and what they have to do with January 4th.

Whip Up Some Science

Experience whipped cream with your sense of touch: try a whipped cream pie-throwing contest. Spread whipped cream on paper plates, wear old shirts or smocks, and have fun throwing the pies. Then, learn about the science of whipped cream.

Prepare an instructive speech that explains why cream becomes fluffy. Whipped cream is a particular type of mixture called a **suspension**. Find out what a suspension is and name several other suspensions.

Some suspensions are edible!

January 5th

- National Whipped Cream Day*
- Twelfth Night
- First Woman Governor (1925, Nellie Ross, Wyoming)
- President Harry Truman Promises a "Fair Deal" for Americans (1949)

23

January 6th

- National Smith Day*
- Creation of Fictional Detective, Sherlock Holmes*
- Organize Your Home Day*
- National Shortbread Day
- Bean Day
- Three Kings' Day (Mexico)
- Epiphany Day or Twelfth Day
- First Around-the-World Commercial Flight (1942)

Birthdays

1412　Joan of Arc
1580　Captain John Smith*
1799　Jedediah Strong Smith*
1878　Carl Sandburg
1912　New Mexico, 47th state

One More Idea

- Create a mime about someone trying to organize his or her home.

Sleuthing After Smiths

Smith is said to be the most common name in America. This day honors the birthday of Captain John Smith.

- Try to get an autograph of at least 20 people named *Smith*.
- Research the roots of the *Smith* name. Brainstorm words and names that contain *"smith" (e.g. blacksmith, silversmith)* and famous *Smiths (e.g. Smith Brothers Cough Syrup, Smith and Wesson Company, Granny Smith apples, Snuffy Smith cartoon, etc.).*
- Find statistics about the number of *Smiths* in your city, state, or country. Count the number of Smiths in your local phone book.
- Memorize the famous poem "The Village Blacksmith" by Henry Wadsworth Longfellow.

5-Minute Mystery

Read at least one story about Sherlock Holmes, or find some other short mysteries to read. Then, create a short mystery. Describe the "crime," give a few crucial clues, and let your reader solve the mystery. These ideas might help you get started with your mystery:

creaking stairs
a broken window
a cat's footprints
chocolate-smeared fingerprints
a muffled cough
a missing chef
a growling stomach
three shadowy figures

January 7th

- Old Rock Day*
- Typewriter Day*
- I'm Not Going to Take It Anymore Day*
- Transatlantic Phoning Began (1927)*

Birthdays

1800　Millard Fillmore

More Ideas

- Use a typewriter to prepare a list of ten things you are "not going to take anymore."
- Simulate a conversation that might have taken place on one of the first transatlantic phone calls.

Rock Paintings

Make a banner that mimics the paintings on the inside of a cave.

Use a toothbrush and piece of wire mesh (such as a screen) to splatter poster paint on butcher paper. This will make the background surface look old and pitted like rock. When the background is dry, add the paintings to the "wall." Use sponges to "paint" primitive animal shapes (horses, bison, antelope) or other symbols. If you put watery paint in a spray bottle, you can spray around your hand to leave a print on the cave wall.

Rock the Day Away

Plan a celebration for the birthday of Elvis Presley, known as the "king" of rock 'n' roll. Find some old 45 RPM records and other recordings of Presley. Listen to several and choose your favorites. Research the dances and clothing styles that were popular in the 1950s. Learn some new rock 'n' roll dances. Interview 25 people to learn their favorite Elvis song. Make a graph to show the results of your survey. Practice for an "Elvis Impersonators" contest. Make up your own new rock 'n' roll songs.

- Rock 'n' Roll Day*
- Earth's Rotation Proved (1851)*
- National Bubble Bath Day*
- National English Toffee Day*
- First Computer Patented*
- Eat Something Raw Day
- Show and Tell Day at Work
- Battle of New Orleans (1815)

Birthdays
1935   Elvis Presley*
1942   Stephen Hawking

More Ideas
- Earth's rotation is responsible for different time zones. Create ten math problems about travel and time zones.
- Write a silly story that includes bubble bath, English toffee, and a computer.

Balloon Designs

Today is the anniversary of the first manned free-balloon flight in America (1793). A balloon filled with hydrogen traveled about 15 miles from Philadelphia to New Jersey at an elevation of almost 6,000 feet. The pilot was Jean-Pierre Francois Blanchard. Today, people travel in balloons for sport, leisure, sightseeing, and adventure. There are balloon clubs, races, and attempts to set new records for balloon flight. Balloons come in all shapes and sizes. Find out how balloons rise and descend, and how they are controlled during flight. Then get out the drawing paper and design a balloon that you would enter in a race or contest.

Make miniature balloon models using latex balloons. Use a marker to add stripes, dots, or other designs. Make a paper band to fit around the balloon.

Attach several strings. Tie the strings to holes punched in a small plastic container. Finally, tape a string to the top of the balloon and let it hang in your room or classroom.

- Aviation in America Day*
- National Static Electricity Day*
- National Apricot Day

Birthdays
1788   Connecticut, 5th State
1913   Richard Nixon
1941   Joan Baez

More Ideas
- Write a sentence about electricity in a shape that (visually) represents something electric. Add color around the words to make a strong visual image.
- Create a song or other rhyme that explains static electricity.

- Peculiar People Day*
- Women's Suffrage Amendment Introduced (1878)*
- "Where's the Beef?" Day*
- Volunteer Fireman's Day
- First Meeting of UN General Assembly (1946)
- First Oil Discovered in Texas (1901)

More Ideas

- Make a timeline of the history of suffrage in America.
- Plan a "Where's the Beef?" Hunt. Hide some beef jerky. Write clues to help searchers track down the beef.

Peculiar People Fun-Book

Make a book that lets you choose different combinations of pages to feature dozens of peculiar people.

Start with six pieces of heavy white paper (5½ x 8 in.) On each piece, draw very light dotted pencil lines 2½ in. from the top and 5 in. from the top. Draw six different characters. Make each one interesting and colorful. Cut a head in the top section of the page, a torso in the middle section, and legs and feet in the bottom section.

How about . . .
- an old man
- a skinny woman
- a chubby baby
- a scuba diver
- a ballerina
- a cowboy
- a baseball player
- a firefighter
- a clown
- a weight lifter

Staple the pages together. Open different sections to enjoy your peculiar creations.

- Secret Pal Day*
- International Thank You Day
- National Milk Day
- Cigarettes Declared Harmful (1964)

Birthdays

1755	Alexander Hamilton
1815	Sir John MacDonald
1934	Jean Chretien

Secretive Messages

Find a way to draw names to get secret pals.
Send a message to your secret pal in invisible ink.

Use a cotton-tipped swab to write a message on white paper with lemon juice. As the writing dries, it will disappear. The secret message will appear when the friend holds the paper near a warm light bulb.
(Take care not to set the paper on fire!)

- National Marzipan Day
- Amelia Earhart—First Woman to Fly Solo Across the Pacific Ocean (1935)
- First Museum in U.S. (1773)
- First Elected Woman Senator (1932, Hattie Caraway, Arkansas)

Birthdays

1628	Charles Perrault*
1737	John Hancock
1876	Jack London

Mother Goose in the News

Charles Perrault was the writer of the Mother Goose Tales. Find a book of these tales. Read some of them aloud to a group. Choose one tale. Make a newspaper headline from the main idea of the story. Then write a news article telling the story as if it were an event that just happened.

King's Guards Fail to Rescue Egg!

Farmer's Wife Arrested for Assault on Mice

London Bridge Collapses

Water Carrier Suffers Mishap on Hill

Who Is Stephen Foster?

Find out! Visit the Internet or your library. Then hunt down some of his most popular songs—and sing them!

Oh! Susanna!

Camptown Races

My Old Kentucky Home

I Dream of Jeannie with the Light Brown Hair

Old Black Joe

Old Folks at Home

Choose one song. Turn it into a picture book, illustrating each line or verse on one page. Add a new verse of your own to the song.

A Dream Come True

Choose one of your dreams (or a dream of someone else's). Make a calendar for the month and write the dream on the last day. On the other days, write "steps" you could take to make the dream come true for you or someone else. Follow the steps with the goal of making a dream come true.

- Stephen Foster Memorial Day*
- Make Your Dreams Come True Day*
- National Clean Off Your Desk Day
- Introduction of Frisbee™ *(1957)*

Poetic Pastrami

Turn a pastrami sandwich (or a Reuben) into a delectable poem. Write a line that describes each layer of the sandwich. Stack the lines on paper, just as if you were putting the sandwich together. Add art to strengthen the visual image created by the written lines. Try this with other kinds of sandwiches, too.

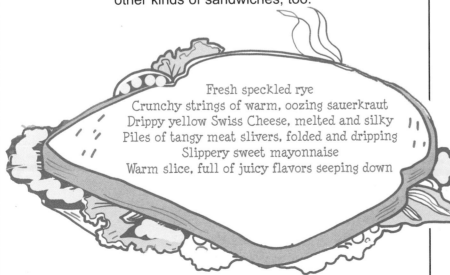

Fresh speckled rye
Crunchy strings of warm, oozing sauerkraut
Drippy yellow Swiss Cheese, melted and silky
Piles of tangy meat slivers, folded and dripping
Slippery sweet mayonnaise
Warm slice, full of juicy flavors seeping down

- National Hot Pastrami Sandwich Day*
- Ratification Day*
- Signing of the *Kremlin Accords (1994)*
- National Dress Up Your Pet Day
- *Soyuz 4*—First Docking of Two-manned Spacecraft *(USSR, 1969)*

One More Idea

- Define the words *ratify* and *accord*. Find out what was ratified on this day, in what year, and what difference that ratification has made.

January 15th

- National Humanitarian Day*
- National Strawberry Ice Cream Day*
- Elementary School Teacher Day*
- National Fresh-Squeezed Juice Day
- Pentagon Completed *(1943)*
- First Super Bowl *(1967)*

Birthdays

1929   Dr. Martin Luther King

Be a Humanitarian

Celebrate National Humanitarian Day by learning what humanitarians do. Then make an effort to get involved in some humanitarian activities.

(You can start by taking some strawberry ice cream to a teacher!)

What is a humanitarian? Make a list of humanitarian organizations. Tell what they do. Make a list of things you could do to be a humanitarian. Tell why it is important to have humanitarian activities in the world. (And, by the way, thanks for the ice cream!)

January 16th

- International Hot & Spicy Food Day*
- National Nothing Day
- National Fig Newton Day
- National Religious Freedom Day
- 18th Amendment to the *U.S. Constitution* ratified *(1919)*
- Persian Gulf War began *(1991)*

Sassy Salsa

Red hot chili peppers are cool, too!

3 fresh tomatoes, seeded and chopped
1 small onion, chopped
1 t minced garlic
3 T lime juice
1–3 T canned green chilies, chopped
1 t salt
2 T fresh cilantro, chopped
Toss all together in a bowl (not metal), cover, and chill for at least an hour.

Enjoy and share your favorite hot and spicy foods today. Make a recipe book of hot and spicy foods. Include some salsa in your menu. In Mexico, **salsa** means *sauce*. Salsa is a sauce with snap! It usually has something hot and spicy. The traditional salsa has tomatoes, peppers, cilantro, and lime. But you can also make salsa with beans, cucumbers, artichokes, avocados, corn, or fruits (e.g., mangos, papayas, cherries, peaches). Try this traditional salsa with chips, crackers, veggies, burritos, or eggs.

January 17th

- Pig Day
- Cable Car First Patented *(1871)*
- First Nuclear-Powered Submarine Voyage *(1955)*
- Earthquake in Southern California *(1994)*
- Earthquake in Japan *(1995)*

Birthdays

1706   Ben Franklin*
1942   Muhammad Ali (Cassius Clay, Jr.)*

Two Wise Guys

Ben Franklin and Muhammad Ali both loved to play with words. Ben is famous for his wise proverbs. Ali loved to make up short, funny rhyming poems. Find one of Ali's poems and write more like them. Find 20 of Franklin's proverbs and finish them with a new twist today.

A bird in the hand is worth . . .
Strike while . . .
A fool and his money are . . .
Don't count your chickens until . . .
It never rains but it . . .
A rolling stone gathers no . . .
Better late than . . .
A penny saved is . . .
Look before you . . .
Don't change _____ in the middle of the stream.
Fools rush in where . . .

wham

POW

POW

slammo

Map the Expedition

Follow the travels and discoveries of Lewis & Clark. Find or draw a large map of the North American continent (or the current U.S.). Mark the route and the key discoveries or places along the way. Write a diary of the expedition as if you were one of the members of the party.

Use globs of clay and toothpicks with tiny flags to make map markers for key places along the route.

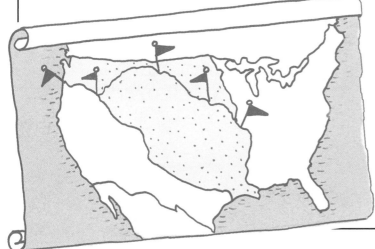

Connect the flags with red string or markers along the map.

January 18th

- Lewis & Clark Expedition Re-created *(2003)**
- Pooh Day
- Maintenance Day
- Eagle Days (18th&19th)

Birthdays
  1882   A. A. Milne

Pass-Around Stories

Edgar Allan Poe wrote wonderfully scary stories. Sit in a circle with friends or classmates. Each person should write a smashing first sentence for a scary story. Then pass your papers to the next person. Write a second sentence or two. Keep doing this six more times. On the last pass, write a great ending. Always keep the writing scary. When you're done, the group will end up with some of the strangest (and scariest) stories ever!

Flying-Arrow Math

Archery takes physical, mental, and math skills! What is the total score shown on this target? (You'll need to learn how the game of archery is scored.) Draw ten more targets with arrows. Then calculate the scores.

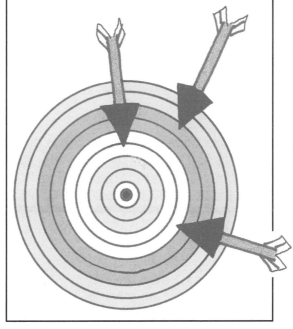

January 19th

- Archery Day*
- Penguin Awareness Day
- Tin Can Patented *(1825)**
- Confederate Heroes Day
- Indira Gandhi Became Prime Minister of India *(1966)*

Birthdays
  1807   Robert E. Lee
  1809   Edgar Allan Poe*
  1839   Paul Cezanne

More Ideas

- Prepare a choral reading of Poe's poem "The Raven."
- Make a list of 100 things (besides foods) that could be kept or caught in a tin can.

January 20th

- Cheese Day*
- U.S. Presidential Inauguration Day*
- Vanilla Milkshake Day
- National Buttercrunch Day
- U.S. Hostages Freed by Iran After 444 days in Captivity (1981)

Birthdays
1896   George Burns
1930   Buzz Aldrin

Homemade Cream Cheese

It's not too hard to make your own cream cheese. All you need is some plain yogurt (not too thick), cheesecloth, some string, and patience. If you want to add flavor to your cheese, you'll need some fruit, too!

Make a double thickness of cheesecloth. Spoon the yogurt into the center of the cheesecloth. Tie it up in a bundle and fasten it shut with string. Hang the bundle over the faucet in a sink. Leave it overnight. The moisture will drip out, leaving a soft cream cheese. When the cheese is done, flavor it with berries or other chopped fruit.

What is the oath taken by a U.S. President on Inauguration Day? Find out.

January 21st

- Gimmicks Day*
- Squirrel Appreciation Day*
- Granola Bar Day*
- First Flight of Concorde* (1976)
- National Hugging Day

Birthdays
1824   Thomas "Stonewall" Jackson

Get a Gimmick

A gimmick is a hidden or tricky condition in a plan OR any small device, especially one used in a sneaky or secretive manner. Brainstorm a list of common gimmicks. Think of a gimmick for appreciating squirrels, making a paper Concorde fly, or baking prize-winning granola bars!

My *gimmick* is to pull a **squirrel** out of my hat instead of a rabbit!

January 22nd

- Answer Your Cat's Questions Day*
- Celebration of Life Day
- Come in From the Cold Day
- National Blonde Brownie Day
- National Compliment Day

What's the Question?

Try to think like a cat. Make a thoughtful list of questions you think a cat would ask. Then get together with a friend and role-play cats with questions. Take turns pretending to be a cat. The listener should try to answer the questions. You may have to do some research to find the answers to the questions.

Why do cats like fish so much?

What is the reason for these whiskers?

Why do people talk baby talk to cats?

Measure Your Feet

Measure your feet today in centimeters, inches, and meters. Measure each toe. Draw a diagram and label the measurements.

Next, use your feet as measuring units. Look around and find 25 things or distances to measure with your feet. Make a chart to show the measurements.

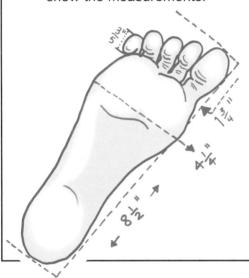

Analyze This!

Search in the library or on the Web to learn basic techniques for analyzing handwriting. Join with a friend and take turns analyzing each other's writing.

- Measure Your Feet Day*
- National Handwriting Day*
- National Pie Day
- 24th Amendment to the *U.S. Constitution* ratified *(1964)*
- First M.D. Received by an American woman *(1849, Elizabeth Blackwell)*

Birthdays
1832   Edouard Manet

All-Day Peanut Butter

Use peanut butter to learn all day long. Think of ways you can study math, science, language, social studies, art, and music with peanut butter. Here are a few ideas to get you started:

- Find out where peanuts are grown, who imports them, and who exports them. Make a "Peanut Locator" Map of the U.S. (or the world) to show where they're grown.
- Read the labels on four different kinds of peanut butter jars. Look for differences in ingredients. Write five questions that can be answered by careful label reading.
- Estimate the number of peanuts in a large jar. Count to check your estimate.
- Do a mime of someone trying to get peanut butter off the roof of her mouth.
- Research the history of peanuts and learn about George Washington Carver.
- Design a peanut butter jar and label. Give a new name to your peanut butter.
- Calculate the calories and different nutrients in a peanut butter sandwich.
- Compare weights of a spoonful of peanut butter from different jars.
- Grind peanuts in a food processor to make peanut butter.
- Write ten rules for eating peanut butter.
- Write a peanut butter tongue twister.
- Finger paint with peanut butter.
- Write a peanut butter dream.
- Do a peanut butter dance.

The First Rule for Eating Peanut Butter: Take out your false teeth!

- National Peanut Butter Day*
- Just Do It Day*
- Eskimo Pie Patented *(1922)*
- Gold Discovered in California at Sutter's Mill *(1848)*

More Ideas

- An Eskimo Pie is ice cream dipped in chocolate. Make your own today. Put a chunk of hard ice cream on a small wooden stick. Melt a package of chocolate chips over a pan of hot water. Dip the ice cream chunk and roll it in nuts or sprinkles.
- Choose one thing that you have been putting off. Write it down. Then just DO IT—TODAY!

- Opposite Day*
- Weather Day
- A Room of One's Own Day
- Nelly Bly's Around-the-World Trip Completed *(72 days, 6 hours, 11 minutes, 1890)*
- First Winter Olympics *(1924)*
- First Transcontinental Commercial Flight *(1959)*
- First Televised U.S. Presidential News Conference *(1961)*
- Apple Macintosh Computer Debut *(1984)*

"Oppositely" Speaking

Solve this opposite puzzle. Each clue says the opposite of what it means, so the answer will be the opposite of what you might think from the clue! Create your own opposite puzzle.

Across
   4   the day after today
   7   lose track of
   9   a large sum
  10   gave up
  11   affirmative

Down
   1   sadness
   2   words with opposite meanings
   3   low temperature
   5   grow a beard
   6   to go up
   8   12 a.m.

- Dental Drill Patented *(1875)**
- Australia Day*
- National Peanut Brittle Day

Birthdays
   1837   Michigan, 26th state

The Fearsome Drill

The dental drill was a great invention for the health of teeth. Yet, many people are terrified of the dentist and the drill. *Dentophobia* is a fear of the dentist. *Algrophobia* is the fear of pain. Find out about these fears:

- heliophobia
- ailurophobia
- demophobia
- eisoptrophobia
- catoptrophobia
- aviophobia

- claustrophobia
- gephyrophobia
- monophobia
- ornithophobia
- mysophobia
- arachibutyrophobia

- acrophobia
- apiphobia
- cynophobia
- sciophobia
- belonophobia
- lachanophobia

Mini Boomerangs

You don't have to go to Australia to throw a boomerang and enjoy watching it return right back to you. You can make one today and practice throwing it right away. Trace the pattern onto thin cardboard, cut it out, and decorate it.

Lay the boomerang on the first finger of your left hand. Hold it out in front of your body. With your right hand, flick it with a quick snap of your index finger and knock it off. This will send it flying!

Lemon Power

You can get enough power from lemons to light up a bulb!
Here's how to make a lemon battery.

1. GENTLY squeeze and roll two lemons to make them juicy. Do not break the skin.
2. Cut a 10-inch (25 cm) strip of copper wire and steel wire. Also, cut a 3-inch (8 cm) strip of each wire. Remove insulation from the ends of the wires so they are bare.
3. Twist the end of the two 3-inch (8 cm) strips together.
4. Place the ends of the wires deep into the lemons as shown in the diagram. Attach one end of the steel wire to a socket containing a small light bulb. Touch the free end of the copper wire to the other side of the socket. The bulb should light up.

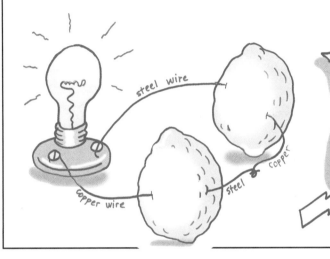

steel wire
copper
steel
copper wire

How it works!
A battery has a liquid or paste chemical inside and an electrolyte that reacts to produce electricity. The lemon contains natural electrolytes. The chemical reactions between the lemon juice and the two metals push electrons to flow through the circuit you have made.

January 27th

- Electric Lightbulb Patented *(1880)**
- National Chocolate Cake Day
- Remembrance of Victims of Nazism
- *Apollo I* Spacecraft Fire *(1967)*
- Vietnam Peace Agreement Signed *(1973)*

Birthdays
1756   Wolfgang Mozart
1832   Lewis Carroll

Can You Kazoo?

Organize your own kazoo band.
Start by making and mastering your kazoos.

1. Get a cardboard tube about 5–6 inches (13–15 cm) long. Decorate the tube with markers, crayons, or other colorful stuff.

2. Cut a 5-inch square (13 cm) from waxed paper. Wrap this over one end of the tube and secure it with a rubber band.

3. To play your kazoo, hum a tune gently into the open end.

The sound of your voice will cause the waxed paper to vibrate, resulting in the unusual kazoo sound.

January 28th

- National Kazoo Day*
- Bubble Wrap Appreciation Day*
- U.S. Great Seal Approved *(1782)**
- Christa McAuliffe Day
- *Challenger* Space Shuttle Explosion *(1986)*
- National Blueberry Pancake Day

More Ideas
- Create a sculpture with bubble wrap. Then write a rap about bubble wrap. Use plenty of *r-* and *wr-* words.
- Draw a picture of the Great Seal. Explain what all the words mean.

January 29th

- National Rattlesnake Roundup Day*
- National Puzzle Day*
- Baseball's American League Organized *(1900)**
- National Corn Chip Day

Birthdays

1874   John D. Rockefeller, Jr.*

1897   William McKinley

1861   Kansas Entered the Union as a Free State

One More Idea

- Learn the meanings of the words *entrepreneur* and *philanthropist*. Find out how these words apply to John D. Rockefeller.

Rattlesnake Puzzler

Draw a huge rattlesnake (6–8 feet long) on mural paper. Color or paint it brightly with diamond-shape patterns. Draw jigsaw puzzle lines on the whole paper. Cut out the puzzle pieces and put them into a large envelope. Challenge a friend to put the puzzle together.

Baseball Mishaps

Prepare an apology about a mishap in baseball (a game you forgot, a broken bat, a missed fly, an accident in the bleachers, etc.). Give the apology orally or in writing.

The baseball has broken your dining room window,
And I know you're having company for dinner.
Forgive me!
It was, after all, a fine hit
And I got a home run!

January 30th

- Escape Day*
- National Croissant Day*
- National Inane Answering Message Day

Birthdays

1882   Franklin Delano Roosevelt

1912   Barbara Tuchman

Cliffhangers

A cliffhanger is a story that is unfinished. The story stops abruptly—leaving the reader "hanging" and anxious to know what happens next. Write a cliffhanger that is an **escape** story. Write enough of the story to grab the reader. Fasten the cliffhanger to a hanger. Leave it for someone else to come along and finish.

Borrowed Foods

Many of the foods we enjoy are borrowed from different cultures. Track down the cultural sources of as many foods as you can.

croissants and éclairs *(French)*
jambalaya *(Creole)*
borscht *(Russian)*
enchilada *(Mexican)*
sauerkraut *(German)*
falafel *(Greek)*
tortilla *(Spanish)*
sushi *(Japanese)*
lasagna *(Italian)*
chow mein *(Chinese)*
trifle *(English)*
tiramisu *(Italian)*
sauerbraten *(German)*
bruschetta *(Italian)*
paella *(Spanish)*
quesadilla *(Mexican)*
hummus *(Middle Eastern)*
kuchen *(German)*
moussaka *(Greek)*

Popcorn History

Many sources list today as National Popcorn Day. Check the Internet for the date in your area—it may vary from place to place. While you're on the Web, look up the history of popcorn. There might have been popcorn back as far as the days of cave dwellers.

Here's an old popcorn legend: One summer it got so hot that fields of corn popped. The cows in a nearby field thought it was a snow blizzard, so they lay down and froze to death.

Write more weather legends beginning with, "One winter, it got so cold that . . ."

January 31ˢᵗ

- National Popcorn Day*
- Inspire Your Heart with Art Day*
- National Backwards Day
- Tape It Day
- Fun at Work Day
- First Social Security Check Issued *(1940)*
- *Explorer I*, First Successful U.S. Satellite *(U.S., 1958)*
- *Luna 9*, First Soft Landing on the Moon *(USSR, 1966)*

Birthdays
1919   Jackie Robinson

Kernel Calculations

Count 500 kernels of popcorn. Weigh the kernels and record the weight. Heat 1/3 C cooking oil in a heavy saucepan or popcorn popper. Pour the kernels into the oil. Cover, and cook over medium heat, shaking constantly. Start a stopwatch or timer as soon as you put the kernels into the pan. Record the time the first kernel pops. Record the time the last kernel pops. Weigh the popped corn. Then . . .

. . . Calculate the average time it took for a kernel to pop.

. . . Count unpopped kernels and calculate the percent of kernels that popped.

. . . Compare the weights of the popped and unpopped corn.

Inspiring Heart Pendant

Celebrate Inspire Your Heart with Art Day by making this unusual pendant. Once you perfect the technique, you can repeat the process with other shapes to make a variety of beautiful jewelry.

1. Sketch a heart shape and cut about 30 exactly the same size from colored paper. Use several colors.

2. Use white glue to glue the shapes on top of each other, making sure each one is thoroughly stuck to the one beneath it.

3. Wait several hours or overnight until the glue is completely dry.

4. With sandpaper, sand around the edges at an angle. Sand a few spots on the top. The sanding does not have to be even. Be patient! The sanding will take time.

5. Coat the pendant with shellac or clear nail polish.

6. When the heart is dry, drill a hole and hang it on a chain, twine, or leather strip.

Easy Caramel Corn

15 C popped popcorn   1/4 C corn syrup
1 C brown sugar   1/2 t salt
1/2 C butter   1/2 t baking soda

1. Put popcorn in large roasting pan.
2. Heat oven to 200°.
3. Heat sugar, butter, corn syrup, and salt in saucepan until bubbly.
4. Cook over medium heat 5 minutes.
5. Remove from heat, stir in soda.
6. Pour slowly over popcorn and stir.
7. Bake 1 hr, stirring every 15 min.
8. Remove from oven; cool on waxed paper.

February

1
- Robinson Crusoe Day*
- Wear Red Day*
- Supreme Court Convened for the First Time*
- National Freedom Day
- Women's Heart Health Day
- Serpent Day
  Birthdays: Langston Hughes, Hattie Wyatt Caraway, Louis St. Laurent

2
- Groundhog Day*
- Bottle Cap Patented*
- Candlemas (Mexico)*
- Bonza Bottler Day
- National Baseball League Formed
- California Kiwi Fruit Day
  Birthdays: James Joyce

3
- Halfway Point of Winter*
- 15th & 16th Amendments Ratified*
- Carrot Cake Day
- Endangered Species Act
  Birthdays: Norman Rockwell*, Elizabeth Blackwell*, Horace Greeley

4
- Thank a Mail Carrier Day*
- Create a Vacuum Day*
- George Washington Elected 1st U.S. President*
- USO Formed
  Birthdays: Rosa Parks, Charles Lindbergh*

5
- National Weatherperson's Day*
- Wiffle Ball Introduced
- National Girls & Women in Sports Day
- Disaster Day
- Constitution Day (Mexico)
  Birthdays: Hank Aaron

6
- Crayola Crayons Debuted*
- Pay a Compliment Day
- Lame Duck Day
- 20th Amendment Ratified
  Birthdays: Babe Ruth, Ronald Reagan, state of Massachusetts

7
- 11th Amendment Ratified*
- Wave All Your Fingers at Your Neighbor Day
- Send a Card to a Friend Day
- Ballet First Introduced in the U.S.
  Birthdays: Charles Dickens, Laura Ingalls Wilder

8
- Boy Scouts of America Founded
- Shovel Race Championships
  Birthdays: Jules Verne*

9
- Toothache Day*
- Hershey's Chocolate Founded*
- National Weather Service Established*
- Pizza Pie Day
  Birthdays: William Henry Harrison

10
- Umbrella Day*
- 25th Amendment Ratified
- French and Indian War Ended
- The First Singing Telegram

11
- National Inventor's Day*
- Be Electrific Day*
- National Science Youth Day*
- Don't Cry Over Spilled Milk Day*
- White Shirt Day
- Make a Friend Day
- Monopoly Board Game Introduced
- Nelson Mandela Released from Prison
- *Yalta Agreement* Signed
  Birthdays: Thomas Alva Edison*

12
- First Puppet Show in America*
- National Lost Penny Day
- National Plum Pudding Day
- NAACP Founded
  Birthdays: Abraham Lincoln, Charles Darwin

13
- Final Warning Day*
- First Magazine Published in America
- Get a Different Name Day
- Value Friendship Day
  Birthdays: Bess Truman

14
- Valentine's Day*
- Ferris Wheel Day
- Race Relations Day
- Read to Your Child Day
- National Have a Heart Day
- First U.S. Presidential Photograph
  Birthdays: Frederick Douglas, state of Oregon, state of Arizona

15
- National Gumdrop Day*
- Flag Day (Canada)
- National I Want Butterscotch Day
- Susan B. Anthony Day
- National Sea Monkey Day
  Birthdays: Galileo Galilei, Susan B. Anthony, Cyrus McCormick

16
- Do a Grouch a Favor Day*
- Nylon Patented
- Fidel Castro Became Cuba's Premier

17
- Champion Crab Races Day*
- Random Acts of Kindness Day*
- American PTA founded*
- My Way Day
  Birthdays: Michael Jordan*

18
- Thumb Appreciation Day*
- First Cow Milked While Flying in an Airplane*
- National Battery Day
- Phonograph Patented
- Pluto Discovered

19
- *Mir* Space Station Launched*
- National Chocolate Mint Day*
- *Mr. Roger's Neighborhood* Debuted*
  Birthdays: Nicolaus Copernicus*

20
- Toothpick Patented*
- Hoodie Hoo Day–Northern Hemisphere*
- John Glenn Day
- National Student Volunteer Day
- First American Orbited Earth
  Birthdays: Ansel Adams, Sidney Poitier

21
- Samuel Morse's Telegraph Demonstrated*
- Lucy Hobbs Became First Female American Dentist*
- Love Your Pet Day
- Washington Monument Dedicated
- First U.S. Telephone Book Circulated
- President Nixon Visited Communist China

22
- World Thinking Day*
- Be Humble Day
- First Chain Store Opened
  Birthdays: George Washington

23
- Banana Bread Day*
- Sticky Bun Day
- International Dog Biscuit Appreciation Day
- First Cloning of an Adult Animal
- Diesel Engine Patented
- Battle at the Alamo
  Birthdays: George Frederick Handel, Emma Hart Willard

24
- National Tortilla Chip Day*
- Flag Day (Mexico)
- Gregorian Calendar Created

25
Quiet Day*
Spay Day USA
  Birthdays: "Texas Rose" Bascom

26
- National Pistachio Day*
- Tell a Fairy Tale Day
- FCC Created
- Grand Canyon National Park Established
- Bomb Exploded at World Trade Center
  Birthdays: Buffalo Bill, Levi Strauss

27
- International Polar Bear Day*
- No Brainer Day
- 22nd Amendment Ratified
- American Indian Movement Occupied Wounded Knee
  Birthdays: Henry W. Longfellow, John Steinbeck, Marion Anderson

28
- Public Sleeping Day*
- Floral Design Day
- *USS Princeton* Exploded
  Birthdays: Mario Andretti

29
- Leap Year Day*
- Bachelor's Day*
- Sadie Hawkins Day*
- National Surf and Turf Day
- First Arrests in Salem Witch Hunt

Month-long Celebrations
African-American History Month*
American Heart Month*
American History Month*
Bake for Family Fun Month*
Canned Food Month
Children's Dental Health Month
International Boost Your Self-esteem Month
International Expect Success Month
International Friendship Month*
Library Lover's Month*
National Bird-Feeding Month*
National Blah Buster Month*
National Caffeine Addiction Awareness Month
National Cat Health Month
National Cherry Month*
National Embroidery Month
National Grapefruit Month*
National Hot Breakfast Month*
National Sign Up for Camp Month
National Snack Food Month*
National Sweet Potato Month*
National World Understanding Month*
Plant the Seeds of Greatness Month
Potato Lover's Month*
Return Shopping Carts to the Supermarket Month*
Scouting Month
Spay or Neuter Your Pet Month
Wise Health Care Consumer Month

February was named for the Roman festival February.
This was a period of time for purification.
February Flower: violet
February Birthstone: amethyst

Weekly Celebrations

First Week: National New Idea Week*, Children's Authors & Illustrator's Week, National Consumer Protection Week

Second Week: National Hero Week*, Homes for Birds Week*, Boy Scouts Week, Big Brothers/Sisters Week, Celebration of Love Week, Live to Give Week, Kraut & Frankfurter Week, Pickle Time Week, National Flirting Week, Love May Make the World Go 'Round, But Laughter Keeps Us from Getting Dizzy Week

Third Week: Nostalgia Week*, The Great Backyard Bird Count*, Health Education Week, International Friendship Week, African Wildlife Week, Engineering Week

Fourth Week: Golf Week*, Kids Love a Mystery Week*, Read to Me Week

Dates That Vary: Presidents' Day*, Chinese New Year*

February's Month-long Celebrations

African-American History Month

- Investigate the history of the people, places, and events on the list shown here. Learn something about the significance or accomplishments of each one.

- Find out about the history of the slave song "Follow the Drinking Gourd."

- Track down performances of black performers. During February, listen to their music: jazz, blues, rock, rap, and old time gospel. Enjoy the creations of black artists such as Teenie Harris and Romare Bearden. Make a collage that mimics Bearden's style. Read and share literature by black writers such as Langston Hughes, Maya Angelou, the Delany sisters, and Toni Morrison.

- See how many "famous firsts" you can learn about from African-American history.

Investigate these . . .

Underground Railroad	Muhammad Ali
Rosa Parks	William H. Lewis
Abolition	Matthew Henson
13th, 14th, 15th Amendments	Martin Luther King, Jr.
Selma, Alabama	*Missouri Compromise*
Uncle Tom's Cabin	*The Black Codes*
Black Civil War Soldiers	*Brown v. Board of Education*
Benjamin Banneker	Little Rock, Arkansas
Ku Klux Klan	Jesse Jackson
Emancipation Proclamation	Mary Ann Shadd
Harriet Tubman	*Civil Rights Act of 1964*
Montgomery, Alabama	Shirley Chisholm
Frederick Douglass	Patricia R. Harris
Nat Turner	*Plessy v. Ferguson*
Sojourner Truth	Phyllis Wheatley
Gay Byron	Oprah Winfrey
Richard Allen	Booker T. Washington

Life is short, and it's up to you to make it sweet.
-Louis Armstrong

Freedom is never given, it is won.
-Booker T. Washington

Anger used, does not destroy. Hatred does.
-Audre Lorde

African-American Quotations

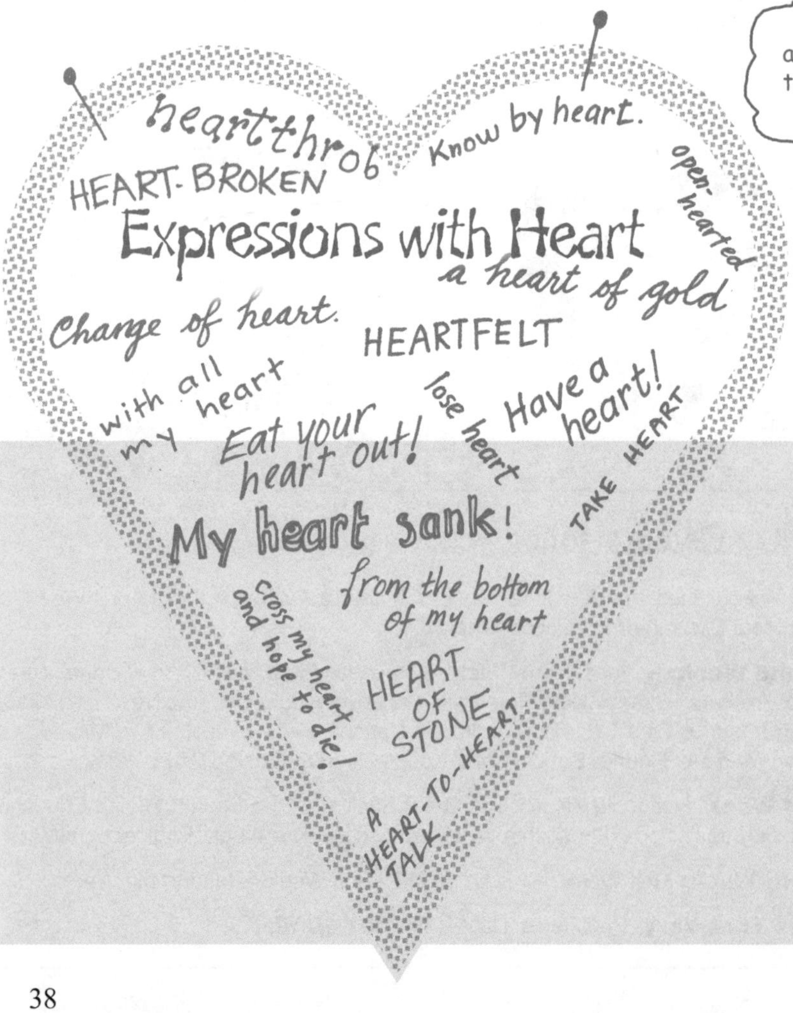

heartthrob
Know by heart.
HEART-BROKEN
open-hearted
Expressions with Heart
a heart of gold
change of heart.
HEARTFELT
with all my heart
Eat your heart out!
lose heart
Have a heart!
My heart sank!
TAKE HEART
from the bottom of my heart
cross my heart and hope to die!
HEART OF STONE
A HEART-TO-HEART TALK

American Heart Month

- Brainstorm expressions that contain the word *heart*. Scrawl or print them on a wall-sized heart shape, a T-shirt, a banner, or a poster.

- Find out how your heart works. Prepare a speech or written explanation, accompanied by a clear diagram.

- Write a recipe for a healthy heart.

International Friendship Month

• Make a walkie-talkie to use for fun communication with a friend. Follow the instructions on this page. Then use it to send bright ideas, private plans, deep secrets, or other special messages back and forth.

• Collect quotes or proverbs about friends or friendship. Write each one on a link of a paper chain to build a long friendship chain. Write a few original quotes and proverbs.

• How many songs about friends can you find? Track down at least ten and write their titles.

• Write some instructions for how to be a friend. Do at least one thing on the list every day this month.

• Compose a song about things friends DON'T do.

Easy Walkie-Talkies

1. Make a hole in the center of each of two tin cans by hammering the nail part way in with a hammer or a rock.
2. String one end of a long piece of twine into each hole. Tie a large knot inside each can.
3. Paint designs on the cans.
4. To use the walkie-talkie, pull the line tight between the two of you. Talk into the can.

Can you hear me?

It works!

How does it work? Learn about the science of sound. Explain how the sound travels between the two cans.

National World Understanding Month

Broaden world understanding with this "Where in the World?" quiz. Try to answer each of these questions before the end of February. (Name a city, region, or nation for each one.) You can increase your world understanding by creating more questions for the quiz. Try to add 20 or more to challenge your friends. (Make sure you learn the answers.)

Where in the world could you find . . .

. . . hundreds of tribes speaking hundreds of different languages?
. . . an area where vast numbers of people are facing starvation?
. . . population density greater than 250 people per square mile?
. . . people who have adapted to living a life below sea level?
. . . a nation that has been split into two nations by conflict?
. . . a culture of people who make their living from the sea?
. . . vast acreages of land are devoted to sheep ranching?
. . . tension and violence caused by religious differences?
. . . millions of people who practice the religion of Islam?
. . . people who must move frequently to make a living?
. . . pollution from industry threatening wetland wildlife?
. . . an economy that is heavily dependent on tourism?
. . . Aborigines who hold title to large areas of land?
. . . many treasures of the Renaissance art world?
. . . millions of people who practice Buddhism?
. . . a city that is located in two continents?
. . . people carrying goods on their heads?
. . . a mostly-socialistic economic system?
. . . a parliamentary form of government?
. . . women who have no voting rights?
. . . people performing Noh plays?

National Blah Buster Month

Bust those blahs with one (or more) of these.

1. Hang balloons all over your room.
2. Learn to play the harmonica.
3. Clean enough stuff out of your room to fill a large trash bag.
4. Write things that make you feel *blahhhhh* all over a paper bag. Wad the bag up and throw it away.
5. SING to yourself every morning as soon as you get up.
6. Do something surprising and kind for someone else once a week.
7. Stand on your head for ten minutes a day.
8. Eat one less item (than usual) of junk food every day.
9. Drink two quarts of water a day.

10. Walk, bounce, jump rope, jog, hop, or skip at least 10 minutes every day!

National Bird-Feeding Month

Create a way to feed birds during the winter. Here are a few good ideas. Make one (or all of these). Hang it on your windowsill or any place where you can watch the birds enjoy a winter picnic.

A Picnic in a Pinecone

Twist a piece of thick twine around a pinecone and tie it securely to make a hanging loop. Mix 1 cup of peanut butter with 1/2 cup salad oil in a bowl. Spread the mixture between the petals of the pinecone. Drop the pinecone into a paper bag 1/4 full of birdseed. Close the bag and shake it gently to coat the cone with seeds.

A Peanut Butter Sandwich

Use a large nail to make a hole in the center of one jar lid. Drive the nail through the center of another jar lid of the same size. Leave the nail in place. Put a stale donut over the nail. Top the donut with the other lid to make a donut sandwich. Spread the sides of the donut with peanut butter. Tie a string securely around the nail to make a hanging loop.

A Corn Feast

Use a hanger to make a hanging loop for an ear of dried corn. Push the ends of the wire into the corn so the birds won't hurt themselves while feasting.

A Tasty Garland

Thread a large needle with a long length of heavy thread. String small chunks of uncooked animal fat and pieces of apple, leaving a little space between each of the chunks. Tie brightly colored ribbon or yarn in the spaces to attract the birds' attention.

American History Month

Solve all these history mysteries during the month. Write 20 mysteries for someone else to solve.

U.S. History Mysteries

1. What president had a candy bar named after his daughter?
2. Who was the real Johnny Appleseed?
3. What happened to the original White House?
4. After whom is America named?
5. What president was married in the White House?
6. What president served all or part of three terms in office?
7. How many people were killed in Nagasaki and Hiroshima, Japan, when the U.S. dropped atomic bombs on those cities in 1945?
8. What U.S. presidential candidate accepted an endorsement from a fictitious Canadian Prime Minister?
9. What American woman has the most statues in the U.S. made to honor her?
10. What president is responsible for the addition of the words "under God" to the Pledge of Allegiance?
11. What state was the first to outlaw slavery?
12. What president had a term that was only one day long?
13. When did the Liberty Bell ring for the first time?
14. What do the Latin words mean that are found on the nation's Great Seal?
15. What was the original name of Memorial Day?
16. How many presidents died in office?

Bake for Family Fun Month

Make a special effort to bake with the whole family. Commit to doing this at least once a week in February. Bake favorite family recipes. Try some new recipes. Make something heart-shaped (a meatloaf, cake, cookies, gelatin treats, a loaf of bread, rice cereal treats, or muffins).

Ice-Cream Cones Without Ice Cream

1. Prepare a cake mix according to directions on the package.
2. Spoon cake batter into flat-bottom ice-cream cones until they are almost full.
3. Set the cones in a cake pan or in muffin tins and bake according to the package instructions for cupcakes.
4. Prepare frosting from a mix, can, or your own recipe.
5. When the ice-cream cone cakes are cooled, frost and decorate them with sprinkles, candies, colored sugars, etc.

National Hot Breakfast Month

To celebrate Hot Breakfast Month, choose oatmeal for your breakfast. It's fast, tummy-warming, tummy-filling, healthy, and oh, so versatile! Make your oatmeal taste different every day!

Lovable, Versatile Oatmeal

Make a bowl of warm oatmeal. Add milk or water until it is just the right consistency that you love. Then mix in any combination of these goodies for a healthy hot breakfast.

almonds	dried peaches	pecans	walnuts
granola	currants	apple chunks	raisins
dried apples	cinnamon	banana slices	coconut
nutmeg	brown sugar	syrup	jam
chocolate chips	sunflower seeds	peanut butter	berries
sesame seeds	apple butter	molasses	cherries

National Snack Food Month

Trade in all those ordinary, sugary snacks for a unique batch of custom-designed gorp. GORP is a mixture of all kinds of good foods. You choose the ingredients, so yours will be like none other!

Gorp for a Group

Ask everyone to bring a bagful of a gorp ingredient. Put the foods into large bowls. Give every person a small zip-top bag. Circulate among the foods and take small handfuls of the ones you like. Zip up your bag and shake it until everything is mixed. Enjoy it anywhere!

Try these . . .

almost any kind of dry cereal	granola	oatmeal
sesame seeds	corn nuts	pretzels
sunflower seeds	peanuts	pecans
chocolate chips	walnuts	raisins

And, if you plan to eat it soon . . .

dates	chunks of cheese	wheat germ
bits of dried meat	tiny crackers	dried fruit

National Grapefruit Month

Don't be fooled by the tart taste—grapefruit is good for you. Here's a way to prepare a grapefruit treat that takes away the tang with a bit of sweetness.

Sweet Broiled Grapefruit

Cut a grapefruit in half. Loosen the sections for easy eating. Sprinkle some brown sugar, cinnamon, and a few splashes of vanilla on top. Put the grapefruit under the broiler for a few minutes—just until the sugar melts and begins to bubble.

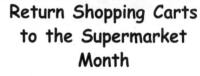

Return Shopping Carts to the Supermarket Month

While you're inside the grocery store, sharpen your math skills by estimating the total that will show up at the register. When you leave the store, don't let your cart stand around lonely in the parking lot. Return it to the store. Return other carts, too.

National Cherry Month

A famous story told in February is about George Washington and the cherry tree. As the story goes, the boy George (whose birthday is in February) chopped down a cherry tree without permission. When he was asked about the tree, he told the truth about what happened. His well-known line is, "I cannot tell a lie." So February is a good month to think about lies. Choose one of the activities here. Write your list. Then share it in writing, on a banner, on a poster, or in a speech.

I cannot lie. Those cherries were delicious!

10 Lies

Write . . .

- **10** worst lies you have ever heard
- **10** lies you will never believe
- **10** dumbest lies you have ever told
- **10** reasons to avoid lying
- **10** ways lies get you into trouble
- **10** lies that backfired

Potato Lover's Month & Sweet Potato Month

- Learn the difference between a potato and a sweet potato. Compare the nutritional values of white potatoes and sweet potatoes.

- Find a new recipe for a soup or other dish with potatoes or sweet potatoes.

- Do a taste test with different kinds of potatoes. Cut a cube of several kinds. Create a chart to describe and rate the potato tastes.

- Fall in love with a potato or sweet potato by following the "For the Love of a Potato" exercise. Do this with a group of at least 10 people.

For the Love of a Potato

1 Get a supply of potatoes or sweet potatoes. Let each person in the group reach into a bag and choose a potato. Then, do these things to get to know your potato:

   a. Look closely at each distinguishing feature of the potato. Notice the shape, size, and color. Notice any cracks, holes, or oddities.

   b. Close your eyes and feel your potato. Let your hands memorize every curve, bump, lump, or indentation.

   c. Name your potato.

   d. Write an ode to your potato, or write a song or poem about your potato.

   e. Take your potato everywhere you go.

2. After two days, put all the personal potatoes into a bag. Add a few new potatoes. Mix them up. Then place all the potatoes on a table. Each person must go to the table and find his or her personal potato from the group. This will be a good test of how well you really know your own potato!

Library Lover's Month

How can you tell a REAL library lover? You decide! Finish this phrase 15 different ways:

A real library lover _____

See page 37 for other month-long holidays to celebrate in February.

Special Weeks In February

National New Idea Week

• Take time this week to think about the wonderful new ideas that have changed life in this world. Draw a huge "Bright Idea" light bulb. Fill it with your favorite ideas that once were new!

• Work on some new ideas of your own! Think of a new way to . . .

butter your toast	make music
save money	eat a s'more
tie your shoes	fasten your clothes
campaign for the presidency	

Light bulb labels: going to the moon, SAFETY PINS, toothpicks, crossword puzzles, GPS, freezer, BAND-AID, Yo Yo, Toilet Paper, Q-tips, crayons, ironing things, trying to fly, camera, RUBBER BANDS, teabags, starting a fire, COMPASS, MRI machines, forks, skiing on water, fireworks, LIQUID PAPER, holidays, DVD

National Hero Week

• Design a hero. Make a list of the characteristics that you believe identify a hero. Draw a life-sized person on mural paper. Cut it out, and write the characteristics on the shape.

• Create a short book (10–20 pages) about real-life heroes. On each page, describe someone you know who has the attributes of a hero. Add photos, pictures, and a good title (such as *Heroes Without Capes*).

• For decades, heroes have been featured on cereal boxes. Think of and design another way to honor a hero of your choice. Or, design a cereal box with a new hero.

Homes for Birds Week

There are many possibilities for a good bird home. Visit your library or the Internet for ideas about building different kinds. Find an idea that appeals to you, make up your own design, or try this easy birdhouse.

Quick & Easy Birdhouse

1. Cut two round holes across from each other in the widest part of a large plastic (well-rinsed) bleach bottle.

2. Glue an aluminum pie tin to the bottom of the bottle to make a ledge.

3. Tie a strong cord or string around the neck or handle of the bottle to make a loop for hanging.

4. Put some birdseed inside the bottle and hang the bottle from a tree branch or from a windowsill.

Tweet

Nostalgia Week

Nostalgia Week falls on different dates in different parts of the country. If there is no set celebration in your area, celebrate it this week. *Nostalgia* means being sentimental about or yearning for something in the past. Get nostalgic this week. What are you nostalgic about? (You might also notice what things, remembered from your past, bring NO nostalgia!) Choose one or more of the following starters to begin writing a memory.

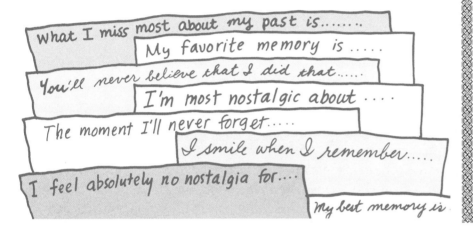

What I miss most about my past is.......
My favorite memory is .....
You'll never believe that I did that......
I'm most nostalgic about . . . .
The moment I'll never forget.....
I smile when I remember.....
I feel absolutely no nostalgia for····
My best memory is

The Great Backyard Bird Count

The Great Backyard Bird Count is held every year over the Presidents' Day Weekend. People all over North America can take part in the four days of counting the birds they see. In recent years, almost 50,000 people joined in the count. Bird-watchers of all ages and experience levels are welcome to participate. People count the birds they see and report to a website. Over 500 species of birds were spotted last year. To find out how to join in on the counting, visit the website of the Audubon Society.

Golf Week & Kids Love a Mystery Week

Celebrate these two occasions by solving a golf mystery. (You'll need to learn about how the game is scored.) Then, create your own golf mysteries.

Mystery on the Green

Alex and Zelda just finished competing with each other in stroke play at Grunion Green. Somewhere along the way, their scores from the 14th hole disappeared from the score sheets.

Alex had birdies on holes 2, 9, and 13. He hit a bogie on hole 18 and an eagle on 15 and 16. On all other holes (except 14), he came in at par.

Zelda hit bogies on holes 2, 7, and 8. She birdied on 6, 9, and 10. Holes 15 and 16 were eagles for her, and she had a double bogie on hole 4. She scored par on all other holes (except 14).

Alex won the game by one stroke.

What were the 14th hole scores that had disappeared?

Hole	Par
1	3
2	4
3	3
4	4
5	3
6	5
7	3
8	3
9	5
10	4
11	3
12	4
13	4
14	5
15	4
16	4
17	4
18	3

See page 37 for other weeklong holidays to celebrate in February.

The Days Of February

Mardi Gras, Shrove Tuesday, and Ash Wednesday have variable dates. These holidays can be found in the March chapter.

Presidents' Day *(third Monday in February)*

In 1997, President Richard Nixon proclaimed Presidents' Day as a national holiday. George Washington and Abraham Lincoln are both honored on this day.

• Read about past presidents who were in office before you were born. Select your favorite. Prepare a speech, telling why he is your choice.

• Create patriotic designs using red, white, and blue paint, chalk, markers, or other medium. Use bold stripes, stars, and other shapes in these colors. Design a pendant, windsock, mobile, pinwheel, banner, hat, T-shirt, wall-hanging, poster—or anything else you choose!

Chinese New Year *(January or February)*

The Chinese New Year falls on a different date each year. The holiday begins with the 2nd new moon after winter solstice. It lasts for 15 days. Each day has traditional celebrations. Each of the 12 years in the Chinese lunar calendar is named after a different animal. The 15th day of the Chinese New Year is called the Lantern Festival. The end of the holiday celebration is marked with festive parades. There's always a dragon in the parade. The Chinese Dragon is called *Gum Loong*, or *Golden Dragon*. He comes at the end of the parade to wish everyone good luck, prosperity, and peace. You and your friends or classmates can make this *Gum Loong* long enough to circle your whole room!

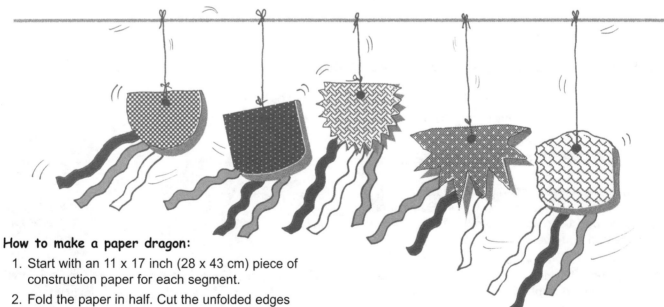

How to make a paper dragon:

1. Start with an 11 x 17 inch (28 x 43 cm) piece of construction paper for each segment.

2. Fold the paper in half. Cut the unfolded edges to shape a pattern (as shown.)

3. Cut scales from bright bits of wrapping paper, colored tissue, or colored foil.

4. Create a collage of scales on the segment. Glue the papers and add generous amounts of glitter.

5. When the glue is dry, staple colorful crepe paper streamers to the bottom.

6. Punch a hole 1 inch (3 cm) from the center fold of each segment. Tie varying lengths of string (1–3 feet or 30–90 cm) onto the segments.

7. Hang a sturdy string or clothesline across the room.

8. Tie the segments to the clothesline. They should hang at different heights, so the dragon looks as if it is undulating in the air.

Survival!

Robinson Crusoe is one of the most famous fictional survivors. Read his story! Then take these survival challenges. Create some of your own.

February 1st

- Robinson Crusoe Day*
- Wear Red Day*
- Supreme Court Convened for the First Time *(1790)**
- National Freedom Day
- Women's Heart Health Day
- Serpent Day

Birthdays

1902 Langston Hughes
1878 Hattie Wyatt Caraway
1882 Louis St. Laurent

Shipwrecked!

You've washed up on an island with your clothes, boots, belt, and a backpack that has a plastic bag full of nuts, a yo-yo, a can of sardines, a pack of bubble gum, a checkers game, a softball, and 3 pencils. In your pocket, you have two $5 bills, 4 quarters, and a pen-knife. Figure out two ways that you could signal for help.

Lost in the Desert!

Wearing only lightweight clothes, you are lost on a desert hike. Your backpack has 2 quarts of water, a sandwich, a towel, a magazine, matches, a jackknife, a bandana, a cup, sunglasses, extra socks, a can of soda, and a large plastic zipper bag. There is plenty of sand, cacti, and lizards in sight. How can you protect yourself from the sun?

Stranded in the Woods!

The shortcut home seemed like a good idea. Now it's getting dark, and you have no idea where you are. You're wearing sandals, shorts, a T-shirt, a hat, and a belt. In your backpack you have 3 candy bars, nail file, binoculars, bottle of water, math textbook, two notebooks, markers, a ruler, a CD player with batteries, a camera, and extra shoelaces. How would you get a fire started?

More Ideas

- Think red today! Eat red food. Paint red designs. Write down every sight, sound, smell, feeling, taste, or experience that is red.
- Find out what it takes to become a Supreme Court Justice. Then learn about some of the most famous cases decided by the Supreme Court.

Use red construction paper for fire.

How to make the dragon's head:

1. Use 2 pieces of 11 x 17 inch (28 x 43 cm) construction paper. Draw a head using the picture as a model. Cut both pieces exactly the same.

2. Draw matching eyes, nostrils, and teeth on both sides.

3. Decorate with a collage of bright scales and glitter to match the body.

4. Punch 2 holes in the center of one side of a small cereal box (as shown). Thread and knot a 2-foot (60 cm) long string through the holes.

5. Glue the pieces of the head to both sides of the box. Hang the head from the line.

For each starred* holiday on pages 47–59, you will find at least one activity.

February 2nd

- Groundhog Day*
- Bottle Cap Patented *(1892)*
- Candlemas (Mexico)*
- Bonza Bottler Day
- California Kiwi Fruit Day
- National Baseball League Formed *(1876)*

Birthdays
1882   James Joyce

One More Idea

- How is Candlemas celebrated in Mexico? Learn about this holiday. Then find a simple recipe for making your own candles.

Catch Your Shadow!

Here's a quick and easy way to see your shadow (and keep it) on Groundhog Day.

Tape a large piece of black paper on a wall. Set up a light to shine on the paper. Sit between the light and the paper while someone draws around the shadow with white chalk. Cut around the shadow carefully, and mount the silhouette on white paper.

Bottle Cap Tambourine

Shake up some rhythm with this do-it-yourself tambourine. Remove the rubber circles inside the caps to get the best sound. Paint decorations on the caps.

Use a hammer and large nail to poke a hole in the center of 50 bottle caps. Untwist the hook of a hanger and bend the hanger into a diamond shape. "Thread" 50 caps onto the hanger. Finally, tie a strip of colorful cloth or yarn between each group of 5 bottle caps. Leave some space between the caps so they will rattle. Re-twist the hanger hook back together and use it as a handle for shaking.

February 3rd

- Halfway Point of Winter*
- 15th & 16th Amendments to the *U.S. Constitution* Ratified *(1870 & 1913)*
- Carrot Cake Day
- Endangered Species Act Became Law *(1973)*

Birthdays
1821   Elizabeth Blackwell*
1811   Horace Greeley
1894   Norman Rockwell*

More Ideas

- Find a copy of a Norman Rockwell painting. Write the story you think is depicted in the picture.
- Tell how Elizabeth Blackwell might have felt about the 15th Amendment.

White Out!

Today is the halfway point of winter. Celebrate by creating an unusual winter scene with plenty of white in it.

1. Cover your work surface with newspaper. Lay dark-colored construction paper on the newspaper.
2. Pour some bleach (carefully) into a glass dish.
3. Dip a cotton swab in the bleach and "draw" a winter scene.
4. Wait and watch while the bleach removes the color from the paper.
5. Wash your hands well after working with the bleach. Do not wipe your hands on your clothes!
6. When the scene is dry, add details with fine-point markers.

Airborne Thank-You

Here's a way to enjoy two holidays at once. Make this paper airplane to remember the accomplishments of Charles Lindbergh (born today). Then turn it into a gift to sail to your mail carrier!

1. Fold a piece of typing paper in half, crease it, then open it up.

2. Fold the long edge of the paper in ³/₄ inch. Repeat this 10 times until the paper is about 4¹/₂ inches long.

3. Fold in half again along your first fold and cut a line like the one shown.

4. Open up the plane and fold the wing tips toward the center.

5. Turn the plane over and fold the tips of the tail wings in toward the center.

6. Decorate the plane and write a thank-you note on it to your favorite mail carrier.

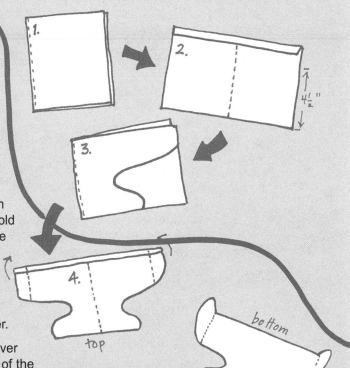

February 4th

- Thank a Mail Carrier Day*
- Create a Vacuum Day*
- George Washington Elected 1st U.S. President *(1789)**
- USO Formed *(1941)*

Birthdays
  1913 Rosa Parks
  1902 Charles Lindbergh*

More Ideas

- It is not easy to create a vacuum. Do some research to find out how it can be done.
- See if you can find two household tools that use a vacuum or partial vacuum to do their job.
- Design a president. Write a job description that describes qualifications you think are needed in a president.

Weathergrams

A weathergram is a very short non-rhyming poem that is not done when you finish writing. As your weathergram hangs outside, it is finished by the sun, rain, and wind. In a few months, it will be a true weathergram.

Cut a 3 x 10 inch strip of paper from a brown grocery bag. Fold over the top, punch a hole, and thread it with a piece of twine. Use ink to write a short winter poem. Write carefully with very good handwriting. When the writing is done, hang it on a bush or branch in your yard, or along a trail.

February 5th

- National Weatherperson's Day*
- Wiffle Ball Introduced *(1953)*
- National Girls & Women in Sports Day
- Disaster Day
- Constitution Day (Mexico)

Birthdays
  1934 Hank Aaron

49

February 6th

- Crayola Crayons Debuted (1903)*
- Lame Duck Day
- 20th Amendment to *U.S. Constitution* Ratified (1933)

Birthdays
1895	Babe Ruth
1788	Massachusetts, 6th state
1911	Ronald Reagan

February 7th

- 11th Amendment to *U.S. Constitution* Ratified (1795)*
- Wave All Your Fingers at Your Neighbor Day
- Send a Card to a Friend Day
- Ballet Introduced in U.S. (1827)

Birthdays
1812	Charles Dickens
1867	Laura Ingalls Wilder

February 8th

- Shovel Race Championships
- Boy Scouts of America Founded (1910)

Birthdays
1828	Jules Verne*

Iron-on Symmetry

Crayons—what a great invention!
Even when you wear them away to stubs, they are still useful tools for wonderful art. Gather up those broken and worn-away crayons to make an imaginative symmetrical creation.

Cover a work area with newspaper. Fold a large piece of drawing paper in half. Open it. On half the paper, shave crayons with a small pencil sharpener and arrange the bits into a picture or design. Fold the other half over the picture. Cover the whole paper with newspaper and iron with a warm iron. (Get an adult to help with the hot iron.)

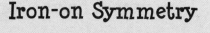

Making Changes

This is the day (in 1795) when the 11th Amendment to the U.S. Constitution was ratified. On February 6, 1933, the 20th Amendment was ratified. It is known as the **Lame Duck Amendment**. Use your research skills to answer these questions today:

1. *What is an amendment?*
2. *How many amendments to the U.S. Constitution are there?*
3. *How does an amendment get added to the Constitution?*
4. *What does the 11th Amendment do?*
5. *What does the 20th Amendment do?*
6. *Why is the 20th Amendment called the Lame Duck Amendment?*

Deep-Sea Search

Jules Verne is known as the father of science fiction. One of his most well-known books is *20,000 Leagues Under the Sea*. Remember Verne's work today while you practice coordinate geometry skills. Find the locations of some mysteries of the deep.

Make your own deep-sea grid and questions.

1. Give the coordinates of:
   the seahorse
   the sea star
   the octopus eye
   the crab

2. What is at
   3, 3 ?
   −1, −3 ?
   −5, −1 ?
   0, 2 ?
   4, −3 ?
   5, 3 ?

50

Homemade Remedies

How can you get rid of that toothache? Many remedies have been invented to cure all kinds of ailments—including toothaches. Write your own cure for that aching tooth. Then concoct remedies for other ailments, too. Put all the remedies into a book that everyone will want to own.

How to Cure a Toothache

When a toothache nags at your jaw, with pains shooting out in all directions, try this cure. Get a freshly-caught, cleaned codfish. Chill it well. Coat it with hot mustard. Hold the fish firmly between your sore tooth and your other teeth. Tear an old T-shirt into long strips. Tie the strip around your head to hold your mouth closed. Tie the cloth tightly. After about 20 minutes, the soreness will come out of the tooth into the fish. Don't eat the fish, or you'll get a stomachache.

Also write cures for... a broken heart; a sore throat; bad grades; headaches; ingrown toenails; chickenpox; hiccups; indigestion; indecision; jealousy; getting rid of a bully; the flu; a fever; sunburn.

February 9th

- Toothache Day*
- Hershey's Chocolate Founded (1927)*
- National Weather Service Established (1890)*
- Pizza Pie Day

Birthdays
1773   William Henry Harrison

More Ideas

- Read the wonderful book *Cloudy With a Chance of Meatballs*. Then write your own zany weather forecasts.
- What do you think the words on the little paper in a Hershey's kiss should say? Hold a contest to come up with the best phrase.

Umbrellas Without Rain

It's Umbrella Day, but it may not be raining. Not to worry—there are other ways to use that umbrella. Use your ingenuity. Make a list today of 100 uses for an umbrella. Put them into a song (maybe to the tune of "Singing in the Rain"). Sing the song while you demonstrate the uses.

February 10th

- Umbrella Day*
- The First Singing Telegram Sent (1933)
- 25th Amendment to the *U.S. Constitution* Ratified (1967)
- French and Indian War Ended by the *Treaty of Paris (1763)*

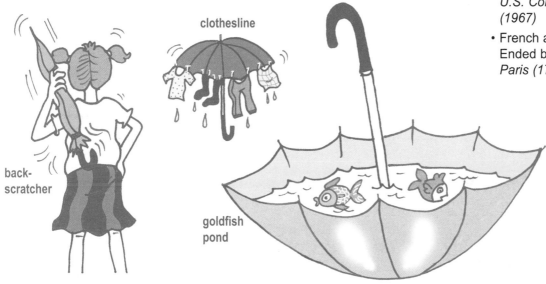

back-scratcher

clothesline

goldfish pond

February 11th

- Be Electrific Day*
- National Inventor's Day*
- National Science Youth Day*
- Don't Cry Over Spilled Milk Day*
- White Shirt Day
- Monopoly Board Game Introduced *(1935)*
- Nelson Mandela Released from Prison *(1990, after 27 1/2 years)*
- *Yalta Agreement* signed *(1945)*

Birthdays
1847   Thomas Alva Edison*

One More Idea
- Find ten idioms besides "Don't cry over spilled milk" that begin with "Don't." Act them out or illustrate them.

Be Electrific!

Try out these science tricks and watch the powers of electricity! It's a great way to celebrate Be Electrific Day, National Science Youth Day, and Thomas Edison's birthday all at once. For each of these tricks, you will need to "charge" a clean, hard rubber comb by rubbing it vigorously on a wool scarf or sweater. Learn enough about static electricity to explain the "magic" in each event.

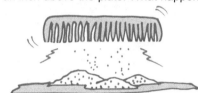

Swinging Cereal

Use heavy thread and tape to hang **O**-shaped cereal from a door frame or table ledge. Charge the comb. Bring it gradually near the **O**. Watch what happens. Charge the comb again, bring it near the cereal again. What happens?

Leaping Pepper

Sprinkle salt and pepper on a plate, and mix them well. Charge the comb. Hold it an inch above the plate. What happens?

Bending Water

Turn on a water faucet so that the water runs in a thin, steady stream. Charge the comb. Gradually bring the comb near the water. What happens? Recharge the comb and try it again!

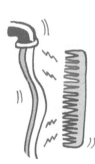

February 12th

- First Puppet Show in America *(1738)**
- National Lost Penny Day
- National Plum Pudding Day
- NAACP Founded *(1909)*

Birthdays
1809   Abraham Lincoln
1809   Charles Darwin

One Pattern, Many Puppets

Use this puppet pattern to make just about any character or creature you can imagine.

1. Create a pattern similiar to this one on 8" x 11" cardstock.

2. Trace the pattern onto construction paper or fabric. Make a front and a back.

3. Draw or cut out eyes, ears, arms, legs. tails, and noses from paper or felt. Glue them to the puppet. Add yarn, buttons, sequins, or other items you need.

4. Glue or stitch the front and back pieces together, leaving an opening at the bottom for your hand.

Consider Yourself Warned!

On Final Warning Day, spend some time thinking about warnings. What have you been warned to do or not to do (or to say or eat or not to say or eat)? Start remembering. You'll be surprised at how long your list is. Turn some warnings into posters. Include a consequence with each of your warnings.

You MUST eat your vegetables or you'll never be smart enough to go to college.

BEWARE! If you cross your eyes, they'll probably stick.

NEVER tickle an elephant. You don't want to be close to a falling elephant.

WARNING! Don't ever put watermelon seeds in your ears. or your head will turn green and get stripes like a rind and sweet pink juice will drip into your mind.

Read these poems by Shel Silverstein: "Early Bird" and "Warning."

February 13th

- Final Warning Day*
- Get a Different Name Day
- Value Friendship Day
- First Magazine Published in America (*The American Magazine*, 1747)

Birthdays

1885   Bess Truman

Valentines with Heart

Are you stumped about what to write in your valentines? Use candy conversation hearts to help you create original, clever valentines.

With a tiny dab of white glue, fasten a heart to each numbered square. Find the birth month of each person on your valentine list. Follow the month code to lead you to the words and phrases to include in your valentine for that person.

Month Codes

Jan: 13, 35, 27, 29, 24

Feb: 3, 19, 23, 4, 16

Mar: 6, 16, 19, 30, 9

Apr: 12, 26, 33, 15, 30

May: 11, 17, 16, 14, 1

Jun: 8, 28, 31, 27, 35

July: 5, 13, 32, 30, 6

Aug: 14, 9, 36, 22, 7

Sept: 2, 7, 20, 29, 21

Oct: 4, 15, 22, 25, 36

Nov: 10, 18, 20, 34, 16

Dec: 8, 21, 34, 3, 11

February 14th

- Valentine's Day*
- Ferris Wheel Day
- Race Relations Day
- Read to Your Child Day
- National Have a Heart Day
- First U.S. Presidential Photograph (*James Polk, 1840*)

Birthdays

1817   Frederick Douglas

1859   Oregon, 33rd State

1912   Arizona, 48th State

53

February 15th

- National Gumdrop Day*
- Flag Day (Canada)
- National I Want Butterscotch Day
- National Sea Monkey Day
- Susan B. Anthony Day

Birthdays
1564　Galileo Galilei
1820　Susan B. Anthony
1809　Cyrus McCormick

Gumdrop Molecules

Use gumdrops to sharpen your knowledge about compounds.

Create models to show the make-up of common compounds. Use one color gumdrop for each element. Connect the gumdrops with toothpicks. Try to show some of these:

water	sugar
salt	baking soda
chalk	gasoline
sand	methane
soap	candle wax
lime	crayons
bleach	butter

NH_3

Ammonia has one nitrogen and three hydrogen atoms.

CO_2

Carbon dioxide has one carbon and two oxygen atoms.

February 16th

- Do a Grouch a Favor Day*
- Nylon Patented (1937)
- Castro Becomes Cuba's Premier (1959)

Advice for Grouches

Write an advice column or notes of advice for a grouch. Give helpful suggestions that might get a grouch to be less grouchy. Pass the advice along to a grouch. Include a coupon offering to do a favor for the grouch.

This COUPON is good for one back rub. Must be used by a certified grouch.

Advice to a Grouch
Start the day by drinking a cup of vinegar. After that, everything that happens during your day will seem a little sweeter.

February 17th

- Random Acts of Kindness Day*
- Champion Crab Races Day*
- American PTA Founded (1897)*
- My Way Day

Birthdays
1963　Michael Jordan*

More Ideas
- Do at least 5 random acts of kindness today.
- Learn how to do the crab walk. Start some crab races.
- Get autographs from three people who belong to a PTA.

Big Money in Basketball

Michael Jordan scored 2,491 points for the Chicago Bulls in the 1995–1996 season. Then he was offered a 1-year contract for $25 million. That's about $10,000 per point! Do some research on NBA salaries. Then create math problems for friends to solve.

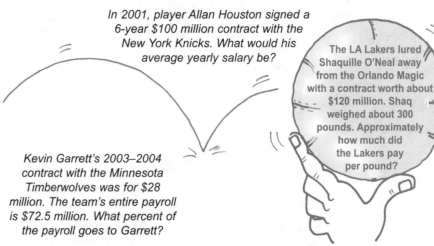

In 2001, player Allan Houston signed a 6-year $100 million contract with the New York Knicks. What would his average yearly salary be?

The LA Lakers lured Shaquille O'Neal away from the Orlando Magic with a contract worth about $120 million. Shaq weighed about 300 pounds. Approximately how much did the Lakers pay per pound?

Kevin Garrett's 2003–2004 contract with the Minnesota Timberwolves was for $28 million. The team's entire payroll is $72.5 million. What percent of the payroll goes to Garrett?

Thumbs with Personality

Appreciate your thumb by spreading your thumbprint around!

Get your thumbs inked up on a stamp pad. Make thumbprints all over a piece of drawing paper. Use fine-point markers to turn each print into a character or creature with personality.

February 18th

- Thumb Appreciation Day*
- First Cow Milked While Flying in an Airplane *(1930)**
- National Battery Day
- Phonograph Patented *(1878)*
- Pluto Discovered *(by Clyde Tombaugh, 1930)*

Wacky Firsts

February 18th marks the first time a cow was milked while flying in an airplane. Just picture that! Find or make up other wacky firsts that might have happened. "Draw" a snapshot of each one. Put them together in a book to share.

Can You Speak Space?

Two events are commemorated today that have affected our understanding of the wonders in outer space: the launch of the space station and the birth of Nicolaus Copernicus. Honor these by brushing up on your fluency in space talk. Identify, describe, and explain each of these:

asteroid belt	magnitude	lunar eclipse	solar wind
chromosphere	nebulae	solar eclipse	shooting star
coma	dwarf stars	moon phases	meteor shower
comet	white dwarf	total eclipse	red giant
corona	red dwarf	partial eclipse	blue giant
falling star	black dwarf	wormhole	supergiant
fireball	supernova	clusters	main sequence star
inner planets	neutron star	universe	binary stars
galaxy	pulsars	cosmology	meteor
outer planets	protostar	Big Bang Theory	meteorite
solar flares	giant star	Big Squeeze Theory	meteoroid
sunspots	quasar	black hole	

February 19th

- *Mir* Space Station Launched into Orbit (U.S.S.R., 1986)*
- *Mr. Roger's Neighborhood* Debuted *(1968)**
- National Chocolate Mint Day*

Birthdays
1473   Nicolaus Copernicus*

More Ideas

- Find out what Copernicus contributed to our knowledge about space.
- Find out who Mr. Rogers really was.
- Don't let Chocolate Mint Day go by without dipping some apple slices into melted chocolate mint!

- Toothpick Patented *(1872)**
- Hoodie Hoo Day in Northern Hemisphere*
- John Glenn Day
- National Student Volunteer Day
- First American Orbited Earth *(John Glenn, 1962)*

Birthdays
1902 Ansel Adams
1927 Sidney Poitier

Toothpick Math

Toothpicks have many talents and uses worth celebrating today. For one thing, they make great props to practice reading and writing Roman numerals. Use tiny bits of clay or chewed-up bubble gum to stick them together and form the numerals.

(Then think of 100 other uses for toothpicks.)

Holler Hoodie-Hoo *(Northern Hemisphere)*

This is the day for people to go outside at noon and yell "Hoodie Hoo" to chase away winter and get ready for spring. Think of other things you could holler to chase away winter or welcome spring.

- First Public Demonstration of Morse's Telegraph *(1838)**
- Lucy Hobbs Became First Female American Dentist *(1866)**
- Love Your Pet Day
- Washington Monument Dedicated *(1885)*
- First U.S. Telephone Book Circulated *(1878)*
- President Richard Nixon Visited Communist China *(1972)*

One More Idea
- Track down your state's requirements for practicing dentistry.

Dot-Dash Messages

The telegraph sends messages with a series of sound signals. All messages are made from different combinations of the same two sounds—a short one (dot) and a long one (dash). Think of a short and loud sound you can create to send messages in Morse Code. Make the noises by tapping, vocalizing, or playing an instrument.

MORSE CODE

A .-	H	O ---	V ...-
B -...	I ..	P .--.	W .--
C -.-.	J .--	Q --.-	X -..-
D -..	K -.-	R .-.	Y -.--
E .	L .-..	S ...	Z --..
F ..-.	M --	T -	
G --.	N -.	U ..-	

Decode this message. There is a space after each letter.

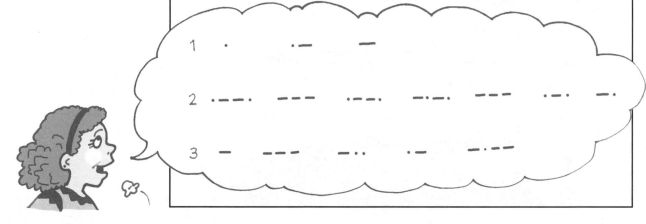

56

Brain Busters

Stretch your brain on World Thinking Day! Solve these brain busters. Write some more and challenge someone else to solve them.

- *Three hours ago, it was as long after 1 PM as before 1 AM. What time is it now?*

- *Five friends raced their lawnmowers. Van beat Stan but not Anne. Nan finished between Dan and Stan. Stan finished sooner than Dan. Who won the race?*

- *A painter was hired to paint all the numbers on the doors of rooms 900–999 on the 9th floor of a hotel. How many times did he paint the number 9?*

- *Sherry is six years older than Terry. Five years ago, Sherry was four times Terry's age. In five years, Terry will be $\frac{2}{3}$ of Sherry's age. How old are they now?*

- *What geometric figure has six edges, four vertices, and four faces?*

- *Al has ten U.S. coins equaling 75¢. What could they be?*

- *Think of ten questions never to ask someone who is defusing a bomb.*

- *What is the smallest number evenly divisible by all digits, 1–9?*

February 22nd

- World Thinking Day*
- Be Humble Day
- First Chain Store Opened *(Woolworth's, 1879)*

Birthdays
1732 George Washington

Hard thinking makes me humble.

Go Bananas!

Invite a friend to help you make banana bread, but prepare the bananas ahead of time to surprise your friend when it's time to peel them. When the peelings come off, the bananas will already be sliced!

1. Stick a threaded needle into one ridge of the banana skin and poke it out at the next ridge. Pull the thread tight but leave some sticking out of the first hole.
2. Push the needle back into the second hole and bring it out at the next ridge. Keep doing this until you bring the needle out of the original hole.
3. Hold both ends of the thread and pull the thread out of the banana. (The thread cuts banana slices inside the skin!)
4. Do this at 6 to 8 more places along the banana.

February 23rd

- Banana Bread Day*
- Sticky Bun Day
- International Dog Biscuit Appreciation Day
- First Cloning of an Adult Animal *(1997)*
- Diesel Engine Patented *(1893)*
- Battle at the Alamo *(1836)*

Birthdays
1685 George Frederick Handel
1787 Emma Hart Willard

Homemade Tortilla Chips

The average American eats almost 6 pounds of tortilla chips a year. That's a lot of chips! Make your own tortilla chips today to celebrate Tortilla Chip Day and Mexican Flag Day.

Brush cooking oil on both sides of tortillas, then cut the tortillas into wedges. Spread the wedges in a single layer on an oiled cookie pan. Sprinkle them with salt. Bake the wedges at 350° until crispy. *(Watch closely!)* Enjoy your chips with salsa, melted cheese, guacamole, or any of your favorite dips.

What is the favorite dance of tortilla chips?

The salsa, of course.

February 24th

- National Tortilla Chip Day*
- Flag Day (Mexico)
- Gregorian Calendar Created *(1582)*

February 25th

- Quiet Day*
- Spay Day USA

Birthdays
  1922 "Texas Rose" Bascom

Quiet Sprouting

Quiet Day is a good time for a science experience that will keep you "mum." When you try this trick, you must keep your mouth closed for a long time. A mung bean contains a seed that will sprout fairly easily in a warm, dark, moist place. Your mouth is the perfect place!

Put a mung bean seed on the center of your tongue. Keep your mouth closed for a long time. Check with a mirror after an hour to see what's happening with the bean. Keep it in your mouth until it sprouts.

February 26th

- National Pistachio Day*
- Tell a Fairy Tale Day
- FCC Created *(1934)*
- Grand Canyon National Park Established *(1919)*
- Bomb Exploded at World Trade Center, NY City *(1993)*

Birthdays
  1846 Buffalo Bill (William Cody)
  1829 Levi Strauss

No-Bake Pistachio Dessert

Get to know more about this tasty little nut. Research to find out all you can about pistachios. Then whip up this easy pistachio dessert.

1. Follow the directions on the boxes to make and cool two boxes of pistachio pudding.
2. Put a layer of ladyfingers in the bottom of a glass pan.
3. Spread half the pudding on the ladyfingers. Top with half a large container of prepared whipped cream.
4. Sprinkle with crushed pistachios and crushed Butterfinger candy bars.
5. Repeat steps 2–4, wrap the pan, and chill.

When pistachios mature, the shells of the nuts split. Because of this, they can be roasted and salted without removing the shells.

February 27th

- International Polar Bear Day*
- No Brainer Day
- 22nd Amendment to the *U.S. Constitution* ratified
- American Indian Movement Occupied Wounded Knee *(1973)*

Birthdays
  1807 Henry W. Longfellow
  1902 John Steinbeck
  1897 Marion Anderson

Scenes from Polar Bear Territory

Polar bears get to enjoy a particular natural phenomenon more often than most of us. They are lucky enough to live in the Arctic, where the northern lights put on spectacular displays of color in the cold north sky. You can create scenes that mimic the colors of the northern lights.

1. Spread watercolor paper on top of newspaper.
2. Use a wide brush to thoroughly wet the paper with water.
3. Choose watercolors such as pink, purple, dark blue, and black.
4. Load your widest brush with color and swipe across the top. Let the color ooze and feather. Clean the brush well and swipe with another color.
5. Leave a little white space between each color. The wet paper will cause the colors to feather into each other and create new colors.
6. At the bottom of the page, paint a black ocean with white icebergs.
7. When your painting is dry, use marking pens to draw a polar bear enjoying the northern lights.

Dreams

Keep your eyes open today for people falling asleep in public. How many sleepers can you find? Think about what someone might be dreaming as he or she is riding the bus, sitting in a train station, taking a lunch break, or riding in a stroller. If you can't find real sleepers, use imaginary characters as your subjects for made-up dreams.

1. **Search magazines** for pictures of people, animals, or other characters doing interesting things.

2. **Cut out the pictures** and paste each on a larger piece of colored paper.

3. **Use markers to alter** their eyes so they appear to be asleep.

4. **Draw a "dream bubble"** about each head. Use the bubble space to write or draw a dream you think they might have.

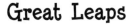

- Public Sleeping Day*
- Floral Design Day
- *USS Princeton* Exploded *(1844)*

Birthdays
1940   Mario Andretti

Great Leaps

What would you do on a day that happens only once every four years? Here are a few ideas. You think of more!

- It's Leap Year! (Leap Year Day)*
- Bachelor's Day*
- Sadie Hawkins Day*
- National Surf and Turf Day
- Salem Witch Hunt Led to First Arrests *(1692)*

- **Find some answers:**
  Why do we have leap year?
  How is leap year related to the history of the Roman calendar?
  How did Julius Caesar affect the calendar?
  Who made the final calendar adjustment that resulted in the leap years we now have?
  When did this happen?
  What is Sadie Hawkins Day?
  Why is February 29 called Bachelor's Day?

- Learn about 10 famous people born on Leap Day. List their accomplishments.

- Plan a Leap Year Day party. Create a menu (how about frog legs?) and choose games and activities fitting a once-in-four-years celebration.

- Make a list of "**Things to Do ONLY Once Every Four Years.**" (DO some of them on this day.)

- Interview someone who is a leap year baby. Find out when and how he or she celebrates.

- Find out about the Honor Society of Leap Year Babies, the Worldwide Leap Year Birthday Club, and the Worldwide Leap Year Festival held in Anthony, Texas.

- Decide how and when you would celebrate a February 29 birthday.

- Find and read *The Leap Year Book* by Barbara Sutton Smith.

59

March

1
- First U.S. Census*
- Peanut Butter Lovers Day
- Share a Smile Day
- Get Caught Reading Day
- Silly Putty Debuted
- Vietnam Peace Treaty
- U.S. Land Mine Ban
- Yellowstone National Park Established
- Peace Corps Established
  Birthdays: Ohio & Nebraska

2
- Pyramid Day*
- Old Stuff Day
- Texas Independence Day
- National Banana Cream Pie Day
- Read Across America Day
- Highway Numbers Introduced
  Birthdays: Dr. Seuss

3
- I Want You to Be Happy Day*
- School Principals Day*
- Girls' Day (Japan)*
- Peach Blossom Day*
- Fun Facts About Names Day*
- National Anthem Day*
- What If Cats & Dogs Had Opposable Thumbs Day*
- Missouri Compromise Introduced*
- Bonza Bottler Day
  Birthdays: Florida*, Alexander Graham Bell*

4
- *U.S. Constitution* Went into Effect*
- National Pound Cake Day
- Unique Names Day
- March 4 Yourself Day
- First Meeting of U.S. Congress

5
- Personality Day*
- Dr. Doolittle Day
- Learn What Your Name Means Day
- National Cheese Doodle Day
- National Fiery Foods & Barbeque Show
- "Iron Curtain" Speech
- Boston Massacre
- "Siege of the Alamo" Ended

6
- Alamo Day
- Dentist's Day
- Oreo Cookies Introduced*
- National Frozen Food Day
  Birthdays: Michelangelo*

7
- Telephone Patented*
- Middle Name Pride Day
- Name Tag Day
- Purim
- Suez Canal Opened
- Monopoly Patented
  Birthdays: Luther Burbank

8
- Plant a Flower Day*
- Commonwealth Day (Canada)*
- Farmers' Day
- Working Woman's Day
- International Women's Day

9
- False Teeth Patented*
- Panic Day*
- International Cabin Fever Day*
- Barbie Doll Introduced
  Birthdays: Amerigo Vespucci

10
- First U.S. Paper Money*
- Mario Day
  Birthdays: Harriet Tubman, Kim Campbell

11
- International Dream Day*
- Johnny Appleseed Day
- Camp Fire USA Day
- Worship of Tools Day
- Bureau of Indian Affairs Established
  Birthdays: Ezra Jack Keats*

12
- American Crossword Puzzle Tournament*
- Alfred Hitchcock Day*
- Blizzard of 1888*
- Girl Scout Day

13
- National Open an Umbrella Indoors Day*
- Good Samaritan Day
- Earmuffs Patented
- Uranus Discovered
- First Uncle Sam Cartoon Published

14
- National Potato Chip Day
- National Preschoolers Day
- Learn About Butterflies Day
- Pi Day
- World Ice Art Championships
- Cotton Gin Patented
  Birthdays: Albert Einstein*

15
- National Quilting Day*
- Ides of March
- Buzzards Day
- Everything You Think Is Wrong Day
- National Pasta Days
- First Blood Bank
  Birthdays: Andrew Jackson, Maine

16
- Vitamin C Discovered*
- Everything You Do Is Right Day
- Lips Appreciation Day
- West Point Academy Established
  Birthdays: James Madison

17
- St. Patrick's Day*
- World's Smallest St. Patrick's Day Parade*
- Rubber Band Invented*
- Submarine Day
- Freedom of Information Day

18
- Awkward Moments Day*
- First Walk in Space
  Birthdays: Grover Cleveland

19
- Swallows Return to Capistrano*
- Poultry Day*
- National Chocolate Caramel Day

20
- National Common Courtesy Day*
- Teenagers Day
- Snowman Burning Day
  Birthdays: Fred Rogers, Brian Mulroney

21
- Children's Poetry Day*
- Memory Day*
- International Astrology Day
- Bird Appreciation Day
- UN Day for the Elimination of Racial Discrimination
- First Round-the-World Balloon Flight
  Birthdays: Benito Juarez, Johann Sebastian Bach

22
- World Water Day*
- International Goof-off Day
- International Day of the Seal
- Laser Patented
  Birthdays: Randolph Caldecott*

23
- World Meteorological Day*
- Liberty Day*
- Near Miss Day
- Toast Day
- National Chip & Dip Day
- *Mir* Space Station Abandoned

24
- National Chocolate-Covered Raisins Day*
- National Family Day
- World Tuberculosis Day
  Birthdays: Harry Houdini

25
- First Color TV Produced*
- Pecan Day*
- Waffle Day*
- First Pancakes Made
- National Medal of Honor Day

26
- Spinach Festival Day*
- Make Up Your Own Holiday Day*
- Camp David Peace Accord
- Polio Vaccine Invented
  Birthdays: Robert Frost*, Sandra Day O'Connor

27
- Quirky Country Music Song Title Day*
- National Joe Day
- Photography Day
- Fly a Kite Day
- World Theater Day
- First Long-Distance Phone Call

28
- 23rd Amendment Ratified
- Something on a Stick Day*
- Respect Your Cat Day
- Save a Spider Day
- Three-Mile Island Nuclear Power Plant Accident
- First Performance of *The Greatest Show on Earth*

29
- Niagara Falls Stopped Flowing*
- Coca-Cola Invented*
- America's Subway Day*
- Vietnam Veteran's Day
- First Anesthetic Used

30
- Pencil with Eraser Patented*
- Doctor's Day
- National Hot Dog Day
- Take a Walk in the Park Day
- U.S. Purchased Alaska from Russia
  Birthdays: Vincent Van Gogh

31
- First Map of the U.S. Patented*
- Bunsen Burner Day
- National Clams on the Half Shell Day
- Eiffel Tower Completed
- U.S. Air Force Academy Established
  Birthdays: Newfoundland, Cesar Chavez, Franz Joseph Haydn

Month-long Celebrations

American Red Cross Month

Deaf History Month

Ethics Awareness Month

Foot Health Month*

Hamburger Month

International Listening Awareness Month

International Mirth Month*

Irish-American Month

Keep Your Shoelaces Tied Month*

Music in Our Schools Month*

National Baby Month

National Craft Month*

National Eye Donor Month

National Frozen Food Month

National Kidney Month

National Kite Month*

National Noodle Month*

Nutrition Month

National Optimism Month*

National Peanut Month

National Umbrella Month

Play the Recorder Month

Poison Prevention Month

Save Your Vision Month

Women's History Month*

Youth Art Month*

Weekly Celebrations

First Week: National Procrastinators Week* Newspapers in Education Week*, Autograph-Collecting Week*, National School Breakfast Week, Celebrate Your Name Week, Return Borrowed Books Week, National Foreign Language Week, Volunteers of America Week

Second Week: National Bubblegum Week*, Camp Fire Girls and Boys Week, Music in Our Schools Week, Girl Scout Week

Third Week: American Chocolate Week*, Anonymous Giving Week*, International Goof-Off Week*, National Smile Week*, Spring Fever Week, Sports Trivia Week, National Art Week, National Clutter Awareness Week

Fourth Week: National Bubble Week*, National Poison Prevention Week, Clean Your Closet Week

Dates That Vary: Easter*, Mardi Gras*, Lent*, Ash Wednesday*, Shrove Tuesday*, Carnival*, Purim*, First Day of Spring*, No Homework Day*, Genealogy Day*, Celebrate Your Name Day*, Iditarod*, World's Largest Rattlesnake Roundup*, Commonwealth Day (Canada)*, International Pancake Day, Maple Syrup Day

March's Month-long Celebrations

National Optimism Month

- Are you an optimist? Find the definition for the word *optimist*. Then decide the answer to the question.

- The projects carried on by Optimist Clubs focus on helping young people become the best that they can be. Learn more by visiting this website and others about optimists: *www.optimist.org*.

- Write a short (illustrated) book called *How to Tell an Optimist from a Pessimist*. Alternate pages with these beginnings:

*An optimist*_____

_____

*A pessimist*_____

_____

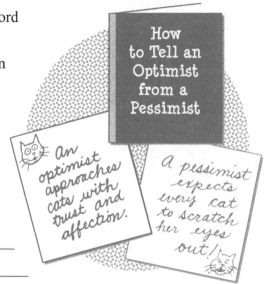

National Kite Month

- What actually causes a kite to fly? Prepare a written or spoken explanation. Use diagrams or a real kite to demonstrate.

- Make a list of *Rules for Kite-Flying Safety*.

- Find out about different kinds of kites.

- Find some music that makes you think of flying kites.

- Track down names, dates, and locations of kite festivals around the world.

- Most important of all, make and fly some kites this month!

National Noodle Month

• Find and draw as many different kinds of noodles as you can. (You might need to visit a grocery store.)

• *Science:* Investigate the ingredients and nutritional value of noodles. Find out how long it takes to cook a noodle until it's soft enough to stick to a wall (when you throw it against the wall). Learn about how noodles are made.

• *Math:* Estimate the number of noodles in an unopened bag; count them to check your estimate. Use noodles for probability problems. Compare weights of different noodles. Find out how many noodles it takes to weigh one ounce or one gram.

• *Art:* Make noodle scenes, necklaces, key chains, sculptures, or collages. Write your name in noodles.

• *Language:* Write noodle poems, noodle jokes, noodle biographies, noodle notices, noodle ads, noodle tongue twisters, noodle riddles, recipes with noodles, or a love song to a noodle. Use noodles to practice writing your spelling words.

National Craft Month

Windy March is the perfect time of year for hanging up some wind chimes. Celebrate National Craft Month by making wind chimes of your own, and enjoy their music right outside your door. You can make wind chimes with several different kinds of materials. Here are a few to try. Decorate your chimes with enamel paints.

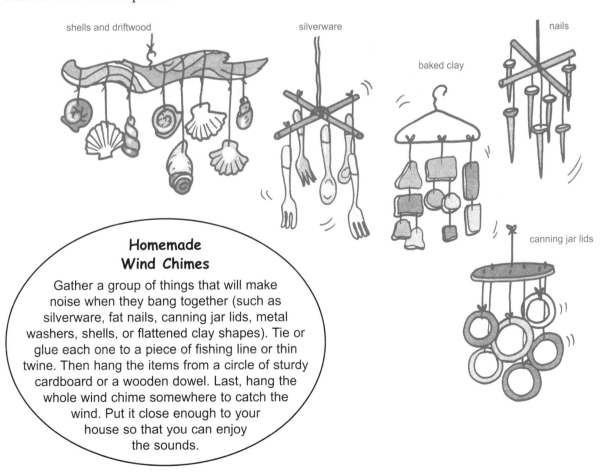

shells and driftwood

silverware

nails

baked clay

canning jar lids

Homemade Wind Chimes

Gather a group of things that will make noise when they bang together (such as silverware, fat nails, canning jar lids, metal washers, shells, or flattened clay shapes). Tie or glue each one to a piece of fishing line or thin twine. Then hang the items from a circle of sturdy cardboard or a wooden dowel. Last, hang the whole wind chime somewhere to catch the wind. Put it close enough to your house so that you can enjoy the sounds.

Youth Art Month

Enjoy all kinds of art this month. Look for art all around you. (You might find it in some unexpected places!) Keep a log of different works of art you see in March. Try as many different kinds of art as possible during the month. Use many kinds of media (paint, sand, glue, chalk, crayons, ink, junk, food, paper, yarn, string, wire, foil, plaster, soap, sticks, stones, dough, fabric).

Keep Your Shoelaces Tied Month

This is a month to think about shoelaces. If you can't keep your shoelaces tied, pull them out and use them for these shoelace paintings in honor of Youth Art Month.

Paint with Your Shoelaces

1 Fold a large piece of drawing paper in half. Open it up.

2. Use a brush to coat a shoelace with tempera paint.

3. Lay the painted shoelace on one half of the paper, leaving the ends hanging over the edge. Twist and curl the shoelace as you lay it on the paper.

4. Fold the paper closed. Hold down the paper firmly with one hand.

5. With the other hand, grab both ends of the shoelace and quickly pull it out from between the layers of paper.

6. If you want to add another color, repeat the steps after the first color is dry.

What will happen if you don't keep your shoelaces tied? Write and illustrate a book for young children about the possible consequences of untied shoelaces.

If you can fingerpaint, you can footpaint. Here's a way to put your best foot forward as you celebrate Youth Art Month.

Foot Health Month

• What can you possibly do to keep your feet healthy? Find out. Then make a comic-book style *Manual for Foot Care*.

• Find out how many bones there are in the foot. Learn their names.

• Be able to describe 5 different diseases that can affect feet.

PAINT WITH YOUR FEET

1. Spread a big piece of paper on top of several newspapers.
2. Pour some paint into a pan.
3. Dip your toe in and use it as a tool to paint. OR, dip your foot into the pan and make whole footprints.
4. You can also try dipping different colors of paint onto different parts of your foot with a sponge before making the prints.

Music in Our Schools Month

Celebrate music by listening to as many different kinds of music as you can find. Listen to a different kind of music every day. Look for music from different cultures and times in history.

As you listen, keep a large piece of paper handy, along with a variety of drawing and art materials. Use lines, designs, shapes, and colors to express on paper the feeling that is inspired by the music. Label each creation with the kind of music. Share your creations with others.

OR . . . respond to each kind of music by moving your body to match its rhythm and mood.

Women's History Month

Research women who contributed to history and make your own *Encyclopedia of Notable Women.* Include at least 25 women. Write a short biography for each one. Here are a few names to get you started:

Amelia Earhart	Rosa Parks
Mae Jemison	Maria Tallchief
Sally Ride	Queen Lilluokalani
Melba Pattilo	Jody Williams
Rachel Carson	Mary Harris Jones
Jane Adams	Harriet Tubman
Geraldine Ferraro	Sandra Day O'Connor
Eleanor Roosevelt	Dolores Huerta
Madam C. J. Walker	Mother Teresa
Chien-Shinun Wu	Susan B. Anthony
Golda Meir	Jovita Idar
Lise Meitner	Stephanie Kwolek
Margaret Thatcher	Mary Anderson
Barbara McClintock	Grace Hopper

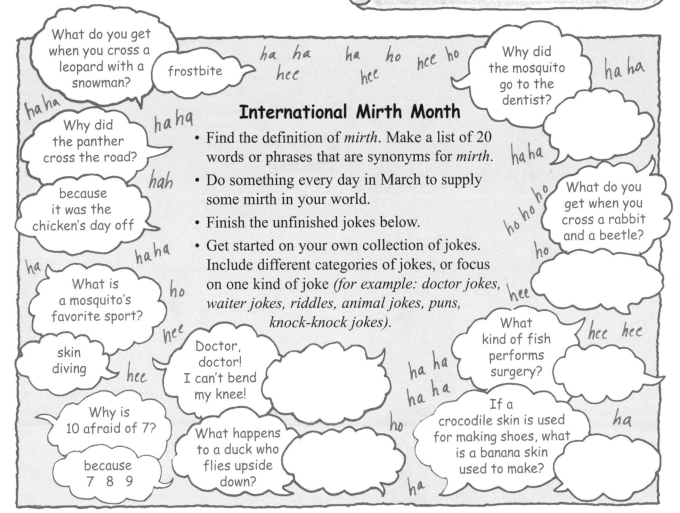

International Mirth Month

- Find the definition of *mirth*. Make a list of 20 words or phrases that are synonyms for *mirth*.
- Do something every day in March to supply some mirth in your world.
- Finish the unfinished jokes below.
- Get started on your own collection of jokes. Include different categories of jokes, or focus on one kind of joke *(for example: doctor jokes, waiter jokes, riddles, animal jokes, puns, knock-knock jokes).*

See page 60 for other month-long holidays to celebrate in March.

Special Weeks in March

National Procrastinators Week

• What is a *procrastinator?* Find out!

• Think of 30 excuses a procrastinator might use.

• Write a list with each line beginning:
You're a procrastinator if _____

• Check out these websites:
www.procrastinator.com and
www.enprocrastination.com.

Autograph-Collecting Week

Collect unusual autographs this week. Combine them into your own personal autograph book. (Make a page for each kind of autograph.) Try to get five autographs from someone fitting each of these descriptions:

    . . . reads a newspaper daily
    . . . is a procrastinator
    . . . chews bubblegum constantly
    . . . is a vegetarian
    . . . has no appendix
    . . . doesn't wear a watch
    . . . lives on a third floor
    . . . wakes up at 5 a.m.
    . . . is an insomniac
    . . . won't eat chocolate
    . . . does a crossword puzzle daily

Newspapers in Education Week

Get acquainted with your local newspaper this week. Try to read newspapers from other towns and cities, too. Pay close attention to the way news articles are written. Notice the style and the vocabulary that reporters use to tell about an event. Use your observations to help you write your own reports about events. Choose one or more of these headlines. Write a news article in the style of a newspaper report.

Sun Times
ASTEROID HITS EARTH

Daily Tidings
Diamonds Discovered in Pastries

Morning Gazette
Pigs' Home Destroyed by Wolf

EVENING NEWS
TOWN OF LANSING DISAPPEARS

METRO NEWS
PYTHONS DISCOVERED IN CITY SEWER

Lakewood Journal
Local Boy Blows Biggest Bubble

You can use a wad of chewed bubblegum to..

...stop up a leak in your waterbed, or plug a hole in your boat...

...or hang a poster on your wall, or...

Bubblegum Week

It's a good week for bubble-blowing challenges. But don't just CHEW the gum. Get creative. Think of at least 25 other ways to use bubblegum. Illustrate your ideas.

American Chocolate Week

• Find out what the top ten chocolate-consuming countries are. Make a graph showing the results of your research.

• Gather a bunch of friends and enjoy some chocolate fondue.

Easy, Perfect Chocolate Fondue

1. Melt a stick of butter or margarine with a large package of chocolate chips over low heat. Stir constantly.
2. Carefully stir in one can of Eagle brand condensed milk. Stir until everything is mixed.
3. Keep the sauce warm in a fondue pot.
4. Dip all sorts of food into the chocolate and enjoy. *(Try cubes of cake, chunks of any fruit, or pretzels. Experiment with unusual dippers!)*

I'm so glad it's **International Goof-off Week**. I've decided to make chocolate a part of my goofing off.

It's **Anonymous Giving Week**. Try to give something unexpected to someone this week. Make absolutely sure that your gift remains anonymous. It's also **National Smile Week**. Think of a way to make someone smile each day.

Fourth Week

National Bubble Week

Mix up a batch of bubble soup, gather a group of friends, and have a good time blowing bubbles. While you're having fun, do some research to learn the science of bubbles. Find out how they are formed.

BUBBLE SOUP

1 C liquid dishwashing soap
1 C glycerin
3 C water
Gently mix all ingredients.

TABLE BUBBLES

1. Cover a table with plastic.
2. Pour some bubble soup on the table.
3. Blow on the soup with a straw.

GIANT BUBBLES

1. Pour a batch of bubble soup into a flat pan.
2. Shape wire or a wire hanger into a circle or other shape to create a bubble-maker. Dip it in the soup.
3. Practice blowing gently to make gigantic bubbles. Or, wave the wire shape through the air.

See page 61 for other weeklong holidays to celebrate in March. 67

The Days of March

Easter, Mardi Gras, Lent, Ash Wednesday, Shrove Tuesday, Carnival

The date of each of these holidays depends on the date of Easter. **Easter** is a Christian holiday that celebrates the return to life of Jesus, the founder of Christianity. Easter is observed on the first Sunday after the first full moon following the first day of spring in the Northern Hemisphere. It can fall on a Sunday anytime between March 22 and April 25. **Lent** is a religious period that prepares for Easter, beginning 40 days before Easter. There is a practice of self-sacrifice during Lent. People often give up certain luxuries (such as rich foods) for the 40-day period. **Ash Wednesday** is the day Lent begins. In some churches, worshippers have ashes placed on their foreheads as a symbol of purification and repentance. The day before Lent begins is called **Shrove Tuesday**. (Shrove Tuesday is also **International Pancake Day**.) The **Carnival** season begins about a week before Shrove Tuesday. Fancy parades and parties mark this week; people parade in wonderful masks and wild costumes. **Mardi Gras** is the last day of Carnival. It falls on Shrove Tuesday. In French, the words *Mardi Gras* mean *Fat Tuesday* because it is a time of celebrating and partying before the sacrifices of Lent begin.

Mardi Gras Masks

Purim

Purim is a festive Jewish holiday celebrated with stories, noisemakers, gifts, and treats to remember a Jewish victory over oppression told in the story of Esther. It is held on the 14th and 15th days of the 12th month in the Jewish calendar. During Purim, children dress up in costumes and masks, and families share gifts and food. One of the Purim traditions is the use of *graggers*. These are noisemakers used during the story. Every time one character, Haman, is mentioned, the listeners twirl their graggers, hiss and boo, and stamp their feet.

Homemade Graggers

Homemade Graggers

Decorate a raisin box with paint, fabric, stickers, markers, and glitter. Put something noisy inside (such as small bells, rice, or beans) and tape the box shut. Cut holes to insert a wooden dowel. Put rubber bands above and below the box. Shake and twirl the gragger.

First Day of Spring

The first day of spring, also known as the *vernal equinox*, occurs on a day when the sun is directly above the Earth's equator. In the Northern Hemisphere, this happens on March 19, 20, or 21. In the Southern Hemisphere, this happens on September 22 or 23. Observe the holiday by getting a close look at the creatures of spring and making a few of your own.

Rites of Spring Piñata

1. Blow up a large, sturdy balloon. Cover it with newspaper strips dipped in liquid starch or thin flour & water paste.

2. Apply enough smooth layers of strips to make a solid covering. Let this dry for several days.

3. Carefully cut a small opening at the top of the dry piñata and push in wrapped candies, dried fruits, and small favors. Use masking tape to cover the hole securely.

4. Glue leaves, flowers, and other natural materials all over the piñata. (These can be real, artificial, or made from paper.)

5. When it's ready, gather some friends, and take turns trying to break the piñata open!

Commonwealth Day
(2nd Monday)

On this day, people in Canada and other Commonwealth countries hold parades to celebrate their common bonds with other Commonwealth countries. (See March 8 for celebration ideas.)

World's Largest Rattlesnake Roundup
(2nd Weekend)

About 30,000 people attend the rattlesnake roundup each year in Sweetwater, Texas. Farmers and ranchers set out to catch and bag every rattlesnake they can find. To honor this day, create a recipe that uses rattlesnake meat.

Iditarod
(begins on 1st Saturday)

This is the world's most famous sled dog race. Sleds, drivers (known as *mushers*), and dogs travel over 1,000 miles along trails of snow and ice from Anchorage to Nome, Alaska. Draw a map of Alaska that shows the Iditarod route.

No Homework Day
(Last Friday)

Gather some friends. Take turns finishing this statement:

The only thing worse than doing homework is _____ .

Celebrate Your Name Day
(1st Monday)

Focus on your name today. Find out what it means. Celebrate it. Sing it. Shout it. Illustrate it. Write about it.

Genealogy Day
(1st Saturday)

Learn the meanings of the words *genealogy* and *ancestry*. Then find out everything you can about your ancestry. Create a family tree with the information you locate.

- First U.S. Census *(1790)**
- Peanut Butter Lovers Day
- Share a Smile Day
- Get Caught Reading Day
- Silly Putty Debuted *(1950)*
- Vietnam Peace Treaty Signed *(1973)*
- U.S. Land Mine Ban *(1999)*
- Yellowstone National Park Established *(1872)*
- Peace Corps Established *(1961)*

Birthdays

1803 Ohio, 17th State
1867 Nebraska, 37th State

Count Me In!

A census is a count of the population. In 1790, the U.S. government began counting the people in the country. The census does not only count the people. The counting process gains many other kinds of information about the people: things such as locations where people live, sizes of households, ages, race, and income levels. Create your own census. Make a plan to count the people in your school or neighborhood. Decide what factors you will look at as you count. Make graphs to display the data you collect.

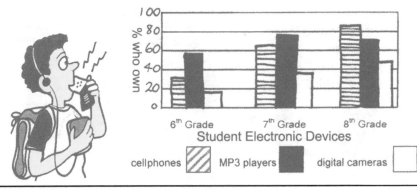

- Pyramid Day*
- Old Stuff Day
- Texas Independence Day
- National Banana Cream Pie Day
- Read Across America Day
- Highway Numbers Introduced *(1925)*

Birthdays

1904 Dr. Seuss (Theodore Geisel)*

One More Idea

- Write a Dr. Seuss-style story about a frog on a log, a snake with a cake, a cook with a book, a witch with an itch, or an owl with a scowl.

Instant Pyramid

In honor of Pyramid Day, find a clear definition of *pyramid*. Find out how, when, and where the pyramids of Egypt were built. Then, trace the pattern below, cut it out, and follow the directions to make a pyramid.

Then answer these questions:
- *How many faces, vertices, and edges does this pyramid have?*
- *What is its surface area?*
- *What is its volume?*
- *What kind of a pyramid is this?*
- *How is a pyramid named?*

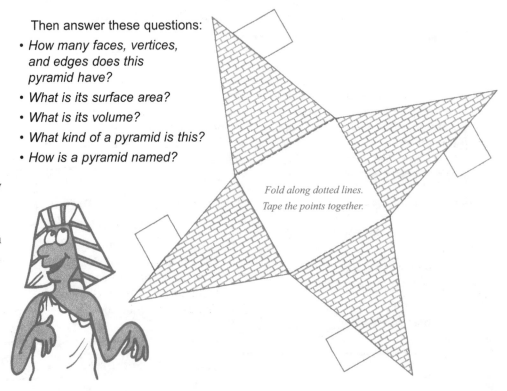

Fold along dotted lines.
Tape the points together.

For each starred holiday on pages 70–83, you will find at least one activity.*

Let's Talk!

Today is the birthday of a man best known as the inventor of the telephone. Celebrate this day with conversations custom-made for the telephone. Imagine a brief telephone conversation for each purpose.

Then write a conversation that. . .

. . . discusses what it takes to **be happy**

. . . interviews a **school principal** about her/his views

. . . explains how **Girls' Day** is celebrated in Japan

. . . exchanges two views about the best way to eat a **peach**

. . . shares interesting **facts about names**

. . . sings and elaborates on the words to the **national anthem**

. . . includes some ideas about what would happen
   if cats and dogs had opposable thumbs

. . . explores and explains the purpose of
   the **Missouri Compromise**

. . . asks and answers some questions
   about **Florida**

- I Want You to Be Happy Day*
- School Principals Day*
- Girls' Day *(Japan)**
- Peach Blossom Day*
- Fun Facts About Names Day*
- National Anthem Day*
- What If Cats & Dogs Had Opposable Thumbs Day*
- Missouri Compromise Introduced *(1820)**
- Bonza Bottler Day

Birthdays

1904   Florida, 27th State*
1847   Alexander Graham Bell*

Constitution Trivia

Make up your own trivia game with questions and answers about the *U.S. Constitution* (or the constitution from your country). Write clear rules telling players how to play the game. *(Here's a sample game board.)*

- *U.S. Constitution* Went into Effect *(1789)**
- National Pound Cake Day
- Unique Names Day
- March 4 Yourself Day
- First Meeting of U.S. Congress *(NY City, 1789)*

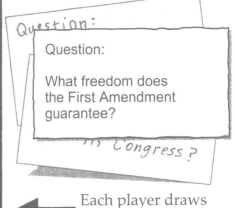

Each player draws a card on each turn.

71

March 5th

- Personality Day*
- Dr. Doolittle Day
- Learn What Your Name Means Day
- National Cheese Doodle Day
- National Fiery Foods & Barbeque Show
- "Iron Curtain" Speech Given (Winston Churchill, 1946)
- Boston Massacre Occurred (1770)
- "Siege of the Alamo" Ended

Create a Personality!

On Personality Day, get ready to create a character with personality! All you need (besides a clever imagination) is a stack of magazines, scissors, some glue, and drawing paper. After you're finished, name the person and write some words or phrases to describe the personality.

Cut parts of faces from different pictures. Put them together to create a brand new character.

March 6th

- Oreo® Cookies Introduced (1912)*
- Dentist's Day
- National Frozen Food Day
- Alamo Day

Birthdays
1904   Michelangelo*

Oreo® Posters

There are many different ways to eat an Oreo®. Make a poster that describes step by step what **you** think is the best way!

How to Eat an Oreo
Gently twist the cookies apart. Break one in half. Use that to scoop frosting into your mouth, then . . .

Simple Sculptures

Michelangelo de Lodovico Buonarroti-Simoni is one of the most famous artists of all times. He masterfully portrayed the human form in drawings, paintings, and sculptures. On his birthday, try your hand at representing the human form with this easy wire sculpture technique.

Sketch a figure on paper. Shape wire (copper, aluminum, or telephone wire) into the shape of the figure. Use a wire cutter when needed. Nail the figure to a block of wood for support. Leave the figure as it is, or cover it with strips of gauze that have been soaked in wet plaster of Paris mixture.

Dial-up Math

You know the telephone is a wonderful invention.
Did you know you could use it to practice math skills?
Get a touch-tone telephone and use it to solve these problems. Find the "value" of each letter by matching it with the number on the keypad. To find the value of a word, add the values of all the letters. After you solve these, make up ten problems of your own.

1. Which name has the greater value? How much greater?
   Luther Burbank   Alexander Bell

2. What is the sum of these words?
   canal   Monopoly

3. What is the average of the digits in this phrase?
   one name tag

4. Find the product of these words.
   patent   game

5. Find the median of the digits in this phrase.
   middle name pride

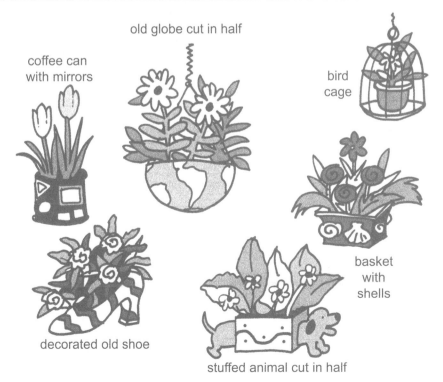

1	ABC 2	DEF 3
GHI 4	JKL 5	MNO 6
PRS 7	TUV 8	WXY 9
*	Oper 0	#

March 7th

- Telephone Patented (1876)*
- Middle Name Pride Day
- Name Tag Day
- Purim (March 7 & 8)
- Suez Canal Opened (1869)
- Monopoly Game Patented (NY City, 1934)

Birthdays
1904   Luther Burbank

Clever Containers

This is a day for planting flowers. If you're planting flowers indoors, the container can be as important as the flowers. Let your imagination go wild to create wonderful places for flowers to grow.

old globe cut in half

coffee can with mirrors

bird cage

decorated old shoe

basket with shells

stuffed animal cut in half

Sniff!

Ahhh

fishbowl

March 8th

- Plant a Flower Day*
- Commonwealth Day (Canada)*
- Farmers' Day
- International Women's Day
- Working Women's Day

One More Idea

- Answer these questions about Commonwealth Day:
  What is the commonwealth?
  Who is a part of it?
  What is its purpose?
  Who is the head of it?
  What happens?

73

- False Teeth Patented *(1822)**
- Panic Day*
- International Cabin Fever Day*
- Barbie Doll Introduced *(1959)*

Birthdays

1451   Amerigo Vespucci

More Ideas

- Write a list of "Good Reasons to Panic."
- Brainstorm at least ten cures for cabin fever.

GOOD REASON TO PANIC #3: GOING TO THE DENTIST.

Do-It-Yourself False Teeth

Make yourself a set of false teeth, then count and identify the incisors, bicuspids, canines, and molars.

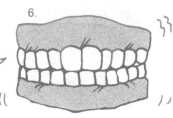

1. Shape modeling clay into a 3/4" (2 cm) thick cookie to fit into your mouth.

2. Press your top teeth into the clay. Make sure the clay is pushed up tightly to your gums on all sides. Carefully pull it away from the teeth.

3. Repeat this with a new cookie on the bottom teeth.

4. Tape a cardboard collar 2" (5 cm) tall snugly around each mold.

5. Mix plaster of Paris according to directions. Pour it into each mold using a toothpick to poke plaster into the tiny spaces. Tap the molds to get rid of air bubbles.

6. After ten hours, remove the collars and gently pull the clay away from the teeth.

- First U.S. Paper Money Issued *(1862)**
- Mario Day

Birthdays

1820   Harriet Tubman
1947   Kim Campbell

Visit the U.S. Bureau of Engraving and Printing website for for more information about money: www.bep.treas.gov

Dollar-Wise

Get to know your way around a dollar bill. Examine a "paper" dollar carefully. Identify each of the features (1–8), and be able to tell what the different symbols, pictures, numbers, and signatures mean.
(Paper money today is not really paper. Find out what it is!)

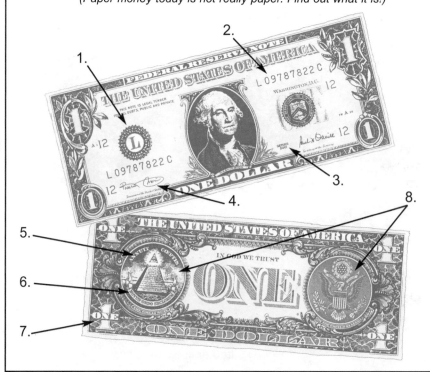

Keats-Inspired Collages

Ezra Jack Keats is an award-winning author of children's books. He uses an interesting collage technique to create wonderful illustrations.

Find and read a few of his books. Then imitate his technique and create one or more collages to illustrate a dream of yours.

March 11th

- International Dream Day*
- Johnny Appleseed Day
- Camp Fire USA Day
- Worship of Tools Day
- Bureau of Indian Affairs Established *(1824)*

Birthdays
  1916 Ezra Jack Keats*

Mystery Puzzler

Alfred Hitchcock was a movie producer, famous for his thrilling mysteries and suspense films. To celebrate him, create a crossword puzzle with a mystery theme.
Start with a graph paper grid. Use several mystery words and names of mystery writers to create a puzzle.
(You'll have to do some research about the mystery writers.)
Add your own mystery words or names. Write the clues for the puzzle.

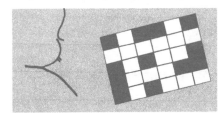

Here are a few to get you started:

suspect	mystery	detective
suspense	thriller	clues
investigate	alibi	escape
Hitchcock	Holmes	Poe
Christie	Chesterton	Hillerman

March 12th

- American Crossword Puzzle Tournament *(Stamford, CT)*
- Alfred Hitchcock Day*
- Blizzard of 1888 Began
- Girl Scout Day

Under the Umbrella

There is a superstition that opening an umbrella indoors is bad luck, especially if you stand under it. A *superstition* is a belief or practice that results from trust in chance, ignorance, or fear. Make a catalog of superstitions from A to Z. Draw illustrations for some or all of the entries.

March 13th

- National Open an Umbrella Indoors Day*
- Good Samaritan Day
- Earmuffs Patented *(1887)*
- Uranus Discovered *(1781)*
- First Uncle Sam Cartoon Published *(NY City, 1789)*

E-Ear
If your right ear itches, someone is speaking ill of you.

A-Ambulance
It is bad luck to see an ambulance unless you pinch your nose and hold your breath until you see a black dog.

S-Seizures
To avoid seizures, wear the dried body of a frog in a silk bag around your neck.

It's not really true that black cats are bad luck.

How can opening an umbrella indoors be so bad if it has its own holiday?

- National Potato Chip Day
- National Preschoolers Day
- Pi Day
- Learn About Butterflies Day
- World Ice Art Championships
- Cotton Gin Patented (*Eli Whitney, 1794*)

Birthdays

1879   Albert Einstein*

The Spectacular Trained Can

Albert Einstein made some marvelous discoveries about energy. Show off some of the miracles of energy with this amazing can that will obey your commands!

1. Remove both ends from a coffee can.
2. Get two plastic lids, one for each end of the can.
3. Punch two holes 3 inches (or 8 cm) apart in the center of each lid.
4. Cut a long rubber band at one spot. Thread it through the holes in one lid. Put the lid on the can.
5. Cross the ends of the rubber band to form an X in the middle. Use a short piece of string to tie a heavy metal nut to the center.
6. Thread the two ends through the holes in the other lid. Put the lid on. Tie the two ends in a knot outside the lid.
7. Roll the can away from you. Say, **"Can! Return to me!"** The can will come back to you! Try rolling the can down a gentle slope; it will climb uphill to you!

Can, come back to me.

How it works . . .

As the can rolls, the weight of the nut causes the rubber band to twist and store energy. When it has stored all the energy it can, it will stop. The rubber band will untwist and release the stored energy, causing the can to roll back to its starting place.

- National Quilting Day*
- Ides of March
- Buzzards Day
- Everything You Think Is Wrong Day
- National Pasta Days (*15th and 16th*)
- First Blood Bank Established (*1937*)

Birthdays

1767   Andrew Jackson
1820   Maine, 23rd state

No-Stitch Quilts

National Quilting Day is the perfect time to find out about different quilting patterns and make your own quilt square. You can combine your square with others made by you or by your friends to create an entire quilt.

Make a grid that divides a 6-inch square paper into 2-inch square spaces (or a 15-cm square into 5-cm spaces). Plan a pattern on the grid that uses three colors. Color in the spaces with crayons, markers, or paint. Or, glue on pieces of colored paper or cloth.

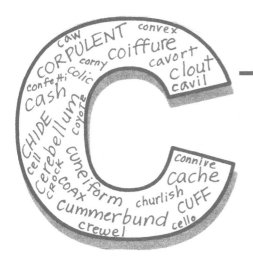

Captivating C

Celebrate **C** by collecting **C** words. Then use some of the words to write a biography of **C**, a **C** poem, an advertisement for **C**, a thank-you letter to **C**, a **C** birth announcement, a menu for an all-**C** café, or an ode to **C**.

- Vitamin C Discovered *(1932)**
- Everything You Do Is Right Day
- Lips Appreciation Day
- West Point Academy established *(1802)*

Birthdays
1451   James Madison

Leprechauns, Limericks, & Pots O' Gold

Get in the spirit of St. Patrick's Day by doing all of these things today:
- Wear green, for sure!
- Find, read, recite, and enjoy some limericks.
- Finish the limerick below or write one of your own.
- Design a trap to catch a leprechaun.
- Design an outfit for a leprechaun.
- Explain how to find the pot o' gold at the end of a rainbow.

A Parade for One

Every year since 1933, the town of Enterprise, Alabama, holds the world's smallest St. Patrick's Day Parade. Only one person marches. A different person of Irish descent is chosen each year. She or he carries a pot o' gold, holds the Irish flag, and recites limericks while marching around the Boll Weevil Monument and past the courthouse.

- St. Patrick's Day*
- World's Smallest St. Patrick's Day Parade*
- Rubber Band Invented *(1845)**
- Submarine Day
- Freedom of Information Day

*The story has often been told
Of a laddie named Patrick McBold
A rainbow he saw_____
_____
_____*

Rubber Band Characters

Celebrate the anniversary of the amazing, versatile, flexible rubber band! Make a cast of characters using rubber bands of all sizes and colors.

Arrange rubber bands of all sizes and colors on a piece of sturdy paper or cardboard, forming any design you like. Try to create faces, people, strange creatures, or animals. Lightly draw around each rubber band with your pencil. Lift the rubber band, squeeze white glue along the pencil line, and lay the rubber band carefully on the glue. When the glue is dry, color inside spaces with markers or crayons.

March 18th

- Awkward Moments Day*
- First Walk in Space *(USSR, 1965)*

Birthdays
1879   Grover Cleveland

Awkward Moments

Who doesn't have awkward moments? Take time to collect the most awkward moments you can imagine or that you have had. Take turns with friends miming these moments (showing with movements and without words). Friends can try to guess what the miming suggests.

March 19th

- Poultry Day*
- Swallows Return to Capistrano*
- National Chocolate Caramel Day

Chicken Jokes

Celebrate Poultry Day with some poultry humor. *"Why did the chicken cross the road?"* is one of the most frequent joke starters of all time. Find or make up at least ten good chicken jokes today.

cluck cluck cluck

Why did the chicken cross the road?

because he was ex-"peck"-ted to

to see what the "eggs"-citement was all about

to boldly go where no chicken had gone before

Mapping the Mission Trail

San Juan Capistrano is about 60 miles south of Los Angeles, California. Each year, thousands of swallows return to the San Juan Mission on March 19th. They stay until late October, when they leave to spend the winter in the south. The Mission at San Juan Capistrano is part of a chain of 21 missions built along *El Camino Real* (The Royal Highway). Research California missions to learn about their history. Then make a map of California showing the missions along El Camino Real.

March 20th

- National Common Courtesy Day*
- Teenagers Day
- Snowman Burning Day

Birthdays
1928   Fred Rogers (Mr. Rogers of TV)
1939   Brian Mulroney

Directory of Common Courtesies

Find a definition of **courtesy**. Get together with some friends or family members and think of everyday, ordinary things people could do to show courtesy to others.

Select the best courtesies from your list. Combine them into an original **Directory of Common Courtesies**.

Write a common courtesy (a suggested behavior) on each page. Illustrate each courtesy in a serious or comic style.

Memory Poems

Share special memories on Memory Day. Since it's also Children's Poetry Day, write some of your memories in the form of poems. Try one of these forms for a poem, or create your own.

> Today, remember to recite some favorite poetry and memorize some new poems.

A happy memory is the championship soccer game.
A sad memory is losing a friend.
A silly memory is dressing up like cockroaches.
A serious memory is getting caught cheating.
A scary memory is being lost at the circus.
A reassuring memory is being found by clo
My favorite memory is holding a baby kitt
My least fa   etting my braces on

I remember an embarrassing dance recital.
I remember my surprise birthday party.
I remember my aunt's funeral.
I remember when I used to hate boys.
I remember fingerpainting with puddles.

Things Worth Remembering
Grandma's sugar cookies, and kindergarten.
on warm summer nights.
ishing on the pond.
hake sundaes w/cherries.
raiding my piggy bank.
sleeping late on Saturday.
jack-o-lanterns.
Christmas stockings.

- Children's Poetry Day*
- Memory Day*
- International Astrology Day
- Bird Appreciation Day
- UN Day for the Elimination of Racial Discrimination
- First Round-the-World Balloon Flight Completed *(1999)*

Birthdays

1806   Benito Juarez
1865   Johann Sebastian Bach

Water Witching

Some people seem to have a special ability to find water. They often help farmers and other people know where to find water pipes or where to dig for water. They are called *dowsers* or *water witches* or *water diviners*. They often use a forked stick called a divining rod to point to the source of the water. Try out your water-witching skills. Find yourself a divining rod and go on a search for water.

EUREKA!

Find a forked stick or branch on the ground. Hold this divining rod in front of your body. Walk around slowly. Hold the rod loosely in your hands and think of water. Do you feel special vibrations? Do your hands begin to tingle? Does the rod suddenly point downwards? If one of these happens, there may be a water pipe, well, or underground stream beneath you. Follow the path of the water. Go where the rod leads you.

- World Water Day*
- International Goof-off Day
- International Day of the Seal
- Laser Patented *(1960)*

Birthdays

1846   Randolph Caldecott*

- World Meteorological Day*
- Liberty Day*
- Near Miss Day
- Toast Day
- National Chip & Dip Day
- *Mir* Space Station Abandoned (1991)

One More Idea
- Find a copy of the famous speech given on Liberty Day.

Easy Weather Vane

On this World Meteorological Day, make your own weather vane to keep a check on wind direction.

1. Glue a wooden spool to a block of wood. Mark N, S, E, W, NE, NW, SE, and SW at intervals on the block.
2. Cut an animal shape and an arrow from heavy cardboard. Cover them both completely with foil.
3. Tape the animal securely to the top of a sturdy drinking straw. Tape the arrow below the animal. Place the straw inside the spool.
4. Set the weather vane in a spot where it will catch the wind. Use a compass to find North and place the N on the block facing North.
5. Watch the vane each day. Remember that a wind is named according to the direction from which it flows.

- National Chocolate-Covered Raisins Day*
- National Family Day
- World Tuberculosis Day

Birthdays
1874   Harry Houdini*

Dancing Raisins

This is a day that celebrates raisins and a famous American magician. So it's a good day to eat raisins and do a good magic trick. While you eat the chocolate-covered kind, get some plain raisins and make them dance!

1. Stir in 2 T of baking soda into a half-filled glass of water.
2. Drop in five raisins.
3. Add 2 T of vinegar and watch the raisins dance!

- First Color TV Produced (1954)*
- Pecan Day*
- Waffle Day*
- First Pancakes Made
- National Medal of Honor Day

One More Idea
- Find out how waffles were invented. Find a recipe for pecan waffles. Make and eat some today!

Add the Color

Can you imagine TV without color? After you find out about the first color TV shows, see if you can "turn off" the color on our own TV. This will give you an idea of what TV was like before color. Then draw some "before" and "after" pictures to compare the two experiences.

Draw two TV screens. Inside one, draw a black-and-white scene. In the other, draw the same scene with color added.

Speak Up for Spinach

Spinach sometimes has a less-than-excellent reputation. On Spinach Festival Day, do something to promote spinach.

- Plan your own Spinach Festival. Wear green; make signs to celebrate spinach; write spinach slogans, tongue twisters, bumper stickers and jokes; serve spinach dip, spinach salad, and spinach soup; make Spinach Festival Day cards.
- Find out why spinach is good for you.
- Prepare a speech that will convince someone to eat spinach.
- Find out why Crystal City, TX, calls itself "The Spinach Capital of the World."
- Make a poster that advertises the virtues of spinach.
- Plan a "Hooray for Spinach" Web site.

March 26th

- Spinach Festival Day*
- Make Up Your Own Holiday Day*
- Camp David Peace Accord Signed *(1979)*
- Polio Vaccine Invented *(Jonas Salk, 1953)*

Birthdays

1874   Robert Frost*
1930   Sandra Day O'Connor

One More Idea

- It's *Make Up Your Own Holiday* Day. Definitely take time today to create your own holiday. Then find a way to share ideas for how to celebrate the holiday.

Promises to Keep

Robert Frost's famous poem, "Stopping By Woods On A Snowy Evening," has a fascinating ending. Part of that ending is this: *". . . and I have promises to keep."* Find the poem and read it. Then think about promises and write a list of some that should be kept.

Quirky Titles

There's much fun in country music song titles! They're fun to hear and fun to invent. Here are a few of the quirkiest (real) titles. Make up several of your own today. Then, choose one of your titles or one of these titles and write the lyrics for the song.

Billy Broke My Heart in Walgreens and I Cried All the Way to Sears
Does Your Chewing Gum Lose Its Flavor on the Bedpost Overnight?
Am I Double Parked by the Curbstone of Your Heart?
Don't Strike a Match to the Book of Love
How Can I Miss You If You Won't Go Away?
I Changed Her Oil, She Changed My Life
I Keep Forgettin' I Forgot You
If the Phone Doesn't Ring, It's Me
I Like Bananas Because They Have No Bones
Redneck Martians Stole My Baby
She Made Toothpicks Out of the Timber of My Heart
Trainwreck of Emotion
You Done Stomped on My Heart
You're the Ring Around My Bathtub

March 27th

- Quirky Country Music Song Title Day*
- National Joe Day
- Photography Day
- Fly a Kite Day
- World Theater Day
- First Long-Distance Phone Call *(1884)*

March 28th

- 23rd Amendment to the *U.S. Constitution* Ratified *(1961)*
- Something On A Stick Day*
- Respect Your Cat Day
- Save a Spider Day
- Three-Mile Island Nuclear Power Plant Accident *(1979)*
- First Performance of *The Greatest Show on Earth* Circus *(1881)*

Happy Anniversary to the "Greatest Show on Earth!"

Something on a Stick

How many things can you think of that come on a stick? Celebrate this day with these activities:

- Make a list of 100 things on a stick.
- Make some stilts and put yourself on sticks!
- Eat at least three things on a stick today.
- Make these easy banana treats:

Frozen Bananas

Put a craft stick in a peeled banana. Wrap the banana in foil and freeze it for an hour. Dip the banana in melted chocolate chips, roll it in crushed nuts, and freeze it for another hour. Then enjoy it!

March 29th

- Niagara Falls Stopped Flowing *(1848)**
- Coca-Cola Invented *(1886)**
- America's Subway Day*
- Vietnam Veteran's Day
- First Anesthetic Used *(1842)*

More Ideas

- See how many empty Coca-Cola cans or bottles you can balance on top of each other. Hold a contest with friends.
- Lots of people perform music in subway stations. Write a *Song for the Subway* today.

Tall Tales

To the great surprise of everyone in the area, Niagara Falls stopped flowing (except for a trickle) on March 29, 1848. Find out why this happened and how long the water was stopped.

This is a true tale, but it sounds like a **tall tale**—because it seems impossible.

In the spirit of this outlandish tale, write some "impossible" tales of your own today. Make sure you do plenty of exaggerating. Write your tale on a long strip of adding machine paper. Glue it on black paper. Add long legs and a tall hat to make the tale even taller!

Some topics for tall tales:
weather, wild creatures, strange animals, fights, strange people, people with unusual powers, food, fishing trips, storms, waves, fights, noses, vehicles, camping trips, school, scary incidents

EARS THAT HEARD AROUND THE WORLD

Earle was born with big ears. But it wasn't until he was twelve that he realized how unusual his ears really were. When someone sneezed in China, Earle could hear it as if a train were running through his ears. When his sister whispered secrets into her telephone, he could hear them through the walls of the house . . .

The Honorable Eraser-topped Pencil

A pencil may seem like one of the simplest things in the world. Yet, as Nobel laureate Milton Friedman once said, "There's not a single person in the world who actually knows how to make a pencil." His point is that it takes many people to make a pencil. Use the Internet to find Friedman's "Pencil Story" and a clever family history of a pencil in the story "I, Pencil" written by Leonard Read. Write your own tribute to a pencil or to its eraser.

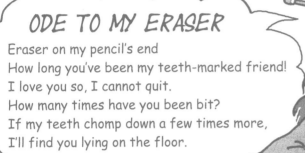

ODE TO MY ERASER

Eraser on my pencil's end
How long you've been my teeth-marked friend!
I love you so, I cannot quit.
How many times have you been bit?
If my teeth chomp down a few times more,
I'll find you lying on the floor.

March 30th

- Pencil with Eraser Patented *(1858)**
- Doctor's Day
- National Hot Dog Day
- Take a Walk in the Park Day
- U.S. Purchased Alaska from Russia *(1867)*

Birthdays
1853   Vincent Van Gogh

Where in the USA?

Where in the U.S. would you find a town called Sassafras or Two Egg? These towns really exist! Get a blank map of the U.S. Use your best research skills to locate as many of the listed towns as you can and place them on the map. Add any others with unusual names.

Accident	Cowlic	Hungry Horse	Rainbow
Alligator	Cowpens	Igloo	Rolling Fork
Antelope	Crooksville	Left Hand	Rough and Ready
Bad Axe	Devil's Lake	Looking Glass	Sandwich
Beaver Dam	Diamond Hill	Magnet	Santa Claus
Bird in Hand	Dinosaur	Monkey's Eyebrows	Sassafras
Blowing Rock	Difficult	Mystic	Smackover
Boring	Ducktown	Nag's Head	Soldier
Bowlegs	Embarrass	Needles	Spillville
Braintree	Fireworks Station	Ninety Six	Squirrel
Broken Arrow	Flowing Rock	Owl's Head	Steamboat
Bumble Bee	Fly	Painted Post	Surprise
Burnt Corn	Forks of Salmon	Pelican	Tarzan
Cash	Frogtown	Pie Town	Tomato
Cheesequake	Gnaw Bone	Pigeon	TumTum
Chews	Good Thunder	Pine Apple	Tuxedo Park
Chicken	Grasshopper	Pitchfork	Twin Sisters
Chilly	Gusher	Plaster City	White Swan
Coconut	Helper	Porcupine	Wink
Coffee Springs	Hershey	Potato Creek	Zigzag
Coon Trap	Horseshoe Beach	Quicksand	

March 31st

- First Map of the U.S. Patented *(1784)**
- Bunsen Burner Day
- National Clams on the Half Shell Day
- Eiffel Tower Completed *(1889)*
- U.S. Air Force Academy Established *(1954)*

Birthdays
1949   Province of Newfoundland
1927   Cesar Chavez
1732   Franz Joseph Haydn

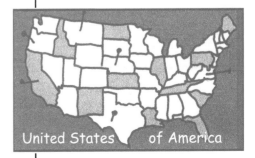

United States of America

April

1
- April Fools' Day*
- One Cent Day*
- National Fun at Work Day
- Reconciliation Day
  Birthdays: Province of Nunavut

2
- Green Day*
- U.S. Mint Created*
- National Sleep Day
- International Children's Book Day
- National Peanut Butter and Jelly Day
  Birthdays: Hans Christian Andersen

3
- Find a Rainbow Day*
- Pony Express Service Began*
- American Circus Day
- Tweed Day
- National Chocolate Moose Day
  Birthdays: Washington Irving

4
- National Reading a Road Map Day*
- Walk Around Things Day*
- Bonza Bottler Day
- School Librarian's Day
- Student Government Day
- NATO Created
  Birthdays: Maya Angelou

5
- German-American's Day*
- Dandelion Day
- Go for Broke Day
  Birthdays: Booker T. Washington

6
- First Modern Olympics*
- Jump Over Things Day*
- Check Your Batteries Day
- Teflon Invented
- Army Day
- U.S. Entered WWI against Germany
- Twinkies Introduced
- Perry & Henson Reached North Pole

7
- World Health Day*
- No Housework Day
- Museum Day
- National Teacher Appreciation Day
  Birthdays: William Wordsworth

8
- International Bird Day*
- Draw a Picture of a Bird Day*
- Kambutsu-e*
- 17th Amendment to the *U.S. Constitution* Ratified
  Birthdays: Sonja Henie

9
- All Over Again Day*
- 100th Day of the Year (in Leap Year)
- Prisoners of War Remembrance Day
- Thank a School Librarian Day
- Winston Churchill Day
- Listening Day
- Name Yourself Day
- Civil War Ended

10
- 100th Day of the Year*
- Safety Pin Patented*
- National Sibling Day
- Golfer's Day
- Commodore Perry Day
- National Teach Children to Save Day
- Encourage a Young Writer Day

11
- U.S. Navy Acquired Its First Submarine*
- Jackie Robinson Day
- Barbershop Quartet Day
- National Youth Service Day

12
- First Launch of Space Shuttle *Columbia**
- First Person Traveled in Space*
- Look Up at the Sky Day
- Reach as High as You Can Day
- Vaccine for Polio Developed
- Civil War Began

13
- Scrabble Day*
- National Peach Cobbler Day
  Birthdays: Thomas Jefferson

14
- First Edition of an American English Dictionary Published*
- Pan American Day
- Abraham Lincoln Shot at Ford's Theater
- Lincoln Monument Built
- *RMS Titanic* Struck an Iceberg

15
- Remembrance Day
- Rubber Eraser Day
- Tax Day
- *RMS Titanic* Sank (1912)
- First MacDonald's Opened
  Birthdays: Leonardo da Vinci*

16
- National Stress Awareness Day*
- National Eggs Benedict Day
- President Lincoln Signed an Act Abolishing Slavery

17
- *Columbia Neurolab* Launched*
- Blah Blah Blah Day
- National Cheeseball Day
- Daffy Duck's Birthday
- Verranzano Day
- Bay of Pigs Invasion in Cuba
- Ford Mustang Introduced

18
- International Jugglers Day*
- National Animal Cracker Day*
- Historical San Francisco Earthquake and Fire*
- Third World Day
- Pet Owner's Day

19
- Patriots Day*
- Paul Revere's Ride*
- First Boston Marathon (1897)
- Federal Building in Oklahoma City Bombed (1995)
- National Garlic Day
- Revolutionary War Began (1775)

20
- Look-Alike Day*
- Cuckoo Day
- Holocaust Remembrance Day
- National Pineapple Upside-down Cake Day
- Volunteer Recognition Day

21
- Kindergarten Day
- San Jacinto Day
  Birthdays: John Muir, Queen Elizabeth II*

22
- Earth Day*
- National Jellybean Day*

23
- Blue Day*
- World Laboratory Animal Day
- International Sing Out Day
- Sneaker Day
- First Public School in America
  Birthdays: William Shakespeare, Lester B. Pearson

24
- First License Plates Issued*
- Pigs in a Blanket Day*
- National Puppetry Day
- Library of Congress Established

25
- Hubble Space Telescope Deployed*
- National Zucchini Bread Day
- Anzac Day
- World YMCA Day
- National Hairball Awareness Day
- Spanish-American War Began

26
- Sense of Smell Day*
- Richter Scale Day*
- Read to Me Day
- Hug a Friend Day
- National Static Cling Day
- National Pretzel Day
- U.S. Holocaust Museum Opened
- Great Plague Began in London
- Chernobyl Nuclear Reactor Exploded
  Birthdays: Charles Richter*

27
- Tell a Story Day*
- Matanzas Mule Day*
- Babe Ruth Day
- National DJ Day
- Playground Safety Day
  Birthdays: Ulysses S. Grant, Samuel Morse

28
- Poetry Reading Day*
- Costume Day
- Puppet Day
- Texas Wildflower Day
- National Day of Mourning (Canada)
- First Tourist Launched in Space
  Birthdays: Maryland, James Monroe

29
- Zipper Patented*
- Moment of Laughter Day*
- National Shrimp Scampi Day
- Los Angeles Riots Erupted
  Birthdays: Duke Ellington

30
- National Hairstyle Appreciation Day*
- International Walk Day*
- Louisiana Purchase Day
- National Honesty Day
- No Spanking Day
- National Oatmeal Cookie Day
- Raisin Day
- George Washington Inaugurated
  Birthdays: Louisiana

Month-long Celebrations

Anxiety Month
Autism Awareness Month
Cancer Control Month
Holocaust Remembrance Month*
International Guitar Month*
Keep America Beautiful Month
Mathematics Education Month*
Month of the Young Child
National Child Abuse Prevention Month
National Frog Month*
National Garden Month
National Grilled Cheese Sandwich Month*
National Humor Month*
National Kite Month
National Pecan Month
National Poetry Month*
National Smile Month
National Soft Pretzel Month*
National Woodworking Month
Pets Are Wonderful Month
Prevention of Cruelty to Animals Month
Soyfoods Month
Straw Hat Month
Stress Awareness Month
Tackle Your Clutter Month
World Habitat Awareness Month*
Youth Sports Safety Month
Zoo and Aquarium Month*

Weekly Celebrations

First Week: Golden Rule Week*, National Dark Sky Week*, Egg Salad Week, National Laugh Week, National Public Health Week, National Reading a Road Map Week, National Straw Hat Week, Week of the Young Child

Second Week: National Week of the Ocean*, Young People's Poetry Week, National Garden Week, National Guitar Week, National Library Week, Reading Is Fun Week, World Wildlife Week

Third Week: National Coin Week*, Pan American Week*, Jewish Heritage Week, Bike Safety Week

Fourth Week: National TV-Turnoff Week*, National Karaoke Week*, National Volunteer Week*, National Secretary Week, Forest Week, National Playground Safety Week

Dates That Vary: Easter*, Good Friday*, Passover*, White House Easter Egg Roll*, Egg Salad Week*, Daylight Savings*, National Arbor Day*, Boston Marathon*, Rattlesnake Derby, Holocaust Remembrance Day (Yom Hashoah), National Secretaries Day, No Excuse Sunday

April's Month-long Celebrations

National Poetry Month

Fill your month with poetry. Read and write poetry every day in April.

How to Create a Diamonte
(diamond-shaped poem of opposites)

Start with a pair of opposite words.

Line 1: Write the first word in the pair.

Line 2: Write two adjectives to describe the word in line 1.

Line 3: Write three participles (ing words) related to line 1.

Line 4: Write two nouns related to the first word in the pair and two words related to its opposite.

Line 5: Write three participles related to the opposite of line 1.

Line 6: Write two adjectives to describe the opposite.

Line 7: Write the word that is the opposite of line 1.

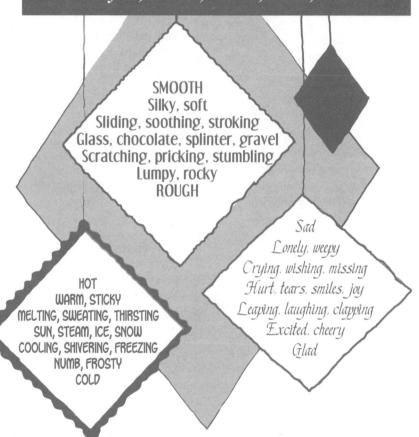

Learn about these different kinds of poems. Try to read or write all of these during April.

acrostic poem, ballad, chorus, cinquain, couplet, diamonte, epigram, free verse, haiku, limerick, nursery rhyme, ode, pantoum, rhymed verse, riddle rhyme, sestina, sonnet, tercet, villanelle

SMOOTH
Silky, soft
Sliding, soothing, stroking
Glass, chocolate, splinter, gravel
Scratching, pricking, stumbling
Lumpy, rocky
ROUGH

HOT
WARM, STICKY
MELTING, SWEATING, THIRSTING
SUN, STEAM, ICE, SNOW
COOLING, SHIVERING, FREEZING
NUMB, FROSTY
COLD

Sad
Lonely, weepy
Crying, wishing, missing
Hurt, tears, smiles, joy
Leaping, laughing, clapping
Excited, cheery
Glad

Holocaust Remembrance Month

This month honors the memory of people who were killed, terrorized, harmed, or discriminated against during Hitler's Nazi era. It also reminds the world of the horrors that can happen if citizens are not actively aware of them. In Israel, Holocaust Day (Yom Hashoah) was established as a day to remember the Jewish people who died in World War II. The day is the anniversary in the Jewish calendar of Nisan 27, 5705: the day on which the Allied troops liberated the first Nazi concentration camp (Buchenwald, near Weimar, Germany). About 56,000 prisoners, mostly Jewish, died in Buchenwald.

On April 26, 1993, the United States Holocaust Memorial Museum opened in Washington, D.C. Since then, millions have visited the exhibits. If you can't visit this museum, look for a Holocaust museum in your state, or visit the USHMM website at www.ushmm.org.

International Guitar Month

- Invite a guitar player to visit with you. Enjoy singing some songs to the accompaniment of the guitar. Learn how to play a few chords.

- Listen to your favorite music. Can you hear any guitars? Find five songs that have guitar accompaniment. Share these with someone.

- Brush up on the science of sound. Be able to explain how the strings on a guitar produce sound, and how sound travels.

- Use the phone book or newspaper ads to find out about the cost of learning to play the guitar. Do the math to figure out how much it would cost to buy a basic guitar, purchase some music, and take some lessons.

- Find out the difference between kinds of guitars (classical guitar, steel guitar, bass guitar, etc.).

- Track down some trivia about famous guitars and guitar players.

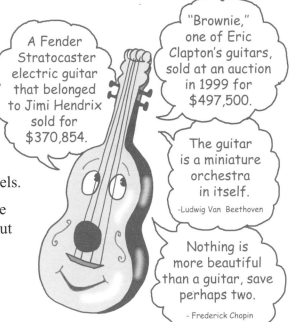

A Fender Stratocaster electric guitar that belonged to Jimi Hendrix sold for $370,854.

"Brownie," one of Eric Clapton's guitars, sold at an auction in 1999 for $497,500.

The guitar is a miniature orchestra in itself.
-Ludwig Van Beethoven

Nothing is more beautiful than a guitar, save perhaps two.
- Frederick Chopin

National Soft Pretzel Month

Ingredients	
1/2 C	warm water
1 pkg	dry yeast
1	egg
1/4 C	honey
1 tsp	table salt
1/4 C	margarine
1 C	milk
5 C	flour
	coarse salt
	mustard

Soft pretzels are a favorite snack in America and other countries. Americans alone eat over 700,000,000 soft pretzels each year.

- Make a list of all the places you can buy soft pretzels.

- Try making your own soft pretzels with this recipe.

1. Put the warm water in a bowl and sprinkle the yeast over it. Stir until the yeast dissolves.

2. Separate the egg yolk from the white. Keep the white in a small dish.

3. Mix the egg yolk, honey, margarine, and milk into the yeast mixture.

4. Add salt and enough flour to make a stiff, but easy-to-handle dough.

5. Knead the dough on a floured surface for five minutes. Let the dough rise for one hour in a covered bowl.

6. Cut the dough into strips about 1-inch wide. Roll each strip into a rope.

7. Shape the ropes into traditional pretzel shapes or any creative shapes you wish.

8. Beat 1 tablespoon of water into the egg white and brush the mixture over the pretzels.

9. Sprinkle the pretzels with coarse salt.

10. Bake them on a cookie sheet at 425° F until they are golden brown (about 15–20 min.).

Dip me in mustard. I'm yummy!

Mathematics Education Month

In 1995, to celebrate the organization's 75th anniversary, the National Council of Teachers of Mathematics named April as Mathematics Education Month. That makes this a great month to enjoy the wonders of math and to think about all the ways you use math in your everyday life. Here are two great math "tricks" to get you started on your celebration of math this month.

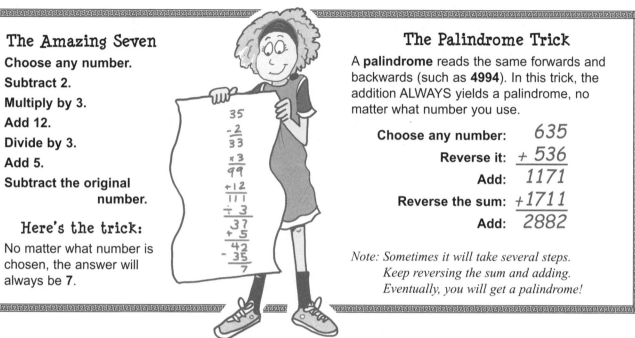

The Amazing Seven

Choose any number.

Subtract 2.

Multiply by 3.

Add 12.

Divide by 3.

Add 5.

Subtract the original number.

Here's the trick:

No matter what number is chosen, the answer will always be **7**.

$$
\begin{array}{r}
35 \\
-\ 2 \\
\hline
33 \\
\times\ 3 \\
\hline
99 \\
+12 \\
\hline
111 \\
\div\ 3 \\
\hline
37 \\
+\ 5 \\
\hline
42 \\
-35 \\
\hline
7
\end{array}
$$

The Palindrome Trick

A **palindrome** reads the same forwards and backwards (such as **4994**). In this trick, the addition ALWAYS yields a palindrome, no matter what number you use.

Choose any number:	*635*
Reverse it:	*+ 536*
Add:	*1171*
Reverse the sum:	*+1711*
Add:	*2882*

Note: Sometimes it will take several steps. Keep reversing the sum and adding. Eventually, you will get a palindrome!

National Frog Month

- Track down frog trivia this month. Find out the difference between frogs and toads. Find out about the biggest, smallest, and oldest frogs.

- There are many myths about frogs and toads. Find some myths about frogs and the weather, frogs and luck, or frogs (or toads) and warts.

- Can it really rain frogs? There are tales of raining frogs. Find at least one of these tales.

- The Center for Global Environmental Education has a program called "A Thousand Friends of Frogs." Visit their website to learn about this and become a friend of frogs.

- Find the word that means "a fear of frogs." Find the word that means "a fear of toads." Find the word that means "a fear of amphibians."

- Write or find a frog joke every day this month.

- Get some friends together and play leapfrog in April.

- Make a friend "hoppy." Send her or him a pop-up *Happy Frog Month* card.

April is National Humor Month—a great reason to tell frog jokes.

JOKE: What happened to the frog's car when the parking meter expired?

It got toad!!

Make a frog card pop-up by gluing a folded strip to the back of the frog.

World Habitat Awareness Month

Every organism (plant or animal) has a particular place within the environment where it lives. This place is called its *habitat*. Identify five or more organisms of interest to you. Describe and draw their habitats. For instance, what kind of habitat would be home to a(n) . . .

tarantula?

sea star?

fern?

toadstool?

crocodile?

inchworm?

crab?

dandelion?

tick?

pineapple?

seaweed?

sorrel cactus?

grasshopper?

sea cucumber?

centipede?

walrus?

Rattlesnake Records

Mangum, Oklahoma, hosts a Rattlesnake Derby the last full weekend in April. There is a prize for the longest rattlesnake brought to the derby. According to **Guinness World Records**, Jackie Bibby (USA) holds the record for the most live rattlesnakes held in the mouth (eight). He also holds the record for sitting in a bathtub with the most poisonous snakes (35 rattlesnakes).

Zoo & Aquarium Month

• Try to visit a zoo or aquarium this month.

• Track down facts about zoos and aquariums around the world. Here are a few fun facts to get you started:

— There are over 1,500 zoos across the world.

— The Berlin Zoo is the largest zoo in the world, with 13,000 animals.

— The Vienna Zoo, which opened in 1752, is the world's oldest zoo.

— The London Zoo opened the first public aquarium in 1849.

— The Philadelphia Zoo, opened in 1874, is the oldest zoo in the U.S.

— Su Lin was the first giant panda infant to reach a U.S. zoo alive (Brookfield Zoo in Chicago).

— Ming Ming, born at the Bejing Zoo in 1963, was the first giant panda born alive in captivity.

— The Waikiki Aquarium in Hawaii (opened in 1904) is the oldest aquarium in the U.S.

National Grilled Cheese Sandwich Month

• Make a list of as many different kinds of cheese as you can find.

• Invite your friends over for a grilled-cheese-making party. In honor of Zoo & Aquarium Month, make your sandwiches in different animal shapes. Gather as many different animal cookie cutters as you can find. Use your favorite bread and cheeses to put sandwiches together. Cut the sandwiches into animal shapes before or after you grill them.

• Think of 30 edible things you could put on a grilled cheese sandwich. Then decide what different animals might put on their favorite grilled cheese sandwiches. (What would a bear, crocodile, iguana, tarantula, anteater, lion, hippo, mouse, or snake have on a sandwich?)

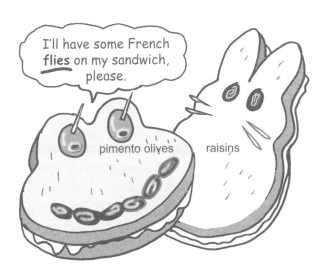

I'll have some French **flies** on my sandwich, please.

pimento olives   raisins

Special Weeks in April

First Week

Golden Rule Week

The Golden Rule is **"Do unto others as you would have them do unto you."** Make a *Golden Rule Log* for the week. Be alert for occasions to practice the Golden Rule. Every day, use the log to record situations in which you use the Golden Rule or see someone else practicing it. Make sure you practice it yourself at least once a day this week.

National Dark Sky Week

National Dark Sky Week is an event that was the idea of Jennifer Varlow, a high school student from Virginia. It began in 2002. The purpose of National Dark Sky Week is to temporarily reduce light pollution and raise awareness about the effects of artificial light on the night sky. Another goal is to promote an interest in astronomy and encourage appreciation of the universe. Reducing the lights around people on Earth lets us better see the wonder of the universe in the night sky. Read and learn something new about astronomy. Visit the Dark Sky site at www.nationaldarkskyweek.htm. Hold a star party in your neighborhood. Turn off the lights, get out the telescope, and enjoy the night sky.

Second Week

National Week of the Ocean

Celebrated since 1983, this event was established to encourage year-round exploration of the ocean. Learn something new about the ocean this week. Visit www.national-week-of-the-ocean.com.

• Make a list of 100 plants and animals that live in the ocean.

• Investigate the foods that come from the ocean.

• Find out about dangers that human activities pose to the ocean or its inhabitants.

• Create a work of art inspired by the ocean.

Salt Resist

1. Draw a picture of underwater life in light pencil on art paper.
2. Carefully paint around the outlines of all the creatures with clear water. Make sure all the ocean area is wet, but keep the sea life dry.
3. Drop blue, green, and purple watercolor carefully into the wet areas.
4. Sprinkle table salt lightly over the colored areas. Let the painting dry.
5. Brush away the salt and see the wonderful patterns.
6. Carefully paint the underwater plants and creatures.

National Coin Week

Here's a great way to celebrate coins. Stretch your brain with these coin questions. After you try these, make up several of your own.

- Sam has 235 coins that are all the same. Their total value is between $5.00 and $50.00. What could they be?
- Moe has 25 U.S. coins totaling $2.00. What could they be?
- Sally has eight U.S. coins. None of them are quarters. She has more dimes than nickels and more nickels than pennies. What two amounts of money could she have?
- Charlie has 14 U.S. coins totaling $0.96. What could they be?
- What is the least number and the greatest number of coins that total $1.35 (no pennies)?
- There are 293 different combinations of U.S. coins that add up to $1.00. Can you find them all?

Pan American Week

Just what does "Pan American" mean? Find out! Who is included in the concept "Pan American"? Make a map of all the countries and/or regions included in Pan America. Then create a game or contest to remember what these countries are and where they are.

Fourth Week

National TV-Turnoff Week

Turn off the TV for a week, and see what happens. You'll be surprised! What can you do instead of watching TV? Make your own list or try some of these:

- Make a sculpture from sand, wire, plaster, or junk.
- Plan a great scavenger hunt or treasure hunt for a group of friends.
- Get a taffy recipe and have a "taffy pull."
- See if you can think of 50 words or phrases that have the letters T and V in them.
- Figure out how to make a working volcano with household items.
- Make up a game that involves popcorn, a bell, and a blindfold.
- Make a map of the night sky.

National Karaoke Week

Practice up on your karaoke skills. Borrow a video camera and make a music video to match a karaoke performance.

National Volunteer Week

- Get the autograph of 25 people who regularly do some sort of volunteer work.
- Make a list of practical, safe volunteer activities that kids your age can do.
- Be a volunteer yourself. Offer at least three hours this week for some good purpose.

See page 85 for other weeklong holidays to celebrate in April.

The Days of April

Easter, Holy Week, Palm Sunday, Maundy Thursday, Good Friday

Easter is a Christian holiday that celebrates the return to life of Jesus, the founder of Christianity. Easter is observed on the first Sunday after the first full moon following the first day of spring in the Northern Hemisphere. It can fall on a Sunday any time between March 22 and April 25. Palm Sunday, the Sunday before Easter, celebrates the entry of Jesus into Jerusalem, when people spread palm branches along the path before him. **Palm Sunday** marks the beginning of **Holy Week**, which includes events leading up to the death and resurrection of Jesus. **Maundy Thursday,** or **Holy Thursday**, remembers Jesus' last meal before his arrest. **Good Friday** is a remembrance of the death of Jesus.

Natural Tie-Dye Eggs

One of the non-religious Easter traditions is the coloring of hard-boiled eggs.
Find out how this tradition began. Then try these all-natural dyed eggs.

1. Find items to make natural dyes *(grass or spinach for green, cranberries for red, tomatoes for orange, blueberries for blue, coffee grounds or walnut shells for brown, daffodils for yellow).*

2. Put the natural material in a pot and cover it (barely) with water. (Use one color at a time.) Boil it until you get the color you want.

3. Pour the dye through a strainer into a glass bowl. Wash the pot well and make another dye. Save each dye in a deep glass dish.

4. Wrap each egg in a piece of thin, white cloth. Cut strips of cloth and tie them tightly around the egg in several places.

5. Dip each egg in a dye. Let it dry for several hours, then unwrap the egg.

On pages 112 and 113, you can find other things to do with eggs.

Egg Salad Wee
(the week after Easter)

| Note: Use only eggs that have been properly refrigerated. |

Find a way to spice up those leftover eggs. Mix chopped eggs with mayonnaise or plain yogurt. Try adding some "extras" such as chopped nuts, curry powder, dill weed, chopped pickles, relish, deviled ham, raisins, sunflower seeds, shredded cheese, or olives.

White House Easter Egg Roll
(the Monday after Easter)

Each year, children race to roll a hard-boiled egg across a finish line on the south lawn of the White House. This tradition began in 1878. Read about it on the Internet. Then plan your own egg roll with friends and neighbors. Or, organize an egg roll for some younger children.

For each starred* holiday, you will find one or more activities on pages 92–107.

Passover *(the 15th Day of the Hebrew month of Nisan)*

Passover (or *Pesah*) is a seven- or eight-day Jewish festival that celebrates the escape of the Israelites from slavery under the Egyptians. The story of Passover is told in the book of Exodus in the *Bible*. The word *Passover* refers to the part of the story about ten plagues brought on Egypt. According to the story, while the first-born child in each Egyptian home was killed, the homes of the Israelites were passed over. Their children were spared from the horrible fate.

The feast of Seder is an important part of the Passover celebration. One of the foods eaten is unleavened bread (bread that is not raised). The Israelites had to flee from Egypt in such a hurry that they did not have time to let their bread rise. During Passover, Jewish people eat a kind of unleavened bread called *matzo* (or matzah). Try this special recipe for matzo balls.

Lots O' Matzo Balls

Combine the matzo meal, salt, and pepper. Gradually stir in the soda. Chill the batter for an hour. Form small balls from the dough. Boil the stock or water. Drop the balls in carefully. Cover the pot and boil the liquid gently for 30 minutes. Do not remove the cover until the cooking is done. Enjoy the matzo balls alone or in soup.

1 C	matzo meal
4	eggs, slightly beaten
1/2 C	melted margarine
1/2 C	club soda
dash	salt
dash	pepper
3 qts	chicken stock or salted water

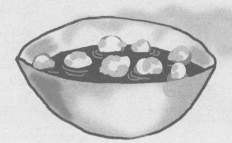

National Arbor Day *(Last Friday in April)*

This is a day for remembering the importance of trees in our lives.

• Think about trees today. Think of ways that trees have played a part in your life. Write a memoir or story about a tree you have known.

• Visit the arboretum nearest you.

• Interview a local nursery owner.

• Visit your library to look for books about trees. Find a children's picture book tree story. Find a nonfiction book with tree information.

• Find the location of the tallest tree and the oldest tree in your country.

• Choose a tree to visit. Stand under the tree. Sit under the tree. Find other ways to enjoy the tree. Find out what kind of a tree it is. Using your senses, examine the tree closely. Create a short diary: ***My Day with a Tree***. Describe what you did and observed during your tree visit.

• Try to climb a tree and plant a tree today.

Boston Marathon *(Third Monday)*

For over 100 years, runners have joined this 26.2-mile running event that begins in Hopkinton and finishes in downtown Boston. Today, over 20,000 compete in the race. Find out how a runner qualifies for this marathon.

Running Logic

Celebrate the marathon day with some logic problems about races. Solve this one. Then make up several of your own.

Five runners raced. Andy finished before Mandy, but after Sandy. Sandy finished ahead of Randy. Randy came in between Mandy and Andy. Who won the race?

April 1st

- April Fools' Day*
- One Cent Day*
- National Fun at Work Day
- Reconciliation Day

Birthdays
1999 Province of Nunavut*

More Ideas

- It's One Cent Day! Drop pennies around your neighborhood. Hide and watch to see if anyone picks them up.
- Find out when, why, and how Nunavut was formed.

April Fools

Fool your friends today, but make sure your fun is not harmful to anyone. Get together with some friends and think of great April Fools' Day gags. What are the best ones you've seen or heard about? What is the most shocking or surprising April Fools' joke that was ever played on you?

TRICKY IDEAS!
GLUE QUARTERS TO THE SIDEWALK.
SECRETLY SET SOMEBODY'S WATCH
   TO THE WRONG TIME.
SNEAKILY OPEN A PAPER CARTON OF MILK
   AND ADD A FEW DROPS OF FOOD COLORING.
SWITCH THE SALT AND PEPPER SHAKERS.
PUT SUGAR IN THE SALT SHAKER AND
   SALT IN THE SUGAR BOWL.
CAREFULLY SLIDE GUMMY WORMS INTO
   SMALL HOLES IN A FRIEND'S APPLE.
SNEAK A RUBBER DUCK INTO
   THE WATER COOLER.

Gummy worms

April 2nd

- Green Day*
- U.S. Mint Created *(1792)**
- National Sleep Day
- International Children's Book Day
- National Peanut Butter and Jelly Day

Birthdays
1805 Hans Christian Andersen

More Ideas

- How can you tell where a U.S. coin was minted? Find out.
- Visit the website of the U.S. Mint at www.usmint.gov.

Get Green

Think green today. Wear green to school. Put some green goop in your hair. Create green designs on your skin with washable markers. Make green hats. Take something green wherever you go. Try to eat only green things. Be on the lookout for things green!

Make lists of all the things you can think of that look, taste, smell, feel, or sound green. Include events, ideas, or experiences that seem green. Combine your ideas into a green poem.

Green is the chirping of crickets,
The way a pickle pinches your tongue,
And the way you feel when your heart is broken.
Green is a math test when you didn't study.
A golf course is a velvet stretch of green.
Green is mold and jealousy,
* and having the flu.*
Going to the dentist is green.

Green stains the seat
* of your baseball pants,*
Paints a forest of pine trees,
* Coats the skin of a slippery frog,*
Drips slime on algae,
Lends music to a rushing stream.

Quiet is green. So is spinach.
* Sundays, lizards, and loneliness*
*   are green, too.*
*   Green is sour, cold, and crunchy.*
*   You can take it to the bank.*

Make a Rainbow

Rainbows occur naturally on a cloudy day when the sun shines at just the right angle through a certain concentration of water drops. If you can't find a rainbow, you can make one. Here's one way:

Do this on a sunny day. Stand with the sun behind you. Have a friend use a hose to spray a fine mist in front of you. Position yourself so you are looking at the spray at a 45-degree angle. You should be able to see a rainbow.

Eat a Rainbow

Get a recipe for refrigerator cookies. Make a batch and divide it into seven parts. Use food coloring to color each part one of the rainbow colors. Roll each portion into a strip. Stack the strips in rainbow order (ROYGBIV). Refrigerate, slice, and bake as directed in the recipe.

April 3rd

- Find a Rainbow Day*
- First Pony Express Service Began *(1860)**
- American Circus Day
- Tweed Day
- National Chocolate Moose Day

Birthdays
1783   Washington Irving

INTERESTING FACT: NO PONIES WERE EVER RIDDEN IN THE PONY EXPRESS.

Road Map Mysteries

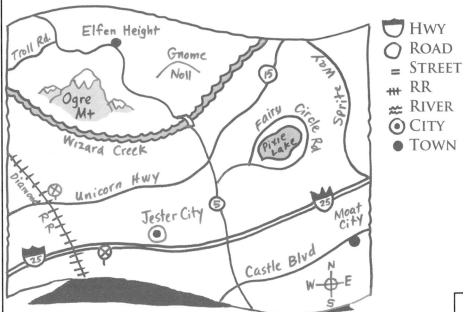

HWY
ROAD
STREET
RR
RIVER
CITY
TOWN

Polish up your road-map reading skills today by making (and solving) road map mysteries. Get any road map. Choose a particular "mystery" location. Write clues that someone else can follow to find the mystery spot. Make use of the map's symbols, key, directions, and scale as you create the clues. If you have time, make and use an original road map.

April 4th

- National Reading a Road Map Day*
- Walk Around Things Day*
- Bonza Bottler Day
- School Librarian's Day
- Student Government Day
- NATO Created *(1949)*

Birthdays
1928   Maya Angelou

One More Idea

- Keep a list of the things you walk around today. Can you put as many as 100 things on your list?

What direction is Pixie Lake from Troll Road?

Which highway is closest to Ogre Mountain?

Give someone two different routes for driving from Moat City to Elfen Height.

95

- German-American's Day*
- Dandelion Day
- Go for Broke Day

Birthdays
1856   Booker T.
        Washington

A Puffy Pfannkuchen

The puffy *pfannkuchen* is a German tradition. This unusual pancake is baked in an oven. You'll be amazed at how big and puffy it gets! Enjoy it with syrup, powdered sugar and lemon juice, fruit and yogurt, or brown sugar. Share it with four people, and serve it right away.

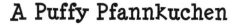

1. Preheat oven to 450°F. Grease a 13" x 9" baking dish.
2. Combine 6 beaten eggs with 1 C flour in a blender.
3. Beat in 1 C milk, 3 T melted butter, and a pinch of salt.
4. Pour into baking dish.
5. Bake 20 min. or until fluffy and brown.
6. Cut into squares and serve with toppings.

- First Modern Olympics *(1896)*
- Jump Over Things Day*
- Check Your Batteries Day
- Army Day
- Teflon Invented *(1938)*
- U.S. Entered WWI Against Germany *(1914)*
- Twinkies™ Introduced *(1930)*
- Perry & Henson Reached the North Pole *(1909)*

Neighborhood Olympics

Plan your own marathon to include many friends and events.

1. Invite friends and neighbors to take part in a Neighborhood Olympic Marathon. Choose the events that will make up the course. Decide on a time and place to hold the marathon.

2. Divide participants into two teams. Teams should be balanced. Assign individual team members to perform events according to individual ability. Give team members a chance to practice their events.

3. Choose a wide open space and set up a course so all the equipment is in place. The marathon works like this: First, participants take their places along the route. Those doing the first event begin at the starting line with a baton in hand. When they finish, they run to the next station and hand off the baton. This continues until all events are finished.

On **Jump Over Things Day,** jump rope 50 times without missing.

Disease Detectives

Today, get familiar with the World Health Organization. Find out about the work done, the events sponsored, and the health issues tackled by the organization. (Visit www.who.int/en/.) Learn about the symptoms, problems, and treatments of some major world health issues.

For example:

lyme disease	*diphtheria*	*typhoid fever*	*SARS*
encephalitis	*malnutrition*	*cholera*	*leprosy*
	tuberculosis	*ebola*	*polio*

April 7th

- World Health Day*
- No Housework Day
- Museum Day
- National Teacher Appreciation Day

Birthdays
1770 William Wordsworth

How to Draw a Bird

What better day is there to learn to draw a bird than this one— International Bird Day and Draw a Picture of a Bird Day? Follow the easy steps to start drawing a whole flock of birds!

Draw a standing bird:

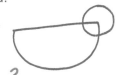

Draw a flying bird:

April 8th

- International Bird Day*
- Draw a Picture of a Bird Day*
- Kambutsu-e*
- 17th Amendment to the *U.S. Constitution* Ratified *(1913)*

Birthdays
1912 Sonja Henie

One More Idea

- Find out how and where *Kambutsu-e* is celebrated.

All Over Again–or Not?

Think about what you would want to do over again. Think about what you would NOT want to do over again. Make a list, poster, or booklet. Include "50 Things to Do All Over Again" and "50 Things Not to Do All Over Again."

April 9th

- All Over Again Day*
- 100th Day of the Year (in Leap Year)
- Prisoners of War Remembrance Day
- Thank a School Librarian Day
- Winston Churchill Day
- Listening Day
- Name Yourself Day
- Civil War Ended *(1865)*

April 10th

- 100th Day of the Year*
- Safety Pin Patented *(1849)*
- Golfer's Day*
- National Sibling Day
- Commodore Perry Day
- National Teach Children to Save Day
- Encourage a Young Writer Day

Hooray for 100!

On this 100th day of the year, have fun with the number 100.

- Collect 100 of something.
- Eat 100 of something.
- Paint a design using repetitions of the numeral 100.
- Try to find someone who is 100 years old. Get his or her autograph.
- List 100 things that have happened since a 100-year-old was born.
- Write a sentence that has 100 syllables.
- Think of 100 things you could do with $100.
- Find out how to say or write 100 in ten different languages.• Shake hands with 100 people.
- Try to get 100 on a test or quiz today.

Safety Pin Sagas

What a wonderful invention the safety pin is! What would life be like without it? Use your imagination to create a saga of one safety pin's life. Tell tales of all the things the safety pin has held together.

Make a collage or sculpture to go with your writing.

April 11th

- U.S. Navy Acquired Its First Submarine *(1900)*
- Jackie Robinson Day
- Barbershop Quartet Day
- National Youth Service Day

Bathtub Submarine

A submarine takes water into tanks to increase its density so it can dive. When it's time to surface, air is blown into the tanks, forcing out the water, and decreasing the density of the submarine.

1. Remove the top from a plastic bottle. Carefully cut the bottom off the bottle.

2. Cut a 1-ft (30 cm) and a 1½-ft (45 cm) piece of plastic tubing. Place both inside the neck of the bottle and secure them with adhesive tape.

3. Push modeling clay into the opening to completely seal the bottle shut.

4. Bend the short piece of tubing and tape it to the outside of the bottle.

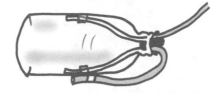

5. Put a large chunk of clay inside the bottle to give the submarine balance. Keep this away from the end of the tubing.

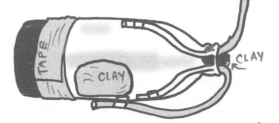

6. Tape the bottom back on the bottle. Make sure the bottle is sealed well at both ends so no water can enter except through the tube.

7. Float the submarine in the bathtub. Suck air out of the long tube. Water will come in through the bottom tube and the submarine will sink. To make the submarine surface, blow air into the bottle. This will force some water out.

Do-It-Yourself Rocket

Two major rocket launches occurred on this date.
So it's a good day to make a rocket. Try this simple one.

1. Set up two chairs several feet apart. Get some sturdy string long enough to reach between the chairs.
2. Blow up a long, sturdy balloon. Fasten it with a spring-type clip.
3. Use scotch tape to fasten two curtain rings to the top of the balloon.
4. Thread the string through the rings and tie it so it is taut between the chairs.
5. Pull the clipped end of the balloon toward one chair.
6. Carefully and quickly take the clip off the balloon and watch the rocket zoom.

April 12th

- First Launch of Space Shuttle *Columbia (1981)**
- First Person Traveled in Space *(Yuri Gagarin, 1961)**
- Look Up at the Sky Day
- Reach as High as You Can Day
- Vaccine for Polio Developed *(Jonas Salk, 1955)*
- Civil War Began *(1861)*

Scrabble Math

Enjoy playing the game of Scrabble today, of course. Scrabble takes some math skills, because scores must be calculated. The game board and pieces can also be used in other ways to create and solve math problems. Make up your own problems using the Scrabble pieces. See if your friends can solve the problems.

April 13th

- Scrabble Day*
- National Peach Cobbler Day

Birthdays
1743   Thomas Jefferson

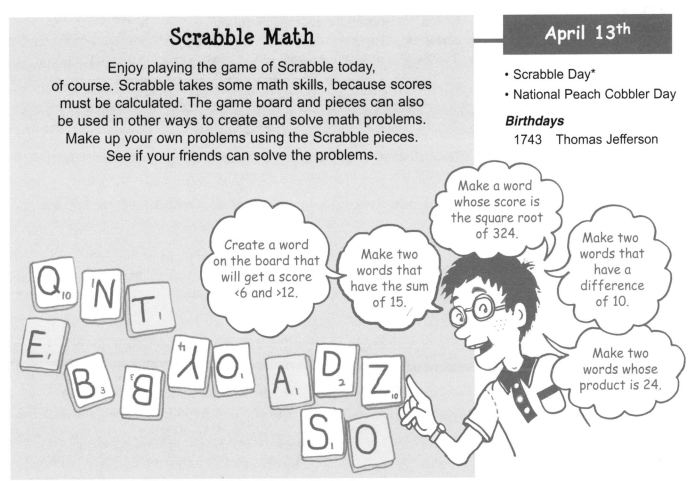

99

April 14th

- First Edition of an American English Dictionary Published *(Webster's, 1828)**
- Pan American Day
- Abraham Lincoln Shot at Ford's Theater *(1865)*
- Lincoln Monument Built *(1976)*
- *RMS Titanic* Struck an Iceberg *(1912)*

Dictionary Discoveries

Spend a little time sleuthing through your dictionary today. Track down the answers to challenging questions such as these. Then make up more questions for other dictionary detectives to pursue.

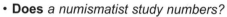

- **Does** *a numismatist study numbers?*
- **Would** *you eat a guffaw for dessert?*
- **Is** *a lackadaisical runner likely to win the race?*
- **Should** *you promulgate a secret?*
- **Could** *you dance with a tycoon?*
- **Could** *you gargle with a gargoyle?*
- **Where** *might you share a repast with a friend?*
- **When** *was the last time you were obstreperous?*

April 15th

- Remembrance Day
- Rubber Eraser Day
- Tax Day
- *RMS Titanic* Sank *(1912)*
- First MacDonald's Opened *(Des Plains, Il, 1955)*

Birthdays
1452   Leonardo da Vinci*

Amazing Leonardo

Leonardo da Vinci is known as one of the greatest painters of all time, yet he only finished a few paintings. You probably know about his famous painting, the *Mona Lisa*. Did you know that he also was an inventor, an illustrator, a scientist, an architect, a military engineer, and a sculptor? He had journals full of sketches for inventions, but he did not publish the journals. Find out about the inventions of da Vinci. Read about, sketch, and describe at least ten of them.

Why do YOU think the Mona Lisa is smiling? Explain your guess in a paragraph.

April 16th

- National Stress Awareness Day*
- National Eggs Benedict Day
- President Lincoln Signed an Act Abolishing Slavery *(1862)*

De-Stress

Take 15 minutes today to practice this relaxing motion. It will help combat stress and chase the tension away.

Find a quiet space. Lie on your back on a mat or carpeted surface. Lie with your hands resting at your sides. Notice each group of muscles in your body. Focus on them one at a time and let them go limp. Start with your head and move down to your neck, shoulders, chest, arms, hands, hips, legs, feet. Let your body melt into the floor.

Ahhhhh!

Then slowly slide your arms out to the side and overhead on the floor as you breathe in deeply. Hold your breath for five seconds. Then slowly breathe out through your mouth as you slide your hands back to your sides. Repeat this slowly several times, breathing in deeply and out fully.

100

Neuro-Search

In 1998, 2,000 animals (fish, mice, snails, and crickets) and seven astronauts were launched on a mission to study the nervous system in space. Make sure you know how the nervous system functions here on Earth.

- Explain the difference between the central nervous system and the peripheral nervous system.
- Draw a model of a neuron, label it, and explain how neurons carry signals.
- Be able to define and explain the function of each of these parts of the nervous system:

brain	spinal cord
cerebrum	cerebellum
medulla	impulses
receptors	synapse
motor neurons	axons
sensory neurons	dendrites

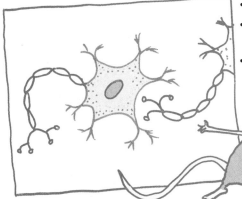

Mice are not nervous in space.

April 17th

- *Columbia Neurolab Launched (U.S., 1998)**
- Blah Blah Blah Day
- National Cheeseball Day
- Daffy Duck's Birthday
- Verranzano Day
- Bay of Pigs Invasion in Cuba *(1961)*
- Ford Mustang Introduced *(1964)*

Learn to Juggle

Don't let International Jugglers Day pass without trying your hand at juggling. (Actually, you will need both hands!)

One Ball:
Throw the ball in an arc from one hand to the other at about eye level.

Two Balls:
Toss the ball in your right hand in an arc toward your left hand. When the ball reaches the highest point in the arc, throw the ball in your left hand in an arc. Catch the first ball in your left hand, then catch the second ball in your right hand. Practice this motion many times before continuing to juggle the balls.

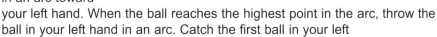

Three Balls:
Start with balls 1 and 3 in your right hand and ball 2 in your left hand. Throw ball 1 in an arc toward your left hand. When it reaches the highest point, throw ball 2 toward your right hand. Catch 1 in your left hand. Throw ball 3 toward your left hand. Catch ball 2 in your right hand. Catch ball 3 in your left hand. Keep practicing!

Oops!

April 18th

- International Jugglers Day*
- National Animal Cracker Day*
- Historical San Francisco Earthquake and Fire *(1906)**
- Third World Day
- Pet Owner's Day

More Ideas

- Get a bag of animal crackers and use them to build a model of a zoo or some other 3-D scene with animals.
- Find out what happened to San Francisco during the great earthquake and fire that followed.
- Create a graph of the worst earthquakes in the 20th and 21st centuries.

April 19th

- Patriots Day*
- Paul Revere's Ride*
- First Boston Marathon *(1897)*
- Federal Building in Oklahoma City Bombed *(1995)*
- National Garlic Day
- Revolutionary War Began *(1775)*

Paint-Can Lantern

Patriots Day remembers the beginnings of the Revolutionary War and the Americans who fought for freedom from British Rule. One patriot, Paul Revere, took a famous ride on April 19, 1775. His ride warned other patriots about the plans of the British forces. Part of the Revere story involves a system of warning using lanterns flashed from the steeple of the Old North Church in Boston. Find out exactly what a patriot was. Find the story of Revere's ride. Find the meaning of the phrase "one if by land, two if by sea."

Find a clean paint can. Use a sturdy nail to poke holes around the outside in any pattern you like. Make sure there are enough holes evenly spaced to allow for good air flow through the can.

Set a fat candle inside the can. Secure it with some clay. Light the candle to turn the can into a lantern.

Develop a code system with friends and use the lantern to send signals.

April 20th

- Look-Alike Day*
- Cuckoo Day
- Holocaust Remembrance Day
- National Pineapple Upside-down Cake Day
- Volunteer Recognition Day

Get a group of friends together ahead of time and arrange to dress alike for the day.

Look-Alikes

Track down these words that look alike (but have different meanings and sometimes sound different). Here are some clues:

- I _____ that you'll find the _____ hiding in the closet.
  (surmise)   *(alleged culprit)*

- We might _____ up sailing into the _____.
  (happen to)   *(moving air)*

- Please don't _____ me in the _____.
  (abandon)   *(wasteland)*

- Will the lady with a _____ please take a _____?
  (fancy ribbon)   *(curtsy)*

- The skater wanted to _____ the results of the _____.
  (argue against)   *(competition)*

- I _____ to your pointing that dangerous _____ at me!
  (protest)   *(gadget)*

- It took only one _____ to eat this _____ cream puff.
  (60 seconds)   *(tiny)*

- Are you going to _____ me with a _____ at the _____?
  (give to)   *(gift)*   *(current time)*

Royal Blood

Today is the birthday of Queen Elizabeth II of England. Brush up on your royal skills. Get to know more about Queen Elizabeth and the line of succession that brought her to the British Throne.

Find out . . .

- *What is a monarch?*
- *What are her official titles?*
- *When did she become queen?*
- *Where does she live?*
- *What is her real name?*
- *How does succession work in the royal family?*
- *What is the line of succession after Queen Elizabeth II?*
- *Who is the Queen Mother?*
- *Does someone who marries a queen become king?*
- *Does someone who marries a king become queen?*
- *Can the monarch abdicate?*

I'm sitting in my royal family tree.

- Kindergarten Day
- San Jacinto Day

Birthdays
1838   John Muir
1926   Queen Elizabeth II*

Put Your Nose to the Earth

April 22nd

You'll have to get close to the ground today to do this investigation. Get down on your belly to get familiar with a small patch of the earth.

1. Find a spot of ground to investigate. Make sure it is a spot where it will be okay to do a little digging.

2. Bend a hanger so that it is nearly square. Lay this on the ground.

3. Find out everything you can about that square. Watch closely. Use a magnifying glass for a closer look. Touch things gently. Use your senses of sight, smell, hearing, and touch. Write down everything you see. Is anything moving?

4. Carefully dig into the soil with a spoon. Notice different layers in the soil. What do you find below the surface? Write down everything you see. Describe the soil.

5. Draw some of the things you saw.

- Earth Day*
- National Jellybean Day*

More Ideas:

- Use jellybeans as art objects. Create mosaics by gluing jellybeans in patterns and shapes to create pictures. Use a cement-type glue.

- Some jellybeans and a bag are all you need to practice probability problems. Put a mixture of colors in the bag. Keep a record of what's in the bag. Calculate the probability of drawing different combinations of two beans.

- Blue Day*
- Sneaker Day
- World Laboratory Animal Day
- International Sing Out Day
- First Public School in America *(1635)*

Birthdays

1564   William Shakespeare
1897   Lester B. Pearson

I'm So Blue

It's Blue Day! Get into a blue mood by doing lots of blue things.

- Wear blue. Put blue streaks in your hair. Paint your face blue.
- Listen to some blues music. Sing the blues.
- Write titles for blues songs. Make up your own blues song.
- Listen to some bluegrass music.
- Make a list of words that name the color blue. (cobalt, for example)
- Find titles of songs, movies, books, or other things that have blue in them.
- Create a blue work of art.
- Write an explanation for each of these "blue" expressions:

blue chip	bluestocking	blue ribbon	blue-blooded
blue-collar	blue Monday	blueprint	blue flu
blue streak	true blue	blue funk	bluebonnet
bluegrass	Bluebeard	blue mood	sing the blues
out of the blue	once in a blue moon		
between the devil and the deep blue sea			

Why did the little shoe cry?

Because his mom was a sneaker and his dad was a loafer.

Blue Masterpieces

Find several different blue paints. Dip a large sheet of paper in water until it is fairly damp. Paint blue streaks, blobs, and designs on the wet paper. Lay it on newspaper to dry. When it is dry, use a dark blue marker to write blue phrases, words, or ideas on the painted design.

- First License Plates issued *(1901)**
- Pigs in a Blanket Day*
- National Puppetry Day
- Library of Congress Established *(1800)*

Easy Pigs in a Blanket

Cut hot dogs in small sections to make "pigs." Cut a slit in each section. Place a strip of cheese in the slit. Wrap each pig in a strip of prepared crescent roll dough. Place the wrapped pigs on a cookie tin. Bake at 375°F for 20 minutes. Dip the treats into mustard, catsup, ranch dressing, or barbeque sauce.

Homemade License Plates

Make your own clever license plate. Use letters and/or numbers to put a message on the plate. Start with a rectangle of wood, styrofoam, metal, glass, or stiff cardboard. Use paints or other materials to create the plate.

1STR8

2B2BDO

AJOY2CU

2JAZ-E4U

2N2R4

LV2SK8

L84DINR

IBGOLFN

IFXUR2TH

These ideas are taken from real plates.

104

Scenes from Space

The Hubble Space Telescope is a powerful telescope that orbits Earth and provides amazing images of heavenly bodies. In honor of its launch into space, learn as much as you can today about Hubble.

Get on the Internet and view some of the wonderful images from Hubble. Use paints or colored chalk to re-create one or several of the scenes from outer space. Hang them on your bedroom or classroom ceiling.

Visit the official Hubble website at www.hubblesite.org.
Find out . . .

- who the person, Hubble, is
- what kind of telescope it is
- what it is used for
- how it works
- who owns it
- how it was launched
- how it is maintained
- plans for Hubble's future
- what pictures are currently being sent to Earth from Hubble

- Hubble Space Telescope Deployed *(1990)**
- National Zucchini Bread Day
- Anzac Day
- World YMCA Day
- National Hairball Awareness Day
- Spanish-American War Began *(1898)*

Smelling Bee

Sense of Smell Day was started by the Sense of Smell Institute to educate people about the wonders, mystery, and importance of the sense of smell. Use this day to raise your awareness of all the things that are enhanced and experienced by your sense of smell.

Get some friends together for a smelling bee. Gather 20 or more items that have a scent. Put them in separate small paper bags. Number each bag. Blindfold two contestants. Give each one a chance to sniff each bag. Keep time with the timer and see which contestant can correctly identify all the smells the fastest. Put liquids into small paper cups inside the bags. Use items such as these:

orange slices
talcum powder
hand lotion
strawberries
banana chunks
mustard
mint leaves
flower petals

apple slices
pine needles
chocolate chips
cinnamon
blue cheese
soap
catsup
pepper

April 26th

- Sense of Smell Day*
- Richter Scale Day*
- Read to Me Day
- Hug a Friend Day
- National Static Cling Day
- National Pretzel Day
- U.S. Holocaust Museum Opened *(1993)*
- Great Plague Began in London *(1665)*
- Chernobyl Nuclear Reactor Exploded (USSR, 1986)

Birthdays
1900   Charles Richter*

More Ideas
- Study the Richter Scale.
- Find out how to prepare for or survive an earthquake.
- Visit the government's earthquake website for kids: www.fema.gov/kids.

April 27th

- Tell a Story Day*
- Matanzas Mule Day*
- Babe Ruth Day
- National DJ Day
- Playground Safety Day

Birthdays

1791 Samuel Morse
1822 Ulysses S. Grant

Matanzas Mule Day

commemorates a day during the Spanish-American War (1898) when the U.S. bombed Matanzas, Cuba. There was only one casualty resulting from the bombing—a mule.

A Good News–Bad News Story

Don't let *Tell A Story Day* go by without concocting a great story or two. A kind of story that is fun to tell and challenging to create is a Good News–Bad News story. The story begins with a good news event, followed by an unfortunate event, followed by a good one, and so on. Hopefully, the story ends on a good news note. You can create such a story with a friend—passing the story back and forth, with one of you writing the good news and one writing the bad news.

1.
Good News
The day dawned clear and bright.

2.
Bad News
By noon, a tornado was heading for the town.

3.
Good News
At the last minute, the tornado's path turned, and missed the town.

4.
Bad News
The tornado struck a campground north of town.

5.
Good News
No tents, RVs, or trailers were destroyed.

6.
Bad News
Ned's tent, however, was picked up—with Ned in it.

Good News! You finish the story.

April 28th

- Poetry Reading Day*
- Costume Day
- Puppet Day
- Texas Wildflower Day
- National Day of Mourning (Canada)
- First Tourist Launched in Space (*Dennis Tito, 2001*)

Birthdays

1758 James Monroe
1788 Maryland, 7th state

Here's a good poem for choral reading. Find others.

A Poetry Party

Increase your poetry-reading skills by planning a poetry party for today. Get a group of friends or students together. Gather all kinds of favorite poems— serious, silly, short, long, original, or borrowed. Practice reading them. Memorize some. Choose some that can be read by a group (choral readings). Decide on the order of the poems. Invite parents or other classes to listen to your presentations. Serve cookies or other goodies.

Someone

by Walter de la Mare

Someone came knocking
At my wee, small door;
Someone came knocking;
I'm sure-sure-sure;
I listened, I opened,
I looked to left and right,
But nought there was a stirring
In the still dark night;
Only the busy beetle
Tap-tapping in the wall,
Only from the forest
The screech-owl's call,
Only the cricket whistling
While the dewdrops fall,
So I know not who
came knocking,
At all, at all, at all.

106

Zipper-Mania

The first zipper was invented in 1851 by Elias Howe, the man who invented the sewing machine. Although he received a patent for an "automatic, continuous clothing closure," Howe never sold his invention. The modern zipper, as we know it today, was invented by Canadian Gideon Sundback in 1913. He received the actual patent for a "separable fastener" in 1917. The name "zipper" was given to the device by the B.V. Goodrich Company in the 1930s when they decided to use it to fasten tobacco pouches and boots.

- Make a list of 100 things that zip.
- Write the life story of a particular zipper from the zipper's point of view.
- Since today is Moment of Laughter Day, write a joke about a zipper that is sure to bring a moment of laughter to your friends.

If everything seems to be going right today, check your zipper.

April 29th

- Zipper Patented *(1913)**
- Moment of Laughter Day*
- National Shrimp Scampi Day
- Los Angeles Riots Erupted *(1992)*

Birthdays
1899 Duke Ellington

Outrageous Hairstyles

It's a great day to think about hairstyles! Look at hairstyles. Imagine new hairstyles. Visualize people with different hairstyles. Think about what hairstyle you'd like to try on yourself or someone else.

Cut out pictures of people from magazines or photographs. Cut away the hair. Glue the pictures on drawing paper and give each person a new hairstyle.

April 30th

- National Hairstyle Appreciation Day*
- International Walk Day*
- Louisiana Purchase Day
- National Honesty Day
- No Spanking Day
- National Oatmeal Cookie Day
- Raisin Day
- George Washington Inaugurated as First U.S. President *(1789)*

Birthdays
1812   Louisiana, 18th state

Walking Feats

Take a walk on International Walk Day and appreciate these amazing feats from the *Guinness World Records.*

- The longest backwards walk was 8,000 miles (12,800 km).
- The longest walk in 24 hours was 142.25 miles (228.93 km).
- The longest nonstop walk was 418.49 miles (673.48 km).
- The longest walk on stilts was 3,008 miles (4841 km).
- The longest walk on water (on flat skis) was 3,502 miles (5603.2 km).
- The longest walk on hands was 870 miles (1392 km).

107

May

1
- May Day*
- Hawaiian Lei Day*
- Cheerios First Produced*
- Loyalty Day
- Labor Day (Mexico)
- Mother Goose Day
- Save the Rhino Day
- Empire State Building Finished

2
- Fire Day*
- Sibling Appreciation Day

3
- Sun Day*
- Sears Tower Opened*
- First Automobile Speed Law*
- Lumpy Rug Day*
- National Public Radio Day
- Hug Your Cat Day
- National Scrapbook Day

4
- Space Day*
- America Comedy Day*
- Kite Day
- National Kids Fitness Day
- National Weather Observers Day
- Kent State University Killings

5
- Cinco de Mayo*
- First U.S. Train Robbery*
- Slow Down Day
- Totally Chipotle Day
- National Hoagie Day
- Bonza Bottler Day
- First American in Space
- First Perfect Baseball Game

6
- Beverage Day*
- National River Cleanup Day
- International No Diet Day
- National Nurses Day
- Dirigible *Hindenburg* Exploded

7
- First Stamp Collection*
- International Tuba Day
- Paste Up Day
- Fire Escape Ladder Day
- Pulitzer Prizes Awarded
- German Submarine Sank the British Ocean Liner *Lusitania*
  Birthdays: Peter Tchaikovsky

8
- World Red Cross Day*
- No Socks Day
- First Coca-Cola Sold
  Birthdays: Harry S. Truman

9
- Lost Sock Memorial Day*
- Hooray for Buttons Day*
- Former POW Recognition Day
- Peter Pan Day
- Tear the Tags off the Mattress Day
- Mother's Day Proclaimed

10
- U.S. Transcontinental Railroad Completed*
- Clean Up Your Room Day
- Trust Your Intuition Day
- Landing at Jamestown
- First U.S. Planetarium

11
- Jigsaw Day*
- Eat What You Want Day
  Birthdays: Irving Berlin, Salvador Dali*, Minnesota

12
- Limerick Day*
- National School Nurses Day
  Birthdays: Florence Nightingale, Edward Lear*

13
- Frog-Jumping Day*
- Leprechaun Day
- Cough Drop Day
- Tulip Day
- Mexican War Declared

14
- Smallpox Vaccine Discovered*
- Dance Like a Chicken Day*
- Motorcycle Day
- Crazy Day
- Jamestown Settlement Established
- Israel Declared an Independent Nation

15
- National Chocolate Chip Day*
- Over the Rainbow Day*
- International Day of Families
- Peace Officer Memorial Day

16
- Canned Spam First Sold*
- Biographers Day*
- First 5-cent Piece Minted and Circulated*
- Wear Purple for Peace Day
- National Bike to Work Day
  Birthdays: Liberace

17
- New York Stock Exchange Established*
- Pack Rat Day
- Merry-Go-Round Birthday
- Child's Safety Awareness Day
- Kids Helping Kids Day
- First Kentucky Derby Held
- Racial Segregation in Public Schools Declared Unconstitutional

18
- Loch Ness Monster First Discovered*
- Mt. St. Helens Erupted*
- International Museum Day
- Visit Your Relatives Day

19
- Circus Day*
- Ringling Brothers Circus First Performed*
- First Department Store Opened

20
- Strawberries Day*
- Levi's Jeans First Produced*
- Amelia Earhart Flew Solo Across the Atlantic*
- Charles Lindbergh Departed on the First Solo Transatlantic Flight*
- Homestead Act Signed

For each starred* holiday, you will find one or more activities on pages 110–135.

21
- Lewis & Clark Expedition Began
- National Memo Day*
- National Waitresses/Waiters Day
- First Test Explosion of Hydrogen Bomb Conducted in Pacific Ocean
- American Red Cross Established

22
- National Maritime Day*
- Toothpaste Tube Invented*
- Victoria Day (Canada)*
- Flag Day (Australia)
- Buy a Musical Instrument Day

23
- National Taffy Day*
- Penny Day*
- World Turtle Day
  Birthdays: South Carolina

24
- Scavenger Hunt Day*
- National Escargot Day
- Asparagus Day
- Brother's Day
- Morse Code First Used
- Brooklyn Bridge Finished

25
- National Something Day*
- First *Star Wars* Movie Released*
- National Tap Dance Day
  Birthdays: Ralph Waldo Emerson

26
- Grey Day*
- Smallpox Epidemic
  Birthdays: Sally Ride*

27
- Body-Painting Arts Festival*
- First Supposed Witch Executed in America
- Golden Gate Bridge Opened
- Masking Tape Patented

28
- Sierra Club Organized*
- National Hamburger Day

29
- Summit of Mt. Everest First Reached*
- International Jazz Music Day
  Birthdays: John F. Kennedy, Bob Hope, Patrick Henry, Wisconsin, Rhode Island

30
- First Indianapolis 500 Car Race Held*
- My Bucket's Got a Hole in It Day
- Water a Flower Day
- First Arctic Expedition Organized

31
- Worldwide Anti-Boredom Day*
- National Macaroon Day
- World No-Tobacco Day
- U.S. Copyright Law in Effect
  Birthdays: Walt Whitman

Month-long Celebrations

American Bike Month

Asian/Pacific American Heritage Month*

Asparagus Month

Better Sleep Month

Blossom Month

Breathe Easy Month*

Clean Air Month*

Correct Posture Month*

Creative Beginnings Month*

Flower Month*

Get Caught Reading Month*

Hearing and Speech Month

Mental Health Month

Modern Dance Month

Moms Are Marvelous Month

National Barbecue Month

National Beef Month

National Duckling Month*

National Egg Month*

National Hamburger Month*

National High Blood Pressure Month

National Motorcycle Safety Month

National Photo Month*

National Promote Your Ideas Month

National Radio Month*

National Salad Month*

National Salsa Month

National Scrapbooking Month*

National Strawberry Month*

Older Americans Month*

Physical Fitness Month*

Responsible Pet Owners Month

Skin Cancer Awareness Month

Teacher Appreciation Month*

Transportation Month

Weekly Celebrations

First Week: Cartoon Appreciation Week*, National Nurses Week*, Clean Air Week, National Be Kind to Animals Week, National Computer Education Week, National Herb Week, National Pet Week, National Postcard Week, National Safe Kids Week, National Wildflower Week

Second Week: National Etiquette Week*, National Bike Week*, National Historic Preservation Week, National Hospital Week, National Music Week, National Police Week, Teacher Appreciation Week, Universal Family Week

Third Week: Hurricane Awareness Week*; National Backyard Games Week*; Buckle Up America Week; National New Friends, Old Friends Week; National Transportation Week; Running & Fitness Week

Fourth Week: National Shoe Week*, International Pickle Week*, National Safe- Boating Week, Good Stewardship Week

Dates That Vary: Memorial Day*, Mother's Day*, Shavuot*, International Astronomy Day*, World Laughter Day*, Armed Forces Day*, Good-Neighbor Day*, No Homework Day*, Windmill Day*, Kentucky Derby*, National Teachers Day, National Day of Prayer, Cartoonists Day

May's Month-long Celebrations

Creative Beginnings Month

Throw away all the ordinary beginnings this month. Start something new in a fresh way. One place to practice creative beginnings is in your writing. Rewrite ordinary beginnings to make them more attention-grabbing. When you start a new piece of writing, think extraordinary! Practice by writing a stunning, creative beginning for each of these:

- ✓ **something** curious that happened in the school lunchroom
- ✓ a **story** of a wild lightning storm
- ✓ a **description** of a terrible meal
- ✓ a **newsletter** to an insect-hunting club
- ✓ a **graduation** speech
- ✓ **news** of an alleged alien abduction
- ✓ a **mystery** about a missing gargoyle
- ✓ a **warning** about food poisoning
- ✓ a **news article** about forest fires
- ✓ a **love letter**

For a variation on the theme of creative beginnings, write 10 "Worst Beginnings" for the top-ten beginnings you NEVER want to read!

National Strawberry Month

Enjoy this fresh strawberry pie with whipped cream!

Don't let May pass by without making fresh strawberry pie!

Ingredients:
1 ready-made pie crust, baked
1 C mashed strawberries
5 C fresh whole strawberries
1 C sugar
3 T cornstarch
1 pkg softened cream cheese (3 oz)
$\frac{1}{2}$ C water

Fresh Strawberry Pie

1. Mix the sugar and cornstarch in a saucepan. Stir in the mashed strawberries and water.
2. Cook this mixture over medium heat, stirring constantly until the mixture boils. Boil and stir for one minute. Cool this mixture.
3. Beat the cream cheese until smooth. Spread this in the piecrust.
4. Fill the pie with fresh, whole strawberries. Pour the cooked strawberry mixture over this. Cool in the refrigerator for three hours or more.

Flower Month

This is a month to plant flowers, draw flowers, paint flowers, and enjoy flowers. It's also a good time to make an unusual flower bouquet that will never wilt. First, learn how to blow the raw egg out of an eggshell.

Eggshell Tulips

1. Paint several brown, blown eggshells with tulip colors—red and yellow. Leave some white eggshells white.

2. Use scissors to make the hole in the bottom of the eggshell wide enough for a pipe cleaner.

3. Dip one end of a pipe cleaner in glue and put it into the hole to make a stem for each tulip.

4. Cut out a pointed, jagged opening at the top of each egg to make the egg look like a tulip.

5. Arrange the tulips in a vase. Add leaves cut from green construction paper.

6. Experiment with other kinds of flowers, too. Add paper petals around eggs, as shown.

Don't throw away the raw eggs that you blow out of the eggshells. Use them for delicious egg recipes. (See page 112.)

Get Caught Reading Month

Read, read, read all month. What can you read? Read books, of course, and . . . read at least 25 of the things on this list this month.

advertisements	magazine articles
advice columns	menus
announcements	movie reviews
autobiographies	mysteries
ballads	myths
billboards	news magazines
biographies	newspapers
book jackets	nursery rhymes
book reviews	odes
brochures	pamphlets
bumper stickers	parables
CD covers	picture books
captions	plays
cartoons	poems
catalogs	posters
cereal boxes	problems
comic strips	proverbs
definitions	puns
diaries	puzzles
diets	quotations
directions	recipes
editorials	reports
essays	riddles
explanations	rhymes
fables	signs
fairy tales	slogans
fantasies	song lyrics
folklore	song titles
greeting cards	sports reports
invitations	tall tales
jokes	travel brochures
letters	travel posters
lists	TV guides
	want ads
	weather reports
	weather forecasts
	words
	yellow pages

National Egg Month

• Visit the Incredible Edible Egg website (the American Egg Board) at www.aeb.org.
  You'll find a dozen reasons to celebrate Egg Month, as well as dozens of recipes and other egg ideas.

• Research the cholesterol question. Are eggs good for you, or not?

• Make an omelet, quiche, souffle, frittata, or other interesting egg recipe.

• Track down some "Egg Trivia." Find out the sizes and weights of different eggs, how long they take to cook, where animals lay them, and so on. Become a regular walking "eggs-ample" of egghead brilliance about eggs.

• Use your best thinking skills to figure out how to drop an uncooked egg out of a second-story window without breaking it.

• May is a good month to track down more of those old "Why did the chicken cross the road?" jokes. See if you can come up with a dozen "fresh" jokes!

• Even though it is not Easter season, you can dye or decorate eggs. Learn how to blow out the inside contents of eggs. Then use egg dyes, paints, glue, glitter, feathers, fabric scraps, and other materials to turn eggs into works of art.

Fancy Brown Eggs

1. Wash and dry some fancy, lacy leaves. Hard-boil some white eggs.

2. Cut pieces of cheesecloth into circles big enough to wrap the eggs.

3. Place leaves on the eggs to form designs. Hold them in place against each egg while you tie the bundle with a string.

4. Put the eggs in a pan and cover them with water. Add five onion skins to the water. Simmer over low heat for 15 minutes. Let the eggs cool in the pan.

5. Unwrap the eggs and admire the fancy white leaf designs on your eggs!

Did you know? It takes 40 minutes to hard-boil an ostrich egg!

Try all four of these fascinating science "eggs"-periments this month!
Write an explanation for each happening.

The Fascinating Floating Egg

Pour two cups of water into a glass quart jar. Gently set a raw egg into the water. What happens? Remove the egg and mix six tablespoons of salt into the water. Put the egg back in the water. What happens?

SALT   FRESH

The Egg-in-a-Bottle Trick

Grease the mouth of a glass baby bottle with cooking oil. Fold a 5-inch (12-cm) square of paper accordion-style. Light it with a match and drop it into the bottle. Right away, set a peeled, hard-boiled egg in the mouth of the bottle. What happens? Then, fill the bottle with water to rinse out the burned paper. After the bottle is rinsed and the water poured out, hold the bottle upside down. Blow into the bottle past the egg as hard as you can. Keep the bottle upside down so the egg blocks the opening. What happens?

The Baffling Bouncing Egg

Place a hard-boiled egg (in its shell) in a glass jar. Cover the egg entirely with vinegar. Let the egg sit overnight. Dry the egg off and drop it. What happens?

The Spinning Eggs

Get a raw egg and a hard-boiled egg. Mark a stripe on the hard-boiled egg so you can tell them apart. Stand each egg on one end and spin it. What happens? Next, spin each egg on its side. Try to stop them both with one touch of your finger. What happens?

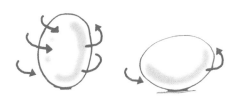

Asian/Pacific American Heritage Month

In 1979, U.S. President Jimmy Carter signed a resolution declaring the first Asian/Pacific American Heritage Week. In 1990, President George H. Bush extended that resolution to a month-long celebration. The purpose of the event is to promote awareness and increase understanding of the Asian-American culture. Get a map of the Asian-Pacific region. Try to identify all the countries from which Asian-Pacific Americans have come.

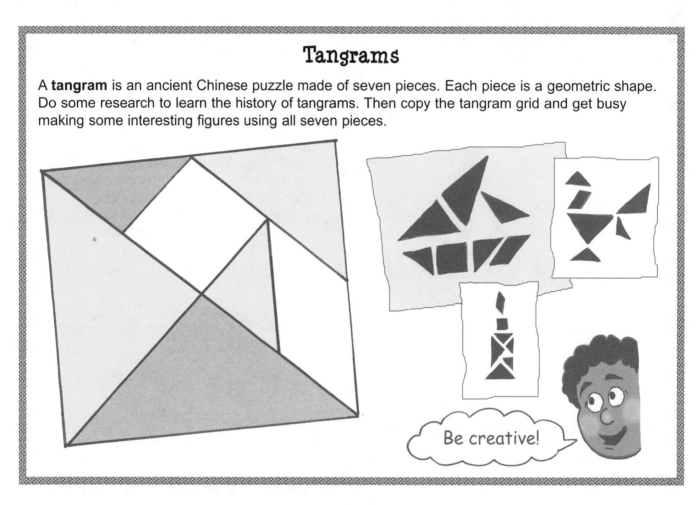

Tangrams

A **tangram** is an ancient Chinese puzzle made of seven pieces. Each piece is a geometric shape. Do some research to learn the history of tangrams. Then copy the tangram grid and get busy making some interesting figures using all seven pieces.

Be creative!

National Salad Month

Enjoy your favorite salads this month. Make sure you try some new salads.

Mandarin Salad

Put the dressing ingredients into a covered jar. Shake well. Toss the salad ingredients with the dressing, and enjoy the salad right away.

Salad ingredients:		Dressing ingredients:	
6 C	bite-sized pieces of lettuce (mixed varieties)	1/2 C	vegetable oil
1 C	shredded cabbage	4 T	sugar
1/2 C	chopped celery	5 T	vinegar
1/4 C	toasted almonds	dash	salt and pepper
2 cans	mandarin oranges		
2 T	sesame seeds		
1/2 C	chopped peanuts		
1 C	chow mein noodles		
1 T	chopped parsley		

Teacher Appreciation Month

Show your appreciation for a teacher this month with a custom-made booklet of comic strips full of teacher jokes. Track down teacher jokes on the Internet, or make up some of your own.

National Photo Month

Gather a collection of many different photos. Ask students each to bring ten photos or copies of photos to school. Brainstorm a list of things that can be written about a picture. Mix up the photos, and distribute ten to each student. Ask them to write something different about each picture.

For example . . .

• Write a diet for the animal in this picture.

• Write what the person in this photo wrote in her/his diary last night.

• Write a conversation that recently took place between two of the people in this photo.

• Pretend you are introducing this person as a banquet speaker. Write your introduction.

• Write ten questions you would ask the person in the photo.

• Write a secret that the person in the photo is keeping.

• Write ten reasons you would NOT like to meet someone in this photo.

Clean Air Month and Breathe Easy Month

Make your own pollution catcher to get a look at some of the stuff that's interfering with clean air and easy breathing. Use a magnifying glass to check the particles that appear on your pollution-catcher.

Two Easy-to-Make Pollution-Catchers

Take the label off a heavy, full can of food. Use double-sided tape to cover the can. Touch the tape as little as possible. Place the can outside in an open space. Check it after several days.

Hang a white coffee filter on a clothesline or other spot where it will catch the wind. Fasten it securely so it doesn't blow away. Check it after several days.

National Scrapbooking Month

What better month is there to make a scrapbook than National Scrapbooking Month? There is no limit to the subjects or themes for a scrapbook. Create a short one, or one that covers a lifetime. Choose a theme, get some supplies, and start! Visit websites or stores for ideas. Here are some sample topics for your scrapbook:

- a Mother's Day memory book
- a collection of favorite inventions
- a record of a vacation trip
- your 6th-grade year (or any one school year)
- a poem/photo collection
- your growing-up years
- field trip memories

- a collection of favorite movies, songs, or artists
- just a book about your friends
- a book of great words or phrases
- history of a broken bone (or other injury)
- a Christmas gift
- graduation memories
- a birthday gift for a friend

Physical Fitness Month

- What does it mean to be "physically fit"? Find a good definition.

- Find out about all three kinds of exercise that your body needs: strength, flexibility, aerobic. Write a description of each kind, including ideas for kinds of activities to do to become FIT!

- Make a personal fitness plan for yourself. Create a month-long calendar. Write the things you will do each day to promote your own fitness. Follow the plan!

...seven... e-eigh-t... ni-i-

Counting Comes in Handy

Exercise often involves math. You count the number of repetitions of an exercise. Or, you count the number of times a week you do something or keep track of the length of time spent on an activity. Use your math skills to solve these fitness problems. Then make up some more problems like these.

On Monday, Sue did 11 push-ups. Each day, she increased the number by two over the day before. How many push-ups did she do on the following Monday?

Sam ran twice as far as Dan yesterday. Dan ran twice as far as Greg. The combined distance for all three friends was 14 miles. How far did each boy run?

Lulu faithfully spends 40 minutes three times a week at a yoga class. At this rate, how much time will she spend doing yoga in a year?

Max does approximately 15 sit-ups a minute. Today he is listening to music as he does his exercises. He does sit-ups throughout three songs. One is 2 min., 20 sec. The second song is 3 min., and the third song lasts 3 min., 45 sec. How many sit-ups does Max do during these songs?

Correct Posture Month

Pay attention to your posture every day this month, and you're likely to end up improving it. Think about this several times a day:

Imagine that there is a string that goes from above your head, down past your ears, shoulders, hips, and knees. Keep this imaginary string in a straight line.

National Radio Month

After Rudolph Hertz demonstrated radio waves in 1886, the invention of the radio followed quickly. In 1895, Guglielmo Marconi proved that it was possible to communicate with radio signals. In 1902, he sent the first successful telegraph of a radio message across the Atlantic. The "magic" of communication by radio waves was that the communication needed no wires. The many radio broadcast programs we enjoy today are the outcomes of this discovery.

• Find out how a radio works. Find out how a two-way radio works.

• Create your own radio broadcast. Write, organize, record, and share an original program. Be sure to give it a name. Include:

> current news stories
> favorite musical pieces
> original advertisements
> community announcements
> entertainment highlights
> commentaries
> weather reports

Ladies and gentlemen, it's a beautiful day in the ballpark . . .

AL MacFLY, THE SPORTS GUY

National Duckling Month

Duckling is the name given to baby ducks. Do you know the names of other baby animals? Find the adult names to match these baby names.

calf	farrow
foal	cub
whelp	kindle
cygnet	poult
kit	fledgling
yearling	eaglet
fry	polliwog
cheeper	goslet
pullet	joey
par	cockerel

Older Americans Month

A presidential proclamation in 1963 set May as a month to honor older citizens. Get five autographs from someone over 90 this month. Interview at least three Americans over 75. Ask them these questions and others you create:

• *What do you know now that you didn't know when you were young?*

• *What has changed the most in your lifetime?*

• *What would you like to tell younger people today?*

• *Who influenced your life the most?*

• *What is the most spectacular invention that happened in your lifetime?*

National Hamburger Month

Make a menu for an all-burger café. Name and describe at least 20 different variations on a burger.

See page 109 for more month-long holidays to celebrate.

Special Weeks in May

Cartoon Appreciation Week

• Find out how cartoons are created.

• Track down the history of cartoons

• Find out about different kinds of cartoons

• Find the website of the International Museum of Cartoon Art and learn about your favorite cartoonist.

• Find ten cartoons about current events. Bring them to class. Discuss the issue that is the subject of each cartoon and the message the cartoonist is trying to convey with humor.

• Create a political cartoon or other cartoon about current events.

National Nurses Week

• Interview a nurse this week. Find out what he/she had to do to become a nurse. Ask her/him to tell you a tale about their most memorable nursing experience.

• Create a nurse cartoon.

National Etiquette Week

• Define *etiquette*.

• Create an *Etiquette Handbook for Teenagers*.

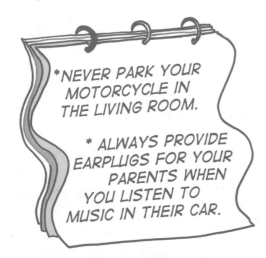

National Bike Week

• The *Tour de France* is the world's most famous bike race. Find out the length and route of this race. Make a map showing the route. Research to find out about the last ten years' winners of the race.

• Find out when the first bicycle was invented and when the first bicycle was used in the United States.

• Use your imagination to design the bike of your dreams. Draw it on paper, design it on a computer, or create a replica with wire.

• Make a list of "Dos and Don'ts for Bicycle Safety."

National Backyard Games Week

This is a great week to get some healthy physical activity in the backyard. Join friends in a kicking game with these easy-to-make giant blocks.

Giant Kicking Blocks

Crumble up a lot of old newspapers. Fill several brown paper grocery bags with the papers. Fold over the top of each bag and tape or staple it securely closed.

Lie on your backs and kick a big block into the air. See who can hold it in the air the longest. Or, "pass" the block around a circle with your feet. Make up other games to play with the giant blocks.

Hurricane Awareness Week

In 2001, President Bush proclaimed Hurricane Awareness Week. The purpose is to save lives and decrease damage to property through better preparedness for hurricanes.

- Visit the website of the National Hurricane Center to learn about safety and preparation for hurricanes.

- Learn about "storm-chasers." Find out why people chase violent storms and what dangers they face.

- Find out the difference between these: *hurricane, hurricane watch, hurricane warning, cyclone, storm surge, tornado.*

Fourth Week

National Shoe Week

This is a week to raise awareness about the number of orphans around the world and their basic needs. Charities collect money to supply shoes for children in over 20 countries.

Find out if there is a charity in your area that accepts donations to supply shoes to orphans.

Shoes come in pairs.
Think of 25 other things that come in pairs.

HOMONYMS   EYES   FEET   SCISSORS

EARS   SYNONYMS   GLOVES

TWINS   SALT & PEPPER SHAKERS

SOCKS   PANTS   PLIERS

International Pickle Week

Become a pickle expert this week.
- Find out exactly what a pickle is.
- Learn how a pickle is made.
- Find five different kinds of pickles. Taste-test and rate the different kinds.
- Visit the grocery store and price pickles.
- Create pickle riddles, pickle jokes, and pickle puns. Write the life story of a pickle from the pickle's point of view.

Why was the cucumber upset?

Because he found himself in a pickle over his wrinkled appearance.

See page 109 for more weeklong holidays to celebrate.

The Days of May

Mother's Day *(2nd Sunday)*

Mother's Day was proclaimed a national holiday by President Wilson in 1914, but a day honoring mothers was celebrated long before that date. Don't wait until the last minute to think about how to honor your mother on this day. One of the best gifts you can give your mom is yourself. Use your own words to tell her what you notice, love, and appreciate about her. Write a letter, note, or poem from your heart. For fun, you might sprinkle your writing with **M** words.

To My Matchless MoM,

You Model MagnaniMity, Moderation, and a Mirthful spirit. Much love to you, MoM,

Your Mischievous son

Memorial Day *(last Monday)*

Memorial Day is a national day of mourning in the United States to honor those who have died in wars.

- Find out what Memorial Day events are scheduled in your area. Attend one.

- Today, read the poem *"In Flanders Fields"* by Lt. Col. John McCrae.

- Learn about the memorials that have been built to honor veterans of specific wars. Make a U.S. map that shows the location of each memorial. Prepare descriptions to accompany the map.

- Thousands who died in wars are buried in Arlington National Cemetery. Find out what qualifies a person to be buried there.

- The book *War Letters* by Andrew Carroll is an amazing collection of 200 letters from several wars. Find a copy of the book and read a few of the letters aloud with a group of friends.

Shavuot *(seven weeks after Passover)*

Shavuot means "Feast of Weeks." Jewish families celebrate the time when the Ten Commandments were given to Moses on Mt. Sinai. The holiday also celebrates the early wheat harvest in Palestine. One Shavuot tradition is to eat rich dairy foods. These blintzes qualify as rich enough foods for a Shavuot treat.

Cheese Blintzes

In a bowl, whisk together 1 C flour, pinch of salt, 1 T oil, 1 egg, and 1 1/2 C milk. Heat a skillet. Add 1 T oil. Pour enough batter to cover the bottom of the skillet. Fry and flip until brown on each side. Fill with the cheese filling and fold up the blintz to form an "envelope." Place all the blintzes in a buttered baking dish. Dot them with butter and bake at 375°F for 30 minutes (until brown).

Filling

Mix 1 egg into an 8-oz container of cottage cheese. Stir in 2 T sugar. Spoon some canned pie filling into the blintz beside the cheese, if you want a sweeter treat.

International Astronomy Day *(between mid-April and mid-May, on a Saturday near the first quarter moon)*

Doug Berger, an astronomer from California, started Astronomy Day in 1973. The goal of the day is to get ordinary people to look into a telescope and to share the excitement and joy of astronomy with everyone! Learn about astronomy today. There are hundreds of books and websites, clubs, museums, planetariums, and observatories where you can see and learn about the stars. Find an Astronomy Day event in your area. Try to look through a telescope today. If you can, find some constellations in the night sky. Choose your favorite constellation, and enjoy it all the time with this *Constellation-in-a-Can*.

Constellation-in-a-Can

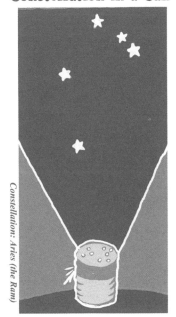

Constellation: Aries (the Ram)

Get a tin coffee can. Leave one end on the can. Draw your favorite constellation on a piece of paper that is about the size of the can bottom. Use the paper as a pattern. Secure it on the can's open end. Poke holes with different-sized nails to show the locations of the stars and the different brilliances of the stars.

Go into a dark room. Put a flashlight into the can and shine it through the constellation. This will project the constellation onto a wall or ceiling.

World Laughter Day *(1st Sunday)*

On this day, members of laughter clubs get together in large places to march for peace and laughter. Marchers chant, "Ho, ho, ha, ha, ha." After the march, people gather for laughter sessions that last ten minutes. Form a laughter club and spend some time laughing with friends to express your happiness.

Armed Forces Day *(3rd Saturday)*

This day honors all men and women who serve in any branch of military service. Get 10 autographs of people who are (or were) in the armed forces. Try to get autographs from all branches of the military.

No Homework Day *(Tuesday of first full week)*

Make sure your teachers know about this day, so you can have a day free of homework.

National Good-Neighbor Day

(Sunday prior to Memorial Day)

This is a day to practice being a good neighbor. Brainstorm a list of things kids or families can do to celebrate this day. Choose at least one thing from the list and DO it!

Kentucky Derby *(1st Saturday)*

This is probably the best-known horse race. Find out these things: when it began, where the race is held, what the Triple Crown is, which horses have won recently, and which horses are favored this year.

Windmill Day *(2nd Saturday)*

Much of the land in the Netherlands is below sea level, so windmills were necessary to drain the land. This day celebrates the history and importance of windmills in the Netherlands. Design your own windmill today. Paint it, draw it, or create a model.

121

- May Day*
- Hawaiian Lei Day*
- Cheerios First Produced (1941)*
- Loyalty Day
- Labor Day (Mexico)
- Mother Goose Day
- Save the Rhino Day
- Empire State Building Finished (New York City, 1931)

More Ideas

- Count the Cheerios in one box. Keep track of how long it takes you to count.
- String leis with Cheerios and other things such as gum wrappers, small candies, styrofoam "peanuts," bottle caps, etc.

May Day

May Day has been around for a very long time. It celebrates the end of winter and the coming of summer. In many countries, May Day is observed as a Labor Day or worker's holiday. The day is observed with festivals, costumes, parades, parties, and dancing around Maypoles. In Hawaii, the lei is featured. People greet each other and the day with long necklaces made from flowers. Greet your friends with leis today. Wear them to your May Day celebrations!

May Day Leis

Use 4-6 pieces of colored tissue paper, 5 x 7 in, or 13 x 18 cm.

Accordion fold

Fold into a fan shape and fluff.

Tie with 4 in, or 10 cm of string.

Tie the loose strings together to form a lei.

Aloha!

- Fire Day*
- Sibling Appreciation Day

One More Idea

- Find the history and lyrics of the Billy Joel song "We Didn't Start the Fire." Learn something about each name or event in the song. Write a new verse containing names and events that have occurred since the song was written.

Fingers of Flame

Don't start any fires on Fire Day, but create a representation of a fire. Use tissue paper in bright flame colors to design a collage of flames.

Cut many flame shapes from tissue paper. Make a thin glue solution with equal parts of water and white glue. Put one layer of flames at a time onto large, stiff drawing paper. Brush the glue solution over the flames, then place another layer. After a few layers, let the creation dry before adding more layers. Keep building layers until you like the design. When it is completely dry, add some "hot" words and phrases to finish the work of art.

Sizzle Scald swelter SMOLDERING torrid Sultry

Blueprints from the Sun

Let the sun's light create pictures and images. All you need is some simple supplies and plenty of sunshine.

1. Lay out leaves, shells, grasses, or other objects in an interesting arrangement on dark blue, black, or purple paper.
2. Lightly tape each item to the paper with a roll of tape behind the item. Try to keep the edges of the items close to the paper so no sunlight "peeks" underneath them.
3. Lay the paper in strong sunshine on a sidewalk or table. Tape the paper down with rolls of tape on the back (so the paper doesn't blow away).
4. Leave the paper in the sun all day. If the paper hasn't faded enough in one day, leave the objects in place and put the paper in the sun for a second day.

May 3rd

- Sun Day*
- Sears Tower Opened (1973)*
- First Automobile Speed Law (1904)*
- Lumpy Rug Day*
- National Public Radio Day
- Hug Your Cat Day
- National Scrapbook Day

More Ideas

- Find the heights of the ten tallest buildings in the world. Create ten math problems from the information.
- Find out what goes on in the Sears Tower.
- What was the first speed limit? Find out.
- Write an explanation for how a rug gets lumpy, or a list of things to do with a lumpy rug, or a story in which a lumpy rug plays an important part.

Space Milestones

Use Space Day to learn about and remember some important moments in space exploration. Track down several dates of major milestones in the exploration of space. Create a timeline on a clothesline or a long piece of paper. Add facts and illustrations.

May 4th

- Space Day*
- America Comedy Day*
- Kite Day
- National Kids Fitness Day
- National Weather Observers Day
- Kent State University Killings (1970)

A few events to get you started:

1671 Newton's Invention of the Reflecting Telescope
1846 Discovery of the Planet Neptune
1926 Launch of First Liquid-Propellant Rocket
1957 Launch of Sputnik 1
1958 Launch of First U.S. Satellite, *Explorer 1*
1961 First Human to Orbit Earth
1962 First American to Orbit Earth
1963 First Woman in Space
1965 First Spacewalk
1969 First Humans on the Moon
1981 First Space Shuttle Launch
1990 Launch of Hubble Space Telescope
1985 Explosion of *Challenger* Space Shuttle
1998 First Part of *International Space Station* Launched
2002 First Tourist in Space
2003 Explosion of *Columbia* Space Shuttle

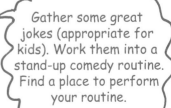

Gather some great jokes (appropriate for kids). Work them into a stand-up comedy routine. Find a place to perform your routine.

May 5th

- Cinco de Mayo*
- First U.S. Train Robbery*
- Totally Chipotle Day
- National Hoagie Day
- Bonza Bottler Day
- Slow Down Day
- First American Launched into Space *(Alan Shepard, 1961)*
- First Perfect Baseball Game *(Cy Young, 1904)*

Write a thrilling story about a train robbery today.

Celebrate the Fifth

Cinco de Mayo means "the fifth of May" in Spanish. It is a Mexican national holiday that honors the Battle of Puebla in 1862, in which Mexican troops defeated the much larger French invading forces. The holiday is observed with parades, dances, parties, and feasts. Celebrate this day with three Mexican traditions: season with chipotle, learn to sing the Mexican folk song like *de colores*, and make a piñata.

A Simple Piñata

1. To get ready, cut many strips of newspaper, blow up a large and sturdy balloon, and mix some papier-mâché.
2. Work on a plastic-covered surface. Soak strips of newspaper in the papier-mâché and lay them on the balloon. Overlap strips in all directions, covering the balloon except for a small hole near the tied end. Make three or four layers.
3. Let the layers dry. Later, add three more layers. Dry the balloon completely.
4. Pop the balloon and pull it out. Fill the space inside with small candies and toys. Close the hole with tape or more papier-mâché strips.
5. When it is completely dry, paint the piñata. Decorate it with streamers or other attachments. Use crepe paper or tissue paper to add decoration.
6. Use strings to hang it from a high place. Blindfold the players and take turns hitting the piñata with a stick.

May 6th

- Beverage Day*
- National River Cleanup Day
- International No Diet Day
- National Nurses Day
- Dirigible *Hindenburg* Exploded *(1937)*

Soda-pop Science

Make your own fizzy beverage today. Get some lemonade (or orange juice), powdered sugar, ice cubes, baking soda, and citric acid crystals (from a drugstore). Then stir up some Lemon Fizz (or Orange Fizz). Enjoy it and share it with friends.

1. Mash 2 T powdered sugar, 2 T citric acid crystals, and 1 T baking soda together in a bowl. (Use a spoon.)
2. Put 1 T of the mixture into a glass. Add ice. Pour in lemonade (or orange juice) and stir quickly.
3. Drink the Lemon Fizz before the bubbles disappear.

Lemon Fizz
the tastiest fizz in town
25 cents a cup

How Does It Work?

The baking soda reacts with the citric acid in the crystals and the lemonade to produce the gas carbon dioxide. The carbon dioxide bubbles make the drink fizzy.

124

Stamp Mania

The first stick-on postage stamp was issued for mail delivery in Great Britain on May 6, 1860. The stamp was known as the "Penny Black." The hobby of stamp collecting began immediately. The practice spread quickly, and was referred to as "timbromania" or "stamp madness." It is estimated that 25 million people across the world collect stamps.

Find out what the "Penny Black" looked like. Look up current stamps from different countries. Then design ten new stamps you'd like to see issued. Also design a stamp for each event or holiday on the list for May 6 and May 7.

> Visit the website of **Guinness World Records** to find out about the world's most valuable stamp.

- First Stamp Collection (1860)*
- International Tuba Day
- Paste Up Day
- Fire Escape Ladder Day
- Pulitzer Prizes Awarded
- Sinking of the *Lusitania* (1915)

Birthdays
1840   Peter Tchaikovsky

Ready-to-Go First Aid

> Do some research to find out what should be in a personal or family first-aid kit. Make a list and assemble your supplies in a container that can be carried in your backpack or car.

Commemorate World Red Cross Day by finding out how the Red Cross works and what it does around the world and in your country. Be prepared for small emergencies with your own first-aid kit.

- World Red Cross Day*
- No Socks Day
- First Coca-Cola Sold (1886)

Birthdays
1884   Harry S. Truman

> Was Coca-Cola the first carbonated beverage sold?

Sock Creatures

One sock may be lost, leaving a lonely mate behind. Remember the lost socks by using the other halves of the pairs to make puppets. Celebrate buttons by adding button eyes to the puppets.

> Cut an oval from cardboard. Glue red felt on one side of it. Fold it in half and glue it on the sock to create a mouth.

> Add sequins, felt or fabric scraps, yarn, and other decorations to make a unique sock creature.

- Lost Sock Memorial Day*
- Hooray for Buttons Day*
- Former POW Recognition Day
- Peter Pan Day
- Tear the Tags off the Mattress Day
- Mother's Day Proclaimed (1914)

- U.S. Transcontinental Railroad Completed *(1869)**
- Clean Up Your Room Day
- Trust Your Intuition Day
- Landing at Jamestown *(1607)*
- First U.S. Planetarium *(Chicago, 1930)*

Train Problems

Read the story of the Golden Spike and the completion of the first railroad that crossed the continental U.S. Turn your thoughts and attentions to trains today with the challenge of those pesky, fascinating train math problems. Find, create, and solve as many as you can.

1) Train A, traveling 60 mph, leaves Ashville at noon, heading west. At the same time, Train B, traveling at 70 mph on a parallel track, leaves Center City (520 miles away) heading east. What time will the trains meet?

2) A train is speeding at 95 mph westward. A child is running toward the back of the train at 5 mph. How fast is the child running?

3) Train C leaves the station and travels 30 mph. Two hours later, Train D leaves the same station on the same track, traveling 50 mph. How soon will Train D catch Train C?

4) At midnight, a 3,000-foot train enters a 6,000-foot tunnel at a speed of 30 mph. What time will the rear of the train emerge from the tunnel?

- Jigsaw Day*
- Eat What You Want Day

Birthdays

1858   Minnesota, 32nd state
1888   Irving Berlin
1904   Salvador Dali*

Dali-Inspired Puzzles

Salvador Dali (1904–1989) was a Spanish artist most famous for his surrealistic creations. He described his paintings as "hand-painted dream photographs."

Find out what Surrealism is. Find an art museum, book, or website where you can look at some Dali art. Mimic Dali's style to produce a surrealistic painting of your own. Then, celebrate Jigsaw Day by turning your painting into a puzzle.

Glue the painting (or a color copy of the painting) to a cardboard backing. Draw a jigsaw puzzle pattern on the back. Cut the shapes carefully, and keep the puzzle in an envelope so someone can put it together.

Such Nonsense!

Today is Limerick Day in honor of Edward Lear's birthday. He is most remembered for his limericks and his *Book of Nonsense*. Find his book or read his limericks on the Internet. Learn about the structure of a limerick. Enjoy these limericks, finish those that are unfinished, and create some of your own.

- Limerick Day*
- National School Nurses Day

Birthdays
1820 Florence Nightingale
1812 Edward Lear*

A school cook named Mojo McClure
Thought the health of his students was poor.
He said, "No junk food!
Get stuff that is good—
Like cabbage and spinach, for sure."

There was a teacher named Bill
Who said to his students, "Sit still!
Your report cards are due,"
_____
_____

The school nurse discovered my spots.
There were not just a few; there were lots!
My fever she took,
Gave a glance at her book,
And decided I needed some shots.

A brave matador named Jose
Tried to outwit a bull yesterday.
His shoulder was torn
By the creature's right horn,
_____

Jumping Dollars

On Frog-Jumping Day, read Mark Twain's famous story, "The Celebrated Jumping Frog of Calavaras County." Then turn a dollar bill into a jumping frog.

- Frog-Jumping Day*
- Tulip Day
- Leprechaun Day
- Cough Drop Day
- Mexican War Declared *(1846)*

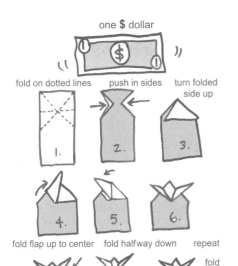

one $ dollar

fold on dotted lines   push in sides   turn folded side up

1.   2.   3.

fold flap up to center   fold halfway down   repeat

4.   5.   6.

fold sides into center   fold bottom up   fold down at center

7.   8.   9.

ribbit!

May 14th

- Smallpox Vaccine Discovered (1796)*
- Dance Like a Chicken Day*
- Motorcycle Day
- Crazy Day
- Jamestown, VA, Settlement Established (1607)
- Israel Declared an Independent Nation (1949)

Learn to dance the 'Funky Chicken'.

Dazzling Discoveries

For centuries, smallpox epidemics plagued Asia and Europe. Edward Jenner's discovery of a vaccine for variola, the smallpox-causing virus, changed history. Today, the disease is virtually nonexistent. Not one case has been documented since 1977. Learn some details about each of these discoveries. Find out who made each of these discoveries and when the discovery was made:

atoms

Halley's comet

antibiotics

electricity

radium

Pluto

X-RAYS

GRAVITY

geometry

combustion

sun as center of the solar system

radio waves

electromagnetic power

quarks

structure of the human genome

May 15th

- National Chocolate Chip Day*
- Over the Rainbow Day*
- International Day of Families
- Peace Officer Memorial Day

Rainbow Chocolate Chip Cookies

Making chocolate chip cookies is a must-do thing for this day. Here's a great recipe. Make a double batch. If it's a hot day, put ice cream between two cookies for a yummy ice-cream sandwich. To honor Over the Rainbow Day, mix M & Ms into the dough for rainbow chocolate chip cookies.

Ingredients:
1 C butter
3/4 C sugar
3/4 C brown sugar
2 eggs
1 t. vanilla
2 1/4 C flour
1 t. baking soda
1/2 t. salt

1. Beat butter and sugars together until creamy.
2. Beat in vanilla and the eggs, one at a time.
3. Mix the flour, baking soda, and salt together.
4. Slowly add the flour mixture to the butter mixture.
5. Drop spoonfuls of batter onto a cookie sheet.
6. Bake for 9–12 minutes at 350F°.

Voila!

Hooray for Spam!

Canned Spam is the first canned ham sold in America. It was developed by Jay C. Hormel. The name Spam was chosen in a contest. Get to know more about Spam today.

- Taste some Spam.
- Think of 20 ways to eat Spam.
- Write a song or rap about Spam.
- Write a Spam limerick.
- Give a speech to convince people to eat Spam.
- Create an advertisement for Spam.
- Investigate the annual Spam Recipe Contest.
- Create and submit a recipe for the Spam Recipe Contest.
- Create a Spam slogan for a T-shirt.
- Find out why Spam was called "the Miracle Meat."
- Find out about the first Spam commercial.
- Find out why Spam was used by the military.

I hate 'spam'!

May 16th

- Canned Spam First Sold *(1926)**
- Biographers Day*
- First 5-cent Piece Minted and Circulated *(1866)**
- Wear Purple for Peace Day
- National Bike to Work Day

Birthdays
1919 Liberace

Be a Biographer

Get ready to write a short biography of someone else. Choose someone as your subject, for example: a neighbor or relative. Think of at least ten questions to ask that will help you gain information about the person's life.

Here's a good idea! Why not try to write the biography in comic book form?

This is the birthday of the nickel. How many things can you do with a nickel?

Follow That Stock!

Learn some basic facts about the New York Stock Exchange. Get someone to give a general explanation of how it works. (Invite a stockbroker to your class, or visit an investment company.) Choose a company that sounds interesting to you. Follow the price and performance of the stock for a month. Create a chart or line graph to show the "behavior" of the stock for that period of time.

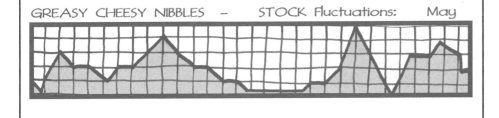

GREASY CHEESY NIBBLES – STOCK Fluctuations: May

May 17th

- New York Stock Exchange Established *(1792)**
- Kids Helping Kids Day
- Pack Rat Day
- Merry-Go-Round Birthday
- Child's Safety Awareness Day
- First Kentucky Derby Held *(1875)*
- Racial Segregation in Public Schools Declared Unconstitutional by U.S. Supreme Court *(1954)*

129

- Head of the Loch Ness Monster First Discovered (1964)*
- Mt. St. Helens Erupted (1980)*
- International Museum Day
- Visit Your Relatives Day

Monster Poems

Definitely find out everything you can about the Loch Ness Monster and other mythical (or possibly real) monsters.

Enjoy the poem about the Loch Ness Monster. Write a poem of your own about Nessie or another famous monster.

I've never shrieked in horror,
Never trembled
Or shook with dread.
Never stopped breathing, or,
Turned white like the dead.
I never knew sheer terror,
Not awake or asleep,
I confess . . .
Until I saw,
For only a moment
The massive
   rising
    gasping
     writhing
    serpent
      of Loch Ness!

Make a Volcano

Here is a simple way to make a volcano.

Put some liquid soap, red food coloring, and a few spoonfuls of flour in a plastic soda bottle. Build a mountain of clay, sand, playdough, plaster, or dirt around the bottle. Carefully but quickly pour some vinegar into the bottle opening and stand back!

- Circus Day*
- Ringling Brothers Circus First Performed (1884)*
- First Department Store Opened (1848)

Just Clowning Around

This is a good day to paint a clown face, create a clown outfit, and get busy with some circus tricks. Here are some easy tin-can stilts for your clowning around.

Remove one end from two large tin cans. Turn them upside down. Punch a hole in each side of each can with a nail and hammer. Cut two pieces of heavy twine (each one about two yards or two meters long). String one through each can. Tie a good knot in both ends. Stand up on the cans, hold the "handles," and walk.

Strawberry Patch Jeans

Combine a celebration of the invention of Levi's jeans and Strawberries Day by decorating your jeans with strawberry patches (or any kind of patch you choose).
How about airplane patches in honor of two famous flights?

Enlarge the strawberry pattern and cut out red berries and green leaves of felt or other fabric. Make seeds with fabric paint or stitches in white.

Sew the patch onto jeans or use it as a pocket on a fabric purse. Use colored thread or yarn, and stitch evenly for a neat look.

- Levi's Jeans First Produced *(1783)**
- Strawberries Day*
- Charles Lindbergh Departed on the First Solo Transatlantic Flight *(1927)**
- Amelia Earhart Flew Solo Across the Atlantic *(1932)**

One More Idea

- Make a map of the flight route for each of today's famous flights.

Memorable Memos

What is a memo, anyway? The word itself stands for "memorandum." It is a short message that has a specific goal. It is a specific instruction or reminder. A memo has a basic structure, containing the "to" and "from" names, the date, the subject, and the message. Make yourself a stack of blank memo cards. Then think of a memo that might be written in each of these situations:

- a mom telling her kids to clean their rooms
- a boss telling an employee she'll get a raise
- a teacher reminding students about a test
- a cook reminding waitresses to wash their hands

Write:

- a cautionary memo
- an instructive memo
- a reminder memo
- a silly memo

- Lewis & Clark Expedition Began *(1804)*
- National Memo Day*
- National Waitresses/Waiters Day
- First Test Explosion of Hydrogen Bomb Conducted in Pacific Ocean *(1956)*
- American Red Cross Established *(1881)*

MEMO

To: *Mom*
From: *Joe*
Date: *May 21*
Subject: *Missing cat*

I found Fluffy! She was in the microwave. Don't worry, she's okay. I put her in the bathtub.

MEMO

To: *Teachers and Students*
From: *Ms. Frank, Principal*
Date: *Jan. 15*
Subject: *Snowballs*
There will be no snowball throwing in the cafeteria whatsoever!

May 22nd

- National Maritime Day*
- Victoria Day (Canada)*
- Toothpaste Tube Invented*
- Flag Day (Australia)
- Buy a Musical Instrument Day

More Ideas

- Find out who invented toothpaste and who invented the toothpaste tube.
- Find out who is celebrated on Victoria Day and how Canadians celebrate the day.

Signals at Sea

Signal flags are used for communication between ships at sea. Mariners have developed a system of international signals. Alphabet flags can spell out short messages. Flags have special meanings when used individually or in combination. Go to your library or to the Internet and search for Maritime Signal Flags. Make a set of signal flags, and have fun passing and reading signals to friends.

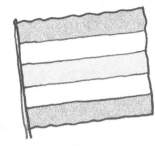

What do each of these signals mean?

May 23rd

- National Taffy Day*
- Penny Day*
- World Turtle Day

Birthdays

1788   South Carolina, 8th state

A penny for your thoughts! (How many expressions have the word penny in them?)

Taffy for Two (or More)

Have a taffy pull on National Taffy Day.

1. Grease a long baking pan.

2. Mix corn syrup, sugar, and water in a saucepan, put in the thermometer, and boil until the mixture reaches 258°F.

3. Remove from heat. Stir in butter, salt, vanilla, baking soda, and food coloring.

4. Pour taffy into the baking pan. Cool 15 minutes.

5. Give a chunk of taffy to two people with buttered hands. Pull the taffy, fold, and pull again until it is light in color.

6. Twist the taffy into ropes and shapes. If necessary, use scissors to cut.

7. Keep pieces wrapped in waxed paper until you are ready to eat them.

Supplies:
1 C light corn syrup
1/2 C sugar
1/2 C water
2 T butter
1/2 t salt
1 t vanilla
1/2 t baking soda
food coloring
butter for greasing hands
long baking pan
stove
saucepan, spoons
candy thermometer
waxed paper
scissors

An Extraordinary Scavenger Hunt

Plan an elaborate scavenger hunt for the day. Make a list of interesting things. Then send off a friend, pairs of students, or a group in search of the items. Set a time limit.

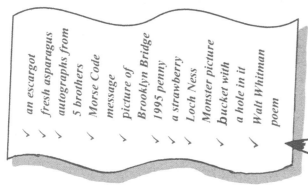

✓ an escargot
✓ fresh asparagus
✓ autographs from 5 brothers
✓ Morse Code message
✓ picture of Brooklyn Bridge
✓ 1995 penny
✓ a strawberry
✓ Loch Ness Monster picture
✓ bucket with a hole in it
✓ Walt Whitman poem

May 24th

- Scavenger Hunt Day*
- National Escargot Day
- Asparagus Day
- Brother's Day
- Morse Code First Used *(1844)*
- Brooklyn Bridge Finished *(1983)*

Star Worthy

Rent and watch the first *Star Wars* movie. Write a movie review or create a different ending.

Now That's Something!

Create a game for Something Day. Name it something like "I'm Thinking of Something," or "Guess Something," or "What Is the Something?" You might make a set of cards with names or pictures cut from magazines. Players could give clues about the "something" on the card while other players guess. Use unusual "somethings" in your game, so it's not too easy.

May 25th

- National Something Day*
- First *Star Wars* Movie Released *(1977)*
- National Tap Dance Day

Birthdays
1803   Ralph Waldo Emerson

Welcome, Grey!

Get into a "grey" mood today. Try to do several "grey" things. Here are a few ideas.

- Collect names that include "grey" or "gray."
- Find out about the correct way to spell this color!
- Write a "grey" poem.
- Eat or make a grey food.
- Find 100 grey things.
- Find a story or piece of descriptive writing. As you read it aloud, substitute the word "grey" or "graying" for every adjective in the written work.
- Find ten people with grey hair. Find out when they turned grey. Ask each one to tell you the best thing that has happened in their life since their hair turned grey.

It's a grey day.

Sally Ride rode!

May 27th

- Mount Hagen Body-Painting Arts Festival*
- First Supposed Witch Executed in America (1647)
- Golden Gate Bridge Opened (1937)
- Masking Tape Patented (1925)

Body Painting

Body painting has been practiced for thousands of years. For ages, people have tried to change their appearance by turning themselves into works of art—painting or tattooing their bodies. Research the art of face painting and other body arts. Plan your own Body-Painting Festival. Get some friends together, collect watercolor paints and paintbrushes, and turn yourselves into works of art.

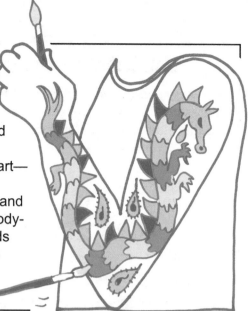

May 28th

- Sierra Club Organized by John Muir (1892)*
- National Hamburger Day

A Great Legacy

John Muir has been called "the father of our national parks" for his work to protect wilderness areas. Born in the 1800s, he had the foresight to understand the need to take good care of the Earth.

- Find out what he accomplished toward the goal of protecting the land.
- Find out about a great disappointment that occurred shortly before he died.
- Describe what John Muir's legacy for young people might be.
- Remember Muir this day by creating a poster or work of art inspired by the great outdoors.
- Explain what he might have meant when he said:
  "Tug on anything at all and you'll find it connected to everything else in the universe."

May 29th

- Summit of Mt. Everest Reached for First Time (1953)*
- International Jazz Music Day

Birthdays

1848	Wisconsin, 30th State
1790	Rhode Island, 13th State
1917	John F. Kennedy
1903	Bob Hope
1736	Patrick Henry

Mountaintop Statistics

Since Sir Edmund Hillary and Tenzing Norgay reached the summit of Mt. Everest on this day in 1953, thousands of people have attempted the climb. Get to know more about the mountain. Learn about what it takes to make an Everest climb today.

Answer some of these questions:

- How is the success of a climb affected by these factors: weather, oxygen supply, avalanches, falls, or human judgment?
- How many people have made it to the summit?
- How high is the mountain?
- Where did it get its name?
- Where is it located?
- Who was the first woman to reach the peak?
- Who was the first American to reach the peak?
- Who was the youngest? Who was the oldest?
- What is the greatest cause of death on the mountain?

Speedy Problems

Celebrate this anniversary of the Indy 500 by inventing math challenges that focus on speed, time, distance, and other things involved in car racing. Make up problems such as the ones below. Trade them with friends for solving.

> **D (distance) = rate (speed per unit of time) x time**
> **R (rate) = D divided by T;**
> **T (time) = D divided by R**

In 1904, the first speed record was set for a land vehicle. It went 91 mph. At this rate, how long would it take to travel 318.5 miles?

A race car's speed is 105 mph. What distance will it cover in 45 minutes?

A car travels 3 1/2 hours at 150 kilometers per hour. What distance is covered?

A race car traveled 88 mph, covering 132 miles in the race. It stopped twice for servicing, at three minutes per stop. How long did this all take?

Fight off Boredom

Fight off boredom today with Glorious Goop. It acts like a liquid. It acts like a solid. Which is it? Whatever it is, it sure is fun. Stir up a batch right away. (Hint: It is a suspension. The solid particles are held up by the water molecules, but are not dissolved in the water.

- Worldwide Anti-Boredom Day*
- National Macaroon Day
- World No-Tobacco Day
- U.S. Copyright Law Went into Effect *(1790)*

Birthdays
1819   Walt Whitman

Glorious Goop

1) Measure 1/2 C cornstarch into a bowl.

2) Add 1/4 C plus 1 T water and mix. It will be VERY hard to stir, but keep working at it.

3) Stir in a few drops of food coloring. This will take a while to mix in, too.

4) Now you're ready to play with your goop.

> Squeeze it. Notice how it feels. Roll it into a ball or a snake. Break it apart. Stop squeezing. Let it lie on your hands. What happens?

June

1
- *Superman* Comic Book Released*
- Stand for Children Day
- International Children's Day
- National Frozen Yogurt Day
- CNN Debuted
  Birthdays: Kentucky

2
- Dinosaur Day*
- Yell "Fudge!" at the Cobras in North America Day
- National Rocky Road Day
- American Indians Granted Citizenship by Congress
- PT Barnum Ran First Major 3-Ring Circus
- Queen Elizabeth II Coronation

3
- National Itch Day*
- Repeat Day*
- Egg Day
- Casey at the Bat Day
- First American Walked in Space
- First Wireless Telephone Message Transmitted
  Birthdays: Jefferson Davis

4
- First *Pulitzer Prize* Awarded*
- National Hunger Awareness Day
- Shopping Cart Introduced
- Wisconsin Cheese Day

5
- National Gingerbread Day*
- National Family Day
- National Attitude Day
- Be-Bop-a-Lula Day
- World Environment Day
- First Hot-Air Balloon Flight
- Robert F. Kennedy Assassinated
  Birthdays: Socrates, Richard Scarry, Joe Clark

6
- National Applesauce Cake Day
- Heart Mania Day
- National Yo-yo Day*
- Bonza Bottler Day
- YMCA Founded
- First Drive-in Movie Theater Opened
- D Day Anniversary

7
- Beginning of Firefly Season*
- June Bug Day
- National Chocolate Ice Cream Day
- Native American Appreciation Day
- Freedom of the Press Day
- Boone Day
- National Trails Day
- Introduction of the VCR
  Birthdays: John N. Turner

8
- Watch Day
- Upsy Daisy Day
- *Ghostbusters* Introduced*
- First Ice Cream Sold
- Suction Vacuum Cleaner Invented

9
- Donald Duck Day*
- National Strawberry-Rhubarb Pie Day
  Birthdays: Donald Duck

10
- First Recorded Tornado in America*
- Ballpoint Pen Patented
- First Public Zoo in World Opened
  Birthdays: Judy Garland*

11
- National Hug Holiday
- Great Barrier Reef Discovered
- *ET* Released
  Birthdays: Jacques Cousteau

12
- Machine Day
- Magic Day
- National Baseball Hall of Fame Opened
- Black Leader Medgar Evers Shot and Killed
  Birthdays: Anne Frank*

13
- National Juggling Day
- Weed Your Garden Day
- Lobster Day*
- Blood Type Awareness Day
- Kitchen Klutzes of America Day
- Blame Someone Else Day
- International Skeptics Day
  Birthdays: Yukon Territory

14
- Family History Day*
- Flag Day*
- Pop Goes the Weasel Day
- Continental Congress Adopted the Design of the American Flag
- U.S. Army Founded
  Birthdays: Harriet Beecher Stowe

15
- 12th Amendment Ratified
- A Friend in Need Day
- National Electricity Day
- Go Fly a Kite Day
- Magna Carta Day
- Family Awareness Day
- Native American Citizenship Day*
- Ben Franklin Proved Lightning Contains Electricity
  Birthdays: Arkansas

16
- National Hollerin' Contest Day
- National Fudge Day
- Fresh Veggies Day
- No Orange Clothes Day
- Helicopter Invented*
- Pepsi Cola First Sold
- Roller Coaster Introduced
- Cracker Jacks Introduced
- Gold Discovered in Alaska
- First Woman Flew in Space

17
- Watergate Day
- Eat Your Vegetables Day*
- Bake Your Own Bread Day*
- Battle of Bunker Hill Began
- Statue of Liberty Arrived in NY Harbor from France*

18
- International Picnic Day*
- Go Fishing Day
- National Splurge Day
- Battle of Waterloo Ended
- War of 1812 Began

19
- World Sauntering Day*
- Juneteenth*
- Julius & Ethel Rosenberg Executed for Wartime Espionage
  Birthdays: Lou Gehrig, Garfield the Cat

For each starred holiday, you will find one or more activities on pages 138–159.*

20
- Ice-Cream Soda Day
- World Juggling Day
- Eat an Oreo Day
- Plain Yogurt Day*
- Great Seal of the United States Adopted
  Birthdays: West Virginia

21
- Baby Boomer's Recognition Day*
- Ferris Wheel Introduced
  Birthdays: New Hampshire, Martha
  Washington

22
- Birthday of the Donut*
- National Chocolate Éclair Day
- Mirthday
- Voting Age Lowered to 18
  Birthdays: Anne Morrow Lindbergh

23
- National Pink Day*
- Let It Go Day*
- U.S. Secret Service Created
- First U.S. Balloon Flight Made
  by 13-year-old Boy
- First Typewriter Patented*
- Berlin Airlift Began

24
- UFO Day*
- Celebration of the Senses Day
- First Report of "Flying Saucer"
- Astronaut Sally Ride, the First U.S.
  Woman in Space, Landed at Edwards
  Air Force Base Aboard the Space
  Shuttle *Challenger*
  Birthdays: John Ciardi

25
- Log Cabin Day*
- Start of the Korean War
- Battle of Little Bighorn Fought*
- Introduction of the Table Fork to
  America from Europe
- Barbed Wire Patented*
- Tennis Shoe Introduced*
- Toothbrush Invented*
- First Color TV Show Broadcast*
  Birthdays: Eric Carle, Virginia (State)

26
- National Chocolate Pudding Day
- Bicycle Patented*
- Human Genome Mapped
- UN Charter Signed
- First Section of the Atlantic City
  Boardwalk Opened
- St. Lawrence Seaway Opened

27
- Sunglasses Day*
- "Happy Birthday to You" Composed*
  Birthdays: Helen Keller

28
- Paul Bunyan Day*
- World War I Began
- Panama Canal Bought by U.S.
  from France
- Treaty of Versailles Signed

29
- Camera Day*
- U.S. Interstate Highway
  System Instituted*

30
- Meteor Day
- Emile Blondin Crossed Niagara Falls
  on a Tightrope*
- President Abraham Lincoln Signed the
  Yosemite Land Grant

Month-long Celebrations

Adopt a Shelter Animal Month*

American Rivers Month*

Children's Awareness Month

Enjoy Candy Month

International People Skills Month

International Men's Month

Italian Heritage Month*

National Accordion Awareness Month*

National Adopt a Cat Month*

National Beef Steak Month

National Dairy Month*

National Drive Safely Month

National Flag Month

National Fresh Fruit and Vegetable
Month*

National Frozen Yogurt Month

National Iced Tea Month

National Papaya Month

National Patriots Month

National Pest Control Month

National Rose Month*

National Safety Month

National Summer Vacation Month*

National Tennis Month

Recycling Month*

Seafood Month

Summer School Month

Turkey Lovers Month

Weekly Celebrations

First Week: National Fishing Week*, National Humor Week, America the
Beautiful Week, National Family Week

Second Week: Anti-Graffiti Week*, National Clay Week*, National Flag
Week, National Hermit Week, National Youth Sport Coaches Week, Pet
Appreciation Week (PAW)

Third Week: National Roller Coaster Week*, National Forgiveness Week,
National Little League Baseball Week, National Tennis Week

Fourth Week: National Camping Week*, Deaf and Blindness Awareness
Week, Eye Safety Awareness Week

Dates That Vary: First Day of Summer*, Father's Day*, Pick Up Some
Litter Day*, Dragon Boat Festival*, National Taco Day*, Muhammad's
Birthday, National Cancer Survivor's Day, Donut Days, Join Hands Day,
America's Kids Day

June's Month-long Celebrations

National Rose Month

The rose is the national flower of the United States of America. It is known as America's favorite flower. Roses are grown in every state, and come in hundreds of varieties. Rose growers are constantly developing new roses.

• Draw and color ten different varieties of roses.

• Find out the cost of roses in your area. Call or visit five or more floral shops to price roses. Determine the average price for a dozen long-stemmed roses.

• Try to find out how many different varieties of roses exist.

• Brainstorm at least 50 names, words, titles, or phrases that contain the word "rose."

The Yellow Rose of Texas
a rose by any other name
a rose is a rose is a rose
Rose Bowl Parade
Red, Red Rose
red as a rose
every rose has a thorn
a bed of roses
Rose Kennedy
Don't throw roses before swine.
A single rose does not mean spring.
bed of roses
Your love is like a rose.
Pete Rose

National Fresh Fruit and Vegetable Month

June is a month to enjoy fresh fruits and vegetables. Besides eating many fruits and vegetables this month, try these three activities:

1. Find out the difference between a fruit and a vegetable.

2. Unscramble the vegetable names.

3. Let your fresh fruit salad teach you a science lesson.

Scrambled Vegetables
1. elycer
2. tarroc
3. srappin
4. eslyrap
5. gababec
6. eclairulowf
7. shapnic
8. kele
9. ape
10. inoon
11. corbicol
12. tebe
13. clarig
14. cerbmuuc
15. ~~glangept~~ eggplant

Munch! Crunch!

Fruit Salad Science

1. Make a fruit salad by combining chunks or slices of fresh pear, apple, banana, peach, and pineapple. Add some grapes.

2. Spread 1/3 of the salad in a flat pan. Do not cover it.

3. Put 1/3 in a bowl. Cover it tightly with plastic wrap.

4. Mix the rest with 1/2 cup of orange or lemon juice. Leave it uncovered.

5. Check all three containers in several hours. Notice what has happened. Compare the salads.

6. Read about the process of oxidation. Draw some conclusions about the oxidation of different fruits under different conditions.

National Summer Vacation Month

June is a month that begins summer vacation for many kids and families. This means time spent in the car or van traveling to vacation spots, visiting relatives, or running back and forth to the park, to camps, to friends' homes, or to the beach. Here's a great game to occupy your time in the car. If you are NOT traveling, you can use your cootie catchers in your backyard, at home, or anywhere else!

How to Make a Cootie Catcher

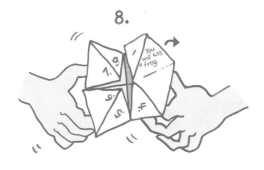

1. Fold a square piece of paper in half (8 x 8 in. or 20 x 20 cm). Mark the center. Open and fold the other way.
2. Fold each corner point into the center.
3. Without unfolding, turn the whole packet over and fold each corner into the center.
4. Number each of the eight triangles on the front side, 1 through 8.
5. Flip over. Color the four square flaps on the reverse side—each a different color.
6. Turn over again. Fold the packet in half. Unfold and fold in half the other way.
7. Under each numbered flap, write a fortune. Be creative!
8. Play the game.

How to Play the Game

Put your two thumbs and two forefingers into each of the four "pockets." Press your fingers together so that the four flaps meet in the center. Have another player choose one of the colors. You spell out the color by opening the cootie catcher up and down, then side to side once for each letter. When you stop, the player looks inside and chooses a number. You open and close the catcher that number of times. When you stop, the player chooses a number. Open that flap and read the fortune!

National Adopt a Cat Month & National Adopt a Shelter Animal Month

The month of June is specially designated to encourage the adoption of pets from a local shelter. Your local animal shelter is a good place to find a free animal that needs your care.

The famous poet T. S. Eliot wrote a wonderful poem about cats. Find a copy of "The Naming of Cats." Read the poem with some friends. Turn it into a choral reading.

• According to Eliot's poem, a cat must have three different names. Find out about the three names a cat must have. Then draw a cat, take a photo of a cat, or find a picture of a cat in a book or magazine. Give the cat three names.

• Write your own poem about cats.

• Create a directory of good names for cats.

• Write a commercial for a new gourmet cat food.

Recycling Month

When you recycle (or reuse) the materials in products, you take less of the Earth's resources to make new products. Educate yourself about waste on the planet and how you can reduce it.

• Get to know the differences between these different kinds of waste: biodegradable, not biodegradable, MSW (municipal solid waste), nonferrous metal, PET (polyethylene terephthalate), styrofoam.

• Find out how different wastes are disposed of or can be recycled (MSW, food waste, paper, aluminum, glass, plastic, styrofoam).

• Use the Internet to track down "waste" trivia. Find out how many rubber tires are scrapped each year, how many trees are cut down for paper, how much food waste is generated, how many aluminum cans are recycled, what is saved by using recycled paper, how much MSW is generated per person per year, and how much glass is thrown away. You will be amazed!

• Make some recycled sandals for yourself.

Recycled Footwear

You'll need an old tire, a tire inner tube, a craft knife or heavy scissors, carpet tacks, paper, pencil, chalk, scissors, hammer, and an adult helper to make these sandals.

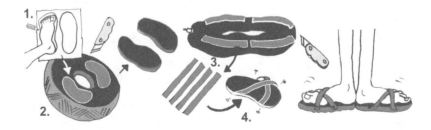

1. Make a pattern for the left and right sandals. Make the sole a little bigger than each foot. Cut out the pattern.

2. Use chalk to trace the patterns onto the tire. Cut out the two soles. Be VERY CAREFUL.

3. Cut four strips from the inner tube, each long enough to reach from the bottom edge of the sole by your ankle OVER your foot to the bottom edge of the sole by your toes.

4. Arrange the straps in a crisscross pattern on each sandal. Fasten the straps to the edges of the soles by hammering carpet tacks in tightly.

American Rivers Month

This holiday was designed to focus on awareness of the importance of rivers to the lives of people, fish, and wildlife.

• Track down some good websites that inform you about the health, protection, and restoration of rivers. Find out if there are any river restoration projects in your area.

• This is a good month to read the river adventures of *Huckleberry Finn*, and to sing a great summertime song like "Up a Lazy River."

• Figure out how to build a miniature raft from craft sticks or other materials. Find a river where you can set your raft off on a voyage.

• Be able to discuss and explain these terms and concepts related to rivers: *tributary, drainage system, drainage patterns, drainage basin, riverbed, river's load, suspended load, river deposits, flood plain, levee, estuary, delta, oxbow lake, meander.*

• Find some river trivia, such as . . .

   . . . Canada's longest river

   . . . a river that runs through more than six states

   . . . South America's longest river

   . . . a river that links the Atlantic Ocean with the Great Lakes

   . . . a river that carries the most water in the world

Italian Heritage Month

Italians are famous for delicious recipes, including rich, tasty desserts. Make this classic Italian dessert for yourself.

Zabaglione just like Mama Mia used to make!

Zabaglione

Combine 6 egg yolks with 2 T sugar in the top of a double boiler. Use a whisk to beat until mixture is frothy. Add 1 T grated orange peel and 2 tsp almond extract flavoring. Set on the bottom of the double boiler over gently boiling water. Stir continuously until the pudding becomes very smooth. Remove from heat, and set the double boiler top into a bowl of ice cubes. Whip 1/2 C whipping cream. Use a rubber spatula to fold the whipping cream into the cooled pudding. Chill the pudding in small serving cups. Sprinkle shaved or powdered chocolate on top, and enjoy!!!

National Dairy Month

Dairy products have an important role in our lives and health. Learn about the nutrients in milk and about the importance of calcium and how dairy products help people get calcium.

Drink a strawberry-banana smoothie.

Blend all these in a blender until smooth:

1 C lowfat milk
1½ C ice cubes
1 pt vanilla yogurt
1 ripe banana, cut in chunks
1 C strawberries
2 T honey

National Accordion Awareness Month

The accordion is an instrument that has been used in many cultures over many years. The purpose of this celebration is to increase awareness of the instrument and its influence on music. Listen to accordion music this month. See if you can find someone who has an accordion and will play it for you or show you how it is played.

Special Weeks in June

First Week

National Fishing Week

Fishermen are famous for their stories about the big fish "that got away." Show off the one that DIDN'T get away. You can make a "trophy" fish for your wall, but first you will need a fresh fish.

1. Line a large pan with foil.
2. Fill the pan with sand. Dampen the sand with water. Smooth it out.
3. Mix plaster of Paris according to directions to form a soft paste.
4. Press a fresh fish firmly into the sand to make a "mold".
5. Quickly fill the impression with the plaster.
6. Make a wire loop and push it into the plaster to form a hanger.
7. Let the fish dry for 2 days.
8. Remove the fish plaque.
9. Paint and shellac it if you want to. Then hang it proudly on the wall.

Second Week

Anti-Graffiti Week

Graffiti is illegal, and is very costly to society to clean up. Don't write on public surfaces. Instead, express yourself on your own Graffiti Mural. Mount a long piece of mural paper on a wall and fill it with any expressions, sayings, jokes, quotes, or puns.

Roller Coaster Week

Roller coasters are fascinating. Visit one of the many roller coaster websites to learn about the history of roller coasters, and collect some mind-boggling facts and trivia.

Roller Coaster Mysteries

See if you can find the information to solve these mysteries.

If it's possible, take a roller coaster ride this week.

- As of July 2004, one roller coaster in Ohio is the world's tallest and fastest and has the greatest drop. What is its name? Where, exactly, is it located? What is its height? What is its speed? What is the drop?

- Do passengers stand up or sit down on the **King Cobra** at Paramount Kings' Island Amusement Park?

- What is the longest roller coaster in the world?

- Where do you have to go to ride the **Desperado**?

- What material makes up the tracks for the **Titan** at Six Flags Over Texas?

- Where can you ride a coaster named **Phantom's Revenge**?

- What is the world's oldest wooden-rail roller coaster still in use?

- What country would you visit to ride **Thunder Dolphin**?

- How long is the **Son of Beast** roller coaster?

- If you rode the **Tower of Terror**, what continent would you be on?

National Camping Week

It's a good week to go camping, visit a day camp, or find out about camps in your area. Even if you can't go camping this week, you can do some "camp" activities.

- Create some great ghost stories that could be read around a campfire on a dark night or told when you're tucked away in your tent.

- Track down some campfire songs. Learn to sing them.

- Get together after dark with some friends, toast marshmallows over a hot plate, sing campfire songs, and tell ghost stories.

- Design a camp. It could be your ideal camp, or it could be "The Camp to Avoid"!

- Write letters from camp as if you were away at camp. Tell tall tales in the letters about your camp experiences.

See page 137 for more weeklong holidays to celebrate.

The Days of June

First Day of Summer *(near the 22nd)*

The first day of summer begins with the summer solstice. This is the longest day of the year, when the sun rises and sets the farthest north on the horizon. Celebrate the beginning of summer by making your own sundial. A sundial tells you sun time. A special pointer, called a GNOMON, casts a shadow that marks the hours. The shadow moves as the sun moves across the sky.

Make Your Own Sundial

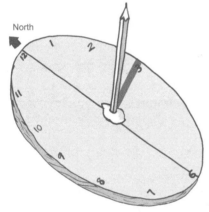

North

1. Cut a circle from wood or very heavy cardboard (15 in. or 40 cm). Mark the center of the circle.

2. Draw a line that passes through the center, dividing the circle in half.

3. Put a glob of modeling clay exactly in the center and stick the fat end of a knitting needle (or pencil) into the clay so that it stands up very straight. This is your gnomon.

4. On a sunny morning, get up with the sun. Set the sundial where it will get sun all day. Use a compass to find north, and point the end of the line on the cardboard toward the north.

5. Throughout the day, add numbers to your sundial. Each hour, look at the board to see where the shadow of the gnomon is. Make a mark and write the hour at the end of the mark. DO NOT MOVE THE SUNDIAL. Do this every hour until the sun sets.

6. On any other sunny day, you can set the dial pointing north and use it as a clock. It will tell the approximate sun time where you live.

Pick Up Some Litter Day
(on the 1st day of summer)

Start a **Litter Brigade** today. Gather some friends to form a parade for cleaning up the neighborhood, park, schoolyard, or any place you have permission to go.

Make some signs to identify your group. Take wagons, carts, large bags, and boxes for collecting litter. Wear sturdy gloves. Pick up paper, cans, bottles, or other trash that is lying where it doesn't belong. Be careful not to touch broken glass or rusty metal with your bare hands.

When your containers are full, meet with all members of the Litter Brigade to sort the litter. Separate kinds of trash and find a place to recycle it.

Dragon Boat Festival
(5th day of the 5th lunar month)

The Dragon Boat Festival is a major holiday in China. It is a time to honor the God of Water, to prevent disasters and bring good fortune. It also commemorates a poet, Chu Yuan, who drowned on this day in 277 B.C. Dragon boat races are a highlight of the festival. Teams compete in boats that look like dragons. The boats race to the rhythm of pounding drums. Dragon Boat festivals and races are held this time of year in many countries.

In some places, people try to stand a raw egg on its end exactly at noon. If the egg stands successfully, it is said to bring good fortune. Try balancing a raw egg on its end at noon today!

- Design a boat for the Dragon Boat races.
- Design a drumbeat to play during the boat race.

National Taco Day *(2nd Tuesday)*

This is a day to celebrate the taco—a convenient, tasty, and portable food. A taco is just about anything you want to eat wrapped up in a corn or flour tortilla. Try some creative tacos today. (How about cream cheese and olives, shredded bologna, strawberries sprinkled with cinnamon and sugar, leftover egg salad, or scrambled eggs?)

Father's Day *(3rd Sunday)*

Father's Day was declared by presidential proclamation (Lyndon Johnson) in 1966, but it started as the idea of a daughter who wanted to honor her dad in 1909. Find out about the history of this day.

Looking for the perfect gift for Dad?

Give him the tool that has hundreds of uses—a roll of duct tape. Include a list of things he can do with the duct tape. You might also write a history of the tape. Find uses and history on the Internet. It's very interesting! There are even whole books of things to do with duct tape. (No, it's not *duck* tape, but it used to be called that! Find out why.)

The Most Versatile Tool
100 Uses For Duct Tape

1. remove lint
2. bandage for huge cuts
3. repair broken windshields
4. catch flies
5. hold remote control batteries
6. patch clothing
7. ankle wrap for sports injuries
8. hold your wig in place
9. sunscreen for bald spots
10. cure warts
11. cover blisters
12. tape annoying people to wall
13. decorate your shoes
14. patch holes in convertible top
15. fix broken glasses
16. replacement for suspenders
17. hold up floppy socks
18. re-attach lost car bumpers
19. girdle replacement
20. keep ears from sticking out

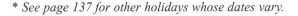

* See page 137 for other holidays whose dates vary.

145

June 1st

- First *Superman* Comic Book Released *(1938)**
- Stand for Children Day
- International Children's Day
- National Frozen Yogurt Day
- CNN Debuted *(1980)*

Birthdays
  1792   Kentucky, 15th State

Design a Superhero

Superman is one of the best known super heroes. But was he the first? This is a good day to explore the history of Superman and to learn about other superheroes. Find out about the superheroes named here and others. Then design your own superhero. Create a comic book or comic strip that introduces your superhero.

Find out about these...
  The Avenger
  The Phantom
  Streaky the Super Cat
  Wonder Woman
  Super Mouse
  Captain Flash
  Batman
  Spiderman
  The Incredible Hulk
  Daredevil
  Rocket Man
  Bulletgirl
  Jungle Girl
  Spy Smasher
  Tarzan
  Phantom Lady
  Miss Victory

Faster than a speeding pullet!

It's a bird! It's a plane! It's Superchicken!

June 2nd

- Dinosaur Day*
- Yell "Fudge!" at the Cobras in North America Day
- National Rocky Road Day
- Queen Elizabeth II Coronation *(1953)*
- PT Barnum Ran First Major 3-Ring Circus *(1835)*
- *American Indians Granted Citizenship by Congress*

Brachiosaurus means "arm lizard." Its front legs are longer than its back legs.

Curious Names

Each dinosaur name was chosen for a reason. Some were named after the places where they were found. Others were named after people who discovered their remains. Most names connect to some feature about the dinosaur's structure or behavior.

Choose a dinosaur. Learn about its features, illustrate it, and write a simple poem that tells something about its name or features.

We turned the corner, and saw before us
The awesome, long-necked Brachiosaurus.
At 80 tons and 40 feet tall,
'Brach' is the largest beast of all.

Which Itch?

On National Itch Day, start thinking about itching. Write stories, poems, tongue twisters, proverbs, advice, or remedies about itches and twitches.

How to Cure an Itch
Make a paste of cream cheese, birdseed, and chopped spinach. Spread it on the itching area. Let it dry. Wash it off with vinegar. Your itch will stop!

Use your left hand to scratch an itch. If that doesn't work, will it help to switch?

BUZZZ

Today is **Repeat Day.**

An itch is something that repeats. Brainstorm a list of other things that repeat: hiccups, telephone rings, eye blinks, heartbeats, SOS signals, honks, swallows, cricket chirps, train whistles, the S in Mississippi . . .

Which witch has the itch?

June 3rd

- National Itch Day*
- Repeat Day*
- Egg Day
- Casey at the Bat Day
- First American Walked in Space *(Gemini 4, Edward White, 1965)*
- First Wireless Telephone Message Transmitted *(1880)*

Birthdays
1808   Jefferson Davis

Neighborhood News

Pulitzer Prizes have been awarded every year since 1917 for excellence in journalism. It's a good day to create a good quality newspaper or newsletter for your neighborhood. Get some friends to take on the different jobs of collecting, reporting, writing, investigating, illustrating, publishing, and distributing your Neighborhood News.

June 4th

- First *Pulitzer Prize* Awarded *(1917)**
- Wisconsin Cheese Day
- National Hunger Awareness Day
- Shopping Cart Introduced *(1937)*

The Maple Street Monitor
Wiggles Biggles Winds Up in the Willows

Wiggles Biggles hangs on.

WEATHER
The weather will be sunny and bright on Thursday and Friday. Watch out for rain clouds on Saturday!

Not again! Last Thursday, Wiggles Biggles, a seven-year-old Persian cat owned by Lorena Biggles of 1723 Maple Street, got himself trapped in the famous Wishing Willow. This 100-year-old willow tree has been designated a historical treasure by the Pleasantville Historical Society.

The mayor, the police department, the fire department, the Historical Society, the Acme Crane Company, and even the Boy Scouts tried in vain to remove Wiggles without damaging the tree.

The cat was finally rescued by Timmy Bright, age 8, who opened a can of tuna fish under the tree. Wiggles wiggled right down!

The traumatized tree was treated by Dr. Twylla Twiggs, Tree Surgeon.

Include features such as . . .
- happenings in the neighborhood
- details on upcoming events
- weather
- crossword puzzle
- sidewalk report
- birthday or birth announcements
- mini biographies of neighbors
- lost pet report
- ads for local services
- introductions of new neighbors
- interviews
- reports of local government or school board issues
- kids corner with games, puzzles, or activities
- editorials
- comic strips
- letters to the editor

June 5th

- National Family Day
- National Gingerbread Day
- National Attitude Day
- Be-Bop-a-Lula Day
- World Environment Day
- First Hot-Air Balloon Flight *(1783)*
- Robert F. Kennedy Assassinated *(1968)*

Birthdays

469 BC	Socrates
1919	Richard Scarry*
1939	Joe Clark

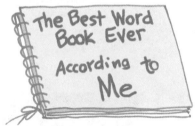

Best Word Book Ever

Richard Scarry is the author of many popular children's books. One of his books that has become a favorite is *The Best Word Book Ever.* Richard Scarry introduces kids to loads of words he thinks they should know. Read his book. Then create YOUR Best Word Book Ever. Choose words that YOU like. Feature a word on each page, or put several words on a page. Explain the meanings, or just show the reader something to help them figure out what the word means.

C WORDS

Which came first, the chicken or the egg? It's a conundrum!

conundrum

The Definition Quiz

A conundrum is

a. a stubborn person
b. a riddle or puzzle that answers a pun
c. two nuns playing a drum

Answer: b

June 6th

- National Yo-yo Day*
- National Applesauce Cake Day
- Heart Mania Day
- Bonza Bottler Day
- YMCA Founded *(1944)*
- First Drive-in Movie Theater Opened *(1944)*
- D-Day Anniversary *(1944)*

A Simple Trick

The yo-yo has been around for centuries—since the days of ancient Greece and ancient China. Since then, thousands of designs have been made and enjoyed around the world. Yo-yos were originally made from wood. Now they're made from many plastic materials. In 1992, a yo-yo was taken on a U.S. space shuttle mission.
If you are not a yo-yo fan, try one out today.
Here's a simple yo-yo trick to practice.

WALK THE DOG

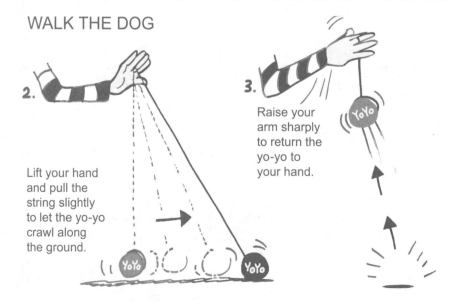

1. Let the yo-yo drop lightly to the ground.

2. Lift your hand and pull the string slightly to let the yo-yo crawl along the ground.

3. Raise your arm sharply to return the yo-yo to your hand.

To Catch a Firefly

Lightning bugs, or fireflies, are not just bugs. They are not flies, either. They are beetles that come in over 100 different species. Find out where fireflies can be found. (They are not everywhere.) Find out how they flash light and why they blink their lights. Learn what bioluminescence means. Some science labs offer money for collected fireflies! So, if you are lucky enough to live in an area that has them, make a firefly catcher. You can observe them and then set them free, or donate them to science for a profit!

Firefly Catcher

Get a quart jar with a lid. Punch holes in the lid. Catch the beetles by scooping them into the jar. Observe their flashing. Count the flashes. Time the flashes. Keep a record of your data. Compare data on groups caught at different times in the evening.

Always return fireflies to the same area where you caught them.

- Beginning of Firefly Season*
- June Bug Day
- National Chocolate Ice Cream Day
- Native American Appreciation Day
- Freedom of the Press Day
- Boone Day
- National Trails Day
- Introduction of the VCR *(1975)*

Birthdays
1929   John N. Turner

Ghostly Art

The first *Ghostbusters* movie was released on this day. It has been one of the most popular movies of all time. Celebrate the day by making your own ghosts with this easy ghost-painting technique.

Ghost Paintings

1. Get a piece of screen or metal strainer, an old toothbrush, dark tempera paints or ink, drawing paper, and plenty of newspaper.

2. Cut a ghost shape out of paper. Lay it on another piece of drawing paper. Place both on newspaper.

3. Hold the screen over the stack.

4. Dip the toothbrush in ink or paint and brush it onto the screen so that it splatters onto the paper.

5. When the paint is dry, remove the ghost shape, and you'll have a white image of the ghost on the paper.

- *Ghostbusters* Introduced *(1983)**
- Suction Vacuum Cleaner Invented *(1869)**
- First Ice Cream Sold *(1786)*

A Radish Vacuum

Make a vacuum with a radish! Cut a radish in half. Scoop out some of the flesh to form a hollow in the half of the radish. Press the radish firmly into the center of a clean, small plate. It will form a vacuum. Lift the radish by its leaves. It will pick up the plate!

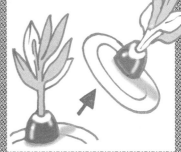

- Donald Duck Day*
- National Strawberry-Rhubarb Pie Day*

Birthdays
1934   Donald Duck*

Definitely Duck Day

June 9 marks the anniversary of the world's introduction to Donald Duck. The charming duck, in his sailor suit, became a favorite Disney character. Celebrate the day with a Duck Party!

Plan a silly Duck Day party.

My new cap is just ducky!

Draw a cap pattern on letter-size cardstock. Color it and cut it out.

Glue or tape eyes to cap.

Draw duck eyes with a notched tab 6 in. (15 cm) wide.

- Plan a silly Duck Day Party.
  — Create a silly menu with "ducky" entrees (*spicy duck wings, quackers and cheese, etc.*).
  — Make duck bill hats for the guests.
  — Plan a rubber duck race in a blow-up backyard pool.
  — Play charades with familiar duck idioms and expressions (*get your ducks in a row, duck out, etc.*).
  — Do some activities that get you into water.

- Find out more about Donald Duck.
  — What was his debut movie of June 9, 1934?
  — What were the names of his nephews?
  — Who created Donald Duck?
- Donald Duck "played second fiddle" to Mickey Mouse.
- Make a list of other famous "second fiddles."

- First Recorded Tornado in America *(1682)*
- Ballpoint Pen Patented *(1943)*
- First Public Zoo Opened *(Paris, 1793)*

Birthdays
1922   Judy Garland*

One More Idea

- It is an interesting coincidence that Judy Garland's birthday is on a day that celebrates a tornado event. Explain why this is a coincidence.

Tornado Watch

Watching for and tracking tornados has become an important activity for saving lives during these destructive storms. Use this day to expand your awareness about tornadoes.

- What, exactly, is a tornado? Explain how a tornado is formed.
- What areas are most likely to have tornados?
- What is a tornado warning? What is a tornado watch?
- Read about people who chase tornados to film them.
- Learn about tornado safety precautions.
- Find and read the poem *"How to Tell a Tornado"* by Howard Mohr.

Tornado Art

1. Use bright crayons to color a large area on a piece of drawing paper.
2. Paint a layer of dark-colored paint over the crayon area.
3. Let the paint dry.
4. Use a pointed instrument like a fork, toothpick, or paper clip to scratch off the swirl of the tornado.

Scenes From a Reef

On this day in 1770, Captain James Cook made the near-tragic discovery of the Great Barrier Reef along the coast of Australia.

- Read about Cook's adventures with the reef.
- Draw a map of the Great Barrier Reef.
- Visit the coral reef website www.coralreef.org. Look at the Photo Bank. If you have a color printer, print out some of the wonderful reef scenes. Use them to make a beautiful reef collage.
- Find pictures of some reef-dwelling fish. Make your own reef scene with a crayon resist.

1. Use bright-colored crayons to create a scene of reef life. Color heavily with the crayons.
2. Prepare a thin mixture of blue tempera paint.
3. Use a wide brush to swipe the paint over the crayon scene, creating an "underwater" effect.

June 11th

- Great Barrier Reef Discovered *(1770)**
- National Hug Holiday
- Movie *ET* Released *(1982)*

Birthdays
1910   Jacques Cousteau

A Homemade Diary

Today is the anniversary of the birth of Anne Frank, a girl whose diary has left a major impact on history and thousands of readers. Get a copy of *The Diary of Anne Frank*. Notice how the keeping of a diary allowed her to think about her life and record her most personal experiences and emotions. If you do not already keep a diary or journal, begin one today. Make a journal by fastening sheets of paper together in a homemade, marbleized cover. Making your own diary will inspire you to keep a regular record of your life experiences.

1. Fill an old dishpan or pail with water.
2. Mix a little turpentine with oil paint until it is thin enough to pour.
3. Pour some of the paint onto the water. Stir slightly.
4. Lay a piece of paper on the surface of the water, and then gently pick it up.
5. Lay it on newspaper to dry.
6. Repeat with another color, if desired.

June 12th

- Machine Day
- Magic Day
- National Baseball Hall of Fame Opened *(1939)*
- Black Leader Medgar Evers Shot and Killed by Snipers *(1963)*

Birthdays
1929   Anne Frank*

June 13th

- Lobster Day*
- National Juggling Day
- Weed Your Garden Day
- Blood Type Awareness Day
- Kitchen Klutzes of America Day
- Blame Someone Else Day
- International Skeptics Day

Birthdays
1898   Yukon Territory

Lobster Manuals

Lobster Day is celebrated in many communities around the world. The dates vary in different areas. Most of the celebrations have to do with eating lobsters. You can use the day to eat a lobster or to appreciate live lobsters. Get to know about lobsters. Then create a manual that instructs someone else on a topic related to lobsters.

Yikes! Who turned up the heat?

The largest documented lobster was 3 to 4 feet long and weighed 44 pounds.

Create a manual that tells . . .

How to Eat a Lobster
The Life Story of a Lobster
All About Lobster Parts
Why Lobsters Are a Delicacy
The History of Lobstering
How to Catch a Lobster
How a Lobster Eats
Tales of the Biggest Lobsters
How to Talk to a Lobster

June 14th

- Flag Day*
- Continental Congress Adopted the Design of the American Flag *(1777)**
- Family History Day*
- Sandpaper Invented *(1834)*
- Pop Goes the Weasel Day
- U.S. Army Established *(1775)*

Birthdays
1811   Harriet Beecher Stowe

Design a Flag

Find out why today is Flag Day. Then visit your library or the Internet to look at pictures of as many different flags as you can find. Read about flags. Notice how the colors, icons, stripes, shapes, and symbols on a flag all have meanings for the state, country, or organization.

Since it is **Family History Day,** think about a flag for your family. Decide on colors, shapes, and symbols that have meaning for the members of your family. Design a flag. Create it on a large piece of fabric cut from an old sheet or pillowcase. Use markers, dyes, or water paints.

The Goldsteins

Italian - American

Rowing   Family

Personal Totem Poles

June 15th celebrates the day in 1924 when the U.S. Congress granted citizenship to Native Americans. Many tribes in Northwestern North America carved totem poles from wood or stone to show family relationships and stories. The poles contained symbols to represent different events and relationships. Read about the history of totem poles before you make your own. Notice the designs. Then make a totem pole that tells your story.

Use sturdy tape to attach juice cans, coffee cans, oatmeal boxes, or cereal boxes into a stack. Attach wings, beaks, or other features securely with tape. Mix papier-mâché paste according to directions, and cover the pole with two layers of paste-covered strips. Let it dry, and then add two more layers. When the pole is thoroughly dry, paint it with designs and symbols. Shellac or varnish it the next day.

- 12th Amendment to the *U.S. Constitution* Ratified *(1804)*
- Native American Citizenship Day*
- A Friend in Need Day
- Magna Carta Day
- Family Awareness Day
- National Electricity Day
- Go Fly a Kite Day
- Ben Franklin Proved That Lightning Contains Electricity *(1752)*

Birthdays
1836   Arkansas, 25th State

A Quick & Easy Helicopter

Commemorate the invention of the helicopter by learning how a real helicopter works. Then fill your sky with these simple mini-whirlybirds that fly with a helicopter-like "blade."

Make copies of the figure. Decorate it. Cut on all the dotted lines. Fold forward along lines 1, 2, and 3. Fold backward along lines 4 and 5.

Hold it high in the air and let it drop. Watch it whirl and twirl.

- Helicopter Invented *(1922)**
- Roller Coaster Introduced *(1884)*
- National Hollerin' Contest Day
- No Orange Clothes Day
- Pepsi Cola First Sold *(1903)*
- Gold Discovered in Alaska *(1897)*
- First Woman Flew in Space *(USSR, 1963)*

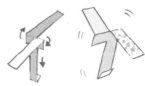

153

June 17th

- Eat Your Vegetables Day*
- Bake Your Own Bread Day*
- Statue of Liberty Arrived in N.Y. Harbor (1855)*
- Watergate Day
- Battle of Bunker Hill Began (1775)

More Ideas

- Learn the history of the Statue of Liberty. Whose idea was it? What is its meaning? How was it made?
- Track down interesting facts about the statue, such as the measurement of its various parts, its height, how many people visit it, and so on.

Zucchini Bread Recipe

Celebrate two holidays today (Eat Your Vegetables Day and Bake Your Own Bread Day) by making this delicious zucchini bread. When it's ready to eat, spread it with soft butter or cream cheese.

Ingredients:
3/4 C sugar
1/3 C oil
2 eggs
1 t vanilla
1 1/2 C shredded zucchini
1 1/2 C white or wheat flour
2 t baking soda
1/3 t baking powder
1 t cinnamon
1/4 t cloves
1/2 C chopped nuts (optional)

1. Mix the sugar, oil, eggs, and vanilla well.
2. Stir in the zucchini.
3. Stir in the remaining ingredients in the order given.
4. Grease the bottom of a loaf pan. Pour in the batter.
5. Bake at 350°F (180°C) for 90 to 100 minutes. *(It's done when a wooden toothpick comes out clean.)*
6. Cool ten minutes, then remove from pan and cool completely before wrapping.

June 18th

- International Picnic Day*
- Go Fishing Day
- National Splurge Day
- Battle of Waterloo Ended (1815)
- War of 1812 Began (1812)

Use a permanent marker to draw axis lines and numbers on an old plastic picnic tablecloth. Draw and cut picnic items from cardboard or paper.

I see my relatives at (-3,-2), (-3,4), (0,2), and (2,-2). Do you see others?

Picnic Table Geometry

Turn a checkered picnic tablecloth into a grid. Then practice your skills at coordinate geometry by placing picnic items on the grid.

154

Superb Sauntering

Set up your own sauntering contest for World Sauntering Day. Get a clear idea of what **sauntering** is. Then design a contest with several categories of sauntering. Gather a bunch of friends, choose some judges, get some measuring tools, and have fun with the competition!

CONTEST CATEGORIES

BEST SAUNTERING ACROSS THE LAWN
BEST SAUNTERING AROUND THE BLOCK
BEST BLINDFOLDED SAUNTERING
BEST BACKWARDS SAUNTERING
BEST SIDEWAYS SAUNTERING
BEST SAUNTERING WHILE WHISTLING
COOLEST SAUNTERING STYLE
COOLEST SAUNTERING OUTFIT

June 19th

- World Sauntering Day*
- Juneteenth*
- Julius & Ethel Rosenberg Executed for Wartime Espionage *(1953)*

Birthdays
1903 Lou Gehrig
1978 Garfield the Cat

One More Idea
- Find out what Juneteenth celebrates. Read the history of this important date.

Homemade Yogurt

Did you know you can make your own yogurt? You don't even need a yogurt-making machine! Try this recipe. You'll need a bit of plain yogurt, a cooking thermometer, milk, small glass jars or dishes, and a large ice chest (cooler).

1. Scald 2 quarts of milk until a film forms on the top.
2. Cool the milk to 110°F. Stir in 4 T plain yogurt (with live acidophilus).
3. Pour the mixture into small jars or glass dishes.
4. Fill a large flat pan with warm water. Set it in the cooler. Set the jars of yogurt into the warm water "bath." Let them sit for 12 hours.
5. Cover the jars and cool them in the refrigerator. The yogurt will finish thickening and be ready to eat.

June 20th

- Plain Yogurt Day*
- Ice-Cream Soda Day
- World Juggling Day
- Eat an Oreo Day
- Great Seal of the United States Adopted *(1782)*

Birthdays
1863 West Virginia, 35th State

Baby Boomer Hunt

Make sure you recognize Baby Boomers today.
Here are some ideas for focusing on baby boomers.

- Find out what a baby boomer is. Find the name of the first baby boomer.
- Get autographs of 50 baby boomers.
- Calculate the present ages of baby boomers.
- List 20 interesting events that happened in history during the period when baby boomers were being born.
- Find the names of some songs, movies, or other entertainment events that were popular when the baby boomers were teenagers.
- Design an advertising poster for a product that might appeal to baby boomers currently.
- Find the names of famous baby boomers.

June 21st

- Baby Boomer's Recognition Day*
- Ferris Wheel Introduced *(1893)*

Birthdays
1788 New Hampshire, 9th State
1731 Martha Washington

June 22nd

- Birthday of the Donut *(1847)**
- National Chocolate Éclair Day
- Mirthday
- Voting Age Lowered to 18 *(1970)*

Birthdays

1906   Anne Morrow Lindbergh

15-Minute Donuts

However you spell the word (*donuts* or *doughnuts*), today is the day to eat them. Here's a quick and simple recipe. Make up a batch, roll them in powdered sugar, and try the donut-eating challenge.

Ingredients:

1 C milk	1 egg	1/2 t baking soda	rolling pin
2 T white vinegar	2 T shortening	1/4 t salt	donut cutter
1/2 C sugar	2 1/2 C flour	1 qt vegetable oil	powdered sugar

1. Mix the vinegar and milk.
2. Beat the shortening with the sugar until smooth. Beat in the egg.
3. Sift the flour, baking soda, and salt together.
4. Gradually add the milk mixture and the sugar mixture to the flour mixture.
5. Roll the dough on a floured surface to about 1/3-in. thick. Cut donuts with the donut cutter. Or, roll the dough into small balls or short "snakes."
6. Heat oil in a deep skillet to 375°F (190°C). Fry the donuts until they are golden brown, turning once.
7. Drain donuts on paper towels. Roll them in powdered sugar while they are warm.

Challenge: Suspend donuts from a string. Try eating them without the help of your hands!

June 23rd

- First Typewriter Patented *(1868)**
- National Pink Day*
- Let It Go Day*
- U.S. Secret Service Created *(1860)*
- First U.S. Balloon Flight Made by 13-year-old Boy *(1784)*
- Berlin Airlift Begun *(1948)*

Story in a Shape

If you're lucky enough to find an old typewriter, use it to create a story in a shape. You can do this on a computer, also. Combine the commemoration of the typewriter patent with National Pink Day by making your story about things pink! OR, celebrate Let It Go Day by typing things people need to let go.

Pink is roses, noses, skin, whimpers, the smell of rhubarb pie baking, going to the circus, bows, ribbons, embarrassment, frilly dresses, a mouse's toes, pansies, the taste of deli ham, the feeling of sun on your skin on a summer morning, fingers, the sound of a whisper, the flavor of strawberry yogurt, petunias, cowardice, a cat's tongue, the sound of a music box, the taste of a lollipop, the smell of bubblegum, a baby's tummy, sunburn and measles and cotton candy ..... and.. sunsets.

1. Lightly draw a shape on typing paper with pencil.
2. Type the words inside the shape.
3. Erase the pencil lines.

On a computer, use your art feature to draw the shape and eliminate the lines after the typing is done.

A UFO Tale

This day marks the first recorded UFO sighting in the U.S. However, for centuries, people have told stories of seeing "flying saucers." This is a good day to let your imagination run wild with a good UFO story. Design your own alien. Design the spaceship the aliens would use for travel. Draw or paint both of these. Then write a tale to go along with your drawings.

June 24th

- UFO Day*
- First Report of "Flying Saucer" (1947)*
- Astronaut Sally Ride Became First U.S. Woman to Complete a Space Mission (1983)*
- Celebration of the Senses Day

Birthdays
1916   John Ciardi

One More Idea

- John Ciardi is a famous poet who has been a favorite of kids because of his humorous poetry. Read several of his poems from *The Monster Den* or one of his other books of poetry for kids.

Things Come Alive

Personification is a technique that writers use to give human characteristics to things that are not human (animals, plants, or nonliving things). Create (or collect) examples of sentences or phrases that include personification. Write a whole story from the viewpoint of a nonhuman character. (For example: Tell the experiences of a table fork, barbed wire fence, tennis shoe, toothbrush, color TV, log cabin, or a horse at the Battle of Little Bighorn.)

June 25th

- Introduction of the Table Fork to America from Europe (1630)*
- Barbed Wire Patented (1867)*
- Tennis Shoe Introduced (1947)*
- Toothbrush Invented (1498)*
- First Color TV Show Broadcast (CBS, 1951)*
- Log Cabin Day*
- Battle of Little Bighorn Fought (1876)*
- Start of the Korean War (1950)

Birthdays
1788   Virginia, 10th State
1929   Eric Carle

The music yanked me to my feet and started me dancing.

An icy wind licked my face raw.

A massive rock bridge raised its arms up to touch the sky.

The fog reached its fingers around corners.

When the little fish saw the submarine, he said, "Look, Mom—it's a tin full of people!"

The toaster grabbed my toast and swallowed it up in its fiery jaws.

157

June 26th

- Bicycle Patented (1918)*
- National Chocolate Pudding Day
- St. Lawrence Seaway Opened (1959)
- First Section of the Atlantic City Boardwalk Opened (1870)
- Human Genome Mapped (2002)
- UN Charter Signed (1945)

The Book of "Bi"

Can you imagine life without bicycles? How fortunate we are to have this convenient two-wheeled transportation device. The prefix "bi" shows up in hundreds of places. Start collecting "bi" words. Write a book of "Bi." Each page can contain a word with a "bi" prefix, an illustration, and a description of the word's meaning.

BICYCLE   BISECT   bifocals   bilingual   BIANNUAL

June 27th

- Sunglasses Day*
- "Happy Birthday to You" Composed (1859)

Birthdays
1880   Helen Keller

One More Idea

- Try to find out who wrote "Happy Birthday to You," how many copies or recordings have been sold, who holds the copyright, who profits from the song, and how much profit has been made?

"Fun"glasses

Celebrate Sunglasses Day by designing your own wacky, creative "funglasses." Start with an inexpensive pair of sunglasses. Decorate them with any materials you find. Create a one-of-a-kind pair that is uniquely "you"!

fabric scraps
cardboard
sequins
pipe cleaners
wire   coins
jewels
feathers
food   bolts
candies
screws   nuts
plastic fruit & flowers

June 28th

- Paul Bunyan Day*
- World War I Began (1914)
- Panama Canal Bought by U.S. from France (1902)
- Treaty of Versailles Signed Ending WWI (1919)

Tall Paul Tales

Who was Paul Bunyan? Find out who created him, and why. Many locations claim him. Find out where his home is supposed to be. See if you can locate all the statues in his honor.

Everything we know about Paul Bunyan comes from "tall tales" about his adventures. Write your own tall tale about Paul Bunyan and his blue ox, Babe. Illustrate your tale.

Do-It-Yourself Camera

Use Camera Day as an occasion to make your own camera. When you point your camera toward an object, a small amount of the light bouncing off the object enters the tiny hole. The tissue paper acts as a screen that shows the picture of the object. The image on the "screen" will be upside down, just as in a real camera.

Make a Pinhole Camera

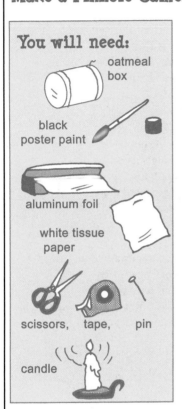

You will need:
- oatmeal box
- black poster paint
- aluminum foil
- white tissue paper
- scissors, tape, pin
- candle

1. Paint the inside of an oatmeal box with black poster paint.

2. Cut a hole in the bottom of the carton about an inch wide.

3. Cover the hole securely with aluminum foil. Prick a hole in the center of the foil with a pin.

4. Tape tissue paper over the open top of the carton.

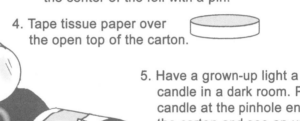

5. Have a grown-up light a candle in a dark room. Put the candle at the pinhole end of the carton and see an upside-down projection of the candle on the tissue "screen."

June 29th

- Camera Day*
- U.S. Interstate Highway System Instituted *(1956)**

One More Idea

- Get to know the amazing U.S. Interstate Highway system. Get a U.S. map and . . . plan a trip from Boston to Albuquerque, Miami to Minneapolis, Chicago to Seattle, and San Diego to Roanoke. In each case, describe the interstate route(s) to follow. Calculate the mileage and the time it will take. Find out the speed limits to calculate the times.

Daring Feats

Crossing Niagara Falls on a tightrope is a rather amazing feat. Read as much as you can find about this accomplishment. Then find out about other amazing feats. Gather them into an illustrated collection (maybe comic-book style) or a *Timeline of Daring Feats.*

June 30th

- Emile Blondin Crossed Niagara Falls on a Tightrope *(1859)**
- Meteor Day
- President Abraham Lincoln Signed the Yosemite Land Grant *(1864)*

Tightrope-Walking Tip: Never look down!

Look for feats such as . . .
walking on a tightrope between airplanes
jumping a motorcycle over 30 limousines
crossing Antarctica alone on skis
traveling almost 25,000 miles in a wheelchair
walking 3,000 miles on stilts
riding a barrel over Niagara Falls
pulling a railroad train with teeth only
lifting an elephant off the ground
standing on one foot for 71 hours
kissing 11 cobras

July

1
- Canada Day*
- Build a Scarecrow Day*
- Creative Ice-Cream Flavor Day*
- Early Bird Day*
- Zip Codes Introduced*
- First U.S. Postage Stamps Issued
- International Joke Day
- Battle of Gettysburg Began
- First U.S. Zoo Opened
- First TV Signal Broadcast
- Medicare Program Established
- 26th Amendment Ratified
    Birthdays: Princess Diana, New
      Brunswick, Nova Scotia, Ontario,
      Quebec, Prince Edward Island

2
- Roswell Incident*
- Amelia Earhart Disappeared*
- I Forgot Day*
- Halfway Point of the Year
- Civil Rights Act Signed (1964)

3
- Dog Days of Summer Begin*
- Stay Out of the Sun Day*
- Compliment Your Mirror Day*
- Eat Beans Day
- First Bank in the U.S.
    Birthdays: Idaho

4
- U.S. Independence Day*
- Declaration of Independence Adopted*
- First Rodeo*
- Earth at Aphelion*
- Tom Sawyer's Fence-Painting Day*
- First Bus Built
- Caesar Salad Invented
- National Country Music Day
- Sidewalk Egg-Frying Day
    Birthdays: Nathaniel Hawthorne,
      Calvin Coolidge, Marc Chagall,
      Stephen Foster

5
- Creativity with a Fork Day*
- Graham Cracker Day
- Caribbean Day
- Debut of the Bikini (1946)
    Birthdays: P. T. Barnum

6
- First Picture Postcard Made*
- National Fried Chicken Day
- National Air Traffic Control Day
- Republican Party Formed (1854)
- First Talking Motion Picture (1928)
    Birthdays: George W. Bush

7
- Chocolate Day*
- First Comic Book Published*
- Chesapeake Turtle Derby*
- Hawaii Annexed
- Bonza Bottler Day
- Macaroni Day
- Father-Daughter Take a Walk Together Day
- National Strawberry Sundae Day
    Birthdays: John D. Rockefeller,
      Nelson A. Rockefeller

8
- Liberty Bell Day*
- First U.S. Passport Issued
- Ice-Cream Sundae Created (1881)
    Birthdays: Michelle Kwan

9
- National Air Conditioning Appreciation Day*
- National Sugar Cookie Day
- Sugar Cane Day
- First Open-Heart Surgery (1893)

10
- Clerihew Day*
- Don't Step on a Bee Day*
- Stone House Day
- Moose Droppings Festival
- Smile Power Day
    Birthdays: Arthur Ashe Jr., Wyoming

11
- UN World Population Day*
- Vegetarian Food Day
- Swimming Pool Day
- Cheer Up the Lonely Day
    Birthdays: John Quincy Adams,
      E.B. White

12
- Paper Bag Day*
- Etch-A-Sketch Invented
- National Pecan Pie Day
- International Criers Day
- National Blueberry Muffin Day
- Eat Your Jello™ Day
    Birthdays: Julius Caesar, Bill Cosby

13
- International Puzzle Day*
- Go West Day
- National French Fries Day
- Embrace Your Geekness Day

14
- Corkboard Invented*
- Bastille Day
- Pick Blueberries Day
- Dynamite First Demonstrated
- Tape Measure Patented
    Birthdays: Gerald Ford

15
- National Tapioca Pudding Day*
- Respect Canada Day
- National Ice-Cream Day
    Birthdays: Rembrandt*, Manitoba,
      Northwest Territories

16
- Parking Meter Invented*
- Fresh Spinach Day
- Washington, D.C. Became Permanent U.S. Capital
- First Atomic Bomb Tested
- First Moon Landing

17
- Wrong Way Day*
- National Peach Ice-Cream Day
- Disneyland Opened
- Air Conditioner Invented
- *Apollo 18* and *Soyuz* Linked in Space

18
- Cow Appreciation Day*
- National Caviar Day
- Railroad Day
    Birthdays: Nelson Mandela, John Glenn

19
- New Friends Day*
- Stick Out Your Tongue Day
- Flitch Day
- Shark Awareness Day
    Birthdays: Edgar Degas

20
- Ugly Truck Contest Day*
- National Lollipop Day
- National Nap Day
- Chess Day
- Special Olympics Day
- *U.S. Viking I* Landed on Mars
- Neil Armstrong Walked on the Moon
  Birthdays: British Columbia

21
- National Tug of War Tournament Day*
- National Junk Food Day
- National Crème Brûlée Day
- National Women's Hall of Fame Began (1979)
  Birthdays: Ernest Hemingway

22
- Spooner's Day*
- Rat Catcher's Day*
- America the Beautiful Day
- National Hot Dog Day
- Summer Leisure Day

23
- Mosquito Day*
- Hot Enough for Ya Day*
- National Vanilla Ice-Cream Day
- Ice-Cream Cone Introduced
- Machu Picchu Discovered

24
- Amelia Earhart Day*
- Coffee Day
- Pioneer Day
- Cousins Day
- Instant Coffee Invented
  Birthdays: Amelia Earhart*

25
- First Birthday Cake Created*
- National Hot Fudge Sundae Day
- Threading the Needle Day
- First Carousel Patented

26
- All or Nothing Day*
- National Coffee Milkshake Day
- Aunt and Uncle Day
- U.S. Postal Service Began
- FBI Founded
  Birthdays: New York

27
- Take Your Houseplants for a Walk Day*
- First Bugs Bunny Cartoon Published
- National Korean War Veterans Armistice Day
- World Youth Day
- Korean War Ended

28
- First Fingerprint Taken*
- Hamburger Day
- National Milk Chocolate Day
- 14th Amendment Ratified
  Birthdays: Beatrix Potter, Jacqueline Kennedy Onassis

29
- National Lipstick Day*
- Chicken Wings Day*
- National Lasagna Day
- NASA Formed

30
- Comedy Day*
- National Cheesecake Day
- Paperback Books Introduced
  Birthdays: Emily Bronte, Henry Ford

31
- Mutt's Day*
- Shredded Wheat Introduced
- Water Skis Used for the First Time
- U.S. Patent Office Established

Month-long Celebrations

American Independence Month*

Blackberry Month*

Blueberry Month*

California Salmon Month

Cellphone Courtesy Month*

Eye Exam Month

Fireworks Month*

Fireworks Safety Month*

Foreign Language Month*

July Belongs to Berries Month*

National Anti-Boredom Month

National Baked Bean Month

National Bison Month*

National Culinary Arts Month

National Doghouse Repairs Month*

National Goat Cheese Month

National Hot Dog Month*

National Ice-Cream Month

National Outdoor Month*

National Peach Month

National Picnic Month

National Recreation and Park Month

Raspberry Month*

Read an Almanac Month*

Red, White, and Blue Month*

Romantic Awareness Month

Tahiti and Her Islands Awareness Month

Wild About Wildlife Month

Weekly Celebrations

First Week: Be Nice to Jersey Week*, Freedom Week*, Great Circus Parade Week, National Canned Luncheon Meat Week, Prevention of Eye Injuries Awareness Week

Second Week: Copious Compliments Week*, Running of the Bulls*, National Farrier's Week, Music for Life Week, National Laughter Week

Third Week: Space Week*, Coral Reef Awareness Week, Lyme Disease Awareness Week

Fourth Week: All-American Soapbox Derby*, Don't Eat Meat Week, National Salad Week

Dates That Vary: National Ice-Cream Day*, Sundae Sunday*, National Get Out of the Doghouse Day*, Barn Day*, Twin-O-Rama*, Parents' Day, UFO Days

July's Month-long Celebrations

American Independence Month, Fireworks Month, & Fireworks Safety Month

July is the month when citizens in the United States of America celebrate the founding of the nation. The Fourth of July is the big day for celebrations, but many commemorations of freedom continue on other days. The most spectacular celebrations come in the form of awesome fireworks displays.

- Find out when, where, and by whom fireworks were invented.

- Make a poster about safety for using personal fireworks.

- Find a piece of music that is a good background for watching fireworks.

- Collect lists of words and phrases that describe the colors, sounds, feelings, smells, ideas, and thoughts connected to watching a display of fireworks. Use these words in a "painted poem" about fireworks.

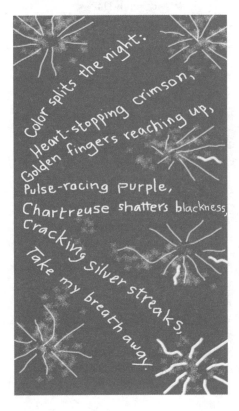

Color splits the night:
Heart-stopping crimson,
Golden fingers reaching up,
Pulse-racing purple,
Chartreuse shatters blackness,
Cracking silver streaks,
Take my breath away.

Painted Poetry

In a "painted" poem, the words and lines are placed on the paper in a way that creates a visual image of the poem's topic. Write a painted poem about fireworks this month. Then try painted poems on other topics, too.

Red, White, and Blue Month

Red, white, and blue are the colors of the American flag. Celebrate *Red, White, and Blue Month* by making a patriotic windsock from crepe paper and poster board.

Patriotic Windsocks

1. Cut a strip of lightweight blue poster board, about 15 x 10 in. (or 40 x 25 cm).

2. Cut out white stars and glue them on the strip.

3. Staple different lengths of red and white crepe paper to the bottom edge of the circle.

4. Form the strip into a circle and tape it securely.

5. Punch two holes in the top edge of the circle. Attach strings so that you can hang the windsock in the wind.

Blackberry Month, Blueberry Month, Raspberry Month, & July Belongs to Berries Month

It's clear that July is the month to celebrate berries. There's no better way to do that than to eat plenty of them. Berries are "berry" good for you. Find out about the nutritional values of berries. Then use some berries to make your own fruit leather.

Mmmmmm

Chewy, Gooey Fruit Leather

1. Wash 2 quarts of very ripe berries. Remove all stems.
2. Combine the fruit in a large cooking pot with $\frac{1}{4}$ C sugar.
3. Cook it over low heat until the fruit is soft. Cool the mixture.
4. Pour off the juice and press the mixture through a sieve.
5. Lay a large sheet of waxed paper on a flat surface outside. Tape the edges so it won't blow away.
6. Pour the mixture on the waxed paper and let it dry for two or more days. The fruit leather is ready to eat when it peels away easily from the waxed paper.

Almanac Mysteries List

What is the home country of the most recent winner of the Nobel Prize in literature?

Which is larger, the current population of Japan or the current population of Russia?

Read An Almanac Month

An almanac is a book that holds an up-to-date collection of statistics and facts. Many almanacs are updated and republished each year. It's a good source for current information. Get some friends together to create *Almanac Mysteries*—questions to be tracked down and solved with an almanac. Each person can make a list of challenging mysteries to solve. Then trade lists and use the almanac to start your detective work

Find a notable quote from last year.

Who is the present treasurer of your state or province?

How many silver medals were won by Swedes in the most recent winter Olympics?

Foreign Language Month

Celebrations for this holiday encourage everyone to appreciate and learn a language that is different from the one that is their first, native language. Take a familiar saying, proverb, or nursery rhyme and find someone who can translate it for you into one or more foreign languages. Then learn to say it!

Humpty Dumpty s'est assis sur un mur.
Humpty Dumpty avait une grande chute.
Tout le roi chevaux et tout le roi homes
Ne pourrait pas mettre Humpty ensemble encore!

National Outdoor Month

Enjoy the great outdoors this month! Start by planning a "Solar Celebration"—an all-day event that takes place outdoors. Plan games and activities that friends of all ages can enjoy outside. Have fun preparing some interesting food right out there under the sun.

Sun Tea

1. Fill a clean quart or liter jar with cold water.
2. Put two teabags in the water. Put the top on the jar.
3. Place the jar in a sunny spot for about three hours.
4. When the tea looks dark enough, take out the teabags. Add crushed mint leaves if you wish.
5. Serve the tea over ice with lemon and sugar or honey.

Sunny Hot Dogs

It's National Hot Dog Month. Eat some hot dogs this month. You can make a solar cooker to prepare hot dogs in the sun.

1. Make cuts in a potato chip can along the dotted lines as shown.
2. Bend the flaps open as shown.
3. Line the opening with aluminum foil. This will catch and reflect the sunlight.
4. Make holes in the center of both ends of the can. (One end is the plastic lid.)
5. Suspend the hot dog in the middle of the can on a wooden skewer.
6. Set the solar cooker in the sun. Position it so the sun is reflected onto the hot dog.
7. The hot dog should be ready to eat in about 45 minutes. Make sure it is hot all the way through before you eat it.

Sidewalk Fried Eggs

1. Grease a piece of aluminum foil with margarine.
2. Place it on a hot spot on the sidewalk.
3. Break an egg directly onto the foil.
4. Watch it until it is cooked to the doneness you like.
5. Serve the egg with salt and pepper.

Sun-Cooked Cinnamon Toast

1. Spread two thick slices of bread with margarine and sprinkle both sides with cinnamon and sugar.
2. Wrap each slice in clear plastic wrap and place them directly on a hot sidewalk in the sun.
3. Turn them after 30 minutes.
4. After another 30 minutes, your toast is ready to eat.

Hot Citrus Cups

1. Cut a grapefruit and an orange in half.
2. Remove the fruit, cut it into chunks, and toss the chunks in a bowl with 1 T of honey.
3. Fill each empty grapefruit half with the fruit mixture. Drizzle with honey.
4. Cover with plastic wrap, and let them cook in the sun for a few hours.

National Recreation and Park Month

Enjoy your favorite forms of recreation as often as you can during this month. In particular, spend time in recreation that is active (and good for your body), as well as recreation that is outdoors (because this is the time of year to be outdoors)! If you have a backyard, or are near a field, park, or playground, gather some friends and make an obstacle course. Creating the course will inspire creativity and ingenuity. Using the course will give you many hours of active fun.

Backyard Obstacle Course

1. Find or make several things to use as obstacles.
2. Decide what activity to do at each obstacle.
3. Plan the course and set up the obstacles.
4. Practice running the course to be sure it is set up well.
5. Time yourself and your friends as you run it. Keep track of your times.
6. Rearrange the obstacle course. Try it several ways.

- *slide through a narrow box*
- *run around a stump*
- *jump over a step stool*
- *turn somersaults over an old mattress*
- *hop across a ladder*
- *run around a slalom formed with sticks*
- *crawl under a row of chairs*
- *step up, on, and over a step stool*
- *climb over a pile of tires*
- *crawl through a series of old tires*

National Bison Month

Find or draw a picture of a bison. Then find out these things about bisons:

- exactly what a bison is
- how fast a bison can run
- how many bison are in North America
- where you could see a bison
- when bison preservation began
- why a bison was once pictured on a U.S. nickel

Cellphone Courtesy Month

Use this month as an opportunity to brush up on cellphone courtesy. Research some basic rules. Make a handbook for courteous cellphone users.

#14. Avoid "Cell Yell"! Don't shout when speaking on a cellphone.

#15. Turn off your phone in restaurants, theaters, churches, and libraries.

See page 161 for other month-long holidays to celebrate.

Special Weeks in July

Freedom Week

Hundreds of organizations around America have joined in the project of Freedom Week. The purpose of this week is to spend several days celebrating the system of government that is powered by the consent of the people who are governed. Plan some activities for your friends, family, class, school, or neighborhood to celebrate freedom this week.

• Interview 25 people of different ages. Ask each one to tell you what *freedom* means to them.

• Create, draw, or find pictures of symbols of freedom. Explain how each one symbolizes freedom.

• Memorize the Preamble to the *U.S. Constitution.*

• Read the "Bill of Rights" from the *U.S. Constitution.*

Be Nice to Jersey Week

Isn't this a curious holiday?

• Speculate about why this holiday exists.

• See if you can find out how it all started that New Jersey became the brunt of jokes.

• Find 100 things to celebrate about New Jersey.

• Write a positive New Jersey joke.

Second Week

Copious Compliments Week

To celebrate the week, you will need to be clear about two things: what *copious* means, and what *compliments* are. Once you know these things, get busy preparing and delivering your own copious compliments. Make sure your compliments are sincere.

Running of the Bulls

The running of the bulls at the annual San Fermin Festival in Pamplona, Spain, starts on July 7 and lasts for eight days. Several thousand people run along cobblestone streets with six bulls for a distance of 902 yards from a corral to the bull ring. This dangerous tradition is called *Encierro.*

• Find the rules for running with the bulls.

• Find out the purpose of the bull run.

• Make some guesses about why someone would choose to take part in this tradition.

Space Week

This week commemorates the day in the third week of July, 1969, when a human stepped onto the surface of the moon for the first time. Read about the *Apollo 11* mission that resulted in the first steps on the moon. Visit NASA's website at www.nasa.gov. Find out which astronauts were a part of the mission, who took the first steps on the moon, and what the astronaut said.

Plaster Moonscapes

Make a model of the scene. Create a moonscape. Mix plaster of Paris in a thick paste. Spread it on a circular piece of heavy cardboard. Mold it into craters and peaks to look like the surface of the moon.

Use cardboard or other materials to make small models of the space module and the astronaut. When the plaster "moon surface" is dry, add these to the scene.

Fourth Week

All-American Soapbox Derby

The All-American Soapbox Derby organization manages the sport of soapbox derby racing. Dozens of cities around the United States and across the world hold qualifying races for the big race at the end of July in Akron, Ohio. Soapbox racing began in 1933 when some kids built and raced homemade cars from junk they found around their houses—even soap boxes. Before long, a soapbox racing championship brought kids and cars from all over the country to Ohio every year.

The sport is open to kids ages 6–16. The important thing about soapbox racing is that kids must build their own cars AND race their own cars. Today, soapbox race car builders can buy a kit, but many kids still build their own cars without kits. Do some research on soapbox racing cars. If you're not up to building a real car for actual racing, design and build a model car during this week of July.

See page 161 for other weeklong holidays to celebrate.

The Days of July

National Ice-Cream Day and Sundae Sunday *(3rd Sunday)*

In 1984, U.S. President Ronald Reagan proclaimed the third Sunday in July as "National Ice-Cream Day." It has also been named "Sundae Sunday." So, don't let this day go by without making your own ice cream. Here's an easy way to do it: Turn your ice cream into a sundae by adding your favorite toppings such as hot fudge, chocolate sauce, butterscotch sauce, jam, sprinkles, nuts, cherries, whipped cream, peanut butter, chopped candy bars, granola, bananas, chocolate chips, and such . . .

Roll Me Some Ice Cream

Supplies:

- a metal can (5-pound coffee can size) with a plastic lid
- a smaller metal can with a plastic lid
  (This must fit inside the larger can with room around the outside of the smaller can for crushed ice.)
- plastic wrap and rubber bands
- milk or cream, sugar, vanilla
- mixing bowl and wire whip (or blender)
- measuring cups and spoons
- finely-crushed ice
- rock salt
- optional flavorings

Put the smaller can inside the larger can.

1. Mix 1 C of milk (or cream) with 3 T sugar and 1 t vanilla.

2. Pour the mixture into the smallest can until the can is about three-fourths full.

3. Gently stir in other flavorings, chocolate chips, or chopped fruit (if you wish).

4. Cover the can with plastic wrap. Put the lid on firmly.

5. Cover the top of the can, over the lid, with plastic wrap and secure it with a rubber band.

6. Set the small can inside the large can.

7. Layer crushed ice and rock salt around the small can. Be generous with the salt.

8. Put the top firmly on the large can.

9. Sit on the floor several feet away from a friend. Roll the can back and forth for about 30 minutes. Eventually, the milk mixture will freeze into ice cream.

Find out why salt is needed on the ice.

National Get Out of the Doghouse Day *(3rd Monday)*

What does it mean to "get out of the doghouse"? What does it mean to "be in the doghouse" to begin with? "She's in the doghouse now" is an example of a figure of speech called an idiom. Like other kinds of figurative speech, an idiom uses words in a way that they mean something different than what they actually (literally) say.

- Since July is National Doghouse Repairs Month, pay attention to your dog's house (if you have a dog). Do something to improve the place where your dog "hangs out."

- If you don't have a doghouse, or if you don't even have a dog, design a doghouse that would be the dream home for a dog. Try to think like a dog. What would a dog want in a home?

- Draw an illustration (comic-book style) to show what the idiom "in the doghouse" means, if taken literally.

- Collect at least 15 other idioms. Illustrate their literal meanings, again in comic-book style. Then put them together with the doghouse illustration into a comic book of your favorite idioms.

Barn Day *(2nd Sunday)*

- Find out what a barn raising is, why someone might hold a barn raising, and how the raising works.

- Do some research on barn painting. Get a large piece of mural paper and use wide brushes and paints to create a design that you would put on a barn.

Twin-O-Rama *(date varies in different locations)*

A Twin-O-Rama is a party-like gathering of twins, complete with games, contests, and other celebratory events.

- See how many sets of twins you can find. Get the autograph of one or both of them.

- Interview twins about what it's like to be a twin.

- Be able to explain how twins are formed. Explain the difference between identical and fraternal twins.

- Twins often look alike. Make a list of other things that look alike, such as things that sound alike, things that smell alike, things that taste alike, and things that feel alike.

- Design a product for twins—something that could be used by two people at the same time.

See page 161 for other holidays with dates that vary.

July 1st

- Canada Day (Dominion Day)*
- Build a Scarecrow Day*
- Creative Ice-Cream Flavor Day*
- Early Bird Day*
- Zip Codes Introduced (1963)*
- First U.S. Postage Stamps Issued (1847)
- International Joke Day
- Battle of Gettysburg Began (1863)
- First U.S. Zoo Opened (Philadelphia) (1874)
- First TV Broadcast (1941)
- Medicare Program Established (1968)
- 26th Amendment to the U.S. Constitution Ratified (1971)

Birthdays

1961 Princess Diana
1867 New Brunswick, Nova Scotia, Ontario, Quebec
1873 Prince Edward Island

More Ideas

- Read the poems "Early Bird" and "Eighteen Flavors" from Shel Silverstein's book Where the Sidewalk Ends.
- Create ten interesting math problems with zip codes.

July 2nd

- Roswell Incident (1947)*
- Amelia Earhart Disappeared (1937)*
- I Forgot Day*
- Halfway Point of the Year
- Spam Town USA Festival
- President Garfield Shot (1881)
- Civil Rights Act Signed (1964)

One More Idea

- Write a Remembering Manual that includes tips for forgetful people.

Salute To Canada

maple leaf pattern

In 1868, Canada's governor proclaimed July 1 as a day to celebrate the formation of the union. Learn about the history of this day and how it is celebrated. Carve Canada's symbol, the maple leaf, into a rubber eraser or a potato to make a stamp. Dip it in paint or onto an ink pad to decorate stationary, posters, T-shirts, or other clothing.

Do-It-Yourself Scarecrow

Don't let this day go by without creating one of your own.

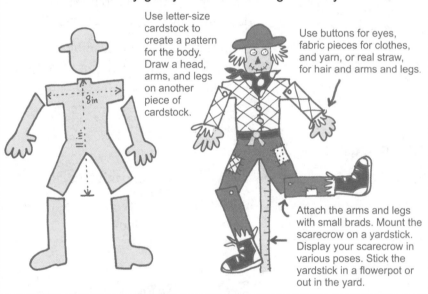

Use letter-size cardstock to create a pattern for the body. Draw a head, arms, and legs on another piece of cardstock.

Use buttons for eyes, fabric pieces for clothes, and yarn, or real straw, for hair and arms and legs.

Attach the arms and legs with small brads. Mount the scarecrow on a yardstick. Display your scarecrow in various poses. Stick the yardstick in a flowerpot or out in the yard.

Strange Occurrences

On this day in 1947, a UFO supposedly crashed in New Mexico. On this same day, Amelia Earhart disappeared on an around-the-world flight. Find out all you can about the "Roswell incident" and the disappearance of Amelia Earhart. Then create a radio news report on each event. Make your report factual, or interview a "pretend" eyewitness to each event, and report their story.

Good evening, from Radio KXYZ.
We have urgent news to report! Amelia Earhart is missing! According to credible witnesses in Roswell, New Mexico, she may have been abducted by aliens! Update at 11:00.

What Are Dog Days?

The Dog Days of Summer span from July 3 – August 11. Find out what they are and how they might be related to Stay Out of the Sun Day. Then, stay out of the sun and whip up one of these cool drinks to get you through this and other "Dog Days."

- Dog Days of Summer Begin*
- Stay Out of the Sun Day*
- International Cherry-Spitting Contest*
- Compliment Your Mirror Day*
- Eat Beans Day
- First Bank in the U.S. *(1819)*

Birthdays
1890 Idaho, 43rd State

One More Idea

- Compliment Your Mirror Day is actually a time for complimenting what you see in your mirror. Find some ways to affirm yourself all day today. Say or write at least 25 compliments to YOU.

Peanutty Shake

Blend 3 T peanut butter with 2 scoops of vanilla ice cream and 1 C of milk.

Whipped Flip

Shake together: 1 C orange juice, 1 C plain yogurt, and 1 T vanilla.

Banana Whiz

Whip in a blender: 1 mashed banana, 2 C milk, $\frac{1}{2}$ C orange juice, and $\frac{1}{2}$ C ice.

Fruit Sodas

Mix $\frac{1}{4}$ C mashed fruit with 1 C soda water and 1 T honey. Top with 1 scoop of ice cream.

Very Berry Blend

Mix strawberries, raspberries, blackberries, or blueberries with 1 C ginger ale, 1 C ice, and 1 T honey. Blend well.

Fruit Floats

Freeze orange slices, lemon slices, peach slices, cherries, or grapes. Float them on top of a tall glass of fruit juice.

Purple Fizz

Add a scoop of ice cream to 1 C grape juice and 1 C ginger ale.

Be creative. Go beyond Dog Days. Make a case for Alligator Days, Cat Days, Snail Days, Tarantula Days, or Octopus Days!

Did You Know? The current world record for cherry pit spitting is 100 feet, 4 inches. Find out who set the record, when, and where.

- U.S. Independence Day*
- Declaration of Independence Adopted *(1776)**
- First Rodeo *(1869)**
- Earth at Aphelion*
- Tom Sawyer's Fence Painting Day*
- First Bus Built *(1829)*
- Caesar Salad Invented *(1924)*
- National Country Music Day
- Sidewalk Egg-Frying Day

Birthdays
1881	Nathaniel Hawthorne
1804	Calvin Coolidge, 30th U.S. President
1887	Marc Chagall
1826	Stephen Foster

More Ideas

- Find out where Earth is when it is at its "aphelion."
- Look for a friend or neighbor who has a fence you can paint. Read about Tom Sawyer's fence-painting experiences.

Rodeo Math

Read about the events that take place at a rodeo. Find out the descriptions and rules for each event. Use that knowledge to invent some proportion problems for friends to solve. Try these examples; then go wild with problems of your own.

A barrel racer was penalized with 6 additional seconds for knocking over barrels in his first minute of riding. At this rate, how many seconds will he be penalized if his race lasts 4.5 minutes?

Joe suffered 12 broken bones riding a bull in his last 48 rodeos. At this rate, how many times will he break something in the next 20 rodeos?

During Stan's first 15 tries at steer wrestling, the steer got away from him 10 times. At this rate, how many times will the steer get away in Stan's next 12 tries?

A "Don't-Miss" Document

The *Declaration of Independence* is a document not to be missed. On this U.S. Independence Day, get to know the document that started it all. Get together with some friends and plan to read it aloud. Divide up the text into solo and "chorus" parts. Read it with gusto! Focus on understanding the meaning of all its sentences.

- Creativity with a Fork Day*
- Graham Cracker Day
- Caribbean Day
- Debut of the Bikini *(1946)*

Birthdays
1810   P. T. Barnum

Fork Sculptures

Use colored plastic forks and super glue to create a one-of-a-kind fork sculpture.

Use the Web to track down information on the art of fork bending!

Get creative with a fork today. Decorate a good fork, or turn old forks (or plastic forks) into sculptures. Add spray paint or other items to the fork sculpture. Think of 100 things to do with a fork.

Picture Yourself

Put yourself in postcards. Gather postcards from different places. Ask friends, relatives, and neighbors if they can contribute postcards. Rummage through family photos to find some pictures from which you can cut images of yourself. Put yourself into the scene in some of the postcards. On the back of the postcard, write a note as though you were visiting the place shown on the postcard. You may have to do some research about the places so that you can write realistic notes!

July 6th

- First Picture Postcard Made *(1873)**
- National Fried Chicken Day
- National Air Traffic Control Day
- Republican Party Formed *(1854)*
- First Talking Motion Picture *(1928)*

Birthdays
1946   George W. Bush, 43rd U.S. President

Crazy About Chocolate

Cool off on Chocolate Day with *Quick & Cool Chocolate Cubes.* Combine a celebration of Chocolate Day with the great idea of comic books by creating a comic book for chocolate lovers. It might include great chocolate sayings and/or chocolate jokes. Enjoy your frozen chocolate treats while you design the book.

Quick & Cool Chocolate Cubes

Follow the directions to make a large package of instant chocolate pudding. Stir in 3 T sugar and 3 extra cups of milk. Pour this thin mixture into ice cube trays.

Cover the trays with plastic wrap. Poke a toothpick through the plastic wrap into each cup of the tray. This will make a little handle for each chocolate cube.

Put the tray into the freezer. When the cubes are frozen, pull them out and enjoy them—one at a time.

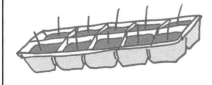

July 7th

- Chocolate Day*
- First Comic Book Published *(1802)**
- Chesapeake Turtle Derby*
- Hawaii Annexed *(1898)*
- Bonza Bottler Day
- Macaroni Day
- Father-Daughter Take a Walk Together Day
- National Strawberry Sundae Day

Birthdays
1839   John D. Rockefeller
1908   Nelson A. Rockefeller

You can imagine how slow the pace is at a Turtle Derby! Think of other things that are slow. Make a list. Can you think of 100? Turn some of your ideas into similes.

173

July 8th

- Liberty Bell Day
  (Liberty Bell Cracked 1835)*
- First U.S. Passport Issued
  (1796)
- Ice-Cream Sundae Created
  (1881)

Birthdays
1980   Michelle Kwan

Who Cracked the Bell?

The Liberty Bell was made in 1751 to commemorate the 50th anniversary of the Pennsylvania colony's constitution. William Penn wrote this document, called the "Charter of Privileges." It is well-known that the Liberty Bell has a large crack in it. Before you brush up on the history of the Liberty Bell, use your imagination to create a story about how the crack occurred. Then read all about the bell, and . . .

. . . find out:
- *what is written on it
- *why Pennsylvania is misspelled
- *how it got cracked
- *where it now hangs
- *when it has been rung

July 9th

- National Air Conditioning Appreciation Day*
- National Sugar Cookie Day
- Sugar Cane Day
- First Open-Heart Surgery Performed *(1893)*

Keep Cool

Air conditioning was a great idea, wasn't it? Or was it? Find out whose idea it was. Get the facts on who invented it and when. Think about *pros* and *cons* of air conditioning. Make a list with at least five arguments on both sides. Of course, air conditioning is not available to everyone all the time, anyway. Here are some ways to keep cool without it:

Get wet. Pour room-temperature water over your head or your whole body, or keep spraying yourself with a spray bottle.

Get a rubber glove. Fill it with water. Tie it securely and freeze it. Carry it on hot days to cool your neck, face, arms, shoulders, or legs.

Make yourself a hat to keep the hot sun off your head.

Play water games with hoses, spray bottles, or water balloons.

Offer to wash someone's car.

Ice a glass by dipping it in water and keeping it in the freezer for half an hour or more. Use it to drink a cool drink. (See page 171.)

Stay in the shade. Sit very, very still.

Dress in light-colored, loose-fitting clothing.

Make yourself some popsicles. *(See page 203.)*

Make a fan from poster board and a ruler.

Think about cool words. Make a list (frigid, icy, frosty, etc.).

Eat watermelon, and drink lots and lots of water.

Who's Who in Your Clerihew?

A *clerihew* is a humorous 4-line biographical poem. It consists of 2 couplets (Lines 1 and 2 rhyme; Lines 3 and 4 rhyme). The first line names the subject. The second line rhymes with that name. A clerihew can be about anyone—real or fictitious. It should be funny. The clerihew is named for its inventor, Edmund Clerihew Bentley. Write some clerihews about people you know, famous people, or fictitious characters.

July 10th

- Clerihew Day*
- Don't Step on a Bee Day*
- Moose Droppings Festival
- Stone House Day
- Smile Power Day

Birthdays
  1943 Arthur Ashe, Jr.
  1890 Wyoming, 44th State

What I like about Clive
Is that he is no longer alive.
There is a great deal to be said
For being dead.
                    -Edmund Clerihew Bentley

Sir Christopher Wren
Said, "I am going to dine with some men.
If anyone calls
Say I am designing St. Paul's."
                    -Edmund Clerihew Bentley

My sister Haley
Cooks breakfast daily.
Her techniques are slick,
But her food makes us sick.

The fame of Mickey Mouse
Is known in every house.
However esteemed his name,
He's a rodent, just the same!

Bee Directory

Bees freeze at zero degrees.

There are 20,000 different species of bees in the world. Do some bee research. Choose 20 different bees to put into a Bee Directory. Make a page for each bee. Include a good illustration, a description of its characteristics, and an explanation of where the species can be found.

I'm moving to Miami.

The World POPClock

The U.S. Census Bureau has a cool clock called the World POPClock. (There's one for the U.S., too.) It is a running clock that shows the growth in the world's population.

Get into the habit of monitoring the POPClock daily. Make your own graph or chart to show the growth in population.

Start a POPClock to monitor the population in your school, neighborhood, or family.

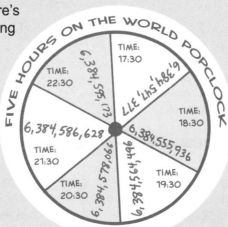

FIVE HOURS ON THE WORLD POPCLOCK

TIME: 17:30   6,384,595,173
TIME: 22:30   6,384,597,377
TIME: 18:30   6,384,555,936
TIME: 21:30   6,384,586,628
TIME: 20:30   6,384,578,090
TIME: 19:30   6,384,544,594

July 11th

- UN World Population Day*
- Vegetarian Food Day
- Swimming Pool Day
- Cheer Up the Lonely Day

Birthdays
  1767 John Quincy Adams, 6th U.S. President
  1899 E.B. White

Visit the popclock at www.census.gov.

175

July 12th

- Paper Bag Day*
- Etch-A-Sketch Invented *(1960)*
- National Pecan Pie Day
- International Criers Day
- National Blueberry Muffin Day
- Eat Your Jello™ Day

Birthdays
102 BC Julius Caesar
1938 Bill Cosby

Celebrate the Paper Bag

There is no limit to the uses for a good old brown paper bag. These are biodegradable, so they're an environmentally friendly resource. Collect some paper bags of different sizes. Then put your imagination to work and put the bags to good use.

Think of 100 uses for a paper bag. Make at least 10 different things from a paper bag today!

July 13th

- International Puzzle Day*
- Go West Day
- National French Fries Day
- Embrace Your Geekness Day

Puzzling Mail

Delight your friends by turning your letters to them into mysteries. Before a friend can read your letter, he or she must solve the puzzle. Your friends will look forward to your letters (although they may find them a little "puzzling"!).

Write your letter on stiff paper. Turn it over and design a jigsaw puzzle. Cut along the lines and mail the pieces off in an envelope.

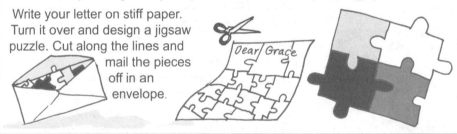

July 14th

- Corkboard Invented *(1891)**
- Bastille Day
- Pick Blueberries Day
- Dynamite First Demonstrated *(1867)*
- Tape Measure Patented *(1868)*

Birthdays
1913 Gerald Ford, 38th U.S. President

Creative Corkboard

Celebrate the invention of corkboard by making your own unusual but individualized cork bulletin boards. (These make great gifts, too!)

Cut lightweight corkboard into a shape of your choice. Decorate the shape with string, yarn, felt, buttons, sequins, or other materials.

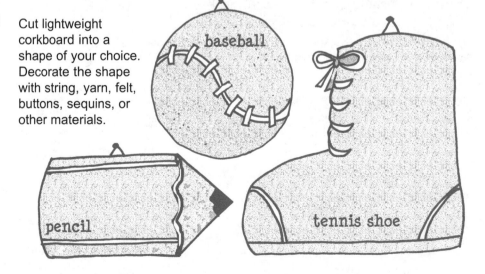

Tapioca for Everybody

Definitely make tapioca pudding on this day. Here's one recipe. Look for others. Every eater can custom-make the tapioca to his or her liking. Just stir a favorite flavoring into the finished pudding *(e.g., jam, berries, orange chunks, raisins, apple chunks, caramel or chocolate sauce)*

Vanilla Tapioca Pudding

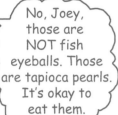

No, Joey, those are NOT fish eyeballs. Those are tapioca pearls. It's okay to eat them.

Gulp!

1. Mix in a saucepan:
   $\frac{1}{2}$ C small pearl tapioca
   3 C whole milk
   $\frac{1}{4}$ t salt
   $\frac{1}{2}$ C sugar
2. Let the mixture sit 5 minutes.
3. Bring the mixture to a boil over medium heat.
4. Lower the heat to very low. Boil 5 minutes. Stir often.
5. Beat 2 eggs well.
6. Pour some of the tapioca mixture into the eggs and mix. Return this to the pan.
7. Boil another 3 minutes over very low heat, stirring constantly.
8. Remove from heat. Stir in $\frac{1}{2}$ t vanilla. Cool and enjoy!

- National Tapioca Pudding Day*
- Margarine Patented *(1867)*
- Respect Canada Day
- National Ice-Cream Day

Birthdays

1606 Rembrandt*
1879 Manitoba, Northwest Territories

One More Idea

- Find pictures of some of Rembrandt's portraits. Re-create one of them as closely as you can. OR, mimic his style as you create a portrait of someone you know. Work from a photograph or get someone to "sit" for a portrait while you draw.

Original Parking Meters

The original parking meter was installed on this day in 1935. Celebrate this day with some parking meter activities.

- Find out who invented and patented the first parking meter, and where it was installed.

- Some people collect parking meters. Read the latest edition of *Guinness World Records* to find out how many parking meters are in the record-holding collection.

- The parking meter has a rather practical, ordinary design. Change that! Design your own **original** parking meter that is extraordinary in some way. Write an explanation of the workings of your parking meter.

- Find and share some good parking meter jokes.

Why have you been standing here watching me for so long?

Because I put my quarter in a long time ago, and I'm still waiting for my gumball to come out.

- First Parking Meter Installed *(1935)**
- Fresh Spinach Day
- Washington, D.C. Became Permanent U.S. Capital *(1790)*
- First Atomic Bomb Tested *(1945)*
- First Moon Landing *(Apollo 11, U.S., 1969)*

- Wrong Way Day*
- National Peach Ice-Cream Day
- Disneyland Opened *(1955)*
- Air Conditioner Invented *(1902)*
- *Apollo 18* and *Soyuz* Linked in Space (1975)

Wrong-Way Stories

This day is named after Douglas Corrigan, who went the wrong way in 1938 and became a celebrated hero known as "Wrong Way Corrigan." Find out where he intended to go, and where he went instead. Everyone goes the wrong way once in a while. Sometimes it turns out okay. Sometimes it doesn't. Write a good "Wrong Way" story. It can be true or imaginary, serious or comical.

July 18th

- Cow Appreciation Day*
- National Caviar Day
- Railroad Day

Birthdays
1918   Nelson Mandela
1921   John Glenn

Appreciate a Cow

Find a way to celebrate cows today. Here are a few ideas. Add some ideas of your own.

- If you have a camcorder or can borrow one, use it to make a "moo"-vie.
- Make, freeze, and enjoy some Purple Cow Moo-Sicles (below).
- Find people who have cow figurines or toys. Interview them to find out why they like cow things.
- Collect or create cow cartoons. (Read Gary Larson's "Far Side" cartoons for ideas.)
- The expression "till the cows come home" means something will go on for a long time. Write 20 sentences that end with that phrase.
- Collect some phrases, figures of speech, or bits of advice that have cow connections.
- Definitely treat yourself to some cookies and milk today.

Always turn the "udder" cheek!

Don't cry over spilled milk.

It is better to be seen and not "herd."

I won't see any increase in my allowance till the cows come home.

Milk every opportunity for all it is worth.

Make a cow knickknack or puppet. Start with a paper towel or toilet paper roll. Add a head, legs, and tail, and color some spots.

The grass is always greener on the "udder" side of the fence.

Purple Cow Moo-Sicles

Blend 1 C milk, 1 C plain yogurt, and 1 C grape juice. Freeze in ice cube trays or frozen pop molds.

Weeklong Sums

Here's a good trick to try on a new friend.
But be sure to show kindness to the friend by revealing the trick, so he or she can succeed at it, too.

Start with today's date (19th). Add it and the next 6 dates to get the sum. Tell your friend you can do the adding faster than he or she. While the friend adds all 7 numbers, you add 3 to the first date and multiply by 7. You'll get the sum fast. This works with ANY 7 consecutive dates.

July 19th

- New Friends Day*
- Stick Out Your Tongue Day
- Shark Awareness Day

Birthdays
1834   Edgar Degas

Ugly Truck Contest

Gather a bunch of friends, grab your sketchbooks, and set out on a hunt for ugly trucks. Walk around your neighborhood or town, or get an adult to drive you around. Find the most ugly truck you can. Sketch it. Describe it. Get back together with your friends, and vote to decide which truck is most ugly. Think of a good prize for the ugliest truck.
If you can't find really ugly trucks, design them yourself!

I'm ugly, and I'm proud!

July 20th

- Ugly Truck Contest Day*
- National Lollipop Day
- National Nap Day
- Chess Day
- Special Olympics Day
- *U.S. Viking I* Landed on Mars *(1976)*
- Neil Armstrong Walked on the Moon *(1969)*

Birthdays
1871   British Columbia

Tug of War Tournament

Plan a Tug of War Tournament today. Get as many friends together as you can. Divide into teams, with at least 4 people on each team. Read up on rules for Tug of War games. Plan a schedule for the contests, and keep the tournament going until you have a final winner. (If you have a variety of sizes and ages of competitors, make different categories for the contests.)

July 21st

- National Tug of War Tournament Day*
- National Junk Food Day
- National Crème Brûlée Day
- National Women's Hall of Fame Began *(1979)*

Birthdays
1899   Ernest Hemingway

- Spooner's Day*
- Rat Catcher's Day*
- America the Beautiful Day
- National Hot Dog Day
- Summer Leisure Day

More Ideas

- Find out why this is Rat Catcher's Day, what it has to do with the Pied Piper of Hamelin, and what a rat catcher is.
- Describe ten good ways to catch a rat.

Spoonerisms

A *spoonerism* is a verbal slip—words or phrases in which letters or syllables get swapped. They are named after an English scholar, Rev. William A. Spooner (1844–1930), who is reported to have made these slips of the tongue (or *tips of the slongue*) frequently.
Have fun coming up with many spoonerisms today.
Try to write a whole story that's full of them!

- *Have you read Beeping Sleauty?*
- *Lurn off the tights before you bo to ged.*
- *I'm pickled tink that you visited.*
- *A hird in the band is worth bwo in the tush.*
- *I'll have a chilled greese sandwich.*
- *Stop and flell the smowers.*
- *Please how your beds and pray.*
- *Sease, be pleated!*

- Mosquito Day*
- Hot Enough for Ya Day*
- National Vanilla Ice-Cream Day
- Ice-Cream Cone Introduced *(1904)*
- Machu Picchu Discovered *(1911)*

Survival for Hot, Buggy Days (or Nights)

The heat is bad enough—but, unfortunately, it's also mosquito season! Create a mosquito shelter for yourself. Then settle into it with a cool handful of homemade "Straw-sicles."

Make a mosquito-proof "tent" for your bed, your yard, or your face. Get inexpensive netting from a fabric store. Or track down old thin, mesh-like curtains from the attic or re-sale shop. Hang this from your bedroom ceiling, from an outdoor umbrella, or from a wide-brimmed hat.

Straw-sicles
Fill straws with pop, punch, or juice. Plug up the ends with chewed bubblegum or putty. Pop them in the freezer for an hour.

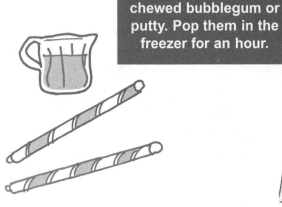

Quick & Easy Whirlybird

Amelia Earhart began her flying career at a young age (24). In 1932, she became the first woman to fly solo across the Atlantic. In 1935, she became the first person to fly solo across the Pacific from California to Honolulu. Her mysterious disappearance on an around-the-world flight in 1937 still fascinates people everywhere. Celebrate the flights of Amelia Earhart with a little flying of your own. Make this easy whirlybird and have fun flying it!

1. Cut slits toward the bottom of a paper cup to form "wings." Fold each strip outward.
2. Cut a small slit about $\frac{1}{2}$ inch from the base of each wing ($\frac{1}{4}$ inch wide). Crease along the dotted line (shown). Fold downward to form a flap.
3. Punch a hole in the center of the cup. Thread a heavy string through the hole.
4. Fasten a large paper clip on the bottom end of the string.
5. Drop the whirlybird from a high place.

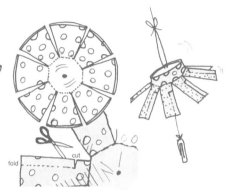

July 24th

- Amelia Earhart Day*
- Coffee Day
- Pioneer Day
- Cousins Day
- Instant Coffee Invented *(1938)*

Birthdays
1898   Amelia Earhart*

Record-Breaking Cakes

Wow! People have been using cake to celebrate birthdays for a long time! Maybe it's because cake is so tasty and such fun to decorate. Visit www.guinnessworldrecords.com or get a copy of the latest edition of *Guinness World Records*. Look up the records for the largest cake, the longest cake, and the most candles on a cake. Then bake a cake with some friends. See how many birthday candles you can crowd onto your cake. Light the candles, but don't set the room on fire!

July 25th

- First Birthday Cake Created *(55 B.C.)**
- National Hot Fudge Sundae Day
- Threading the Needle Day
- First Carousel Patented *(1871)*

All or Nothing

"It's all or nothing!"
This is an expression that is used often. Interview 25 people today. Ask them to tell you what situation would lead them to say, truthfully, that they want "all or nothing."

July 26th

- All or Nothing Day*
- National Coffee Milkshake Day
- Aunt and Uncle Day
- U.S. Postal Service Begun *(1775)*
- FBI Founded *(1909)*

Birthdays
1788   New York, 11th State

- Take Your Houseplants for a Walk Day*
- First Bugs Bunny Cartoon Published *(1940)*
- National Korean War Veterans Armistice Day
- World Youth Day
- Korean War Ended *(1953)*

Hiking with Houseplants

What a strange holiday! See if you can find out whose idea this was. Then think about what a good idea it is. First of all, plants benefit from fresh air and sunshine. So do you! You also get the benefit of exercise. So, get together with some friends and plan a houseplant hike. Gather wagons, carts, strollers, and bikes. Figure out how to get all your houseplants ready to travel. Plan a route. Stop along the way to visit friends and get drinks for yourself and your plants.

- First Fingerprint Taken *(1858)*
- Hamburger Day
- 14th Amendment to the *U.S. Constitution* Ratified *(1868)*

Birthdays

  1866 Beatrix Potter
  1929 Jacqueline Kennedy Onassis

Leave Your Prints!

You see detectives "dusting" for fingerprints in movies. You can "lift" fingerprints, too. Human skin has oil—some of which is left behind when something is touched. You can capture the prints quite easily. After you have fun lifting, saving, and comparing fingerprints, do some research on the structure of fingerprints. Then write a mystery story that uses fingerprints as a major clue. Try to include a hamburger in your story. If you're really clever, you might be able to set the story in the World War I era.

1. Press your finger onto a dark, smooth surface.
2. Sprinkle baby powder or talcum powder over the fingerprint area.
3. Use a soft feather to gently brush the powder across the fingerprint.
4. Place a small strip of clear tape over the print.
5. Lift the powder print gently with the tape.
6. Place the tape on a piece of dark-colored paper.
7. Get prints from all your fingers. Fingerprint your friends. Try dusting frequently-used surfaces to get mystery prints!

Lipstick Art

Collect old lipstick tubes from family members, friends, or neighbors. Try to get a variety of colors. Search to find puns, idioms, figures of speech, or other expressions related to lips, mouths, or smiles. Use lipstick to write these on a poster or window. Add drawings to accompany the words.

July 29th

- National Lipstick Day*
- Chicken Wings Day*
- National Lasagna Day
- NASA Formed *(1958)*

Find out where and when the fad of tasty chicken wings began. Get a recipe and enjoy some chicken wings today.

A " Pane"-ful Joke

Honor Comedy Day with this harmless joke. Play it on a friend or family member today.

Cut a piece of clear plastic wrap the size of a window. Smooth it over the window. Use a wide marking pen to design a large crack across the window. Add a creepy-looking bug or spider to the design.

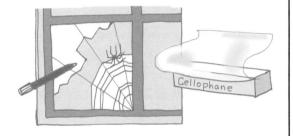

July 30th

- Comedy Day*
- National Cheesecake Day
- Paperback Books Introduced *(1935)*

Birthdays
1818 Emily Bronte
1863 Henry Ford

Mutt's Treats

Delight your dog today with some homemade treats.
(If you don't have a dog, make them for someone else's dog.)

1. Dissolve 1 pkg dry yeast in $3\frac{1}{2}$ C warm beef broth or chicken broth.
2. Mix 5 C whole wheat flour, $\frac{1}{2}$ C oatmeal, 1 C cornmeal, $\frac{1}{2}$ C dried powdered milk.
3. Combine wet and dry mixes.
4. Add $\frac{1}{2}$ C peanut butter.
5. Roll out on a floured surface.
6. Cut into doggie bones or any other shape.
7. Bake on a lightly greased cookie sheet for 45 minutes in a 300°F oven.

July 31st

- Mutt's Day*
- U.S. Patent Office Established
- Shredded Wheat Introduced *(1893)*
- Water Skis Used for the First Time *(1922)*

August

1
- "Chopsticks" (song) Published*
- San Francisco Cable Car Day*
- Respect for Parents Day
- Anniversary of Emancipation of 500
- Homemade Pie Day
- *Spiderman* Published
- U.S. Air Force Established
- World Wide Web Created
  Birthdays: Colorado, Francis Scott Key

2
- First Lincoln Head Penny Issued*
- National Ice-Cream Sandwich Day*
- Hug a Senior Day
- First U.S. Income Tax Enacted
- Kuwait Invaded by Iraq

3
- National Watermelon Day*
- National Park Day
- National Night Out
- National Basketball Association Formed
- Christopher Columbus Voyage Began

4
- National Chocolate Chip Day*
- Hooray for Kids! Day
- Kentucky Fried Chicken Created
- U.S. Coast Guard Established
  Birthdays: Louis Armstrong*

5
- Traffic Light Invented*
- Green Peppers Day
- Take a Walk on the Moon Day
- American Bandstand First Televised
  Birthdays: Neil Armstrong

6
- National Pamper Yourself Day*
- Root Beer Float Day*
- National Fresh Breath Day*
- Wiggle Your Toes Day
- Peace Day
- First Atomic Bomb Dropped
  Birthdays: Lucille Ball

7
- National Lighthouse Day*
- Halfway Point of Summer
- Particularly Preposterous Packaging Day
- Sea Serpent Day
- First Picture of Earth Taken from Space

8
- Dollar Day*
- Sneak Some Zucchini onto Your Neighbor's Porch Night
- The Date to Create
- Middle Children's Day
- Bonza Bottler Day
- Swim Day
- Cheese Cake Day
- Admit You're Happy Day
- Electric Refrigerator Patented

9
- Book Lovers Day
- Celebrate Your Lakes Day
- National Hand-Holding Day
- Dance a Polka Day
- Electric Washing Machine Patented
- Second Atomic Bomb Dropped
- President Richard Nixon Resigned
  Birthdays: Smokey Bear*

10
- *Candid Camera* TV Show Premiered*
- S'mores Day*
- Lazy Day
- Smithsonian Institute Founded
- National Ragweed Day
- Spoil Your Dog Day
  Birthdays: Missouri, Herbert Hoover

11
- Play in the Sand Day*
- Dog Days End
- Presidential Joke Day
- S.O.S. Signal First Used
  Birthdays: Alex Palmer Haley

12
- Truck Driver Day
- Sewing Machine Invented
- Baseball Fans Day
- UN International Youth Day
  Birthdays: Cecil B. DeMille*

13
- International Left-Hander's Day*
- Berlin Wall Built
- Eyeglasses Invented
- Greyhound Bus Introduced
- First Roller Derby
- First Taxicab Introduced
  Birthdays: Alfred Hitchcock, Annie Oakley, Fidel Castro

14
- Oregon Territory Created*
- National Creamsicle Day
- Senior Citizens Day
- Japan Surrendered, WWII Ended
- Wiffle Ball Patented

15
- National Failures Day*
- National Relaxation Day
- Hello Day
- Lemon Meringue Pie Day
- Angel Food Cake Day
- Panama Canal Opened
- *The Wizard of Oz* Premiered
- Woodstock Rock Concert Held
  Birthdays: Napoleon

16
- Vinegar Day*
- Elvis Presley Commemoration Day
- Tell a Joke Day
- Roller Coaster Day
- Anniversary of Major League Baseball No-Hitter
- Antiseptics Discovered

17
- Pencil Day*
- Airmail Balloon Day
- Archaeology Day
- Buttered Popcorn Day
- First Steamboat Trip
  Birthdays: Davy Crockett

For each starred holiday*, find one or more activities on pages 194–207.

18
- Bad Poetry Day*
- Women's Voting Rights Day
- First Mail-Order Catalog Published
- 19th Amendment to the *U.S. Constitution* Ratified
  Birthdays: Meriwether Lewis

19
- Potato Day*
- *Sputnik 5* Carried First Living Organisms into Space
- National Aviation Day
- First Saturday Morning TV Shows for Children Aired
- Indianapolis 500 Speedway Constructed
  Birthdays: Orville Wright, Ogden Nash, William Jefferson Clinton

20
- Summer Cool-off Day*
- Lemonade Invented
- National Radio Day
  Birthdays: Benjamin Harrison

21
- National Spumoni Day*
- Poets' Day*
  Birthdays: Hawaii

22
- National Punctuation Day*
- Be an Angel Day
- Hoodie Hoo Day in the Southern Hemisphere
- National Tooth Fairy Day
- *Mona Lisa* Painting Stolen from *The Louvre,* Paris

23
- National Spongecake Day*
- Eat a Peach Day
- National Gymnastics Day

24
- Strange Music Day*
- Mt. Vesuvius Erupted
- Waffle Iron Patented
- Peach Pie Day
- Washington, D.C. Burned

25
- Banana Split Day*
- National Park Service Established
- Paris Liberated in WWII
  Birthdays: Leonard Bernstein

26
- Toilet Paper Roll Invented*
- Women's Equality Day
- National Cherry Popsicle Day
- First Baseball Games Televised
- Make Your Own Luck Day
  Birthdays: Paul J. Martin

27
- Banana Lovers Day
- Just Because Day
- Motorist Consideration Day
- Creation of *Tarzan*
  Birthdays: Mother Teresa*

28
- National Bow Tie Day*
- First Radio Commercial Aired
- Anniversary of March on Washington
- Oil First Produced Commercially
  Birthdays: Lyndon B. Johnson

29
- First Motorcycle Patented (1885)*
- More Herbs, Less Salt Day
- Chop Suey Invented

30
- National Toasted Marshmallow Day*
- Hotline Established Between U.S. and USSR

31
- Kinetoscope Patented*
- Princess Diana Memorial Day
- Trail Mix Day

Month-long Celebrations

American Artist Appreciation Month*

Admit You're Happy Month

Architecture Month

Brownies at Brunch Month*

Children's Good Manners Month*

Children's Vision & Learning Month

Eat Dessert First Month

Family Eye Care Month

Family Fun Month

International Air Travel Month*

National Back-to-School Month*

National Catfish Month*

National Data Entry Month

National Golf Month

National Immunization Awareness Month

National Inventors Month*

National Little League Baseball Month

National Napping Month*

National Parks Month*

National Sandwich Month*

National Vacation Month*

National Water Quality Month

National Watermelon Month

Romance Awareness Month

Weekly Celebrations

First Week: National Clown Week*, National Mosquito-Control Awareness Weekend*, National Video Game Week, Simplify Your Life Week

Second Week: National Apple Week*, Elvis Week, National Bargain-Hunting Week

Third Week: Weird Contest Week*, American Dance Week*, Don't Wait—Celebrate! Week, National Aviation Week

Fourth Week: National Waffle Week,* Be Kind to Humankind Week, National Veterinary Week, Stepparent's Appreciation Week

Dates That Vary: International Friendship Day*, National Buttered Corn Day*, National Kids Day*, National Forgiveness Day*, National Mustard Day*, National Garage Sale Day*, National Neighborhood Day, American Family Day, Sisters Day, Daughter's Day, National Homeless Animals Day

August's Month-long Celebrations

National Inventors Month

Get to know some new (to you!) inventors this month. Find out what inventions are credited to each of these inventors and when the inventions were created:

- James Faria and Robert Wright
- Jacques Heim and Louis Reard
- Richard Knerr and Arthur Melin
- Byron and Melody Swetland
- Leon Battista Alberti
- Mary Anderson
- Ladislo Biro
- Sara Boone
- Jacques Brandienberger
- Allen Breed
- Nolan Bushnell
- Martin Cooper
- Dr. Harry Coover
- Earle Dickson
- Richard Drew
- Peter Durand
- Michael Faraday

- George W. Ferris
- Sally Fox
- Art Fry
- Bette Nesmith Graham
- Joyce Hall
- Ruth Handler
- Walter Hunt
- Jack St. Clair Kelby
- Willem Kolff
- James Naismith
- O.A. North
- James Ritty
- Benjamin A. Rubin
- Ralph Samuelson
- Charles Seeberger
- Patsy Shuman
- Richie Stachowski

National Sandwich Month

- Make a list of all the different ingredients you can think of that could go in a real sandwich.

- Make a list of ingredients for fun (possibly inedible) sandwiches.

- Buy the longest loaf of bread you can find. Make a sandwich for the whole family.

- Use sandwich ingredients to create some math problems about *combinations*.

How many different sandwiches could you make using 1 meat, 1 cheese, and 2 veggies in each sandwich?

WOW!

Sandwich Menu
Meat: turkey
        roast beef
        ham
Cheese: cheddar
        provolone
        swiss
Veggies: tomatoes
        lettuce
        onions

International Air Travel Month

Use this month as an excuse to create and solve time zone problems. Start by finding a map of Earth's time zones. Solve these; then make up your own.

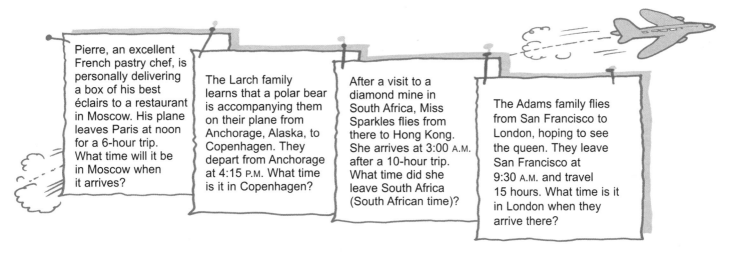

Pierre, an excellent French pastry chef, is personally delivering a box of his best éclairs to a restaurant in Moscow. His plane leaves Paris at noon for a 6-hour trip. What time will it be in Moscow when it arrives?

The Larch family learns that a polar bear is accompanying them on their plane from Anchorage, Alaska, to Copenhagen. They depart from Anchorage at 4:15 P.M. What time is it in Copenhagen?

After a visit to a diamond mine in South Africa, Miss Sparkles flies from there to Hong Kong. She arrives at 3:00 A.M. after a 10-hour trip. What time did she leave South Africa (South African time)?

The Adams family flies from San Francisco to London, hoping to see the queen. They leave San Francisco at 9:30 A.M. and travel 15 hours. What time is it in London when they arrive there?

Children's Good Manners Month

Use a dictionary to find the meaning of the word *etiquette*. Find out about the etiquette of greeting people and making introductions. Practice what you learn by introducing people of different "ranks" and ages to one another.

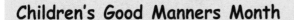

Dr. Marshall, may I present Miss Smith?

Mr. President, I have the honor to present Mrs. Appleby.

American Artist Appreciation Month

Find out about one of your favorite artists this month—a singer, painter, musician, sculptor, commercial artist, comic, dancer, mime, actor, architect, seamstress, chef, designer, circus performer, or other artist. Write a short biography. Create or present something that mimics the art of the person you choose.

A master of mime always keeps mum!

Learn to appreciate the art of *mime*. Mime is a medium of self-expression that uses no words. The artist uses only facial expressions and gestures (along with costume and makeup). Research the history of mime. Read about Marcel Marceau, known as the "master of modern mime." Learn the difference between *abstract mime* and *literal mime*. Try some mime yourself. Use it to express feelings and/or to tell a story.

Back-to-School Month

Get organized for going back to school and brush up on your math skills at the same time. Make a list of the supplies you need for school. (Include clothing items on your list, if you wish.) Then "shop" for the items at 3 or 4 different places (without buying anything at first). The "places" may be stores, catalogs, or Internet sites. Figure out what each item will cost. Compare the individual and total costs. When you do go out to buy supplies, you'll know where to get the best bargains.

Supplies/Clothes	Larson's	Office Supply	Super Saver mart	Web Office
10 pencils	5/.79	.10 ea	10/$1	$.89.95
calculator	$89.90	$94.50	$69.80	$2.79
3 ring binder	$2.99	$2.59	$1.99	$3.00 ea
4 subject notebooks	$3.15 ea	$2.85 ea	$2.75 ea	$1.00
notebook paper (1000)	$1.29	$.99	$.80	
assignment book	$4.50	$5.00	$5.95	$4.50
compass	$3.00	$2.19	$2.05	$3.99
10 pens	10/6.99	$1.99 ea	5/3.99	10/7.50
TOTAL:				

It's Brownies at Brunch Month! Make these extra-easy brownies for brunch.

Prepare a small box of instant chocolate pudding according to directions. Stir in a chocolate cake mix (powdered only). Carefully stir in 2 cups of chocolate chips. Pour into a greased, glass cake pan. Bake for 40 minutes at 350°.

National Parks Month

Find a national park in the U.S. or Canada to answer each question. Use a blank map of North America to star the location of each park and label the spot with the park's name.

In which park would you find . . .

   . . . the last remaining herds of bison in Northern Canada?

   . . . Florida panthers, alligators, and crocodiles?

   . . . the highest mountain in the U.S.?

   . . . the world's greatest geyser, "Old Faithful"?

   . . . Sunwapta Falls and Mt. Edith Cavell (Canada)?

   . . . large granite domes: El Capitan and Half-Dome?

   . . . part of the Painted Desert, petrified food, and Indian artifacts?

   . . . the deepest lake in the U.S.?

   . . . the world's largest tree?

   . . . the highest waterfall in the U.S.?

   . . . white pelican breeding colonies at Lavallee Lake (Canada)?

National Vacation Month

More people take vacations in August than in any other month. Enjoy your August vacation, AND learn about vacationing in your country and state. Find out what the top-ten vacation sites are in your state, your country, and the world! Find the top-ten spots for some specific kinds of vacations (such as hiking, rock climbing, water-skiing, etc).

August 1 is the birthday of Herman Melville, author of **Moby Dick**. Read some or all of Melville's tale about the great white whale this month.

Top-Ten Spots for Whale-Watching

Baja California, Mexico
Cape Cod
California Coast
Vancouver Island, British Columbia
Dominican Republic
Lofoten Islands, Norway
Whale Route, South Africa
Masoala Park, Madagascar
Kaikoura, New Zealand
Shikoku, Japan

National Catfish Month

Celebrate catfish in August (even if you don't have any around)!

• What, exactly, is a catfish? Find out.

• Create a cartoon about a catfish, or about fishing for catfish. Or, write your favorite catfish memory, joke, dream, or story.

• Find a good recipe for cooking catfish.

• Give a speech or make a poster that will convince someone to vote for the catfish as America's official fish.

• Find out which state boasts the highest catfish consumption.

• Write directions for "How to Catch a Catfish" (with a hook, bait, your bare hands, or any other method).

I like to "cat nap" while I'm waiting for the catfish to bite.

National Napping Month

Track down some sleep statistics this month. Find websites that give information about sleep patterns, sleep problems, or sleep experiences. Make a "Did You Know?" brochure or comic book that shares some of the statistics you learn.

51% of America's adults report they have driven while drowsy during the past year.

Almost $\frac{2}{3}$ of Americans report a sleep problem a few nights a week.

Experts recommend 8 hours of sleep a night for adults. The average American adult sleeps less than 7 hours a night during the workweek.

See page 185 for other month-long holidays to celebrate in August.   189

Special Weeks in August

First Week

National Clown Week

Clowns are a favorite part of any circus. However, you don't even need a circus to be a clown or find a clown.

- Design clown faces.
- Design clown clothing.
- Find ten fun ways to "clown around."

Unscramble these circus words
(some may be two words):

grimrestan

theeplan

taereefir

alimorten

zeerpat

prigotthe

glegruj

snokyem

cenulyic

scowln

National Mosquito-Control Awareness Weekend
Find out . . .

- how many kinds of mosquitoes there are.
- the lifespan of a mosquito.
- what diseases are carried by mosquitoes.
- why mosquitoes bite.
- why a lump results from a mosquito bite.
- why some people seem to attract mosquitoes more than other people.
- how mosquitoes can be controlled.

Second Week

National Apple Week

Celebrate apple week with these apple treats. The hot August sun will help you make them easily.

Sun-dried Apples

1. Peel several apples and take out the cores.

2. Slice the apples crossways to form rings.

3. Place an old sheet or pillowcase (or paper towels) on a picnic table or other hard surface in the sun. Spread the apple slices on the sheet and cover them with cheesecloth to keep the bugs away.

4. Turn the apples when the tops are dry to allow the other side to dry. This can take several days. (Take the apples inside at night to protect them from nighttime moisture.)

5. Store the dried apples in tightly closed plastic bags or containers.

     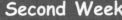

American Dance Week

The word *tarantism* means "the irresistible urge to dance." Experience tarantism this week.

- Read about, watch, or demonstrate at least ten different kinds of dances.
- Find out about dance contests and records (e.g., the largest dance, the longest line dance, the longest Conga line).
- Learn a new dance this week.

    samba
    box step
    two-step
    salsa
    waltz
    fox trot
    jive
    twist
    rock & roll
    tango
    rumba
    square dance
    polka
    swing
    line dancing

Weird Contest Week

Let your imagination go wild as you "concoct" weird contests to hold with your friends. Here are a few existing weird contests. Think of more. Plan at least one to hold during the week.

- light bulb collecting
- cricket spitting
- bed racing
- slug racing
- wall sitting
- onion peeling
- raw egg eating
- mosquito killing
- milkshake drinking
- cow pie throwing
- grape tossing
- bed making
- present wrapping
- balancing on one foot

We're sure to win the Weird Dance Contest!

Let's dance the tarantella!

National Waffle Week

Celebrate this week with a good waffle meal. You can have waffles for breakfast (with syrup), waffles for lunch (with peanut butter and jelly), waffles for dinner (with creamed chicken), or waffles for dessert (with ice cream or fruit—or both). Use the basic waffle recipe for any of these. Or, try the chocolate waffle recipe as a base for ice cream, chocolate syrup, and nuts.

For chocolate waffles, add half a cup of cocoa powder during step 1 in the basic waffle recipe.

Basic Waffle Recipe

1) Mix 2 C flour, 2 t baking powder, $1\frac{1}{2}$ t baking soda, and a pinch of salt together.

2) Separate 3 eggs. Beat the yolks.

3) Gradually add 2 C milk to the eggs. Gradually add 2 T melted margarine.

4) Stir the flour mixture into the egg-milk mixture.

5) Beat the egg whites in a glass or metal bowl until they are stiff.

6) Fold the egg whites into the flour-milk-eggs mixture.

7) Cook on a hot waffle iron.

See page 185 for other week-long holidays to celebrate in August.

191

The Days of August

National Mustard Day *(1st Saturday)*

• Gather up as many different kinds of mustard as you can find. Have a mustard-tasting contest. Devise a way for friends to rate the different mustards. Pick a winner in one or many categories.

• Find out what ingredients make up mustard.

• Hold a mustard-squirting contest.

• Use mustard squeeze bottles to write messages in mustard.

• Make some soft pretzels and enjoy them with mustard.

• Find out about the history of mustard's use as a medicine.

• Write a mystery in which Colonel Mustard is a suspect.

Mustard Mini-Thoughts

In ancient Greece, Pythagoras suggested using mustard as a cure for scorpion bites.

The spiciness in mustard comes from oil released when a mustard seed is mixed with water.

In the first century, someone believed that mustard would make lazy housewives more industrious.

Mustard was produced long before its favorite pal, the hot dog.

It is believed that ancient Egyptians chewed mustard seeds as a seasoning to accompany meals.

More than 400 million pounds of mustard are consumed in the world each year.

International Friendship Day & National Kids Day *(1st Sunday)*

International Friendship Day is a day to reflect on the contribution your friends make to your life. Celebrate your friends in combination with a celebration of all kids on this day.

• Think about who your friends are. Make a list. For each one, make a note of one important contribution that person has made to your life.

• Write a tribute to one or more of your friends.

• Make sure you tell your friends how much you value their friendship.

• Get some friends together and have fun keeping cool on your homemade "Slip & Slide."

Do-It-Yourself Slip & Slide

1. Get a large piece of sturdy plastic sheeting or a tarp.

2. Put the plastic on a smooth, grassy area. Do not put it on any rough or hard surface; this will not be safe.

3. Put smooth, heavy items around the edges of the plastic to keep it from moving or blowing away.

4. Set up a sprinkler so that the water sprays onto the slide.

5. When the plastic is thoroughly wet, start sliding. Keep the sprinkler on the plastic all the time. Slide carefully.

6. Do not leave the plastic on the lawn for more than an hour, or your grass will die.

National Buttered Corn Day *(4th Thursday)*

Be sure to enjoy hot, buttered corn on this day. Steam it on top of the stove, or enjoy the special treat of fire-roasted corn.

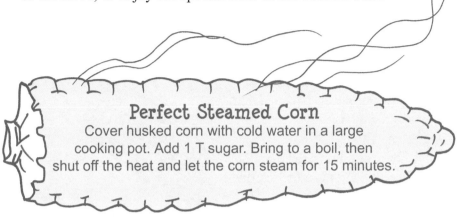

Perfect Steamed Corn
Cover husked corn with cold water in a large cooking pot. Add 1 T sugar. Bring to a boil, then shut off the heat and let the corn steam for 15 minutes.

Fire-Roasted Corn

1. Remove husks and silk from the corn. Soak the husks for $\frac{1}{2}$ hour in salt water ($\frac{1}{2}$ C salt to 1 qt water).
2. Spread corn with butter and salt. Add paprika or hot pepper sauce if you wish.
3. Put ears of corn back into husks.
4. Fold the husks around the corn and tie with string that has been well soaked in water.
5. Place the corn directly on or under coals in a charcoal fire. Roast 30 minutes.

National Garage Sale Day
(2nd Saturday)

Plan your own garage sale. It's a good way to get rid of all that stuff you don't need and make some money at the same time. If you can't have a garage sale, clean out closets, drawers, attics, storage rooms, and playrooms anyway. Pile up all the things you don't use regularly and contribute them to a charity. Save a few of the interesting throwaway items and turn them into creative sculptures.

Garage Sale Junk Sculptures

plastic ball head

mop hair

ping pong ball eyes

plunger arms

old pillow torso

hat box skirt

hockey stick legs

Most cities have rules for garage sales. Find out the rules in your town. Make up some rules of your own.

National Forgiveness Day
(1st Sunday)

Forgiveness is a gift that benefits the giver as much as the receiver. Think about the grudges you are holding. Think about the stress and hurt that results from your anger or resentment. Find at least one "wrong" that you can forgive today. Tell that person. You will feel much better, and the other person will, too.

See page 185 for other days that vary in August.

August 1st

- "Chopsticks" (song) Published (1877)*
- San Francisco Cable Car Day*
- Respect for Parents Day
- Anniversary of Emancipation of 500
- Homemade Pie Day
- *Spiderman* Published (1962)
- U.S. Air Force Established (1907)
- World Wide Web Created (1990)

Birthdays
1876   Colorado, 38th State
1779   Francis Scott Key

New Chopsticks Lyrics

The "Chopsticks" song is one of the world's most recognizable tunes. Find out who wrote the song and whether there are any words (lyrics) written to accompany the original song. Then create your own lyrics to match the tune. (Sing the lyrics below to the tune.)

Ride in a cable car.
Ring the bell every hour.
Up and down steep hills of San
Fran-cis-co and
Laugh on the cable car.
Don't lean out very far.
There's nothing else to compare.
Have fun!

August 2nd

- First Lincoln Head Penny Issued (1909)*
- National Ice-Cream Sandwich Day*
- Hug a Senior Day
- First U.S. Income Tax Enacted (1861)
- Kuwait Invaded by Iraq (1990)

Penny Probability

Read the history of the Lincoln penny. Then use some pennies to brush-up on probability understandings. Visit the U.S. Mint's website for kids at www.usmint.gov/kids.

Prepare to toss two pennies (simultaneously) 100 times. Calculate the probability for each outcome: two heads, two tails, one of each. Then do the toss 100 times, keeping a record of the actual outcomes. Repeat the process, tossing three or four pennies at a time.

Cool Calculations

Make your own ice-cream sandwiches by combining your favorite cookies with your favorite ice cream.

Soften scoops of your favorite ice cream. Press a large spoonful between two cookies. Wrap the sandwich in plastic wrap and store it in the freezer for several hours.

Clean your pennies! Mix 3 tablespoons of vinegar and 1 T salt in a jar of water. Drop your dirty pennies into the jar, wait a few minutes, then rinse and dry them. They'll be clean as a whistle.

Combine ... mint ice cream with chocolate cookies ... or vanilla ice cream with chocolate chip cookies ... or chocolate ice cream with peanut butter cookies ... or strawberry ice cream with oatmeal cookies ... or bubblegum ice cream with sugar cookies.

For each starred* holiday on pages 194–207, you will find at least one activity.

Purple Watermelon Surprise

August 3rd

Any summer day is a great day to eat cold watermelon. Definitely eat watermelon today. But just for fun, turn your watermelon into a surprise that will delight your guests and make them think you are a magician! You'll need a whole watermelon and four cups of purple grape juice.

- National Watermelon Day*
- National Park Day
- National Night Out
- National Basketball Association Formed *(1949)*
- Christopher Columbus Began His First Voyage to the New World *(1492)*

1. The melon must be very cold, so put it in the refrigerator for 2 days.
2. Cut a small square chunk (about 3 cm) out of the rind at one end of the melon. Cut all the way through the rind down to the melon's flesh.
3. Repeat this, cutting another square at the other end, and a square in the center of the melon.
4. Very, very slowly pour grape juice into the holes. This will be a slow process. You will have to wait as the juice soaks down into the melon. Pour about $\frac{1}{2}$ the juice in; then put the melon back in the refrigerator for 2–3 hours to re-chill it.
5. Slowly pour the rest of the grape juice into the holes.
6. Put the pieces of rind back in the holes. Chill the watermelon for a few more hours.
7. Slice the watermelon and serve the purple melon to your amazed friends.

Chocolate Chip Calculations

August 4th

Start with one or more bags of chocolate chips. Find a desk or other flat surface, and sharpen several math skills before those chips find their way into your cookies (or your mouth!).

- National Chocolate Chip Day*
- Hooray for Kids! Day
- Kentucky Fried Chicken Created *(1952)*
- U.S. Coast Guard Established *(1790)*

Birthday
1900   Louis Armstrong*

- "Measure" your height using chips as a unit rather than inches or centimeters. Measure other things, too.
- Estimate the volume of a bag of chocolate chips. Find a way to check the accuracy of your estimate. Compare the volume of a bag of solid chips to a bag of the chips, melted.
- Use the chips to visually represent mathematical expressions.
- Find a way to weigh a chocolate chip. Compare its weight to the weight of ten other things. Find something that weighs the same as the chip.
- Figure out a way to use chips to show an odd number, an even number, a fractional number, an integer, and a decimal number.
- Devise some probability experiments to do with two colors of chips.
- Track down some chocolate chip statistics.

Find Louis Armstrong's recording of "What A Wonderful World," and other pieces of his music. Listen to them while you do chocolate chip math.

- Traffic Light Invented *(1914)**
- Green Peppers Day
- Take a Walk on the Moon Day
- American Bandstand First Televised *(1957)*

Birthday
1930 Neil Armstrong

Talking Traffic Lights

Personification is a technique writers use to make writing interesting. It gives human characteristics or actions to a nonliving item or to an animal. Personification inspires readers to imagine how a nonliving item would think and act if it were alive.

Personify a traffic light. Think about what a traffic light sees, hears, smells, tastes, and feels. Imagine what a traffic light might tell or advise if it could talk. Write a news article, an advice column, a mystery, a diary, or a story from the viewpoint of a traffic light.

I'll be glad when all the cars are electric. Then I won't choke on these fumes.

In the last hour, 3 cars have run my red light.

- National Pamper Yourself Day*
- Root Beer Float Day*
- National Fresh Breath Day*
- Wiggle Your Toes Day
- Peace Day
- First Atomic Bomb Dropped *(Hiroshima, 1945)*

Birthdays
1911 Lucille Ball

More Ideas

Try these natural, low-cost ways to keep your breath fresh:
- Nibble on parsley.
- Floss your teeth daily.
- Brush your teeth often.
- Brush your tongue, too.
- Eat more fruits and vegetables.
- Change your toothbrush once a month.
- Don't smoke!

Homemade Bubble Bath

Pamper yourself with a long bubble bath today. Visit the Internet to find great recipes for bubble bath and bath salts. Or try this recipe. Make fun jars of bubble bath gel to give to friends or keep for yourself.

To use, hold a few tablespoons in hands and run warm water over them into the bathtub.

On Root Beer Float Day, sip a fresh root beer float while you relax in a bubble bath. Pour cold root beer into a cold glass. Add a scoop of hard vanilla ice cream AFTER the root beer is poured.

A Bubble Gel Jar

1. Pour a package of unflavored gelatin into a large bowl.
2. Heat $\frac{3}{4}$ C water until it boils. Remove it from the heat right away, and gradually stir the water into the gelatin. Let the gelatin powder dissolve completely.
3. Slowly stir $\frac{1}{2}$ C of clear, liquid dishwashing soap into the gelatin mixture.
4. Add a fragrant oil of your choice and one drop of food coloring.
5. Pour the mixture into a clean glass jar.
6. Place a small rubber ducky or other item into the gel.
7. Chill the jar in a refrigerator for five hours.

Lighthouse Map

Use your library or the Internet to do some research on lighthouses. Find several that interest you. You can choose from your state, from a particular area, or from your whole country (or the world). Look for different structures and styles of lighthouses. Then make a map that shows the location of each of these lighthouses. Label the spot with the name of the lighthouse and its location. Leave room around the edge of the map for drawings of each lighthouse.

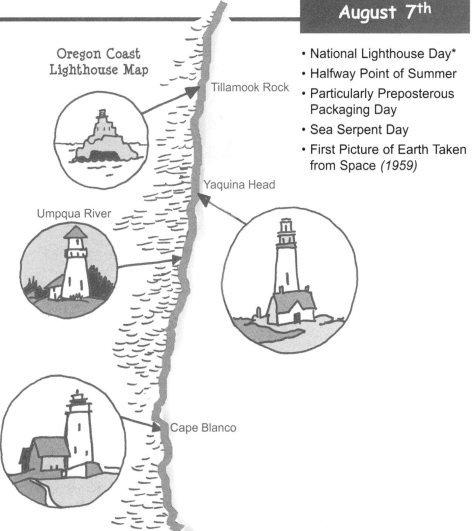

Oregon Coast Lighthouse Map

Tillamook Rock

Yaquina Head

Umpqua River

Cape Blanco

August 7th

- National Lighthouse Day*
- Halfway Point of Summer
- Particularly Preposterous Packaging Day
- Sea Serpent Day
- First Picture of Earth Taken from Space *(1959)*

CATCH!

This time I'll catch it!

Catch a Falling Dollar

Learn a few things about force and motion with this experiment. All you need is a dollar bill and someone who will volunteer to try to catch it.

1. The volunteer stands with arm outstretched, fingers open from the thumb about 1 inch (3 cm), in a position ready to catch the dollar.
2. Hold the dollar bill between the parted thumb and fingers, with half the bill above the hand.
3. Let the volunteer know that the trick is to grab the dollar bill (between fingers and thumb) when it falls.
4. Don't tell the volunteer when you are ready to let the dollar bill go. Just drop it. See if it can be caught.

August 8th

- Dollar Day*
- Sneak Some Zucchini onto Your Neighbor's Porch Night
- The Date to Create
- Middle Children's Day
- Bonza Bottler Day
- Swim Day
- Cheese Cake Day
- Admit You're Happy Day
- Electric Refrigerator Patented *(1899)*

- Book Lovers Day
- Celebrate Your Lakes Day
- National Hand-Holding Day
- Dance a Polka Day
- Electric Washing Machine Patented *(1910)*
- Second Atomic Bomb Dropped *(Nagasaki, 1945)*
- President Richard Nixon Resigned *(1974)*

Birthdays
1944   Smokey Bear*

Smokey's Goals

The Smokey Bear campaign, which began in 1944, advertised a fire prevention message using Smokey Bear as its image. Smokey's slogan was "Only YOU can prevent forest fires!"

On this anniversary of Smokey Bear's creation, learn more about him and the reason he was created.

Happy Birthday, Smokey!

Find out:

- how the idea of Smokey Bear began
- the story of the real bear cub who was the basis for his story
- how he was named
- where the "real" Smokey Bear lived his life after his rescue
  - when the "real" Smokey Bear died
  - the definition of a "wildfire" and the other kinds of fires
- how wildfires get started
- who fights wildfires
- how YOU can prevent wildfires
- how Smokey's message changed in April 2001

- *Candid Camera* TV Show Premiered *(1948)**
- S'mores Day*
- Lazy Day
- Smithsonian Institute Founded *(1846)*
- National Ragweed Day
- Spoil Your Dog Day

Birthdays
1821   Missouri, 24th State
1874   Herbert Hoover, 31st U.S. President

Great Pranks

In the TV show *Candid Camera,* people were caught in hoaxes that were devised by the show's host, Allen Funt, and the show's staff. Strange situations were set up to "catch" unsuspecting people on hidden cameras and concealed microphones. The idea was to see how people would react to these hoaxes.

Do some research to find a few of these tricky situations. Then devise several Candid Camera-like scenarios. Try them out on friends and family members.

Candid Camera Pranks

Make s'mores in the microwave! Put a square of milk chocolate candy bar on half a graham cracker. Top this with a marshmallow. Place the stack on a paper towel and microwave for 10–15 seconds, just until the marshmallow is puffy. Top this with the other graham cracker half, squeeze, and eat!

A customer at a bowling alley rolls a ball. When it comes back, the finger holes are missing.

A woman asks someone for help because her car won't start. When the helpful person lifts up the hood of the car to take a look, the car has no engine.

A person puts mail in her mailbox. The mailbox talks to her.

Someone steps into an elevator full of people. All the people on the elevator are facing the side wall.

Layered Sand Planter

Get some sand, and as you play with it, turn it into a work of art.

1. Get sand from a beach or hardware store. Try to get or create different colors and textures of sand, if you can.

2. Add some fine gravel or crushed shells to some of the sand to create different textures.

3. For different colors, crush some colored chalk and mix it with some of the sand.

4. Fill a fat, glass pickle jar by layering the sand in a pleasing combination of textures and colors.

5. Remove both ends from an aluminum soup can to make a tube. Push this into the center of the sand until the can's top edge is below the top edge of the sand. Scoop out the sand that comes into the can.

6. Drop some rocks or pieces of charcoal into the tube, then fill it with soil.

7. Plant ivy or another house plant in the soil and water it well.

August 11th

- Play in the Sand Day*
- Dog Days End
- Presidential Joke Day
- S.O.S. Signal First Used *(1909)*

Birthdays
1921   Alex Palmer Haley

Silent Movies

Cecil B. DeMille was one of the most successful early movie directors, famous for directing hundreds of short silent films. He is probably most well-known for his film *The Ten Commandments* (1956).

Honor Cecil B. DeMille today by making a short silent film of your own. Gather some friends, borrow a video camera, and plan your movie. Remember: When there's no talking in a movie, the body actions and facial expressions must tell the story.

August 12th

- Truck Driver Day
- Sewing Machine Invented *(1851)*
- Baseball Fans Day
- UN International Youth Day

Birthdays
1881 Cecil B. DeMille*

Handy Considerations

Honor left-handed people today.

- Find out about organizations for left-handed people.
- Get the autographs of 25 left-handed people today.
- Create a list of 20 or more famous people who are/were left-handed.
- If you are right-handed, try using your left hand as your dominant hand all day today. (If you are left-handed, use your right hand.)
- If you are right-handed, write a letter with your left hand. Draw a picture with your left hand also. (If you are left-handed, do these with your right hand.)

August 13th

- International Left-Hander's Day*
- Berlin Wall Built *(1960)*
- Eyeglasses Invented *(1287)*
- Greyhound Bus Introduced *(1914)*
- First Roller Derby *(1935)*
- First Taxicab Introduced *(1907)*

Birthdays
1899   Alfred Hitchcock
1860   Annie Oakley
1927   Fidel Castro

- Congress Created the Oregon Territory *(1848)**
- National Creamsicle Day
- Senior Citizens Day
- WWII Ended *(Japan Surrender, VJ Day, 1945)*
- Wiffle Ball Patented *(1953)*

Oregon, or bust!

On the Oregon Trail

The Oregon Trail played a major role in the development of the young United States of America. It is a colorful part of U.S. history.

Find out exactly what and where the Oregon Trail is.
Draw the route of the Oregon Trail on a map.
Answer these questions:

- What was the use of the Oregon Trail?
- What was the importance of the trail?
- During what years was the trail used?
- About how many people made the trip on the trail?
- Where did the travelers end up settling?
- Who created the Oregon Trail?
- Where did travelers begin the journey?
- What were the dangers of the trail?
- How many people died on the journey?
- How is the Oregon Trail celebrated in recent history?

- National Failures Day*
- National Relaxation Day
- Hello Day
- Lemon Meringue Pie Day
- Angel Food Cake Day
- Panama Canal Opened *(1914)*
- *The Wizard of Oz* Premiered *(1939)*
- Woodstock Rock Concert Held *(1969)*

Birthdays
1769   Napoleon

It's true! Napoleon was a failure at Waterloo.

Famous Failures

Everybody experiences failure. It is a part of learning and growing. National Failures Day is a good day to remember people whose failures contributed to accomplishments in their lives.
Here are a few of the famous folks who experienced failure or were told they were failures. Find out something about the accomplishments of each one. Find other "famous failures."

- *Walt Disney was fired by a newspaper editor who thought he had "no good ideas."*
- *Ludwig Beethoven's music teacher said that he was hopeless as a composer.*
- *Albert Einstein was encouraged to drop out of high school by a teacher who told him, "You'll never amount to anything."*
- *Thomas Edison was once told by a teacher that he was too stupid to learn anything.*
- *Winston Churchill failed sixth grade.*
- *Fred Waring was once rejected from a high school choral group.*
- *Isaac Newton was a poor student in elementary school.*
- *Michael Jordan was cut from his high school basketball team.*
- *Henry Ford was a poor student in high school.*
- *Giacomo Puccini was informed by a music teacher that he had no musical talent.*
- *Charles Darwin was called a disgrace by his father.*
- *Pablo Picasso dropped out of school at age ten because he could hardly read or write.*
- *Enrico Caruso's music teacher told him he had no voice and couldn't sing.*
- *Steven Spielberg dropped out of high school.*
- *Elvis Presley was fired by the Grand Ole Opry and told he would never go anywhere.*
- *Eugene O'Neill dropped out of college after only nine months.*
- *F. Scott Fitzgerald flunked out of college.*

Versatile Vinegar

Do you know how many uses there are for vinegar? It's a useful substance for many science experiments. But that's not all. It has many health benefits and other practical uses.

Pop a Top

POP!

Get a small bottle with a push-on plastic lid.

Put 2 T baking soda in the glass.

Add $\frac{1}{3}$ C vinegar and push the top on the bottle firmly right away.

Watch what happens.

Try this again. This time, have an adult hold a lit match next to the top of the bottle.

Watch what happens.

August 16th

- Vinegar Day*
- Elvis Presley Commemoration Day
- Tell a Joke Day
- Roller Coaster Day
- Anniversary of Major League Baseball No-Hitter
- Antiseptics Discovered (Joseph Lister, 1865)

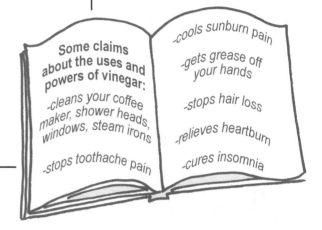

Some claims about the uses and powers of vinegar:
-cleans your coffee maker, shower heads, windows, steam irons
-stops toothache pain
-cools sunburn pain
-gets grease off your hands
-stops hair loss
-relieves heartburn
-cures insomnia

A Pencil Bouquet

Turn a handful of pencils into a handy bouquet. The "vase" will be adorned with pencils, and the "flowers" will actually be pencils. Keep the flower arrangement on your desk or near the telephone so you'll always have a pencil when you need one.

August 17th

- Pencil Day*
- Airmail Balloon Day
- Archaeology Day
- Buttered Popcorn Day
- First Steamboat Trip (1807)

Birthdays
1786   Davy Crockett

Use 10–12 pencils to make flowers. Trim the stems of artificial flowers to about one inch. Use floral tape to tightly wrap a flower to the eraser end of a pencil. Continue to wrap the whole pencil in tape, leaving one to two inches at the pencil's point end unwrapped.

Use thick layers of white glue to attach new pencils (eraser end up) to a metal can. Make sure all pencils are firmly stuck in the glue. Tie string around them until the glue dries.

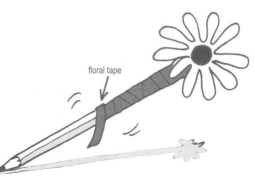

floral tape

August 18th

- Bad Poetry Day*
- Women's Voting Rights Day*
- First Mail-Order Catalog Published *(1872)*
- 19th Amendment to the *U.S. Constitution* Ratified

Birthdays

1774   Meriwether Lewis

Bad Poetry

Find bad poetry, write bad poetry, and enjoy bad poetry today. What is bad poetry? You decide! Get together with your friends and make a list of criteria for bad poetry. Then have a bad poetry contest or a bad poetry reading party. Think of some appropriate prizes for the worst poems.

Bluejays sing and robins chirp. Did you hear that birdie burp?

First Prize for the Worst-Smelling Poem

Dirty Gym Socks

Heart Linked

She smiled at me. I blinked.
My cheeks got red. They pinked.
She walked away. My heart sinked.
"She loves me not," I thinked.

Row, row, row your boat
Gently down the stream
Don't you fool around,
or rock the boat
Or you'll really be sorry.

August 19th

- Potato Day*
- *Sputnik 5* Carried First Living Organisms That Returned from Space *(1960)*
- National Aviation Day
- First Saturday Morning Television Shows for Children Aired *(1950)*
- Indianapolis 500 Speedway Constructed *(1909)*

Birthdays

1871   Orville Wright
1902   Ogden Nash
1946   William Jefferson Clinton, 42nd U.S. President

A Curious Potato Trick

Raw potatoes are tough-skinned and hard as rocks, but you can use your strength and an ordinary straw to penetrate that tough exterior (and interior). All it takes is a little knowledge about force.

1. Get some raw baking potatoes and plastic or paper drinking straws.
2. Soak the potatoes for 5 minutes. Then wash and dry them very well.
3. Hold a straw tightly between your first finger and thumb at a right angle to the potato. Hold a potato in the other hand.
4. Jab the straw hard into the potato. Make sure you jab at a right angle. It should go right through the potato. (You might need to practice this a few times.)

Ouch!

How Does It Work?

When a force is applied along the entire length of the straw, the straw has amazing strength. All the force of your push is concentrated on the small circle at the end of the straw. With so much force at that one spot, the straw is able to pierce the hard potato.

Cool-Sicles

Cool off on a hot August day with one of these frozen delights. Prepare any of these mixtures or invent your own. Pour the mixture into small paper cups or ice cube trays. Freeze until slushy, then insert plastic spoons or Popsicle sticks for handles. Freeze until firm.

Purple Applesicles

Mix 2 C applesauce with 1 C purple grape juice.

Pudding Sicles

Thin your favorite pudding with a little milk. Then freeze it.

Spicy Sicles

Mix 1 C yogurt with 1 t nutmeg, 1 t cinnamon, and 1 T honey.

Banana Cream Pops

Mix mashed ripe bananas with cream or half-and-half.

O-J-Yo-Sicles

Mix 1 C yogurt, 1 small can frozen OJ, and 1 t vanilla.

Tutti-Fruitti-Sicles

Mix 2 C of any kind of fruit (no seeds) with 1 C any kind of juice in a blender.

August 20th

- Summer Cool-off Day*
- Lemonade Invented *(1630)*
- National Radio Day

Birthdays
1833   Benjamin Harrison, 23rd President

Homemade Lemonade

Stir $1\frac{1}{2}$ C sugar into $\frac{1}{2}$ C boiling water. When sugar dissolves, stir in 2 t grated lemon rind, $1\frac{1}{2}$ C fresh-squeezed lemon juice, and 5 C cold water. Chill for several hours.

Easy Spumoni

Spumoni is a 3-colored, 3-flavored ice-cream dessert. Generally the flavors are cherry, chocolate, and pistachio. Try this easy recipe for spumoni. As you eat your spumoni, pay attention to the colors, flavors, texture, and other sensations. Use these spumoni experiences to help you write a poem about spumoni, in honor of Poets' Day.

August 21st

- National Spumoni Day*
- Poets' Day*

Birthdays
1959   Hawaii, 50th State

You will be making the dessert in layers, softening the ice cream enough to spread it into a mold (a metal bowl or pan), and returning each layer to the freezer to harden before spreading the next layer.

Layer # 1: Soften 1 qt vanilla ice cream. Gently fold in sliced maraschino cherries and 2 drops of red food coloring. Spread in mold. Freeze.

Layer # 2: Soften 1 qt vanilla ice cream. Stir in $\frac{1}{2}$ package pistachio pudding mix. Spread on top of first layer. Freeze.

Layer # 3: Soften 1 qt chocolate ice cream. Stir in $\frac{1}{2}$ t almond flavor. Sprinkle top with almond slices. Freeze.

To serve the dessert, invert it (turn it upside down) on a cold plate. Cover and rub the metal mold with a hot towel to loosen it from the dessert. Gently lift the mold away. Serve by cutting wedges or squares.

She'll have the rigatoni.
He'll take zabaglione.
They're having macaroni.
But please make mine spumoni!

August 22nd

- National Punctuation Day*
- Be an Angel Day
- Hoodie Hoo Day in the Southern Hemisphere
- National Tooth Fairy Day
- *Mona Lisa* Painting Stolen from *The Louvre,* Paris *(1911)*

Punctuation Personified

Make punctuation come alive today as you honor commas, colons, semicolons, hyphens, dashes, periods, question marks, exclamation points, parentheses, and quotation marks. Come up with a system of noises to represent punctuation marks—one sound for each of the marks. Then read any article, poem, paragraph, or story aloud. Make the noise for each punctuation mark every time you come to it in your reading. Your listeners will love it!

August 23rd

- National Spongecake Day*
- Eat a Peach Day
- National Gymnastics Day

Sponge Garden

A spongecake has its name because it is light and airy, like a sponge. Its fluffiness comes from beaten egg whites. Find a recipe and make a spongecake today. Enjoy it with peaches. Then continue celebrating the "sponge" theme by starting a garden in a sponge.

Soak birdseed or mustard seed overnight in a cup of water. Dampen a natural sponge and put seeds into the little holes. Keep the sponge in a dark place for a few days. Keep it damp at all times by having its edge touch a pan of water.) After the seeds sprout, hang the garden in a sunny spot. Continue to keep the sponge damp.

August 24th

- Strange Music Day*
- Mt. Vesuvius Erupted *(79 AD)*
- Waffle Iron Patented *(1869)*
- Peach Pie Day
- Washington, D.C. Burned *(1814)*

Make Strange Music

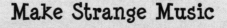

Make strange music by fashioning your own instruments. Use anything you can find that makes notes or "musical" noise. Join with friends to make a band so you can coordinate your sounds into a whole orchestra of strange music.

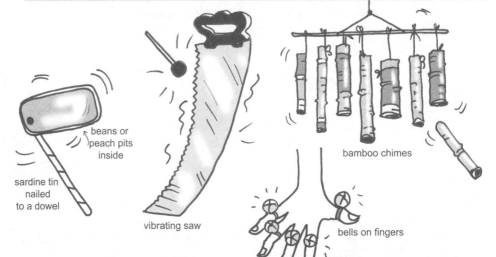

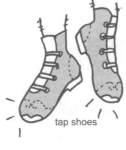

tap shoes

sardine tin nailed to a dowel

beans or peach pits inside

vibrating saw

bamboo chimes

bells on fingers

Terrific Banana Splits

Pull out all the stops and make a grand banana split. Start with a base of split bananas covered with scoops of ice cream. Add lots of toppings: syrups, marshmallows, strawberries, coconut, nuts, cherries, sprinkles, and whipped cream. Share it with several friends.

- Banana Split Day*
- National Park Service Established (1916)
- Paris Liberated in WWII (1944)

Birthdays
1918   Leonard Bernstein

Why did the banana split?

Because it was the gorilla's lunchtime!

Cylinder Scenes

The first toilet paper was produced in 14th century China for the use of the emperor. Before that, people used such things as leaves, moss, wool, sponges, or paper. The first toilet paper on a roll was sold in 1879. Toilet paper was not perforated until the end of the 19th century.

- Toilet Paper Roll Invented (1879)*
- Women's Equality Day
- National Cherry Popsicle Day
- First Baseball Games Televised (1939)
- Make Your Own Luck Day

Birthdays
1938   Paul J. Martin

Use the edge of a toilet paper roll dipped in paint as a stamp.

In 1996, the U.S. Congress tried to pass a tax of 6 cents per roll on toilet paper. President Clinton vetoed the tax.

A toilet paper roll is a cylinder. Create a whole scene with cylinders. Start with a heavy cardboard or wood base. Cut cylinders in different lengths. Use heavy glue or a glue gun to create the scene. Add paint if you wish. Use cardboard tubes, straws, small cans, or any other cylinders you find.

August 27th

- Banana Lovers Day
- Just Because Day
- Motorist Consideration Day
- Creation of *Tarzan* (1912)

Birthdays

1910 Mother Teresa*

Mother Teresa said:

> If we really want to love, we must learn how to forgive.

Wise Words

Mother Teresa was a Catholic nun who spent much of her life working with the poor in India. She was lovingly known as "the saint of the gutters." Her religious order, the Missionaries of Charity, provides food, shelter, and other basic services for sick and dying poor people. Mother Teresa received the Nobel Peace Prize in 1979. Pope John Paul II beatified her in 2003.

- Find a picture of Mother Teresa's face. Draw a charcoal sketch of her.
- Find some Mother Teresa quotations.
- Find out what "beatification" is.
- Learn about charities in your area. Find out who runs them and what kind of work they do or what services they provide.

August 28th

- National Bow Tie Day*
- First Radio Commercial Aired (1922)
- Anniversary of March on Washington (1963)
- Oil First Produced Commercially (1859)

Birthdays

1908 Lyndon B. Johnson, 36th U.S. President

Crazy Bow Ties

Who wears bow ties? Find out! Bow ties are the trademark of certain famous personalities. Some not-so-famous persons love them, too. Find at least five famous persons known for bow tie wearing. Get the autograph of five more not-famous bow tie wearers.

Design a crazy bow tie. Get together with some friends and hold a contest. Award prizes for the wackiest, most creative, craziest, and so on . . .

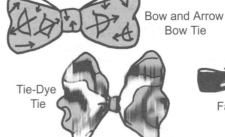

Bow and Arrow Bow Tie

Tie-Dye Tie

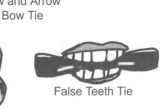

False Teeth Tie

August 29th

- First Motorcycle Patented (1885)*
- More Herbs, Less Salt Day
- Chop Suey Invented (1896)

> On my ride from Fairbanks, Alaska, to Anamosa, Iowa, I stopped at a restaurant to get an order of Chop Suey with more herbs and less salt.

Motorcycle Mania

The U.S. National Motorcycle Museum & Hall of Fame is located in Anamosa, Iowa. Find out what motorcycle memorabilia is in the museum. Then plan a road trip (by motorcycle, of course) to get there. Your trip may start from any place on the North American (or South American) continent. Write clear directions (including route numbers) that someone could follow to ride a motorcycle to Anamosa. Avoid using Interstate highways for the trip. Draw a map and "plot" the course of the trip, or get a real map and outline the trip on the map.

Homemade Marshmallows

You can celebrate National Toasted Marshmallow Day by finding an open fire and toasting marshmallows. If you don't have an open fire handy, celebrate the day by making your own marshmallows. They're good just as they are—no toasting needed!

1. Empty a large package of flavored gelatin into a large bowl. (Use any flavor you like!) Stir in $1\frac{1}{2}$ C boiling water and $\frac{1}{2}$ C light corn syrup. Stir well.

2. Refrigerate the mixture until it begins to thicken.

3. Whip the mixture with a beater until it is fluffy.

4. Pour the mixture into a baking pan and let it set until it is firm.

5. Cut it into small cubes. Roll each cube in sugar.

August 30th

- National Toasted Marshmallow Day*
- Hotline Established Between U.S. and USSR *(1963)*

Moving Pictures

Edison's invention of the kinetoscope paved the way for moving pictures. It was a machine for producing animated pictures with film carrying several views of a scene. In each successive view, the scene has changed a little. Because of *persistence of vision*, an observer's eyes hold onto each image for a split second so that when the next image (with a slight change) is shown, the scene appears to be one continuous motion. This concept can be simply demonstrated with a flip book. Make one to experiment with persistence of vision and the idea of moving pictures.

August 31st

- Thomas Edison Patented the Kinetoscope *(1891)**
- Princess Diana Memorial Day
- Trail Mix Day

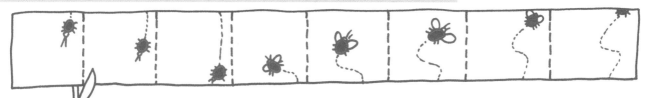

Create a flip book by dividing strips of paper into 3-inch (7.5-cm) squares. Draw a simple object and change the scene slightly in each square. Make between 15 and 20 squares for a really good action flip. Cut the squares apart and staple them together in a book.

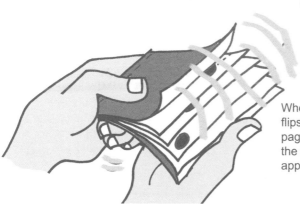

When someone flips through the pages quickly, the images will appear to move.

September

1
- *Mary Had a Little Lamb* Published*
- Pink Cadillac Day*
- American Chess Day
- World War II Began
  Birthdays: Alberta, Saskatchewan

2
- U.S. Treasury Department Established*
- President Teddy Roosevelt's "Big Stick" Speech
- Pierce Your Ears Day
- V-J Day (1945)
- London's Great Fire
  Birthdays: Christa McAuliffe

3
- U.S. Bowling League Day*
- Skyscraper Day
- Legend of Uncle Sam Created
- First Kodak Camera Patented
- *Treaty of Paris* Ends Revolutionary War

4
- Newspaper Carrier Day*
- Eat an Extra Dessert Day
- Los Angeles, CA Founded
- Introduction of Peter Rabbit
- Quaker Oats Trademark Day
- Electric Lighting Power Made Available

5
- Be Late for Something Day*
- National Cheese Pizza Day
- Death of Crazy Horse
- America First Celebrated Labor Day

6
- Great Egg Toss Day*
- Labour Day (Canada)
- Pilgrims Sailed for America
- First Video Recording on Magnetic Tape
- National Iguana Awareness Day
  Birthdays: Jane Addams

7
- First Closed-Circuit Auto Race in U.S.
- Grandma Moses Day
  Birthdays: Grandma Moses

8
- International Literacy Day*
- Pardon Day
- National Date-Nut Bread Day
- Nose Hair Maintenance Day*
- TV Show *Star Trek* Premiered

9
- Wonderful Weirdos Day*
- Bonza Bottler Day
- Aunt's Day
- Teddy Bear Birthday
- Hot Dog Birthday
- Name "United States of America" Adopted
  Birthdays: California

10
- Swap Ideas Day*
- National Grandparents Day
- Sewing Machine Patented

11
- Emergency Services Day*
- Patriot Day*
- Terrorist Attacks on the World Trade Center and Pentagon*
- Make Your Bed Day
- No News Is Good News Day

12
- National Policewoman Day
- Video Games Day
- National Chocolate Milkshake Day
  Birthdays: Jesse Owens*

13
- Defy Superstitions Day*
- National Peanut Day
- Fortune Cookie Day
- Positive Thinking Day
- Middle East Peace Accord Signed (1993)

14
- Write Your Own Headlines Day*
- National Cream-Filled Donut Day
- National Pet Memorial Day
- Handel's *Messiah* Completed
- "The Star-Spangled Banner" Composed

15
- Felt Hat Day
- TV Show *The Lone Ranger* Premiered
  Birthdays: William Howard Taft, Robert McCloskey, Tomie dePaola*, Agatha Christie

16
- Collect Rocks Day*
- Mexican Independence Day
- National Student's Day
- World Peace Day
- Mayflower Day
- Wrinkled Raincoat Day
- General Motors Established

17
- National Constitution Day*
- Citizenship Day
- National Apple Dumpling Day
- George Washington Gave His Farewell Speech
- National Football League Established
- Final Draft of *U.S. Constitution* Signed

18
- National Play Dough Day*
- "Iron Horse" Transcontinental Railroad Began
- George Washington Laid the Cornerstone of Capitol Building
- *New York Times* Newspaper First Published
  Birthdays: John G. Diefenbaker

19
- National Talk Like a Pirate Day*
- POW/MIA Recognition Day
- National Butterscotch Pudding Day
- Assassination of U.S. President James A. Garfield
- First Animated Cartoon

20
• Magellan Began His Voyage
  Around the World*
• National Punch Day
• First Railroad Station Opened
• World's Largest Chicken Dance

21
• Miniature Golf Day*
• Biosphere Day
• World Gratitude Day
• Introduction of the Croissant
• Hurricane Hugo Hit East Coast of U.S.

22
• Dear Diary Day*
• Centenarians Day
• Elephant Appreciation Day
• Band-Aid Invented
• U.S. Post Office Established
• President Lincoln Issued the
  Emancipation Proclamation

23
• Time Capsule Buried
  at 1939 World's Fair*
• Planet Neptune Discovered
• Beginning of Airmail
• Checkers Day

24
• National Bluebird of Happiness Day*
• Hurricane Rita Struck U.S.
• Rabbit Day
  Birthdays: Jim Henson,
    Francis Scott Fitzgerald

25
• National Comic Book Day*
• National Fishing & Hunting Day*
• First Female U.S. Supreme Court
  Justice Sworn In
• Card Game *Uno* Debuted
  Birthdays: William Faulkner,
    Shel Silverstein

26
• Shamu the Whale Introduced*
• First Presidential Debate Aired on TV
  Birthdays: Johnny Appleseed,
    T. S. Eliot, George Gershwin

27
• Crush a Can Day*
• Answering Machine Patented*
• Birthday of Einstein's Famous Formula
• Ancestor Appreciation Day
  Birthdays: Samuel Adams

28
• Ask a Stupid Question Day*
• Family Health & Fitness Day
• First Sighting of California
  by a European

29
• Happy Goose Day*
• Blackberries Day
• U.S. Military Created

30
• Safety Pin Invented*
• Chewing Gum Day
• First Use of Ether as an Anesthetic
• Frisbee Patented
• World's First Hydroelectric Power
  Plant Opened

Month-long Celebrations

American Newspaper Month*

Baby Safety Month

Backpack Safety Month

Be Kind to Writers & Editors Month

Better Breakfast Month

Childhood Cancer Awareness Month

Children's Eye Health & Safety Month

Classical Music Month

Emergency Care Month

Fall Hat Month*

Food Allergy Awareness Month

Library Card Signup Month

National Beach Cleanup Month

National Biscuit Month*

National Chicken Month*

National Coupon Month*

National Courtesy Month

National Ethnic Foods Month*

National Grandparents Month

National Hispanic Heritage Month*

National Honey Month*

National Ice-Cream Sandwich Month

National Jazz Month

National Mushroom Month

National Pediculosis (Lice) Month*

National Piano Month

National Potato Month

National Rice Month*

National School Success Month*

National Sewing Month*

Pink Flamingo Month*

Read a New Book Month

Save the Tiger Month*

Self-Awareness Month

Self-Improvement Month

Women of Achievement Month

Weekly Celebrations

First Week: Child Accident Prevention Week*, National Crime Prevention Week

Second Week: National 5-a-Day Week*, Biscuits & Gravy Week,
    School Bus Safety Week, Substitute Teacher Appreciation Week

Third Week: National Farm Animals Awareness Week*, National School
    Internet Safety Week, Constitution Week, National Childcare Week,
    Deaf Awareness Week

Fourth Week: National Dog Week*, Fall Hat Week, Hooray for Imperfection Week

Dates That Vary: Labor Day*, Native American Day*, Fall Equinox*,
    Rosh Hashanah*, Yom Kippur*, Idaho Spud Day, Good Neighbor Day,
    International Day of Peace, Fight Procrastination Day

September's Month-long Celebrations

American Newspaper Month

Color the News

The visual patterns in newspaper columns make an interesting background for original designs. Turn a newspaper page into a unique design. Plan a design using the heavy black lines of a dark marker or crayon. Or, use bright colors against the black and white print.

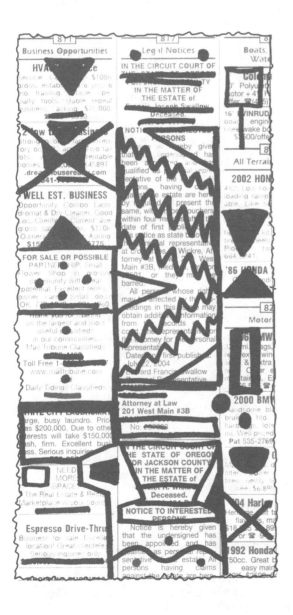

There are many things to learn from your newspaper. There are many ways to use a newspaper. Try a few of these ideas. Add some smart-newspaper-use ideas of your own.

• Ask someone to get a newspaper for you and paste white paper over the captions for all the pictures. You read the articles and write new captions for the pictures.

• Ask someone to paste white paper over the "talking" in all the comic strips. You fill in the "talk balloons."

• Find 25 words in a newspaper that you do not know. Learn their meanings or find synonyms to substitute for those words.

• Rewrite a news article as a poem, diary entry, or first-person story.

• Get an outline map of the world. Find every place in the world that is mentioned in today's paper. Locate that place on your map with a star. Label the spot with the name.

• Choose one person who is featured in a news story. Do some research on that person and write a short biography.

• Cut 50 words or phrases out of the newspaper. (Choose words in large print.) Form a statement, poem, question, or piece of advice by using some of the words. Paste the words onto a piece of drawing paper to form your new writing.

• Find a section of the newspaper that advertises groceries or other things for sale. Create ten math problems that someone could solve using that advertising section.

• Scan the paper for news about upcoming events taking place in your community. Make a list of events that someone could attend. Write the dates, times, and places.

National School Success Month

Get off to a good start with study habits at the beginning of the school year. Organize your time and your space for getting your schoolwork done. Follow these tips for school success.

Top-20 Tips for School Success

In class . . .

1. Pay attention.
2. Write down assignments.
3. Ask questions.
4. Take notes.
5. Turn in your homework on time.
6. Ask for help when you have a problem.

At home . . .

7. Gather study supplies into one place.
8. Plan your study time.
9. Find a quiet place to study.
10. Start early.
11. Do your homework.
12. Turn off the TV.
13. Stay away from the telephone and video games until homework is done.
14. Do the hardest tasks first.
15. Break long assignments into short pieces.
16. Plan ahead for long-term assignments.
17. Don't get behind on your work.
18. Don't make excuses.
19. Get enough rest.
20. Get plenty of exercise.

National Chicken Month

Honor chickens this month! Enjoy chicken stories, chicken jokes, and chicken sounds.

- Think of ten clever ways to answer the question, "Why did the chicken cross the road?"
- Create five tongue twisters with the word *chicken* and other words that have the *ch* sound.

National Rice Month & National Sewing Month

Find out how and where rice is planted, grown, harvested, and dried. Then stitch up a beanbag shape and fill it with rice. Your beanbag can be any shape you like. How about a chicken?

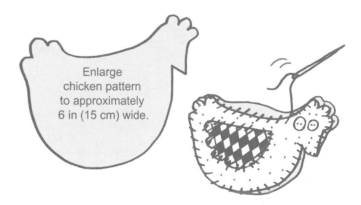

Cut two identical shapes from felt. Use a large needle and heavy thread or yarn to stitch the pieces together. Leave a small opening. Fill the bag with rice, then stitch it shut.

National Biscuit Month

Make and eat biscuits during September. Try different biscuit recipes.

Slice a fresh biscuit and eat it with your favorite "stuffing," such as:
peanut butter, berries, jam, peaches, cream cheese, cheese or meat slices, honey, scrambled eggs, or apple butter.

Easy Cheese Biscuits

1) Mix these ingredients together into a soft dough and beat for $\frac{1}{2}$ minute:

   2 C biscuit baking mix (such as Bisquick)

   $\frac{2}{3}$ C milk

   $\frac{1}{2}$ C shredded cheddar cheese

2) Drop large spoonfuls of dough onto an ungreased cookie sheet.

3) Bake until browned (8–10 min.) at 425°F.

4) Melt $\frac{1}{4}$ C butter.

5) Brush melted butter over the warm biscuits.

National Honey Month

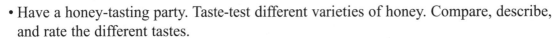

A bee flaps its wings about 300 times per second.

- Find out how bees make honey.

- If you can, pay a visit to a beekeeper who can show you up close how she/he raises bees and collects honey.

- Prepare an illustrated chart or a speech that explains how honey is made.

- Have a honey-tasting party. Taste-test different varieties of honey. Compare, describe, and rate the different tastes.

- Have fun concocting some bee jokes and riddles.

- Use the sound of bees as a starting point for learning about *onomatopoeia*.

zip   crack   whisper   crackle   BUZZ   Bonk

Onomatopoeia is a technique that makes writing interesting. An author uses words whose sounds are the same as their meaning. Bees make this sound: **buzz**. The word *buzz* sounds the same as it means! Think of other words that are onomatopoetic!

POP   ding dong   SWISH   splat   Thunk

Enjoy this poem, then try eating peas off a blunt, plastic knife with the help of some honey!

I eat my peas with honey.
I've done this all my life.
They do taste kind of funny,
But it keeps them on my knife.

Who is a bee's favorite composer?

"Bee"thoven, of course.

What do you call a bee born in May?

A maybe.

Fall Hat Month

Get hat-creative! Combine the sights, traditions, and fruits of fall with your imagination to design some great fall hats. You can make the actual hats or sketch them on paper. They can be practical or outrageous.

National Pediculosis Month

Find out what these things are, how you might catch some, what problems they cause, how to avoid catching them, and how to get rid of them. Find a reference that will show you what they look like. Draw a diagram of one, labeling its parts.

Pink Flamingo Month

Flamingos are known for their long legs, long neck, and ability to stand still for a long time on one leg. Find out everything you can about flamingos. Then try to answer the question, *"Why does a flamingo stand on one leg?"* Suggest ten different answers to the question. Then see if you can find the real answer.

I'm trying to beat a world record set by a man in India in 1995. He stood on one foot (unsupported in any way) for 71 hours and 40 minutes.

National Hispanic Heritage Month

This holiday was declared in 2003 by President George W. Bush to increase awareness, understanding, and appreciation for Hispanic culture and people, and to honor their contribution to American culture. About ten percent of all people living in America are of Hispanic origin. Many names and places in the United States are derived from Hispanic words or names.

Get a map of the U.S. and mark names of states, cities, national parks, or other places that have Hispanic names. If you don't already speak Spanish, find someone who can teach you how to say a few words and phrases. Find out how to say each of these ten words in Spanish: hello, yes, school, lunch, much, music, chocolate, laugh, dance, wonderful.

Ojos de Dios

Ojo de Dios means "eye of God" in Spanish. Mexican Indians made these for good luck. Weave one for yourself. Get two ice-cream sticks (pencils, Q-tips, or other small sticks) and some bright-colored yarn.

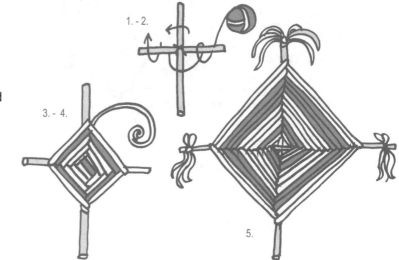

1. Cross the two sticks.

2. Tie the yarn in a knot around the two sticks where they cross.

3. Weave the yarn over one stick, then around and under, then over the stick toward the next stick.

4. Do this on each stick. Continue around the square doing the same thing for each row.

5. Change colors whenever you want. Start a new color by tying it to one of the sticks.

National Coupon Month

Coupons come in all sizes, shapes, and purposes. They can help you save money, introduce you to a new place or product, or offer you a service. Start a coupon-collecting project this month. And while you're in the coupon mood, make some of your own to give away.

• Borrow, beg, and find current magazines and newspapers. Clip out all the coupons with current dates. Organize them by kind and give them to someone who can use them (such as a senior citizen). Before you give them away, do the math to find out how much savings is represented by the coupons.

• Make coupons that offer your own services or homemade surprises. Give a booklet for a birthday gift or for other special occasions.

Save the Tiger Month

The tiger is the largest of all the members of the cat family.

There are eight known species of tigers.

Three species are extinct and three more are seriously endangered.

- Find out where tigers live in the wild.
- Learn about the eight species. Which ones are extinct?
- Find out why tigers are extinct or endangered.
- Learn about efforts to save the remaining tigers from extinction.
- Do some research on poaching. Find out how this affects wild tigers.
- Look into these questions:

    Are zoos good places for tigers?
    How many tigers are in zoos worldwide?
    Are circuses good places for tigers?
    Are tigers dangerous to humans?
    What is a healthy tiger habitat?
    How can an individual help to save tigers?

It's a fact! It is not only the fur of a tiger that is striped. The skin is striped, too.

What do you get when you cross a snowman with a tiger?

Frostbite!

National Ethnic Foods Month

Many of the foods we eat came from other countries or cultures. "Ethnic" food is a broad category that includes any food that originated with or was created by a specific culture or nationality! Eat as many ethnic foods as you can this month. Make a point to try some new ones. Find recipes and make some ethnic food. Try some food from many ethnic backgrounds, such as these:

African	Australian	Latin American	Cuban
Mediterranean	Middle Eastern	Eastern European	Cajun
English	Caribbean	Western European	Polynesian
Irish	Asian	Indian	Italian
Jewish	North American	South American	Scandinavian

Meringue Kisses

Enjoy this French-inspired dessert:

1. Beat 4 egg whites until stiff.
2. Gradually add 1 C powdered sugar. Beat until peaks hold their shape.
3. Fold in $\frac{1}{4}$ C more powdered sugar.
4. Add $\frac{1}{2}$ t vanilla.
5. Drop spoonfuls onto a cookie sheet covered with parchment paper, lightweight brown paper, or typing paper.
6. Bake at 275°F for 30 minutes until the meringues are dry. Let them cool uncovered.
7. Top the cooled meringues with ice cream or fruit.

See page 209 for other month-long holidays to celebrate in September.

Special Weeks in September

Child Accident Prevention Week

Each year, thousands of children die or are seriously injured in accidents. Most of these could be prevented.

• Find statistics about the numbers and causes of accidental deaths and injuries in your country or state.

• Make an *"Accident Prevention Checklist"* for your home. Do a tour of your home to find and fix hazards. Share your checklist and advice with your family.

• Design and make a poster that would help prevent one kind of accident for children.

Hey kids! Try to be careful skateboarding, too!

Find out about these:
drowning
fires
scalds and burns
auto accidents
bicycle accidents
falls
poisoning
electrocution
accidents with guns
suffocation
sports accidents
playground accidents
choking

Second Week

National 5-a-Day Week

This is a national program sponsored by several organizations, including the National Cancer Institute. The goal of the holiday is to encourage people to eat five to nine servings a day of vegetables and fruits for better health. The program encourages a colorful diet. Eat fruits and vegetables in the red, green, white, yellow/orange, and blue/purple categories. Find out what benefits you can gain from each different color of fruit or vegetable.

Find the names of 33 fruits and vegetables in this word search puzzle. Circle each word with its correct color. (Use red, green, white or gray, orange, and purple crayons or markers.)

B	D	A	P	P	L	E	P	U	R	P	L	E	C	A	B	B	A	G	E
L	R	V	R	E	L	E	K	C	H	E	R	R	Y	K	A	L	E	B
U	A	A	L	T	T	U	R	N	I	P	E	A	R	D	L	N	D	O	G
E	N	C	I	F	I	G	M	P	U	M	P	K	I	N	I	A	E	T	C
B	G	A	B	R	O	C	C	O	L	I	K	I	W	I	M	N	P	O	M
E	E	D	A	T	E	C	H	A	R	D	G	R	A	P	E	A	P	M	A
R	Z	O	N	I	O	N	C	O	R	N	G	R	E	E	N	B	E	A	N
R	A	I	S	I	N	X	A	W	K	R	A	D	I	S	H	A	R	T	G
Y	A	M	S	P	I	N	A	C	H	E	G	G	P	L	A	N	T	O	O
L	E	M	O	N	P	E	A	C	H	C	U	C	U	M	B	E	R	B	O

National Farm Animals Awareness Week

Create a list of all the farm animals you can name. Read about farms to identify the animals that are raised on farms. Choose one farm animal name. Turn it around and write it backward to create the name of a "beast." Write a short poem about the backward beast. Then use cut or torn shapes from colored paper, wrapping paper, or wallpaper to create the beast. Add features and decorations with fabric, sequins, glitter, pipe cleaners, feathers, or other "stuff" you find. On the back side of the "beast" picture, draw a picture of the farm animal.

BACKWARD BEASTS

The TELGIP is a terrible beast,
With razor teeth—nineteen at least!
Surprise! She's really very sweet:
A piglet small with muddy feet!

The RETSOOR will make you quake with fear,
Three horns up front, six in the rear.
But turn him frontwards, girls and boys.
He's just a rooster, making noise!

Fourth Week

National Dog Week

Celebrate Dog Week by giving good care to any dog you know. Learn how to draw a fun cartoon dog. Add some wise saying that could come from a dog.

Hot dog!

See page 209 for other weeklong holidays to celebrate in September.

The Days of September

Labor Day *(1st Monday after 1st Sunday)*

Labor Day is a day to honor workers. For many workers, this is a holiday—an additional day of rest during the workweek. Here's the actual scientific definition of work: *the transfer of energy as a result of motion.* The amount of work done depends on the weight of something moved and the distance it is moved. Work is measured in units called Joules. You can calculate work with the following formula:

It takes a force of **15 newtons** for a gorilla to push a box a distance of **1.5 meters**. Figure out how much work is done.

Work (W) = force (F) times distance (d)

15 N X 1.5m = 22.5 J (joules)

Native American Day *(4th Friday)*

This holiday is to honor and celebrate the first Americans in what is now the United States. Before any Europeans arrived, Native Americans populated all parts of the North American continent.

Wampum Beads

Wampum beads are small, short tubular beads made of seashells that were highly valued by many Native American tribes. They were strung onto strings and woven into belts. These beads had great symbolic meanings, were used to keep records of important events, and were believed by some to have mystical powers. Try making these simple paper replicas of wampum beads.

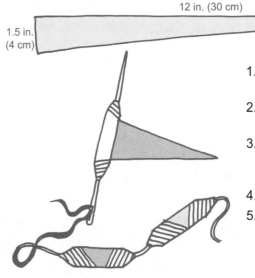

12 in. (30 cm)

1.5 in. (4 cm)

1. Cut long thin triangles from magazine pages.
2. Thread a necklace-length piece of yarn on a large needle.
3. Wrap a triangle around the needle, starting with the wide end.
4. Put glue on the pointed end.
5. Brush the beads on your finished necklace with clear nail polish.

Fall Equinox *(about the 22nd or 23rd)*

On the fall equinox or autumnal equinox (in the Northern Hemisphere), the sun crosses the equator moving south. As a result, day and night are nearly the same lengths. This day is the spring or vernal equinox in the Southern Hemisphere.

Quick Whistle

After the fall equinox, the days will be getting shorter. Enjoy this longer day by getting outside with your quick homemade whistle.

1. Cut a long, thin strip of paper. Fold it in half.
2. Cut a small hole in the folded edge of the strip.
3. Fold the bottom edges of the strip up.
4. Decorate the whistle.
5. GO OUTSIDE! Move away from any other people. Hold the ends of the whistle loosely between two fingers. Blow hard into the folded paper. The air will make the paper vibrate and cause a screeching whistle.

Applesauce Kugel

1. Cook 1 lb wide egg noodles until nearly tender. Drain.
2. Mix these things together: 4 beaten eggs, 2 T sugar, 2 C applesauce, $\frac{1}{2}$ C raisins, $\frac{1}{2}$ C melted margarine, and $\frac{1}{2}$ C melted butter.
3. Add to cooked noodles and pour the mixture into a greased baking dish.
4. Sprinkle some sugar and cinnamon on top.
5. Bake for about 1 hour at 350°F, until brown on top.

Rosh Hashanah and Yom Kippur *(mid-September)*

These are the Jewish High Holy Days, observed over a 10-day period. These days are celebrated during the first ten days of Tishri, the seventh month of the Jewish calendar. They are the most important of all Jewish holidays.

Rosh Hashanah, the Jewish New Year, is celebrated for the first two days with celebrations, family gatherings, and special meals. It is the custom to eat sweet foods, usually foods that contain honey, carrots, or apples. The sweet foods are a symbol of good fortune for the new year.

Yom Kippur is the Day of Atonement. It falls on the 10th day. It is a day of quiet fasting. The belief is that all who have repented of their sins in the days before Yom Kippur will be granted a good New Year.

• Find and read the fuller story of each of these holidays.

• Find out why the Shofar is such an important part of Rosh Hashanah.

• Challah is a traditional bread used for the Rosh Hashanah feast. If you are willing to spend some time baking, find a recipe and make some challah in the shape used for this feast.

• Try this easy recipe for traditional sweet food served at Rosh Hashana. Kugel is actually a pudding made with potatoes or noodles.

See page 209 for other dates that vary in September.

- *Mary Had a Little Lamb* Published *(1830)**
- Pink Cadillac Day*
- American Chess Day
- Beginning of World War II *(1939)*

Birthdays
1905   Alberta
1905   Saskatchewan

New Rhymes, Old Pattern

The popular nursery rhyme *Mary Had a Little Lamb* was first published as a poem by Sarah Hale. It was based on an actual incident in which a girl named Mary took a pet lamb to school.

This poem has a rhyme pattern that is similar to many nursery rhymes. It can be labeled **a, b, a, b**. The first and third lines rhyme. The second and fourth lines rhyme.

Create other poems that have this pattern. OR, start with the first line of two of well-known nursery rhymes. Finish them with two new lines that follow the correct pattern.

On this day in history, someone bought a pink Cadillac for his mother. Find out who and when.

Row, row, row your boat
Gently down the stream...
_____
_____

Jack be nimble.
Jack be quick.
_____
_____

Itsy bitsy spider
Went up a water spout.
_____
_____

- U.S. Treasury Department Established *(1789)**
- U.S. President Teddy Roosevelt Gave his *"Speak Softly and Carry a Big Stick"* Speech *(1901)**
- Pierce Your Ears Day
- V-J Day *(1945)*
- London's Great Fire *(1616)*

Birthdays
1948   Christa McAuliffe

One More Idea

- Find out what President Roosevelt meant when he said, "Speak softly and carry a big stick."

Money Talk

Find out what the U.S. Treasury is all about. Visit the website at www.ustreas.gov or www.ustreas.gov/kids. Use the site or other resources to find the answers to these money questions:

1. *Where are U.S. coins made?*
2. *Where are U.S. dollars made?*
3. *Could you find a foreign phrase on a U.S. dollar bill?*
4. *Where could you get a U.S. Savings Bond?*
5. *How is a money order like a dollar bill?*
6. *Does the U.S. Treasury Department store gold?*
7. *Can you spend money that is out of circulation?*
8. *Could someone mint a $100 bill?*
9. *Where would you get a U.S. $500 bill?*
10. *Could you keep a bond in an envelope?*

There are 293 ways to make change from a dollar. Can you find them all?

100 pennies... 95 pennies and one nickel... 90 pennies and one dime...

For each starred* holiday on pages 220–233, you will find at least one activity.

Leagues Everywhere You Look

There are literally thousands of *leagues* in the world (besides bowling leagues). Spend some time today getting to know more about leagues.

- Find all the meanings of the word *league*.
- Explain the size of a *league* (unit of measurement) and what it measures.
- Find a summary of the book *20,000 Leagues Under the Sea*.
- Look for leagues in your neighborhood or town. Make a list of 25 local leagues and tell what they do. Investigate one of them in detail.
- Find out something about these leagues and others that are interesting to you:
  - **League of Nations**
  - **the Ivy League**
  - **Math League**
  - **National League of Cities**
  - **American Classical League**
  - **Fitness League**
  - **League of Herpetologists**
  - **National Puzzlers League**

I'm a member of the Leapin' Lizards Bowling League and the League of Herpetologists!

September 3rd

- U.S. Bowling League Day*
- Skyscraper Day
- Legend of Uncle Sam Created *(1766)*
- First Kodak Camera Patented *(1888)*
- *Treaty of Paris* Marked the End of the Revolutionary War *(1783)*

A member of a bowling league might be interested to know that a bowling pin needs to tilt only 7.5 degrees to fall.

Tube Creatures

Many newspaper carriers roll up the papers to toss onto doorsteps or stuff into mailboxes. Put your imagination to work turning some rolled-up newspaper into creative creatures and characters.

1. Tape rolls together to make base shapes.
2. Dip newspaper strips into creamy wheat paste or wallpaper paste.
3. Cover the base with overlapping strips.
4. Use two or three layers. Let each layer dry before applying the next.
5. Paint or decorate your creature or character when it is thoroughly dry.

September 4th

- Newspaper Carrier Day*
- Eat an Extra Dessert Day
- Los Angeles, CA Founded *(1781)*
- Introduction of Peter Rabbit *(1893)*
- Quaker Oats Trademark Day *(1877)*
- Power for Electric Lighting Available to Customers *(1882)*

One More Idea

- Find out about the job of delivering newspapers in your area. What is required? How is the carrier paid? What is the pay? What are the hours? Who gets the jobs? How many carriers are there?

221

September 5th

- Be Late for Something Day*
- National Cheese Pizza Day
- Death of Crazy Horse, American Indian Leader *(1877)*
- America First Celebrated Labor Day *(1882)*

Late Again

Who hasn't been late to something? What happens when you're late? Use your imagination to finish this sentence 25 times.
(Finish the sentence differently each time, please.)

She (or he) was so late that.....

September 6th

- Great Egg Toss Day*
- Labour Day (Canada)
- Pilgrims Sailed for America *(1620)*
- First Video Recording on Magnetic Tape *(1958)*
- National Iguana Awareness Day

Birthdays
1860   Jane Addams

Choose Messy or Clean

There are many ways to toss eggs. Some of them can be downright messy and gooey. Choose whatever method you wish, but DO toss eggs today! Stock up on eggs for any of these ventures.

1. Form two teams. Line up half of each team facing the other half with a distance of several feet between. Toss raw eggs to other members of your team. Catch them carefully. The team that can toss two dozen eggs with the fewest broken ones is the winner.

2. Find a way to toss an egg safely. Design different containers that will protect the raw egg when you toss it. Take your eggs in their containers outdoors and toss them a long distance. See which containers work to keep the eggs from breaking.

September 7th

- First Closed-Circuit Auto race in U.S. *(1896)*
- Grandma Moses Day

Birthdays
1860   Grandma Moses

As the 7th son of a 7th son, I love doing math with 7s.

The Amazing Number Seven

The seventh is a good day to watch the powers of seven.
Try these two great math tricks with the number seven.

Pick any number.
Double it.
Add 5.
Add 12 to the total.
Subtract 3.
Divide that by 2.
Subtract the original number.
You will always get 7!

Start with 777.
Multiply by 11.
Multiply by 91.
What do you get?

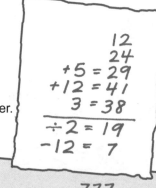

```
        12
        24
   +5 = 29
  +12 = 41
    3 = 38
   ÷2 = 19
  -12 =  7

         777
  x11 = 8547
  x91 = 777,777
```

Love to Read

Literacy is the ability to use language to read, write, listen, and speak. Celebrate this literacy day by reading as much as you can! Get a good book, read it, and share it.

- *Read a book and write a response to the author.*
- *Read a book and write 20 questions that someone else could answer if they read the same book.*
- *Read the ingredients on all the cans in your kitchen cupboard.*
- *Read a recipe to a friend while he or she follows the directions.*
- *Read some poems to an elderly person.*
- *Read a picture book to a younger child.*
- *Read aloud all the signs you see on your way to and from school.*
- *Read all the ads in a magazine. Circle the words they use to try to convince you to buy something.*
- *Read all the titles and headlines in today's newspaper.*
- *Read some jokes to your mom, dad, or other family member.*
- *Read your favorite ad in the yellow pages of the phone book.*
- *Write a letter to yourself and read it aloud to yourself.*

A day with a book is a good day.

September 8th

- International Literacy Day*
- Pardon Day
- National Date-Nut Bread Day
- Nose Hair Maintenance Day
- TV Show *Star Trek* Premiered *(1966)*

One More Idea

- Think of a clever way to maintain nose hair! Write a "Nose Hair Maintenance" brochure, or design an implement for nose hair grooming.

Wonderful Weirdos

Often the word *weird* has a negative meaning. Use this holiday as an opportunity to see the good, the creative, the clever, the interesting, and the wonderful in weird. Design weird characters, houses, cars, clothing, neighborhoods, schools, or anything else you can make weird. Be sure to give your creation a wonderfully weird name. Write about whatever characteristics of the creation that cannot be seen in the design.

September 9th

- Wonderful Weirdos Day*
- Bonza Bottler Day
- Aunts' Day
- Teddy Bear Birthday *(1902)*
- Hot Dog Birthday *(1884)*
- Name "United States of America" Adopted *(1776)*

Birthdays

1850   California, 31st State

Hi, I'm Hot Dog Hannah, your weird, but wonderful friend. It's my birthday today.

steelwool hair

wax lips

paper towel roll

wire arms

cardboard hands

cardboard teddy bear car

Weird Bear-mobile

jar caps for wheels

Make your design from cut-up magazines, paper, wire, cardboard tubes, paper plates and cups, straws, foil, or any other materials you wish.

September 10th

- Swap Ideas Day*
- National Grandparents Day
- Sewing Machine Patented (1846)

Idea-Swap Party

Invite some friends or classmates to bring their bright ideas to an *Idea Swap*. At the party, swap ideas and watch others make, try, or finish the bright idea. Ask kids to write an idea of any kind and bring it to the party. If the idea needs "ingredients," ask them to bring those along.

Suggest that they bring a favorite idea for . . .

something to make
something to cook
something to do
something to try
a great first line for a poem
a great last line for a story
a great opening verse for a song

September 11th

- Emergency Services Day*
- Patriot Day*
- Terrorist Attacks on the World Trade Center and Pentagon (2001)*
- Make Your Bed Day
- No News Is Good News Day

One More Idea

- Find out why this day is called Patriot Day. Make a flier that tells or shows what you believe it means to be a patriot.

Emergency!

Many of us don't think about the emergency care workers in our communities until an accident or disaster strikes. Then we are so glad these people have chosen to do the jobs and volunteer work that they do. A day such as September 11, 2001, shows us how important and dedicated these people are. September is a month to honor them.

- Do some research to compile a list of all the emergency caregivers you can find. Include people and organizations that volunteer their services, as well as people who have regular jobs in the business of providing emergency care.

- Try to find and meet at least ten emergency caregivers this month. Prepare a list of questions to use in an interview with each of these workers. Find out about their work, their experiences, their feelings about their work, their difficulties, their rewards, and their risks. Make a written report of your interview.

Speedy Problems

Jesse Owens was one of the world's fastest runners. This African-American son of a sharecropper and grandson of a slave made history when he became the first American to win four gold medals in track and field during a single Olympics—the 1936 summer games in Berlin.

Solve these running problems and create ten more problems about runners.

Jesse ran the 100-meter dash in 10.3 seconds. How much distance did he cover in one second?

Jesse's time for the 200-meter dash was 20.7 seconds. How much distance did he run per second?

September 12th

- National Policewoman Day
- Video Games Day
- National Chocolate Milkshake Day

Birthdays
1913   Jesse Owens*

Defy Superstitions

If you're going to defy superstitions today, you need to understand what these two words mean: *defy* and *superstition*. Next, do some searching to gather a list of interesting superstitions. Then you can plan ways to defy some of them.

It's bad luck to put a hat on a bed.

If your left ear itches, someone is speaking ill of you.

Three butterflies together mean good luck.

A cricket in the house brings good luck.

chirp chirp

Wishes on shooting stars come true.

Step on a crack, break your mother's back.

OUCH

Breaking a mirror brings seven years of bad luck.

If your nose itches, you will soon be kissed by a fool.

September 13th

- Defy Superstitions Day*
- National Peanut Day
- Fortune Cookie Day
- Positive Thinking Day
- Middle East Peace Accord Signed *(1993)*

Eye-Catching Headlines

Headlines may be short, but that doesn't mean they're easy to write. It takes skill to get the main idea of a story into a short phrase. A headline must also grab the attention of readers. Read headlines in all the papers you can get your hands on today. Then try to write some attention-grabbing headlines for any event—past, present, or future, real or imaginary.

The Tribune---September 14, 2007
PET CAT RESCUES DROWNING ELEPHANT

Evening Gazette..Sept. 14
Mayor Eats 100 Cream-Filled Donuts for Charity

Morning News--September 14, 1814
New Song Honors U.S. Flag

September 14th

- Write Your Own Headlines Day*
- National Pet Memorial Day
- National Cream-Filled Donut Day
- *Messiah* Completed *(Handel, 1741)*
- "The Star-Spangled Banner" Composed (Francis Scott Key, 1814)

- Felt Hat Day
- TV Show *The Lone Ranger* Premiered *(1949)*

Birthdays

1857	William Howard Taft,
1914	Robert McCloskey
1934	Tomie dePaola*
1890	Agatha Christie

Friends Indeed

Tomie dePaola is a popular writer and illustrator of children's books. Some of his books are about two interesting characters: Bill, an Egyptian crocodile, and Pete, his bird friend. Pete cleans Bill's teeth and goes on adventures with him. This relationship is one that exists in real life as well as in fiction. The Egyptian plover eats leeches from between the teeth of a crocodile. The bird gets food and the crocodile gets clean teeth.

I have a very unusual dentist.

This dependent relationship that benefits both creatures is called *mutualism*. Track down and read some of Tomie dePaola's books about Bill and Pete at your library. Find other pairs of organisms that have a relationship that benefits both. Write and illustrate a dePaola-style story about two other characters.

- Collect Rocks Day*
- Mexican Independence Day
- National Student's Day
- World Peace Day
- Mayflower Day
- Wrinkled Raincoat Day
- General Motors Established *(1908)*

Rock Sculptures

Collect rocks on Collect Rocks Day. You can collect rocks to treasure, to display, to use in art projects, or just to hold. Be sure to visit your library to read the book *Everybody Needs a Rock* by Byrd Baylor. Besides convincing you that you NEED your own special rock, the author gives a set of rules for choosing your own rock. Follow her rules and choose a rock to treasure.

Make your creatures from rocks and pebbles using paint and glue.

Gather some smooth rocks and pebbles. Turn one or more of them into something unique.

- Attach rocks together with epoxy glue.
- Add color with markers or acrylic paints.
- Decorate with seeds, string, buttons, felt, foil, bottle caps, flowers, wire, and such.

You can make a whole zoo or neighborhood from rocks!

Constitution Savvy

This day celebrates the signing of the *U.S. Constitution*.
Get to know the Constitution a little better today.
Get some answers to these questions about the Constitution.

- What is the preamble to the *Constitution*?
- What does it say?
- Who signed the *Constitution*?
- How long did it take to write this document?
- In what order did the original states ratify the *Constitution*?
- Who gives the oath of office to the President?
- What is the *Bill of Rights*?
- How is the *Constitution* amended (changed)?
- What amendment has been repealed?
- How many Senators are allowed for each state?
- What are the requirements for being President?
- How long is the term of a Representative?
- Where is the *Constitution* kept today?

I have an eagle's eye for constitutional details.

September 17th

- National Constitution Day*
- Citizenship Day
- National Apple Dumpling Day
- George Washington Gave His Farewell Speech *(1796)*
- National Football League Established *(1920)*
- Final Draft of *U.S. Constitution* Signed *(1787)*

One More Idea

- Make up your own Constitution Trivia game. Scour the Constitution to find questions. Set a timer while friends use a copy of the document to find the answers.

Dough in a Hurry

In honor of National Play Dough Day, mix up this quick, versatile dough. Mold it into all kinds of creatures, "foods," and other creations.

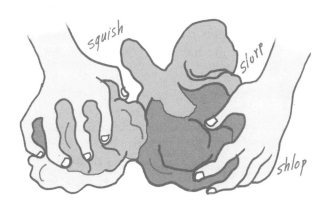

1. Mix 2 C salt, 2 C flour, 2 t cream of tartar, and $\frac{1}{2}$C vegetable oil with your hands. Mix it well.
2. Gradually add enough water to make a dough that is not too stiff and not too sticky.
3. Work in a few drops of food coloring to color the dough.

September 18th

- National Play Dough Day*
- Iron Horse Transcontinental Railroad Began *(1830)*
- George Washington Laid the Cornerstone of Capitol Building *(1793)*
- *New York Times* Newspaper First Published *(1851)*

Birthdays
1895   John G. Diefenbaker

- International Talk Like a Pirate Day*
- POW/MIA Recognition Day
- National Butterscotch Pudding Day
- Assassination of U.S. President James A. Garfield (1881)
- First Animated Cartoon Produced by Walt Disney ("Steamboat Willy," 1928)

Spotlight on Pirates

Ahoy, me hearties! Start yer celebrations of this holiday with a visit to www.talklikeapirate.com. Find out how this day got started and how its popularity has spread. Visit the pirate glossary and learn how to talk like a pirate. Then fill your day with other pirate activities.

- *Choose a pirate name for yourself and dress up like a pirate today.*
- *Design your own pirate flag. Make a spyglass.*
- *Learn the difference between these: fore and aft; starboard and port.*
- *Get a plain white (or black) T-shirt and add your own pirate design with markers or fabric paint.*
- *Get together with some "mateys" and write letters in pirate talk. Trade letters and try translating them into English.*
- *Make some pirate puppets. Put on a pirate puppet show.*
- *Create a name and routine for a pirate comedian, OR create a name and write a song for a pirate band, OR create a name and a poem for a pirate poet.*
- *Read about the history of pirates.*
- *Enjoy a good pirate story in a book or movie. Visit your library or local movie store to find these.*
- *Write a story about pirates that do good things (instead of bad things) on the high seas.*
- *Be sure to visit this cool pirate website for kids from National Geographic: www.nationalgeographic.com/pirates.*
- *Create a pirate puzzle or play some online pirate games.*
- *Bury or hide a "treasure" somewhere. Make a map so someone can find it.*

YO, HO, HO!

Arrrgh!

AVAST, YE SCURVY DOGS.

SHIVER ME TIMBERS, A CHEST FULL OF DOUBLOONS!

Ahoy, me Hearties!

Ahoy, ye landlubbers! Belay eyeing me booty or ye'll walk the plank into the briny deep.

Find out how to make a pirate's telescope on the Internet by typing-

KIDS CRAFTS - TELESCOPE SPYGLASS

Let's be clear about one thing: Pirates were not nice guys! History shows them to be thieves and murderers. These pirate activities are purely for fun. We certainly don't want to suggest any approval of real pirates or their activities.

Getting Around the World

Ferdinand Magellan, a sailor, had a dream to sail around the world. His ship and crew accomplished that goal but, sadly, Magellan did not finish the voyage. Read the story of Magellan's trip. Find out what happened to him. Find out when his travels ended. Get an outline of a world map and draw a path that traces the route of Magellan's voyage.

September 20th

- Magellan Began His Voyage Around the World *(1593)**
- National Punch Day
- First Railroad Station Opened
- World's Largest Chicken Dance

Map another trip around the world. Draw an around-the-world route that would take a traveler to the listed destinations. Name the mode of transportation you would take to complete the different legs of the trip.

Osaka, Japan
Papua New Guinea
Somalia
Uruguay
Medan, Sumatra
Sicily
Helsinki, Finland
Reykjavik, Iceland
El Paso, TX, USA
Madagascar
South China Sea

Havana, Cuba
Yukon Territory, Canada
Cape Horn, South America
The Suez Canal
Lake Victoria, Africa
Kano, Nigeria
Quatar
Tasmania
Fiji
Bering Strait
Northern Ireland

Golf in Your Own Backyard

Turn your backyard, schoolyard, or any other open space (even indoors) into a miniature golf course. Learn the rules for miniature golf. Find out details, such as how many holes there are. Plan a theme for your course. Set up obstacles. Decide on the difficulty (par) for each hole. Get some golf balls or other balls. Figure out what to use for clubs. Invite your friends, and enjoy a game of golf.

September 21st

- Miniature Golf Day*
- Biosphere Day
- World Gratitude Day
- Introduction of the Croissant *(1529)*
- Hurricane Hugo Hit Eastern Coast of U.S. *(1989)*

A miniature golf game was first patented in 1927. It was called "Tom Thumb golf."

The first golf balls were sacks of leather stuffed with feathers.

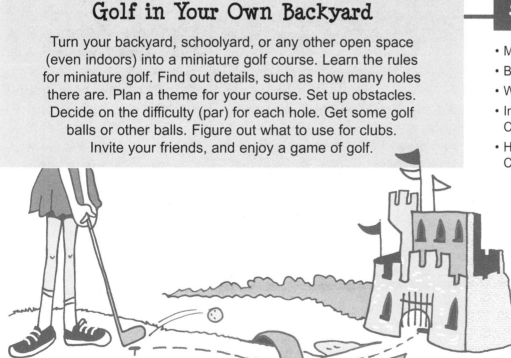

September 22nd

- Dear Diary Day*
- Centenarians Day
- Elephant Appreciation Day
- Band-Aid Invented *(1921)*
- U.S. Post Office Established *(1789)*
- President Lincoln Issued the *Emancipation Proclamation (1862)*

A Good Day for a Diary

A diary is a place to write your private thoughts, experiences, ideas, or memories. If you are not a diary keeper, this is a good day to begin a serious diary for yourself. The process of keeping a diary is a good one. It encourages you to express your most creative thoughts and deepest feelings.

Create an unusual diary today by taking the viewpoint of another character. Make a short diary. Write several entries as they might be written by one of these:

- a centenarian
- an elephant
- a band-aid
- an ice-cream cone
- a mail carrier
- Abraham Lincoln
- a recently emancipated slave

September 23rd

- Time Capsule Buried at the World's Fair *(1939)*
- Planet Neptune Discovered *(1846)*
- Beginning of Airmail *(1911)*
- Checkers Day

Time Capsules

The time capsule buried at the 1939 New York World's Fair held items representative of the society at that time. It was intended that the capsule be opened in 5,000 years by a future civilization.

Another time capsule was buried in 1964. Find out what was in this capsule. What do you think should be put in a time capsule today? Make a list.

Make your own personal time capsule. Get a secure container. Fill it with items and writings that tell about who you are today and what is important to you. Find a place to store it for opening in 5, 10, 20, or more years.

Contents of the 1939 Time Capsule

alarm clock
can opener
eyeglasses
fountain pen
electric lamp
miniature camera
nail file
safety pin
slide rule
toothbrush
watch
baseball
deck of cards
cigarettes
Mickey Mouse cup
Sears Roebuck catalog
dollar bill
seeds
Holy Bible

Curious Phrases

The phrase *bluebird of happiness* has been around for a long time. Where did it begin? Why is a bluebird associated with happiness? There are many curious phrases that have developed in our language. See if you can learn something about the meaning and the origin of each of these phrases.

* barking up the wrong tree * *bring home the bacon*

* putting on the dog * *sold down the river* * **a baker's dozen**

* *a red-letter day* * **let's talk turkey** * *let the cat out of the bag*

* make no bones about it * *bluebird of happiness*

- National Bluebird of Happiness Day*
- Rabbit Day
- Hurricane Rita Struck U.S. Gulf Coast (2005)

Birthdays
1836   Jim Henson
1896   F. Scott Fitzgerald

Sporting Laughs

Fishing and hunting have long been the source for good jokes and comedy. Combine the celebration of comic books with the celebration of fishing and hunting. Do a quick review of some comic books to see how they are written. Then make a short comic book with a fishing or a hunting theme.

Bill and Bob Go Fishin'   by Fisher McFly

- National Comic Book Day*
- National Fishing & Hunting Day*
- First Woman Sworn in as U.S. Supreme Court Justice (*Sandra Day O'Connor, 1981*)
- Card Game *Uno* Debuted (*1971*)

Birthdays
1897   William Faulkner
1932   Shel Silverstein

September 26th

- Shamu the Whale Introduced (1985)*
- First Presidential Debate Aired on TV (Nixon–Kennedy, 1960)

Birthdays
- 1774 Johnny Appleseed (John Chapman)
- 1888 T. S. Eliot
- 1898 George Gershwin

Did you get the letter
my goat wrote?
Don't go out after dark
with a shark.
Would you get in a canoe
with a gnu?

Mail a Whale?

Make a whale of a rhyme (or two or more) today. Create a hilarious picture book for younger children. Make each page a wacky rhyme, starting with one about a whale. Add a fun illustration to each page. Gather some young children around and read your book to them.

Where would you mail a whale?

Should we teach the snake to rake?

September 27th

- Crush a Can Day*
- Answering Machine Patented (1950)*
- Birthday of Einstein's Formula $E = mc^2$
- Ancestor Appreciation Day

Birthdays
- 1722 Samuel Adams

One More Idea

- Offer your services as a provider of answering machine messages. Make a list of 25 different businesses or professions. Devise a unique telephone answering machine message for each one. Record these messages with music or sound effects.

The Astonishing Power of Air

Air can crush a can or bottle without any force or pressure from you! Try this experiment and find out how.

1. Get a gallon-sized metal can with a screw-on lid.
2. Boil water in a teakettle.
3. Carefully pour $\frac{1}{2}$ C boiling water into the can until steam rises out of the top.
4. Immediately screw on the top tightly.
5. Watch the can carefully. It will collapse.

What's Happening?

The heat from the water causes air in the can to expand. When the air cools, it contracts. Now the air pressure inside the can is less than the pressure outside the can. So, the greater air pressure crushes the can.

232

Stupid Questions

September 28th

This is the day to ask all the questions you thought were too stupid to ask. Actually, no question is too stupid. Ponder your questions. Write them down. Try to find a person who can answer one or more of your questions. You might have to choose a different person for each one.

- Ask a Stupid Question Day*
- Family Health & Fitness Day
- First Sighting of California by a European *(Juan Rodriguez Cabrillo of Portugal, 1542)*

Can an oyster sneeze?

Is an acute angle the opposite of an ugly angle?

Why don't freckles line up in rows?

Hooray for Double Os

September 29th

The word goose has **OO** in it. Many other words have the same attribute. Make a list of double **O** words. Create a clue for each word, and give the list of clues to a friend as a **Double O Puzzle**. Or, make an illustrated dictionary of **Double O** words.

- Happy Goose Day*
- Blackberries Day
- U.S. Military Created by Congress *(1789)*

1. You don't want this outcome on your next yacht trip!

2. You can get a cold drink from this.

3. A thick, slimy liquid does this.

4. This always comes back to you.

5. Extraordinary silliness!

1. *marooned*
2. *cooler*
3. *oozes*
4. *boomerang*
5. *foolishness*

Safety Pin Jewelry

September 30th

Find out just how versatile safety pins can be. Use safety pins and plastic pony beads to make necklaces, bracelets, or belts.

- Safety Pin Invented *(1849)**
- Chewing Gum Day
- First Use of Ether as an Anesthetic *(1846)*
- World's First Hydroelectric Power Plant Opened *(1882)*
- Frisbee Patented

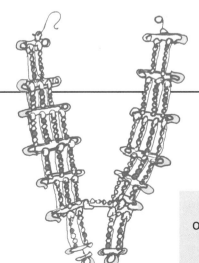

Put plastic beads on the vertical pins. Fasten these pins to horizontal "anchor" pins.

233

October

1
- Homemade Cookies Day*
- First World Series Baseball Game
- Yosemite National Park Established
- Disney World Opened
- CD Player Debuted
- Model T Introduced by Henry Ford
  Birthdays: James Earl Carter

2
- First *Peanuts* Comic Strip Published*
- Name Your Car Day
- World Farm Animal Day
  Birthdays: Nat Turner,
       Mahatma Gandhi, Groucho Marx

3
- Techies Day*
- Virus Appreciation Day
- German Reunification Day
- First *Captain Kangaroo* TV Show

4
- National Taco Day*
- Pumpkin Day
- 10-4 Day
- National Golf Day
- Toot Your Flute Day
- International Frugal Fun Day
- *Sputnik* First Launched

5
- World Smile Day*
- Do Something Nice Day
- First Presidential TV Broadcast
  from the White House
  Birthdays: Chester A. Arthur

6
- First Known Train Robbery
  in the U.S. *
- National German-American Day*
- Child Health Day

7
- National Frappé Day*
- Rose Designated U.S. National Flower*
- National Denim Day

8
- American Tag Day*
- The Great Chicago Fire
- National Fire Prevention Day
  Birthdays: Jesse Jackson

9
- First Two-Way Telephone
  Conversation*
- Leif Erickson Day*
- World Post Day
- Moldy Cheese Day
  Birthdays: John Lennon

10
- Bonza Bottler Day*
- World Mental Health Day
- Billiard Ball Patented
- First Tuxedos Worn
- "Pledge of Allegiance" Written

11
- Wild Turkey Calling Day*
- Bring Your Teddy Bear to School Day
- National Sausage Pizza Day
  Birthdays: Eleanor Roosevelt

12
- Day of Six Billion*
- International Moment of Frustration
  Scream Day
- World Egg Day
- National Gumbo Day
- National School Celebration
- Columbus Day

13
- Cornerstone of the White House Laid*
- First Aerial Photograph Taken*
- National Bring Your Teddy Bear to
  Work Day
- U.S. Navy Established

14
- National Dessert Day
- Sound Barrier Broken
- Martin Luther King, Jr. Awarded
  Nobel Peace Prize
- Elie Wiesel Awarded Nobel Peace Prize
  Birthdays: Dwight D. Eisenhower,
       William Penn, Grace Drayton*

15
- National Grouch Day*
- National Poetry Day*
- First Human Flight
- *I Love Lucy* TV Show Premiere

16
- Dictionary Day*
- National Boss Day
- World Food Day
  Birthdays: Noah Webster

17
- Gaudy Day*
- Black Poetry Day*
- International Day for the Eradication
  of Poverty*
- San Francisco Earthquake

18
- Boost Your Brain Day*
- No Beard Day
- Alaska Day
  Birthdays: Puerto Rico as U.S. Colony,
       Pierre Trudeau

19
- National Forest Products Day
- Evaluate Your Life Day
- "Star-Spangled Banner" First
  Performed*

20
- End of Hurricane Season
- National Fruit Day
- Louisiana Purchase Treaty Ratified
  Birthdays: John Dewey*,
       Mickey Mantle*

21
- National Babbling Day*
- Launch of the *USS Constitution*
- National Reptile Day
- Edison Lamp Day

For each starred holiday, you will find one or more activities on pages 236–243.*

22
- First Parachute Jump*
- National Color Day*
- National Nut Day
- Anniversary of Cuban Missile Crisis
  Birthdays: N. C. Wyeth*

23
- Swallows Leave San Juan Capistrano*
- Canned Food Day
- Terrorist Attack in Beirut, Lebanon
- First Plastic Surgery Operation Performed
  Birthdays: Pele

24
- First Person to Survive a Ride over Niagara Falls in a Barrel*
- United Nations Day
- National Bologna Day
- George Washington Bridge Opened
- United Nations Established

25
- National Sourest Day*
- Punk for a Day Day
- World Pasta Day
- St. Crispin's Day
  Birthdays: Pablo Picasso*

26
- National Mule Day*
- Erie Canal Opened*
- Diwali (Hindu Festival of Lights)
  Birthdays: Steven Kellogg

27
- *Walt Disney* TV Show Premiered*
- Make a Difference Day
- Navy Day
- New York City Subway Opened
  Birthdays: Theodore Roosevelt

28
- Statue of Liberty Dedicated*
- Plush Animal Lover's Day
- St. Jude's Day
- Harvard University Founded
  Birthdays: Jonas Salk

29
- International Internet Day*
- Oldest Human Flew in Space
- U.S. Stock Market Crash

30
- Haunted Refrigerator Night*
- National Candy Corn Day
- Time Clock Patented
- Michael Jordan Returned to the NBA
  Birthdays: John Adams

31
- Halloween*
- Carve a Pumpkin Day*
- National Knock-Knock Day*
- Paper Punch Patented*
- National UNICEF Day
- Mt. Rushmore Completed
- Martin Luther Posted *95 Theses*
  Birthdays: Nevada, Juliette Lowe

Month-long Celebrations

Adopt a Dog Month

Car Care Month

Child Health Month

Computer Learning Month

Consumer Information Month

Country Music Month

Dinosaur Month

Diversity Awareness Month

Do-It-Yourself Month*

Energy Awareness Month

Family Health Month

Family History Month*

Fire Prevention Month

Go Nuts Over Texas Peanuts Month

Hunger Awareness Month

Kids Love a Mystery Month*

National Apple Month*

National Caramel Month*

National Clock Month*

National Cookie Month*

National Crime Prevention Month

National Dental Hygiene Month

National Dessert Month

National Fantasy Month*

National Go on a Field Trip Month

National Literacy Month*

National Pasta Month*

National Pickled Pepper Month

National Pizza Month*

National Pork Month

National Popcorn-Popping Month

National Pretzel Month

National Roller-Skating Month

National Sarcastic Month

National Seafood Month*

National Stamp-Collecting Month

National Vegetarian Month*

Polish American Heritage Month

Scouting Month

World Chocolate Awareness Month*

Youth Against Tobacco Month

UNICEF Month

Weekly Celebrations

First Week: National Pickled Pepper Week*, Fire Prevention Week, Get Organized Week, No Salt Week, Universal Children's Week, National Newspaper Week, World Space Week

Second Week: National Metric Week*, National 4-H Week, National School Lunch Week, National Chili Week, National Wildlife Week, Fire Prevention Week, National Pet Peeve Week

Third Week: National Chemistry Week*, Wolf Awareness Week, National Character Counts Week, Whale-Watching Week

Fourth Week: World Rainforest Week*; National Peace, Friendship, and Goodwill Week

Dates That Vary: Sweetest Day*, Daylight Saving Time Ends*, Canadian Thanksgiving*, Ramadan*, Supreme Court Convenes*, National Children's Day*, World Habitat Day, Sukkot

October's Month-long Celebrations

National Clock Month

Celebrate! Take a whole month to think about **time** and all the tools you use to measure **time**!

• Keep a clock journal. Carry around a pad of paper all month. Draw a picture of every time-keeping device you see. At the end of the month, prepare a great illustration or photograph of the most interesting clock (or other timekeeper) that you found.

• Figure out how many hours, minutes, and seconds there are in the month of October.

• Collect at least 25 different expressions or jokes related to time.

Family History Month

The U.S. Congress has designated October as Family History Month in the U.S. This is a month for people to learn about, appreciate, and celebrate their family histories. Over 80 million people are already searching for their genealogies—mostly thanks to the Internet. Learn something new about your family history this month.

Family Bio-Cube

Find a sturdy box and use it to show and keep some family history treasures.

Glue on the outside:
  • a family tree
  • pictures of family members
  • a family name anagram
  • design using letters of the family name
  • original news headlines about important events in the family history
  • drawing of a family crest
  • a family poem
  • words and phrases describing your family
  • an ode to your family's past
  • an anecdote about some family event

Tuck away inside:
  • interviews of various relatives
  • short biographies of family members
  • family mementos and treasures
  • a book of family recipes

National Pasta Month

Get to know your pastas this month! Do some research to find out about the shape of each of these different kinds of pasta. Make a Pasta Directory. Paste an example of each pasta (or draw a picture) and write a brief description.

fettuccine	capellini	rotini	linguine
macaroni	manicotti	fusilli	ruote
lasagna	spaghetti	penne	orzo
vermicelli	farfalle	ziti	rigatoni

Kids Love a Mystery Month

Kids all over the world have fallen in love with mystery stories. Each year during October, thousands of them take part in a program sponsored by the Mystery Writers of America and the Library of Congress. The program includes all kinds of activities designed to inspire kids and adults to join in a nationwide celebration of the writing and reading of mysteries. Join the celebration by reading several mysteries this month . . . and by writing at least one mystery story of your own to share. Use a character kit to create the face of two or more "suspects" in a mystery. Then write the story using these characters as a part of the mystery. Refer to the characteristics of the suspects, perhaps as a part of eyewitness descriptions.

Character Kits

noses	eyes	mouths	hair	other
				scar
				freckles
				beauty mark
				tattoo

Draw Your Own Suspects

#1

#2

National Seafood Month

Seafood Month provides a great excuse to enjoy the luscious tastes of many kinds of seafood. But there's more to seafood than the delicious tastes. Dozens of scientific studies have found health benefits from seafood. Find at least FIVE good reasons to eat seafood.

Jumbo Shrimp
is an oxymoron (a combination of two words that seem to contradict each other).

Did someone just call me a moron?

Keep a list of good oxymorons. These will get you started:

good grief	small crowd	ill health
old news	act naturally	silent scream
black light	alone together	fresh frozen
bittersweet	modern history	pretty ugly
seriously funny	exact estimate	original copy

Do-It-Yourself Month

This is a month to be on the lookout for things you can do yourself. Think about things you do or use that ordinarily would be bought, provided, or created by someone else.

Make a list of some things you could do yourself this month. Then choose at least one a week and DO it!

My Do-It-Yourself List

Make my own breakfast.

Do my own laundry.

Plan a week's menus (and shopping list) for my family.

Make my own stationery and envelopes from old magazines.

Find a recipe and make soda pop.

Buy a plain T-shirt and decorate it with fabric paints.

I'm making my own boomerang.

National Apple Month and National Caramel Month

Don't let this month go by without combining these two great flavors—apple and caramel.

Easy Caramel Apples

1. Clean six apples. Place a stick in the center of each apple.

2. Place about 20 caramels (unwrapped) in a glass baking dish. Add 2 T milk.

3. Warm the caramels for about two minutes in a microwave oven. Stir the mixture until it is smooth.

4. Quickly dip each apple in the melted caramel.

5. Roll the caramel apple in one of these crushed treats: nuts, peppermints, coconut, or chocolate chips.

6. Set the apple on waxed paper to cool.

National Pizza Month

- Celebrate this holiday by trying some unusual pizzas this month.

- Make your own list of all the possible pizza toppings you can imagine.

- Figure out the number of different three-topping pizzas you could make with these choices:

artichokes	tuna fish
apples	meatballs
walnuts	coconut
snails	radishes
peppers	yams

Vegetarian Pizza? YES!

National Vegetarian Month

- Interview one or more vegetarians to find out why they have chosen this manner of eating.

- Create a day's menu of meals for a vegetarian.

- Find out how a vegan is different from a vegetarian.

National Literacy Month

Literacy refers to the ability to read and write. The goal of this holiday is to spread literacy to everyone in the world.

- Find the literacy rates in your country and five other countries.

- Improve your own literacy by reading a new book this month.

- Write a "How-to" book for younger kids on something YOU know how to do. Use clear language and illustrate the book to make it appealing to younger readers. Share the book with some younger readers.

World Chocolate Awareness Month
National Cookie Month

Celebrate both of these holidays by making and enjoying these no-bake cookies.

Chocolate Peanut Butter No-bake Cookie Balls

$\frac{1}{4}$ C chocolate chips	$\frac{1}{4}$ C peanut butter
$\frac{3}{4}$ C all-bran cereal	$\frac{3}{4}$ C oatmeal

Put chocolate chips and peanut butter in a glass bowl and microwave for about 45 seconds until the peanut butter is melted. Stir to blend. Carefully stir in oatmeal and all-bran. Wet your hands and form small balls. Place on a pan and refrigerate for several hours.

National Fantasy Month

A dictionary definition of fantasy is: *a creation of the imagination*. Enjoy reading and writing fantasies this month. Start right now. Write a fantasy to match this picture.

Special Weeks in October

First Week

National Pickled Pepper Week

Pickled peppers are the subject of the most famous tongue twister. It begins . . . *Peter Piper picked a peck of pickled peppers.* If you don't know the whole tongue twister, look it up and try to say it very fast. Try to master each of these. Then write some tongue twisters of your own.

What noise annoys an oyster? Thieves seize skis.

INCHWORMS ITCHING

Please pay promptly. three free throws The sheik's sixth sheep's sick.

KNAPSACK STRAPS truly rural PALE AILING ALLIGATORS

Second Week

National Metric Week

This week falls during the tenth month and in the week containing the tenth day. It is a week to appreciate a system of measurement based on ten. It is also a week to sharpen your skills with the metric system. Review metric units of measurement for weight, distance, and capacity. Make this metric wheel and use it to measure distances wherever you go. Keep a record of the distances you measure.

1. Make four copies of this pattern.

2. Cut out four quarter-circles and paste them on cardboard to form a wheel. Trim the cardboard to match the circle.

3. Decorate the wheel.

4. Use a ruler to draw an arrow from the center to one edge.

5. Starting at the arrow, label the centimeter marks 1 to 100 cm.

6. Tap a nail loosely through the center of the wheel into the yardstick or meter stick. The wheel should turn easily.

7. Optional: Place a paper clip at the tip of the arrow. As you roll, every bump of the paper clip represents 100 cm (1 m).

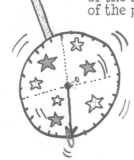

National Chemistry Week

Celebrate this holiday with some good chemistry experiments. Start with these, and then find some other experiments to try. Follow the directions. Then explain the results. (You might have to do some research or interview some other people in order to find your explanation.)

The Baffling, Bending Bone

Astonish your friends. Bend a bone right before their eyes!

1. Get a chicken bone, such as the large bone in a chicken wing. Clean it well. Place it in a wide-mouth glass jar.
2. Pour in enough vinegar to completely cover the bone (about one cup). Stir in six tablespoons of salt.
3. Cover the jar. Let the bone soak for three days.
   Presto! The bone will bend!

The Captivating, Changing Liquid

Show your magic powers! Change colored liquid while your amazed friends watch.

1. Set up the trick before the audience arrives. Make liquid by stirring 3 drops of red food coloring into a glass that is $\frac{3}{4}$ full of water.
2. Put 1 T bleach into the second glass. It will look as if the glass is empty.
3. When your audience arrives, tell them you will change the liquid just by pouring it into another glass.
4. Pour the liquid into the "empty" glass. Say some magic words. In a few minutes, the liquid will become clear instead of colored.

Do not drink the liquid!

World Rainforest Week

Each October, the Rainforest Action Network asks everyone to focus on the world's rainforests. The goal is to build awareness of the beauty and benefits of rainforests and of the threats to the rainforests. During this week . . .

- Do some research to locate the rainforests of the world. Mark them on a world map.

- Find out why rainforests are important to the Earth's health.

- Make a list of resources, plants, and animals that can be found in rainforests.

- Learn all you can about what is being done to preserve rainforests.

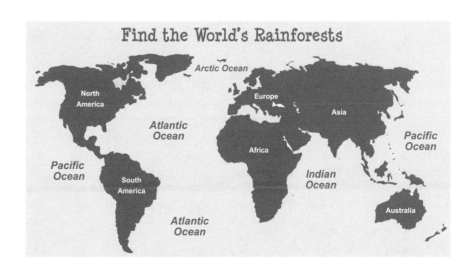

Find the World's Rainforests

See page 235 for other weeklong holidays to celebrate in October.

The Days of October

Sweetest Day *(third Saturday)*

Herbert Birch Kingston worked at a candy company in Cleveland in 1922 when he came up with the idea for this holiday. Herbert was concerned about "forgotten" people such as poor people, orphans, and elderly or sick people in their homes or hospitals. His idea was to set aside a special day to distribute gifts and candy to brighten their spirits. Over the years, more and more people across the country have taken up the Sweetest Day tradition. It has become a day to express appreciation and "sweet" wishes to friends, acquaintances, public servants, and people in need. Make a plan to observe Sweetest Day this year.

Here are a few ideas:

- Take candy or small gifts to someone who would not be able to buy them.
- List the ten sweetest things you have ever eaten.
- List the ten sweetest things anyone has ever said to you or done for you.
- List the ten sweetest experiences you have ever had.
- Write a sweet note to someone, expressing your appreciation.

Daylight Saving Time Ends for Some Countries *(last Sunday)*

Do some research about the origins and reasons for Daylight Saving Time. Be sure you can answer these questions:

"Fall back" in Fall by turning the clock back an hour.

"Spring forward" in Spring by pushing the clock time forward an hour.

DST Quiz

1. Exactly when does Daylight Saving Time begin?
2. Exactly when does Daylight Saving Time end?
3. What are some benefits of DST?
4. When did the U.S. formally adopt DST?
5. How many countries in the world utilize DST?
6. How should your clock be changed when DST ends?
7. What countries do not observe DST?

Supreme Court Convenes *(first Monday)*

Learn more about the U.S. Supreme Court today. Find out . . .

- the names of all current Supreme Court Justices
- how a Supreme Court Justice gets the job
- how long a Justice serves on the Supreme Court
- the subjects of three cases that are scheduled to come before the Supreme Court during this term

Canadian Thanksgiving *(second Monday)*

In 1957, Canada's Parliament set this day as a day for thanksgiving for Canada's "bountiful harvest." For many years, the red maple leaf has been the most recognized symbol for Canada. In 1965, the red maple leaf flag was chosen as the National Flag of Canada. Use the maple leaf or other leaves you find to decorate a tablecloth, table runner, place mats, or banners for your Canadian Thanksgiving celebration.

Splattered-Leaf Decorations

1. Find copper, gold, or silver-colored spray paint or other metallic paint to brush on.
2. Cover your work area with plenty of newspaper.
3. Arrange real leaves or cut-out leaf shapes in patterns over paper (for place mats, tablecloths, or banners).
4. Spray or brush paint around the edges of the leaves. (Or dip a toothbrush in paint and brush it across a piece of screen to splatter paint onto the pattern.)
5. Leave the leaves in place for a few minutes until the paint dries.
6. Remove the leaves to show leaf patterns with paint-splattered edges.

National Children's Day *(second Sunday)*

When President Clinton released a proclamation in 1997 designating National Children's Day, he stated, "With the birth of every child, the world becomes new again. Within each new infant lies enormous potential—potential for loving, for learning, and for making life better for others." National Children's Day is a reminder to encourage all children to make use of their inborn talents. Celebrate this holiday by interviewing other kids to find out what they believe about their talents and potential.

Interview Questions

1. What is your greatest talent?
2. If you were asked to be on TV or the radio, what would you say or do?
3. What would you like everyone to know about you?
4. What would you like to do to make life better for someone else?

Ramadan

Ramadan is the ninth month of the Muslim calendar. The dates vary, with Ramadan beginning in September or October. During this month, Muslims concentrate on their faith and observe certain restrictions. Find out more about traditions of Ramadan, including the reasons for the Fast of Ramadan. Be sure to learn about these things: *the itar, the Taraweeh, the sawm, and Eid ul-Fitr.*

See page 235 for other dates that vary in October.

October 1st

- Homemade Cookies Day*
- First World Series Baseball Game *(1903)*
- Yosemite National Park Established *(1890)*
- Disney World Opened *(1971)*
- CD Player Debuted *(1982)*
- Model T Introduced *(1908)*

Birthdays

1924   James Earl Carter, 39th U.S. president

Draw a picture of the 1st Model-T.

Find out who won first World Series.

Sing all verses of "Star Spangled Banner."

Challenging Cookies

Make fortune cookies with a twist. Instead of a fortune, put a challenge task or question (related to October holidays) inside each cookie. A person must complete the challenge before eating the cookie.

Recipe

1. Write the challenges on strips of paper.
2. Beat 4 egg whites and 1 C sugar until fluffy.
3. Melt $\frac{1}{2}$ C butter and cool to lukewarm. Stir in $\frac{1}{2}$ C flour mixed with $\frac{1}{4}$ t salt, $\frac{1}{2}$ t vanilla, and 2 T water. Beat until the batter is smooth.
4. Grease a cookie sheet very well. Pour batter from a spoon to form 3-in. (8-cm) flat circles.
5. Bake at 375°F for 8 minutes.
6. While the cookies are warm, lay a "fortune" on each circle, fold the circle in half, then bend it gently in the center. If the cookies get too hard to bend, put them back in the oven for a moment.

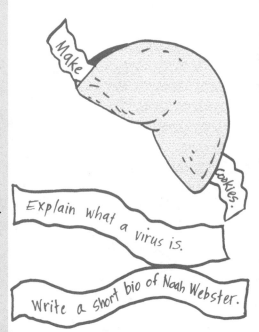

Make cookies.

Explain what a virus is.

Write a short bio of Noah Webster.

October 2nd

- First *Peanuts* Comic Strip Published *(1950)*
- Name Your Car Day
- World Farm Animal Day

Birthdays

1800   Nat Turner
1869   Mahatma Gandhi
1890   Groucho Marx

Finish the Comic Strip

Finish the second comic strip. Then create some of your own original comic strips on your favorite topics.

244

Tribute to Technology

Techies Day was started in 1999 to encourage young people to consider careers in technology. Think about your favorite technological tools. Make a list of ways YOU use technology in a week. Or, write an ode (tribute) to your favorite technological device.

To My Cellphone

Ode to a Keyboard

PRAISES TO MY DIGITAL ALARM CLOCK

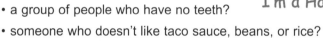

Hooray for Voice Mail!

October 3rd

- Techies Day*
- Virus Appreciation Day
- German Reunification Day *(1990)*
- First *Captain Kangaroo* TV Show *(1955)*

Tacos with Imagination

Take tacos to a new level today. Escape from the ordinary taco. "Design" just the right taco for a special occasion or special person. What would you put inside a taco made for . . .

- Sunday breakfast?
- Christmas dinner?
- a birthday party?
- a sweltering hot July day?
- a visiting king and queen?
- a St. Patrick's Day celebration?
- a mouse?
- a dessert party?
- a group of people who have no teeth?
- someone who doesn't like taco sauce, beans, or rice?

I'm a Halloween taco!

October 4th

- National Taco Day*
- Pumpkin Day
- 10-4 Day
- National Golf Day
- Toot Your Flute Day
- International Frugal Fun Day
- Launch of the First Artificial Satellite *(Sputnik, USSR, 1957)*

Catch a Smile, Cause a Smile

1. "Catch" some smiles. Cut pictures of smiles (just the mouth area) from magazines or newspapers. Glue them on a poster or large drawing paper. Write a caption for each smile, telling what you think has caused this smile. OR, write a "talk bubble," allowing the mouth to tell why she or he is smiling.

2. Do or say something several times today that will **cause** someone to smile.

I THINK MY MOUTH IS FROZEN.

I JUST HAD MY TEETH CLEANED.

IT'S SATURDAY!

October 5th

- World Smile Day*
- Do Something Nice Day
- First Presidential TV Broadcast from the White House *(1947)*

Birthdays
1830   Chester A. Arthur, 21st U.S. President

245

October 6th

- National German-American Day*
- Child Health Day
- The First Known Train Robbery in the U.S. *(1866)**

One More Idea

- Find someone who speaks German. Translate these German phrases into English or your native language:
  - *Zicklein sind wundervoll.*
  - *Nehmen Sie ein Bad.*
  - *Aufenthalt gesund.*

What's Missing?

The first recorded train robbery took place in Indiana in 1866 when bandits took two safes off a passenger train in Indiana. They got away (for a while) with $13,000. For several years, a number of train robberies followed. But railroad companies hired detectives, and most of the thieves were caught. Use your math skills to figure out which bag could hold the money stolen in the 1866 robbery. Calculate the amounts in the other bags as well.

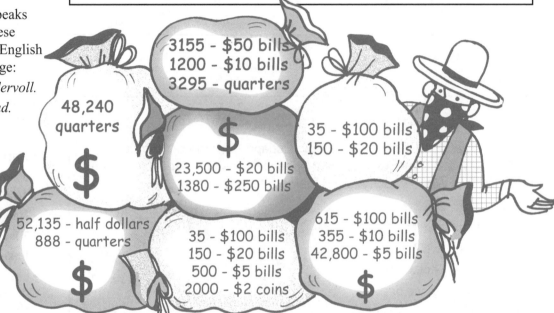

48,240 quarters $

3155 - $50 bills
1200 - $10 bills
3295 - quarters

35 - $100 bills
150 - $20 bills

23,500 - $20 bills
1380 - $250 bills

52,135 - half dollars
888 - quarters $

35 - $100 bills
150 - $20 bills
500 - $5 bills
2000 - $2 coins

615 - $100 bills
355 - $10 bills
42,800 - $5 bills $

October 7th

- National Frappé Day*
- National Denim Day
- President Reagan signed Bill Making the Rose the National Flower of the U.S. *(1986)**

I'm doing the "Frappé."

What's a Frappé?

The original Greek frappé is a cold drink made from instant coffee. In French, the word means shaken. In some places, a frappé is a smoothie or a milkshake with shaken milk and flavoring. In New England, a frappé is a milkshake made with ice cream. Whip up this frappé in your blender, or find a recipe you like better.

Mocha Frappé

Combine . . .
$\frac{1}{2}$ C strong coffee, brewed or instant
2 T sugar
3 T cocoa powder
1 C milk
1 C ice
Blend in a blender until it is smooth.

A Rose Is a Rose

The word *rose* turns up in many quotations. Find out who made these "rosy" statements. Then find other words or expressions that contain the word *rose*.

"Every rose has a thorn."

"A rose is a rose is a rose."

"LIFE IS A ROSE; BEWARE OF THE THORNS."

"LOVE IS LIKE A ROSE."

"I never promised you a rose garden."

Tag with a Twist

Find a new kind of tag to play today. Choose one of these or make up a new version. Just be sure it's a tag that's new to you.

Clothespin Tag

Each player starts with five clip clothespins on the back of the shirt. Each player tries to take as many clothespins (without pushing or pulling clothes), while keeping his or her own clothespins. Players are out of the game when all their pins are gone. Play lasts until only one person remains.

Toes & Noses Tag

At the beginning of each round, players agree on a body part that must be tagged. In the game, a player is caught ONLY if "It" tags that part (nose, toes, elbow, ear, etc).

Shadow Tag

Play in the afternoon when shadows follow players. "It" tags other players by stepping on their shadows.

Night Tag

"It" counts to 50 or 100 while players hide in the dark (at night). Then "It" uses a flashlight to "catch" others in the beam of the light.

October 8th

- American Tag Day*
- The Great Chicago Fire Began *(1851)*
- National Fire Prevention Day

Birthdays
1941   Jesse Jackson

The Other End of the Line

Give some thought today to the wonders of the telephone. "Listen" in on these one-sided conversations. Decide what was said or will be said on the other end of the line. Write the other side of each conversation.

Blah, blah, blah . . .

Caller: _____

Call Receiver: "But that's impossible!"

Caller: "I'm inside the bank and it's being robbed!"

Call Receiver: _____

Caller: _____

Call Receiver: "And how did you get into this situation, anyway?"

Yak, yak.

Caller: "Ma'am, we will be discontinuing your cellphone service right away."

Call Receiver: _____

Caller: "Sue, I need help with my homework. What is the formula for finding the volume of a cylinder?"

Call Receiver: _____

October 9th

- First Two-Way Telephone Conversation *(1876)*
- Leif Erickson Day*
- World Post Day
- Moldy Cheese Day

Birthdays
1940   John Lennon

More Ideas

- Answer these questions: Who was Leif Erickson? Why was October 9th designated as Leif Erickson Day? What U.S. city is home to a statue of Leif Erickson?
- Name three kinds of moldy cheese that are popular to eat.

247

October 10th

- Bonza Bottler Day*
- World Mental Health Day
- Billiard Ball Patented *(1865)*
- First Tuxedos Worn *(1886)*
- "Pledge of Allegiance" Written *(1892)*

I'm heavenly.

Double Numbers

A Bonza Bottler Day is a day for which the number of the month and the number of the day are the same.
(Find out what the Australian term *Bonza Bottler* means.)
Bonza Bottler Day in October is 10/10. On this day . . .

1. Calculate the years, months, and days between now and **10/10/10**.
2. Describe something you like doing well enough to repeat **10** times.
3. Tell **10** things or situations in the world that need to be improved.
4. Create **10** math problems, each having the answer **1,010**.
5. Find **10** situations in which the number **10** is important.
6. List **10** things everyone should do once in a lifetime.
7. Find and write **10** words that contain the word **ten**.
8. Tell what you would do with **10** times $10.
9. Do **10** different exercises in **10** minutes.
10. Find the value of 10^{10}.

October 11th

- Wild Turkey-Calling Day*
- Bring Your Teddy Bear to School Day
- National Sausage Pizza Day

Birthdays
1884   Eleanor Roosevelt

To Call a Turkey

When the National Wild Turkey Federation holds its annual convention, as many as 40,000 people might show up. There are plenty of turkey sounds, but no live turkeys! The **Turkey-Calling Contest** is the highlight of the convention. Callers are required to perform four different sounds in four minutes. A panel of judges picks the winners. "Why call wild turkeys?" you might ask. There are about 7,000,000 wild turkeys in North America. The calling helps to lure turkeys and transfer them to safe habitats.

Set up your own Turkey-Calling Contest today. Decide on the rules, choose some judges, and find some competitors. (Choose some good prizes for the winners—but don't serve any turkey dinners!)

GOBBLE-GOBBLE

October 12th

- Day of Six Billion*
- International Moment of Frustration Scream Day
- World Egg Day
- National Gumbo Day
- National School Celebration
- Columbus Day

Wow! Six Billion!

This day commemorates a population milestone: This is about the time in 1999 when the global population reached six billion.

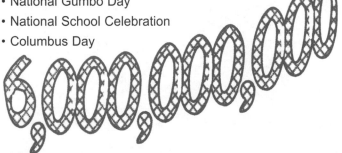

- Time yourself counting to 100. Then figure out how long it would take you to count to six billion.
- Find out how long it took for the world population to grow from three billion to six billion.
- Find out what kinds of factors and decisions affect the rate of population growth.
- Read about population projections. When might the world population reach ten billion?
- Visit www.census.gov/main/www/popclock.html to find today's world population.

248

Inside the White House

President George Washington chose the site for the White House and oversaw its construction, but he never lived in it. The second president, John Adams, and all following presidents have lived in the White House. You can learn about the White House and its history by visiting www.whitehouse.gov. Answer these White House questions:

What happens there? **How many** rooms are there? **How many** bathrooms? **How many** fireplaces? **How many** elevators? **How many** chefs? **How many** presidents have lived there? **What** is its address? **When** did it get the name *The White House*? **How much** paint does it take to repaint the outside? **What** recreational facilities are there? About **how many** visitors see it each year?

October 13th

- Cornerstone of the White House Laid *(1792)**
- First Aerial Photograph Taken *(1860)**
- National Bring Your Teddy Bear to Work Day
- U.S. Navy Established *(1775)*

One More Idea

- Draw a "snapshot" of your home property, city block, neighborhood, or school property as you believe it would look from an aerial photo.

Don't Eat the Soup!

Grace Drayton was the creator of the Campbell's Kids—characters that decorated the ads and labels for Campbell's soups. Celebrate her birthday with this soupy science experiment.

Supplies:
- a can of tomato soup
- soupspoon
- 5 small bowls
- white bread
- plastic wrap
- rubber bands
- sticker labels
- magnifying glass
- tongue depressors

1. Use stickers to label the bowls 1–5.
2. Put four spoonfuls of soup in each bowl.
3. Plant some "seeds" in each bowl:
   - Sneeze in bowl #1
   - Scrape some dirt off the floor with a tongue depressor. Shake this into bowl #2.
   - Sprinkle bread crumbs into #3.
   - Use a tongue depressor to collect some outdoor dirt for #4.
   - Scrape a wet tongue depressor across your arm and shake the skin into #5.
4. Cover each dish with plastic wrap, fastening it with a rubber band.
5. Set the dishes in a warm place. Use the magnifying glass to watch the mold spores grow. Notice the different kinds of mold shapes that grow.
6. Draw five circles, labeled 1–5. Draw what you see growing in each dish.

October 14th

- National Dessert Day
- Sound Barrier Broken *(Captain Chuck Yeager, 1947)*
- Martin Luther King, Jr. Awarded the Nobel Peace Prize *(1964)*
- Elie Wiesel Awarded the Nobel Peace Prize *(1986)*

Birthdays

- 1644   William Penn
- 1890   Dwight D. Eisenhower, 34th U.S. President
- 1877   Grace Drayton*

- National Grouch Day*
- National Poetry Day*
- First Human Flight
  (*Hot-Air Balloon, 1783*)
- *I Love Lucy* TV Show
  Premiered
  (*1951*)

Gallery of Grouches

Draw pictures to match words that name people. Use these words or find others. Choose one and write a poem about the person.

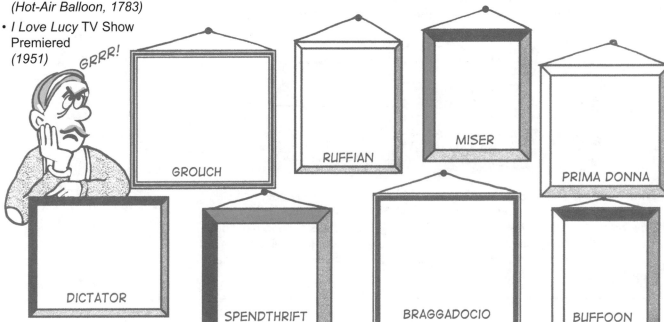

GRRR!

GROUCH

RUFFIAN

MISER

PRIMA DONNA

DICTATOR

SPENDTHRIFT

BRAGGADOCIO

BUFFOON

- Dictionary Day*
- National Boss Day
- World Food Day

Birthdays
1758 Noah Webster

Dictionary Delights

Use your dictionary to track down the meanings of any unknown words so that you can answer these delightful questions.

WOULD IT BE A GOOD IDEA TO EAT A **FRICASSEE** DURING A **FRACAS**?

WHERE WOULD YOU BE MOST LIKELY TO FIND A **SEPTUM?**

HAVE YOU EVER HAD **PECCADILLOES** ON A PIZZA?

COULD YOU TAKE A NAP IN THE MIDDLE OF A **BEDLAM?**

WHAT SUGGESTIONS WOULD YOU MAKE TO A **MOROSE** FRIEND?

WHERE WERE YOU THE LAST TIME YOU TOOK A **SOJOURN?**

WHAT IS ONE THING THAT YOU **VEHEMENTLY** OPPOSE?

CAN YOU THINK OF THREE THINGS YOU MIGHT FIND IN A **GROTTO?**

WHO WORE THE MOST **GARISH** OUTFIT YOU HAVE EVER SEEN?

WHERE WOULD YOU GO TO **PROCURE** A PIG?

HOW WOULD YOU **PLACATE** A **CANTANKEROUS** TODDLER?

WHICH WOULD YOU FIND IN A CANDY STORE: **NOUGATS** OR **ANNUITIES?**

Get Gaudy!

Find out what the word **gaudy** means. Then create the gaudiest outfit, makeup, sculpture, food item, room decoration, painting, hat, pair of shoes, book cover, or jewelry that you can imagine.

GAUDY PARADE

October 17th

- Gaudy Day*
- Black Poetry Day*
- International Day for the Eradication of Poverty*
- San Francisco Earthquake (1989)

More Ideas

- Find out why this particular day is Black Poetry Day. Then find and read five poems written by African-American poets. Start with these poets: **Langston Hughes, Maya Angelou, Gwendolyn Brooks, Countee Cullen**

- Learn what it means to be below the poverty level. Find out how many people in your city, state, and country are *impoverished*.

Boost Your Brain

Boost your brainpower with these three brain boosters. Then find other brain boosters to share with your friends.

Gretchen is moving this morning. She packs nothing, then causes a terrible traffic backup, even though she never leaves her home. Actually, she would cause a traffic jam no matter what time she would have chosen to move. Explain this!

Gretchen lives in a houseboat. To move, she must pass through a drawbridge—which backs up traffic.

Charlie has five coins totaling nine cents. One of them is not a nickel. What are the coins?

Charlie has one nickel and four pennies. One of the coins is NOT a nickel. In fact, four of the coins are not nickels—they are pennies!

What domino is missing from this group?
(Pay attention to the numerical relationships. The arrangement or order of the dominoes is not important.)

The total on each domino follows a pattern of consecutive even numbers: 0, 2, 4, 6, 8, 10. So the last domino will have 6 on top and 6 on the bottom—for a total of 12, to continue the pattern.

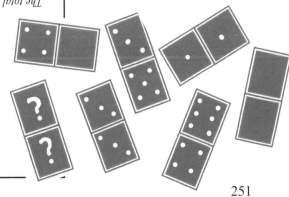

October 18th

- Boost Your Brain Day*
- No Beard Day
- Alaska Day

Birthdays
    1898   Puerto Rico Became a U.S. Colony
    1919   Pierre Trudeau

251

October 19th

- "Star-Spangled Banner" First Performed (1814)*
- National Forest Products Day
- Evaluate Your Life Day

Star-Spangled Banner Art

Use the words from the "Star Spangled Banner" to create some star-spangled art. Create a red, white, and blue design using JUST letters, words, or phrases from the U.S. national anthem. Add glitter to your design to make it sparkle.

OHSAYCANYOUSEEBYTHEDAWN'SEARLY
LIGHTWHATSOPROUDLYWEHAILEDATTHE
TWILIGHT'SLASTGLEAMING?WHOSEBRO
ADSTRIPESANDBRIGHTSTARSTHRUTHEP
ERILOUSFIGHT,O'ERTHERAMPARTSWEWATCHEDWERESO
GALLANTLYSTREAMING?ANDTHEROCKET'SREDGLARE,TH
EBOMBSBURSTINGINAIR,GAVEPROOFTHROUGHTHENIGHT

October 20th

- End of Hurricane Season
- National Fruit Day
- Louisiana Purchase Treaty Ratified *(1803)*

Birthdays
- 1859   John Dewey*
- 1931   Mickey Mantle*

Curious Conversations

Today is the birthday of two influential and interesting people in America's past. It is unlikely that the two ever had a conversation. But, if they had . . . what might John Dewey and Mickey Mantle have discussed?

Write at least two questions each man might have asked the other. Then imagine what the answers would have been. Write the conversations using correct punctuation for quotations.

October 21st

- National Babbling Day*
- National Reptile Day
- Edison Lamp Day
- Launch of the *USS Constitution* (1797)*

One More Idea
- This *USS Constitution* was built for an interesting reason. Find out what it was, what nickname it was given, and where it is now.

Babbling Is Beautiful

Collect as many words as you can that begin with **b**. Gather many different kinds of words (nouns, verbs, adjectives, adverbs, names). Then write beautiful b..b..b..b..babbling phrases and sentences.

Barbara barely bit the bacon.
BORED BOXERS BOYCOTT BUSES.
BACTERIA ON BANANAS?
baboons brandishing balloons
bearded braggarts blundering and bantering
brides' blossoming bouquets
BEFUDDLED BACHELORS WITH BAGGAGE ON BALCONIES
bees barely buzzing
buoys in Bubba's bathtub

Quick Parachute

The invention of the parachute is generally credited to Sebastian Lenornmand (1783). It is believed that Jean Pierre Blanchard was the first to use a parachute (for a dog in a basket.) On this day in 1797, Andrew Garnerin was the first person who actually jumped with a parachute that had no frame. He jumped from hot-air balloons at a height of 8,000 feet. Celebrate this event and National Color Day by creating your own bright parachute.

1. Use a colorful bandana scarf or cut an 8-inch square of bright fabric. Decorate a small paper cup with bright colors.

2. Cut four 8-inch strings. Tie a string in a knot around each corner.

3. Make a small hole in four spots around the rim of a small paper cup. Knot the loose end of a string through each one of these holes.

4. Place some sort of a weight in the paper cup. (Experiment with different kinds of weights.)

5. Stand on a chair and drop the parachute. Use a stopwatch to time its trip to the ground.

October 22nd

- First Parachute Jump *(1797)**
- National Color Day*
- National Nut Day
- Anniversary of Cuban Missile Crisis *(1962)*

Birthdays
1882   N.C. Wyeth*

One More Idea

- Investigate the illustrations of artist N.C. Wyeth. Read one of the great classic novels that include his artwork, such as *Treasure Island, Kidnapped, The Yearling, The Deerslayer*, or *The Black Arrow.*

Celebrate the Swallows

It seems like a miracle. Every year on March 19th, thousands of swallows complete a 7,500-mile trip to build their nests in the Old Mission of San Juan Capistrano, California. After spending the summer in the mission, they circle the building and fly away on October 23. Commemorate this wonderful event by creating your own flock of swallows.

October 23rd

- Swallows Leave San Juan Capistrano*
- Canned Food Day
- Terrorist Attack in Beirut, Lebanon *(1983)*
- First Plastic Surgery *(1814)*

Birthdays
1940   Pele, Brazilian Soccer Player

Paper Birds

1. Trace the bird pattern onto heavy, colored paper.

2. Cut out three or four birds.

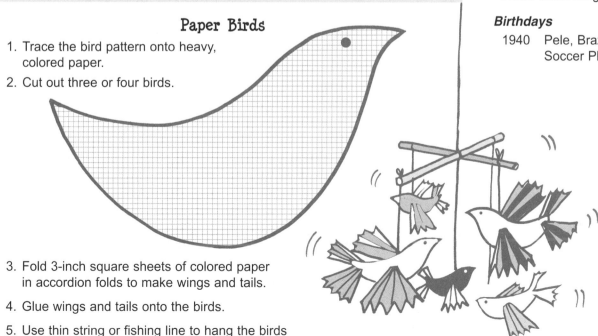

3. Fold 3-inch square sheets of colored paper in accordion folds to make wings and tails.

4. Glue wings and tails onto the birds.

5. Use thin string or fishing line to hang the birds from a clothesline or from crossed dowels.

- First Person to Survive a Ride over Niagara Falls in a Barrel *(Ana Edson Taylor, 1901)**
- United Nations Day
- National Bologna Day
- George Washington Bridge Opened *(1931)*
- The United Nations Established *(1945)*

Believe It or Not!

People have actually gone over Niagara Falls and survived! Annie Taylor was the first to take this trip. She did it at age 63—strapped in a barrel.

- Find out how many other people have survived this feat.
- Who went over the falls in a large rubber ball?
- Who is the most recent person to survive the plunge?
- How many people have **twice** survived this feat?
- Who was the only person to go over the falls (intentionally) with no protection of any kind?
- Imagine yourself going over Niagara Falls. Write a poem or monologue to describe the experience.
- Find out about people who have walked across Niagara Falls on a high wire.

- National Sourest Day*
- St. Crispin's Day
- Punk for a Day Day
- World Pasta Day

Birthdays
1881   Pablo Picasso*

One More Idea

- Think of the **sourest** things you know. Name one for every category: food . . . drink . . . person . . . comment . . . idea . . . place . . . experience . . .

Mimicking Picasso

Pablo Picasso is one of the world's most famous artists—possibly the best-known of all modern artists. He went through different periods of painting in various styles. One of these was *cubism*. Along with Braque and Gris, Picasso is credited with developing a *cubist* style. In cubist art, objects are broken up and reassembled in an abstract form. In a later period of cubism, called *synthetic cubism*, Picasso brought different objects together in colorful collage-like creations.

Try this simplified version of cubism.

1. Find several large pictures of faces.
2. Cut each picture into two-inch squares.
3. Reassemble the faces, overlapping the face parts to create a new "abstract," composite face.

Mule News

Mule Day commemorates the arrival of Spanish donkeys (Spanish Jacks) in the New World in 1785. It is fitting that October 26 is also the day the Erie Canal opened. Do some research to find out about the role of mules in the operation of the Erie Canal.

Animal Similes: Write a descriptive word or an animal name to finish each simile. Then write ten more animal similes of your own.

- as stubborn as a mule
- sneaky like a _____
- as _____ as an aardvark
- as elusive as a _____
- _____ like a scorpion
- _____ like a hippopotamus
- as mysterious as a _____
- as _____ as an anemone
- as _____ as a rat
- as tough as a _____

October 26th

- National Mule Day*
- Erie Canal Opened *(1925)**
- Diwali (Hindu Festival of Lights)

Birthdays
1941   Steven Kellogg

HAW HAW!   HEE HAW!

Do-It-Yourself Animation

Walt Disney is one of the most important figures in the history of film animation. His small company was the first to release a full-length animated musical film *(Snow White and the Seven Dwarfs, 1937)*. The animation process involves drawing a picture over and over again, with just a slight change in each new version. Watch simple animation by putting together this flip book. Then turn the book upside down and draw new pictures to make one of your own.

October 27th

- *Walt Disney* TV Show Premiered *(1954)**
- Make a Difference Day
- Navy Day
- New York City Subway Began Operation *(1904)*

Birthdays
1858   Theodore Roosevelt, 26th U.S. President

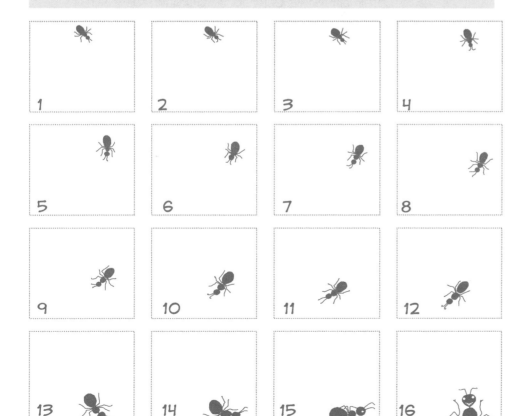

Flip Book

1. Enlarge the 16 pages of the flip book onto an $8\frac{1}{2}$ by 11-inch piece of paper.

2. Color the bug on each square.

3. Cut the squares on the dotted lines.

4. Staple the booklet together on the left side.

5. Flip the pages. Watch the bug move across the page.

6. Turn the book over. Use the blank pages to make your own flip book.

October 28th

- Statue of Liberty Dedicated (1886)*
- Plush Animal Lover's Day
- St. Jude's Day
- Harvard University Founded (1636)

Birthdays
  1814   Jonas Salk

Statue Statistics

Track down some fascinating facts about the Statue of Liberty.

Find the approximate measurements:
  1. from ground to top of torch
  2. length of hand
  3. height of head (chin to top)
  4. distance across an eye
  5. thickness of waist
  6. thickness of tablet
  7. height of pedestal
  8. length of the index finger
  9. length of nose
  10. length of right arm

Also find out . . .
  - what the rays of the crown represent
  - what the statue weighs
  - the number of windows in the crown
  - where the statue resides
  - one thing that is not allowed inside the statue

October 29th

- International Internet Day*
- Oldest Human to Fly in Space (John Glenn, 1998)
- Crash of U.S. Stock Market (1929)

Five Online

On International Internet Day, search the Web to find the answers:

1. What year did the Internet begin functioning?
2. What company first created or sold candy corn?
3. Who is St. Crispin and why is October 25 St. Crispin's Day?
4. National Denim Day is celebrated in October. Who first created denim?
5. October is UNICEF month. What is UNICEF? What is its purpose?

October 30th

- Haunted Refrigerator Night*
- National Candy Corn Day
- Time Clock Patented (1894)
- Michael Jordan Returned to the NBA

Birthdays
  1735   John Adams, 2nd U.S. President

Strange Things in the Fridge

Let those weird, strange-looking and strange-smelling things in your refrigerator be the inspiration for some Hallo-eve poems.

It's fuzzy, rubbery, slightly grey.
The hairs it's grown are wavy.
The odor takes my breath away,
I think it once was gravy.

Bologna groans
With slippery green mold
Creeping slowly,
Wrapping around
The whole sliced-meat
Family

Punch & Paste

Celebrate the paper punch!
Use it to make some interesting holiday creations.

1. Cut one 8-inch square of black paper and two 8-inch squares of yellow paper.
2. Use the paper punch to "punch" a picture in black paper.
   (SAVE all the tiny punched-out black circles.)
3. Mount the punched picture on yellow paper so that the yellow shows through.
4. Paste the tiny black circles on the other piece of yellow paper to form a mirror image of the picture punched from black.

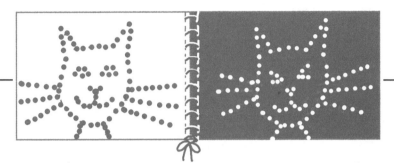

- Halloween*
- Carve a Pumpkin Day*
- National Knock-Knock Day*
- Paper Punch Patented (1893)*
- National UNICEF Day
- Mt. Rushmore Completed (1941)
- Martin Luther Posted His *95 Theses (1517)*

Birthdays
   1864   Nevada, 36th State
   1860   Juliette Lowe

Knock-Knock!

Who's there?

Wanda.

Wanda who?

Wanda go for a broomstick ride?

New Ways with Pumpkins

Try something different this year. Sculpt your pumpkin instead of carving it, or turn a stack of pumpkins into a glowing totem pole.

Sculpting takes less effort than slicing through the whole, thick pumpkin skin. Clean out the inside of the pumpkin. Then draw a pattern on the outside. Sculpt away the tough orange skin around the outside edge of the design and in all the places where you want the light to shine through. Do this with a small knife, Exacto knife, or special pumpkin-sculpting tool. Place a candle inside the pumpkin and watch the design **glow**.

Make a pumpkin totem pole. Cut a small hole in the bottom and top of each pumpkin. Thread a string of Christmas lights through 3 or more pumpkins. Stack them on top of each other and plug in the lights!

November

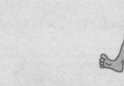

1
- Hockey Mask Invented*
- New York City Marathon
- National Author's Day
- World Community Day
- All Saints Day
- Library of Congress Opened
- Day of the Dead
- European Union Established

2
- Look for Circles Day*
- National Deviled Egg Day
- All Soul's Day
- Anniversary of Spruce Goose Flight
- First Scheduled Radio Broadcast Aired
  Birthdays: North Dakota, South Dakota,
  Daniel Boone, Marie Antoinette,
  James Polk, Warren Harding

3
- Cliché Day*
- National Sandwich Day*
- Give Someone a Dollar Today Day
- Japanese Culture Day
- Public TV Debuted
- First Dog Launched into Space
  Birthdays: John Montague,
  Earl of Sandwich*

4
- Donut Day*
- Candy Day
- First Wagon Train Reached California
- Cash Register Patented

5
- Crossword Puzzles First Published
  in America*
- National Young Readers Day*
- Guy Fawkes Day
- Iran Hostage Crisis Began
- King Tut's Tomb Discovered
  Birthdays: Walter Cronkite

6
- Basketball Day*
- Saxophone Day
- Halfway Point of Autumn
- National Nachos Day
  Birthdays: John Phillip Sousa

7
- Magazine Day
- National Bittersweet Chocolate
  with Almonds Day
- Hug-a-Bear Day
  Birthdays: Marie Curie*, Billy Graham

8
- X-Ray Discovered*
- Dunce Day*
- Cook Something Bold and
  Pungent Day*
- National Ample Time Day
- The Louvre Opened
  Birthdays: Montana, Edward Haley

9
- Go to an Art Museum Today Day*
- National Scrapple Day*
- Astronomy Day
- Parade Day
- Anniversary of Boston Fire
- Berlin Wall Demolished
- Anniversary of Krystalnacht
- Vietnam Veteran's Memorial Unveiled

10
- Telephone Area Codes Introduced*
- Forget-Me-Not Day
- Henry Stanley Found David Livingstone
- U.S. Marine Corps Day
- *Sesame Street* TV Show Premiered
  Birthdays: Martin Luther

11
- Air Day*
- Veterans Day
- Bonza Bottler Day
- Remembrance Day (Canada)
- National Vanilla Cupcake Day
- "God Bless America" First Performed
  Birthdays: Washington

12
- National Sundae Day*
- Mellow Yellow Day
- National Pizza with the Works Except
  Anchovies Day
  Birthdays: Elizabeth Cady Stanton

13
- National Indian Pudding Day
- World Kindness Day
- National Mom's and Dad's Day
- National Community Education Day
- Actor's Day
  Birthdays: Robert Louis Stevenson*

14
- Around the World
  in 72 Days Anniversary*
- Pickle Appreciation Day
- Guacamole Day
- First Streetcar Operated
  Birthdays: Claude Monet,
  Astrid Lindgren

15
- America Recycles Day*
- American Enterprise Day
- Pack Your Mom's Lunch Day
- National Clean Out Your
  Refrigerator Day
  Birthdays: Georgia O'Keeffe

16
- Button Day*
- International Day for Tolerance
- National Fast Food Day
- Animal Day
- Love a Tree Day
  Birthdays: Oklahoma

17
- National Farm Joke Day*
- World Peace Day
- Homemade Bread Day
- Take a Hike Day
- Coping with Uncertainty Day

18
- Push-Button Telephone Debuted*
- William Tell Day*
- Mother Goose Parade
- Debut of Mickey Mouse
- Introduction of the Teddy Bear
- Antarctica Discovered

19
- Have a Bad Day Day*
- Alaska Highway Opened
- Cold War Formally Ended
- Puerto Rico Discovered
- Gettysburg Address Delivered by President Abraham Lincoln
- The Mayflower Docked at Cape Cod, Massachusetts
  Birthdays: James Garfield, Indira Gandhi

20
- Absurdity Day*
- National Parental Involvement Day
- Name Your PC Day
- Universal Children's Day
- Revolution Day (Mexico)
- National Peanut Butter Fudge Day
  Birthdays: Robert F. Kennedy, Edwin P. Hubble

21
- Congress First Met in Washington, D.C.*
- World Hello Day
- The *Mayflower Compact* Signed
  Birthdays: North Carolina

22
- National Stop the Violence Day
- Go for a Ride Day
- Morse Code Signal "S.O.S." Adopted
- John F. Kennedy Assassinated
  Birthdays: Billie Jean King*

23
- National Cashew Day*
- You're Welcome Day
- First Color Photos Released
- Pencil Sharpener Invented
  Birthdays: Franklin Pierce

24
- What Do You Love About America Day*
- Comedy Hall of Fame Established
- Softball Invented
- National Espresso Day
- Lee Harvey Oswald Shot
  Birthdays: Zachary Taylor

25
- National Parfait Day*
- U.S. Department of Homeland Security Formed
  Birthdays: Andrew Carnegie, Joe DiMaggio

26
- First Lion Exhibited in U.S.*
- National Cake Day
- First Holiday Proclaimed by U.S. President
  Birthdays: Charles Schulz

27
- Pins and Needles Day*
- Freckle Pride Day*
- National Bavarian Cream Pie Day*

28
- Red Planet Day*
- National French Toast Day
- First American Automobile Race

29
- Newspaper Day*
- National Chocolates Day
- Electronic Greetings Day
- Square Dance Day
  Birthdays: Louisa May Alcott, C. S. Lewis

30
- National Mousse Day*
- Computer Security Day
  Birthdays: Mark Twain (Samuel Clemens), Sir Winston Churchill

Month-long Celebrations

Aviation History Month

British Appreciation Month

Child Safety and Protection Month

Family Stories Month*

Fun with Fondue Month

Good Nutrition Month

I Am So Thankful Month

International Creative Child and Adult Month

International Drum Month*

Latin American Month

Lung Cancer Awareness Month

National Adoption Month

National American Indian and Alaskan Native Heritage Month*

National Candy Month

National Christmas Seal Month

National Diabetes Awareness Month

National Family Literacy Month

National Georgia Pecan Month

National Healthy Skin Month*

National Ice-Skating Month

National Model Railroad Month

National Pepper Month

National Raisin Bread Month*

National Run Away Prevention Month

National Sleep Comfort Month

Peanut Butter Lover's Month*

Weekly Celebrations

First Week: National Card & Letter Writing Week*, National Cat Week*, Kids Goals Education Week, National Split Pea Soup Week, National Health Information Week, National Fig Week, World Communication Week, National Children's Book Week

Second Week: Random Acts of Kindness Week*, Youth Appreciation Week, Pursuit of Happiness Week, National Farm Week, American Education Week

Third Week: Geography Awareness Week*, National Diabetes Week, Leftover Awareness Week, National Farm-City Week

Fourth Week: National Game and Puzzle Week*, National Family Week, National Cookie Week

Dates That Vary: Thanksgiving Day*, Buy Nothing Day*, Daylight Saving Time Ends*, Election Day*, National Family Caregivers Day, National Adoption Day

November's Month-long Celebrations

National American Indian and Alaskan Native Heritage Month

The first American Indian Day was celebrated in 1916, but it wasn't until 1990 that a whole month was dedicated to the recognition of Native Americans. Today, there are over four million people of American Indian or Alaskan Native heritage. Native American cultures have a rich history in stories: legends, myths, folk tales, and other stories that are passed down from generation to generation. Much of this folklore is passed along orally. The variety of kinds of stories is wide. There are hero stories, warnings, stories about tricksters, creation or origin stories, dream stories, or stories that explain something. Spend some time this month reading many of the wonderful legends and tales that come from of the Native American cultures.

Look for some of these legends or tales:

- *"The Girl Who Climbed to the Sky"*
- *"Coyote's Salmon"*
- *"The Raccoon and the Bee-Tree"*
- *"White Buffalo Calk Pipe Woman"*
- *"How Corn Came to the Earth"*
- *"Grandmother Spider Steals the Fire"*
- *"How the Red Bird Got His Color"*
- *"Gift of the Bear"*
- *"How Coyote Stole Fire"*
- *"Corn Mother"*
- *a creation story*
- *a dreamcatcher legend*
- *a Northern Lights legend*
- *a legend of the Yellowstone Valley Great Flood*

National Healthy Skin Month

Get connected to your skin this month. Read all about skin. Learn about the purpose and function of skin. Find out about all the places in your body that have skin. Then find out what actions keep skin healthy, and make a plan to keep YOUR skin in good shape. Make a list of do's and don'ts of skin care. Share the list with at least five other people.

Family Stories Month

Collect stories in your own family. Choose at least three family members to interview this month. Ask each one to tell you a story. Record the stories, then type a transcript of each story. Add an illustration or photograph of the storyteller. Get each storyteller started by asking them to tell you a story about one of these:

- *something in your life that you will never forget*

- *the best thing that ever happened to you*

- *something you wish you could do over*

- *the most frightening thing that ever happened to you*

- *the funniest thing you ever did*

- *the worst thing that ever happened to you*

- *a person that made a huge difference in your life*

National Raisin Bread Month

Don't let November go by without baking a loaf of raisin bread. (Bake it, try it, and share it.) Try a slice with honey butter, cream cheese, or applesauce. If you're a peanut butter lover, spread peanut butter on raisin bread, too. If you don't have a favorite recipe, here's one to try:

Raisin Bread Recipe

1. Mix these well in a large bowl:

   $\frac{1}{2}$ C sugar   3 C flour

   1 t salt $\frac{1}{2}$ C baking soda

   3 t baking powder $\frac{3}{4}$ t cinnamon

   1 C raisins
2. Make a hole in the center of the above mixture.
3. Beat one egg in a smaller bowl. Mix 1 C milk and $\frac{1}{4}$ C melted butter with the egg.
4. Pour the egg mixture into the hole in the flour mixture. Stir just until the batter is moistened.
5. Pour the batter into a greased bread pan.
6. Bake for one hour at 350°F. Remove from the bread pan and cool the loaf on a rack before slicing.

Peanut Butter Lovers Month

This month . . .

Answer the question: *Is a peanut really a nut?*

Find out how much peanut butter is eaten every year in your country.

Find five other uses for peanuts or peanut shells (besides food uses).

Two U.S. presidents were peanut farmers. Find out who they were.

Make up an original (extremely creative) recipe that contains peanut butter.

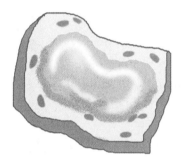

International Drum Month

The purpose of Drum Month is to promote drumming for people of all ages and backgrounds. You don't have to be a musician to drum. You don't even need a drum! There are hundreds of ways to drum using your fingers, toes, or many other things you find. Just about any surface will work for a drumming sound.

• Try to think of 100 different ways to drum. List things you could use for a "drumstick." Also, list different surfaces for drumming.

• Try out at least ten different combinations from your lists. Get together with friends to create a drum corps! Compare the different sounds of different "drumsticks" on different surfaces.

• Make a drum cake today. Stack three or four round layers of cake with frosting between the layers. Decorate the cake with bright colors. Use licorice strips or long pretzels and cherries for the drumsticks.

Everyone is a drummer.
Everyone is a drum.
Theme of the 2003 International Drum Month

See page 259 for other month-long holidays to celebrate in November.

Special Weeks in November

National Card & Letter-Writing Week

In this age of phones, cellphones, computers, e-mail, instant messaging, e-greetings, and text messaging, many people rarely write a card or letter that they actually send through the mail! Change that habit. Make a list of seven people who need to hear from you. Write a card or letter. Then turn it into a puzzle, put it in an envelope, and mail it. Your friends will have fun putting the pieces together before they read the letters.

1. Write a card or letter.
2. If you have written a letter or a card with no picture, find or draw a great picture to paste on the back of the writing.
3. Cut the card or letter into a puzzle—"jigsaw" style.

- Design and describe an ideal cat. Draw a picture of the cat.
- Find 20 words that contain the word *cat*.
- Find ten proverbs or expressions about cats.
- Find and read the poem "The Naming of Cats" by T. S. Eliot.
- Think of 20 names for a cat.
- Find out how many people in your country are cat owners.

Random Acts of Kindness Week

No act of kindness, however small, is ever wasted.
- Aesop

The Random Acts of Kindness Foundation is one of many organizations associated with the World Kindness Movement. The goal of this holiday and these organizations is to promote the spread of kindness and generosity. It is like the Pass It Forward Movement where people who are treated kindly or given a gift pass on the kindness to someone else.

Get together with some friends and make a long list of random acts of kindness that are realistic for you to do alone or together. Then, carry the list around and add more that come to mind. Keep your eyes open for chances to treat someone else with kindness or generosity. Perform at least ONE random act of kindness each day this week. Visit to see what other people are doing or to learn how to start a RAK club.

Sometimes it's smart to be aware of your surroundings.

Geography Awareness Week

U.S. President Ronald Reagan established this special week in 1987. The National Geographic Society has used this to promote the awareness of geography. As a part of this celebration, the Society sponsors a Geography Bee each year to spark interest in geography. Thousands of students in grades 4–8 participate. The national finals of the GeoBee are broadcast on TV. You can learn more about the Bee, find sample questions, and take a sample test (new every day) at www.nationalgeographic.com/geobee/.

Your Own GeoBee

Create your own GeoBee to challenge your friends or classmates. Start with these questions and create more questions like them:

1. Which city would be found at 30°N, 31°E: New Delhi, India; Sydney, Australia; Cairo, Egypt; or Brasilia, Brazil?

2. What is the term for a shallow water area enclosed within an atoll or cut off from the sea by a strip of land?

3. What time is it in Perth, Australia, when it is 9 A.M. in Montreal, Canada?

4. What countries border Cameroon?

5. To see these three sites—Great Sphinx, Stonehenge, and Chichen Itza—which continents must you visit?

National Game & Puzzle Week

Find a new game and a new puzzle for each day of this week. Visit your library for game or puzzle books, or find games and puzzles on the Internet. Mancala is a family of "count and capture" games played around the world. If you have not played a mancala game, make your own "game board" and enjoy this age-old game with friends. Use an egg carton and seeds (or beads, beans, or stones). The object of the game is to capture more "seeds" than your opponent.

Mancala Game Board

Cut an egg carton's lid in half. Tape one section to each end of the bottom of the carton. Put four seeds in each of the egg cups. Leave the two "mancala bins" empty—one for each player.

Play the Game

• Players sit on either side of the game board (the long side), "dividing" the board lengthwise.

• Take a turn by picking up all the seeds in any one of the cups on your half of the board. "Plant" them in a counterclockwise direction around the board, one in each cup. Do not drop seeds in your opponent's mancala bin, but drop one in your own if you pass it. If the last seed falls in an empty bin on your own side, you may take all the seeds from the bin across from it and put them into your bin.

• When all the seeds are gone in one player's bins, the game is over. The opponent puts any remaining seeds into his or her bin. Both players count seeds in their bins. The player with the most seeds is the winner.

See page 259 for other weeklong holidays to celebrate in November.

The Days of November

Thanksgiving Day (fourth Thursday)

Members of the Plymouth Colony celebrated the first American Thanksgiving in 1621. This day was a celebration of the harvest that followed a long, harsh winter. In 1789, U.S. President George Washington declared Thanksgiving a national holiday. In 1941, the U.S. Congress issued a resolution that set Thanksgiving on the fourth Thursday of November.

Prepare for Thanksgiving Day by giving serious thought to the things for which you can be thankful. Cut these large letters from sturdy colored paper: THANKS. On each letter, write some of the answers to one of the following questions. Suspend the letters from string to make a "thankful" mobile.

> T - *For what people am I thankful?*
> H - *For what personal characteristics am I thankful?*
> A - *For what experiences am I thankful?*
> N - *For what things am I thankful?*
> K - *For what situations am I thankful?*
> S - *For what natural wonders am I thankful?*

A Paper Bag Turkey

Decorate your porch, yard, or home with a whole flock of these friendly turkeys. Hide surprise gifts or treats inside them! They are made from brown paper bags, stuffed with newspaper, and decorated with colored paper and red balloons.

1. Make a fist-sized wad of newspaper. Stuff it into the bottom of a medium-sized bag to form the turkey's head. Twist the rest of the bag to form the turkey's long neck.

2. Stuff a large bag with newspapers. Leave about six inches empty at the top of the bag. Tie the bag firmly shut with twine.

3. Turn the bag lengthwise. Near the front of the top, cut a small slit. Slide the turkey's long neck into the slit.

4. Make tail feathers by cutting circle wedges from brown bags or from bright-colored paper. Glue the feathers onto the back of the turkey's body.

5. Draw eyes, glue on paper eyes, or glue on eyes that you buy at a craft shop. Glue the end of a red balloon to the turkey's "chin" (for a wattle).

Turkey Trivia

- Americans eat over 45 million turkeys on Thanksgiving Day.

- Large, old male turkeys taste better than younger turkeys.

- Turkey gobbling is a mating call.

- Each year, the U.S. president pardons two turkeys before Thanksgiving. In 2005, the pardoned turkeys served as grand marshals for Disneyland's Thanksgiving Day Parade.

Buy Nothing Day

(the day after Thanksgiving)

This is THE major shopping day in North America. Consumers run out to buy holiday presents or to take advantage of great sales. The intent of the BND Movement is to cause people to stop and think before they spend money. It is a day to pause—to see what it feels like to NOT shop, and then to consider carefully what really needs to be bought.

Election Day (first Tuesday)

Brush up on Election Day events, processes, and ideas with this scrambled-word challenge. Unscramble these words that are related to elections. Then find and write an explanation for each word.

Make a Buy-Nothing "campaign" poster or button.

NO MORE STUFF!

DO YOU REALLY NEED THAT?

Oak Street School Straw Poll

Vote for Your Favorite Athletic Activity:

___skateboarding
___hiking
___swimming
___cycling
___tennis
___team sports
_____baseball
_____football
_____soccer
_____basketball
_____hockey

SNACIDDATE

STRAPIE

MACAPING

TABSEDE

FOLMPART

BLOTAL

STIRREGE

RYMPIAR

SLOLP

RUNUOTT

Election Challenges

- Track down the names of all the elected representatives that represent YOU (from YOUR district in your city, county, state, country).

- Find the date on which the last presidential election was held.

- Figure out how many days will pass before the next presidential election.

Design-a-Candidate

Design an ideal candidate for any office you choose (mayor, school board member, senator, governor, president, vice president, etc.).

- Develop a straw poll to determine what the candidate should promote.
- Describe the characteristics the candidate would have.
- Write a platform for the candidate.
- Create a slogan, campaign poster, and magazine ad for the candidate.

See page 259 for other dates that vary in November.

- Hockey Mask Invented (1959)*
- New York City Marathon
- National Author's Day
- World Community Day
- All Saints Day
- Library of Congress Opened (1897)
- Day of the Dead (Mexico)
- European Union Established (1993)

Alaskan Raven Mask

This is a good day to combine November's month-long celebration of American Indian and Alaskan Native heritage with remembrance of the invention of the hockey mask. There are many Native American legends about Raven. Find and read some of those today. Then use this pattern to make an Alaskan Raven mask (which actually has some similarities to the protective hockey mask!).

Enlarge this pattern to fit an $8\frac{1}{2}$ by 11-inch piece of white card stock. Cut it out and color it. (Raven's colors are red, white, and black.) Punch holes near the side edges as shown. Fasten a piece of thin elastic to hold the mask on your face.

- Look for Circles Day*
- National Deviled Egg Day
- All Soul's Day
- Anniversary of *Spruce Goose* Flight (1947)
- First Scheduled Radio Broadcast Aired (1920)

Birthdays

1889	North Dakota, 39th State	
1889	South Dakota, 40th State	
1734	Daniel Boone	
1755	Marie Antoinette	
1795	James Polk, 11th U.S. President	
1865	Warren Harding, 29th U.S. President	

Circles Everywhere You Look

Be aware of circles today. Once you intentionally focus on looking for circles, the number of circles you see will probably surprise you. Here's a way to keep track of what you see. Get a notebook or pad of paper. Draw 100 or more circles. Carry these around with you all day. Every time you see a circle out there in your world, "record" it by turning one of the circles on the pad into that circular thing! See how many you can find before the day ends.

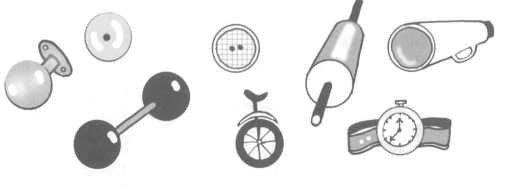

For each starred* holiday on pages 266–279, you will find at least one activity.

Catch a Cliché

November 3rd

A cliché is a phrase or expression which has been used so much that it has lost the force of its original meaning, or even become irritating.

- Track down clichés today. Try to build a long list.
- Include a cliché in every conversation you have today.
- Ask people to name their *least* favorite clichés.
- Think about how clichés are used in advertising. Write an ad using at least five clichés.
- Write a story or dialogue that is full of clichés.
- In honor of National Sandwich Day, find out how the sandwich was invented. Then find some clichés about food.
- Find a few clichés on the same topic. Write them in a way that creates the visual impression of that topic.

- Cliché Day*
- National Sandwich Day*
- Give Someone a Dollar Today Day
- Japanese Culture Day
- Public TV Debuted *(1969)*
- First Dog Launched into Space *(Sputnik II, 1957)*

Birthdays

1718   John Montague, Earl of Sandwich*

Time flies when you're having fun.
Live and let live.
It's as easy as falling off a log.
Rome wasn't built in a day.
What goes around comes around.
There's no time like the present.
Don't worry; be happy!
Every cloud has a silver lining.
Love makes the world go 'round.
There's no place like home.
Life is a bowl of cherries.
Money burns a hole in his pocket.
Money talks.

Today's special: Cliché Sandwich

WHEN YOU BREAK BREAD, SOMETIMES THE BIG CHEESE DOESN'T CUT THE MUSTARD, SO DON'T BITE OFF MORE THAN YOU CAN CHEW!

Dangling Donuts

November 4th

Celebrate Donut Day with this great contest. Use it at a party, or any other time. Don't be fooled by this task; it's not as easy as it sounds.

- Donut Day*
- Candy Day
- First Wagon Train Reached California *(1844)*
- Cash Register Patented *(1879)*

1. Hang donuts from strings. Attach them to mobiles, dowels, door frames, or the ceiling. Hang them at different heights, for people of different heights.

2. Have contestants choose a donut that is about nose-height. They must stand with their hands behind their backs.

3. When the "Start" signal is given, contestants try to eat their donuts. The first person to completely eat the donut (without losing a substantial amount to the floor) is the winner.

- Crossword Puzzles First Published in America *(1913)**
- National Young Readers Day*
- Guy Fawkes Day (*Bonfire Night*)
- Iran Hostage Crisis Began *(1979)*
- King Tut's Tomb Discovered *(1922)*

Birthdays

1916   Walter Cronkite

Classic Crosswords

Crossword puzzles were first published almost a hundred years ago. Soon after their invention, their popularity spread, with books of puzzles popping up everywhere! Try this puzzle with a reading theme—perfect for National Young Readers Day.

It's All About Reading

Clues

Across

3 move eyes across the lines
7 read these and laugh
8 read and enjoy the rhyme
9 room full of books
10 draws the book's pictures

Down

1 pages with a cover
2 comes with headlines
4 writes the book
5 a tale to read
6 the funnies

- Basketball Day*
- Saxophone Day
- Halfway Point of Autumn
- National Nachos Day

Birthdays

1854   John Phillip Sousa

Computations on the Court

James Naismith, a Canadian P.E. teacher, invented the game of basketball in 1891. At first, players dribbled a soccer ball and tossed it into a peach basket. The basketball was patented in 1929. Today, figure out some facts about basketball and other sports balls.

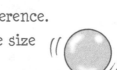

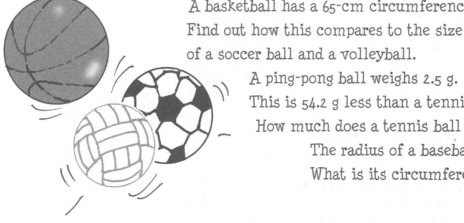

Find the diameter of a bowling ball, a billiard ball, and a golf ball.

A basketball has a 65-cm circumference. Find out how this compares to the size of a soccer ball and a volleyball.

A ping-pong ball weighs 2.5 g. This is 54.2 g less than a tennis ball. How much does a tennis ball weigh?

The radius of a baseball is 0.0320. What is its circumference?

Drinking Straw Physics

Marie Curie, a Polish scientist, was an important figure in the history of physics and chemistry. Along with her husband, Pierre, and Henri Becquerel, she won a Nobel Prize for her work in radiation. Celebrate the day of her birth with this physics experiment.

1. Get a glass soft drink bottle and several drinking straws.

2. Bend a straw about two inches from the top.

3. Push the bent end of the straw into the bottle and wiggle it around until it is wedged between the two sides of the bottle.

4. Carefully pull on the straw, and the bottle will lift!

This is a good trick—but it's hard to drink.

- Magazine Day
- National Bittersweet Chocolate with Almonds Day
- Hug-a-Bear Day

Birthdays
1867   Marie Curie*
1918   Billy Graham

Homemade X-Rays

Investigate the discovery of the X-ray. (Who discovered it? Where? How?) Then make your own easy "X-rays."

1. Stock up on some chicken bones. Clean and dry them.

2. Get some photographic paper from your local camera shop.

3. Arrange the bones on the photographic paper to look like a skeleton or part of a skeleton.

4. Set the arrangement in the sun for several hours.

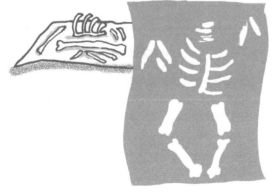

- X-Ray Discovered *(1895)*
- Dunce Day*
- Cook Something Bold and Pungent Day*
- National Ample Time Day
- The Louvre Opened in Paris, France *(1793)*

Birthdays
1889   Montana, 41st State
1656   Edward Haley

One More Idea

- Find out what *pungent* means. Then cook up a good recipe for something bold and pungent.

No Dunces!

A 13th-century philosopher from Duns, Scotland, believed the theory that a cone-shaped hat could funnel knowledge from the point down into the mind of the person wearing the hat. He developed what has come to be known as the "dunce cap." But it was not intended for anyone "slow." It was intended to make smart thinkers even smarter. Design your own dunce cap today. See it if makes you smarter.

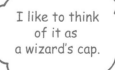

I like to think of it as a wizard's cap.

- Go to an Art Museum Today Day*
- National Scrapple Day*
- Astronomy Day
- Parade Day
- Anniversary of Boston Fire (1872)
- Berlin Wall Demolished (1989)
- Anniversary of Krystalnacht (1938)
- Vietnam Veteran's Memorial Unveiled (1984)

One More Idea

- Definitely find out about *scrapple* today. Draw it, list its ingredients, and taste it (if you can find any!).

Make Your Own Museum

ART is far more than paintings and sculptures. Search for any museums in your area that show collections of things people enjoy viewing. If you cannot find a museum to visit (or even if you can), get together with some friends and make your own art museum. Gather collections of anything that can be displayed in a pleasing way. Make a whole museum of one kind of art, or set up a museum that has many corners and stations to display a variety of any colorful, interesting creations you'd like to show off.

How about a museum for...

hats
T-shirts
rocks
shells
shoes
decorated skateboards
CD or DVD covers
candy wrappers
book jackets
boxes
watches
jewelry
calendars
labels from cans

- Telephone Area Codes Introduced (1951)*
- Forget-Me-Not Day
- Henry Stanley Found David Livingstone (1871)
- U.S. Marine Corps Day (Founded 1775)
- Sesame Street TV Show Premiered (1969)

Birthdays

1483   Martin Luther

Area Code Mysteries

You'll be able to solve these mysteries with the help of a current telephone directory and an atlas of North America. After you answer these questions, create a few more area code mysteries of your own.

1. *A jewel thief makes a call from area code 717. Is she east or west of the Mississippi River?*

2. *Detective Finders needs to call a police department in New Orleans, Louisiana, to get some information about a missing person. Which of these area codes will get him through to New Orleans: 620, 714, 504, or 310?*

3. *An anonymous tip is called into the Los Angeles County sheriff from Medford, Oregon. What is the caller's area code?*

4. *In February, Sergeant Lucy LaSnoop is sent to a city in area code 907 to track down a clue. Should she take her snowsuit or her shorts?*

5. *A citizen reported a train robbery. He called from his cellphone with a 615 area code. What was his home state?*

Airbourne

Air Day falls in Aviation History Month. So this is a good day to make a flying contraption. Try this easy glider, and take it outside where it can catch some air and soar away. (Make several!)

1. Cut one strip of drawing paper $1\frac{1}{2}$ inches wide and 7 inches long. Cut another strip the same width and 9 inches long.

2. Decorate the paper strips.

3. Tape both strips into loops.

4. Tape one loop to each end of a plastic drinking straw.

5. Fly the glider by tossing it forward with the small loop in front.

6. Do some research to find out how gliders and airplanes stay up in the air.

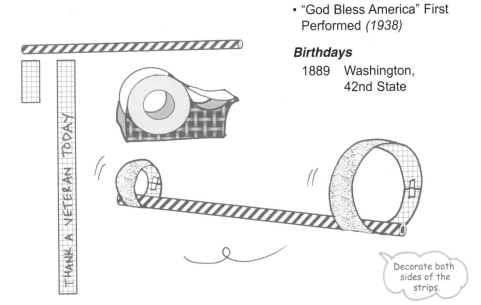

THANK A VETERAN TODAY

Decorate both sides of the strips.

- Air Day*
- Veterans Day
- Bonza Bottler Day
- Remembrance Day (Canada)
- National Vanilla Cupcake Day
- "God Bless America" First Performed *(1938)*

Birthdays
1889   Washington, 42nd State

Delicious Combinations

The great thing about a sundae is that it has a wonderful combination of different flavors, temperatures, and textures. On this National Sundae Day, sharpen your math skills by figuring out how many different combinations of ice cream (one scoop), creamy topping (one kind), and crunchy topping (one kind) can be put together with the following ingredients. DRAW and color each possible combination.

- National Sundae Day*
- Mellow Yellow Day
- National Pizza with the Works Except Anchovies Day

Birthdays
1815   Elizabeth Cady Stanton

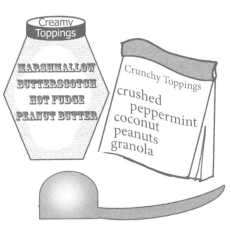

Ice Cream Flavors

vanilla
rocky road
mocha
grape
lemonade
pistachio

Creamy Toppings

MARSHMALLOW
BUTTERSCOTCH
HOT FUDGE
PEANUT BUTTER

Crunchy Toppings
crushed peppermint
coconut
peanuts
granola

November 13th

- National Indian Pudding Day
- World Kindness Day
- National Mom's and Dad's Day
- National Community Education Day
- Actor's Day

Birthdays
1850   Robert Louis Stevenson*

Shadow Show

Robert Louis Stevenson was a Scottish novelist and poet, well-known for his poem collection, *A Child's Garden of Verses*. One of the favorites in this collection is the poem "My Shadow." Read this poem and several other Stevenson poems today. Then find a book about shadows you can make with your hands. Have fun with your own shadow!

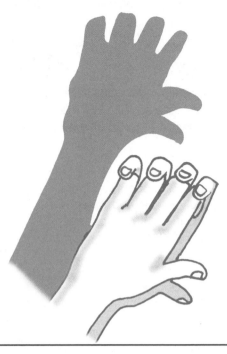

November 14th

- Around the World in 72 Days Anniversary *(1889)**
- Pickle Appreciation Day
- Guacamole Day
- First Streetcar Operated *(1832)*

Birthdays
1840   Claude Monet
1907   Astrid Lindgren

Globe Trotting

On this day in 1889, a young reporter, Nellie Bly, left New York to try to mimic the trip around the world from Jules Verne's famous book, *Around the World in Eighty Days*. She completed the trip in just 72 days! A team of basketball players, the Harlem Globetrotters, is known for its entertaining basketball exhibitions around the world. Plan a 72-day trip around the world for the Globetrotters. Write out an itinerary that includes stops in at least 50 cities around the world.

November 15th

- America Recycles Day*
- American Enterprise Day
- Pack Your Mom's Lunch Day
- National Clean Out Your Refrigerator Day

Birthdays
1897   Georgia O'Keeffe

Recycled for Entertainment

It's a day to recycle, and this may take some imagination. Think about things that are usually thrown away. Find a few of these things and turn them into a game or some other form of entertainment.

Carefully use a knife to cut the top off several plastic soda bottles, leaving five inches at the bottom of each bottle. Use nails or a staple gun to attach the bottle bottoms inside a shallow box. Write different numbers (for points) on stickers to place inside. Fasten the box on a wall or set it on a table. Stand a few feet away from the box. Take turns with friends tossing a ping-pong ball or golf ball into the containers. Keep score. The person who gets the highest point score for ten throws is the winner.

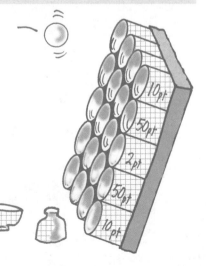

Double the Fun

Button is one of those words with a double letter in the middle. On Button Day, find dozens of words to keep *button* company. Build a list. Then use the words as art to create a *Double Fun* poster. Decorate the poster with buttons.

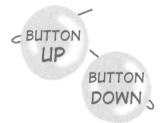

November 16th

- Button Day*
- International Day for Tolerance
- National Fast Food Day
- Animal Day
- Love a Tree Day

Birthdays
- 1907 Oklahoma, 46th State

Chuckles Down on the Farm

Have some good laughs today with jokes about farm animals. See how many good jokes you can find. Many jokes start by asking what you get when you cross two animals. Make the game below to get you started on some of these "animal-crossing" jokes.

November 17th

- National Farm Joke Day*
- World Peace Day
- Homemade Bread Day
- Take a Hike Day
- Coping with Uncertainty Day

What is a pig's favorite ballet? *Swine Lake.*

What do you get when you cross a hen with a dog? *Pooched eggs.*

What do you get when you cross a chicken with a cement mixer? *A brick-layer.*

What do you get when you cross a cow with a camel? *Lumpy milkshakes.*

Great Idea

Draw or glue pictures of animals on cards of the same size. Cut each card in half. Pair up the cards to make wacky new farm animals.

273

November 18th

- Push-Button Telephone Debuted (1963)*
- William Tell Day*
- Mother Goose Parade
- Mickey Mouse Introduced to the World (1928)
- Introduction of the Teddy Bear (1902)
- Antarctica Discovered (U.S. Navy Captain Nathaniel B. Palmer, 1820)

One More Idea

- Find out who William Tell was. Draw a picture to show that you have learned something about his story.

Push-Button Math

A wonderful feature of the push-button telephone is that you can dial by numbers or letters. This supplies great possibilities for math problems that mix words and numbers. Each phrase below has a numerical value. Find the sum of the buttons you pushed to "spell" each of these:

Sample:

Mickey Mouse: 6 + 4 + 2 + 5 + 3 + 9 + 6 + 6 + 8 + 7 + 3 = 59

Solve these:

Mother Goose =

ring tones =

Call me tonight. =

Who's On The Line? =

Answer the phone. =

When is Thanksgiving? =

Can you hear me now? =

I'm getting a busy signal. =

1	2 ABC	3 DEF
4 GHI	5 JKL	6 MNO
7 PQRS	8 TUV	9 WXYZ
	0 OPER	

November 19th

- Have a Bad Day Day*
- Alaska Highway Opened (1942)
- Cold War Formally Ended (1990)
- Puerto Rico Discovered (1493)
- President Lincoln Delivers the Gettysburg Address (1863)
- The Mayflower Docked at Cape Cod, Massachusetts (1620)

Birthdays

1831 James Garfield, 20th U.S. President
1917 Indira Gandhi

The Very Worst Day

Everyone has a bad day once in a while. This is a good day to read a great book about a bad day: *Alexander and the Terrible, Horrible, No Good, Very Bad Day* by Judith Viorst. Find and enjoy this book today. Then make a book to tell about your own bad day. Each page should tell one thing that would make your day an awful day. The pages can be real things that have actually happened or things you can imagine that would make a bad day.

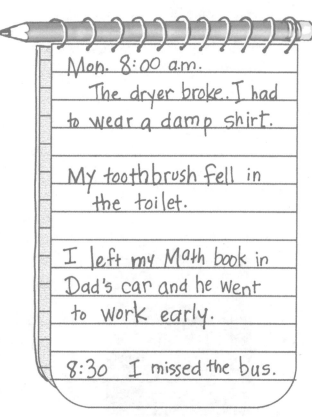

Mon. 8:00 a.m.
The dryer broke. I had to wear a damp shirt.

My toothbrush fell in the toilet.

I left my Math book in Dad's car and he went to work early.

8:30 I missed the bus.

Now, That's Absurd!

World history includes some rather absurd ideas, events, and beliefs. Explore some of these today. First of all, get out a dictionary and make sure you understand what *absurd* means. Then investigate some of these absurd ideas, beliefs, practices, inventions, or superstitions. Choose one that interests you the most, or make up an absurd invention or idea of your own. Draw a picture and write a brief explanation of the idea.

Some absurdities . . .

the idea that the Earth was flat

the invention of a dog umbrella

making wings out of wax to help a human fly

the invention of a drill to create dimples

the belief that finding a 4-leaf clover will bring good luck

the idea of letting blood out of a person to eliminate an illness

the practice of burning suspected heretics or witches at the stake

the practice of dunking a woman underwater to see if she was a witch

I'm lucky a cow hasn't eaten me.

the notion that the number 13 is bad luck

the invention of eyeglasses for chickens

the invention of inflatable greeting cards

the notion that a broken mirror means someone will die

November 20th

- Absurdity Day*
- National Parental Involvement Day
- Name Your PC Day
- Universal Children's Day
- Revolution Day (Mexico)
- National Peanut Butter Fudge Day

Birthdays
1925   Robert F. Kennedy
1889   Edwin P. Hubble

Washington, D.C. Firsts

Today is the anniversary of the first meeting of the U.S. Congress in Washington, D.C. Use your good research skills to track down these other "firsts" in Washington, D.C.

November 21st

- Congress First Met in Washington, D.C. *(1800)**
- World Hello Day
- The *Mayflower Compact* Signed *(1620)*

Birthdays
1789   North Carolina, 12th State

When did the Supreme Court first meet in Washington, D.C.?

Which president was the first to be inaugurated in Washington, D.C.?

Name the first time a woman administered the oath of office to a president?

Who was the first vice president to live in Washington, D.C.?

Who was the first elected mayor of Washington, D.C.?

When was the first televised presidential inauguration?

What president's inauguration was the first to be broadcast live on the Internet?

Which was the first monument built in Washington, D.C.?

November 22nd

- National Stop the Violence Day
- Go for a Ride Day
- Morse Code Signal "S.O.S." Adopted as International Distress Signal *(1906)*
- John F. Kennedy Assassinated *(1963)*

Birthdays
1943   Billie Jean King*

Double Meanings

Billie Jean King was an accomplished tennis player, winning championships in the 1960s and 1970s. Locate a biographical sketch of Billie Jean to find out about her tennis accomplishments, including one important match in 1973.

Please stop all the racket. It's interfering with my tennis game.

Let the word *racket* inspire a word search game. This word has more than one meaning. Find ten other words that have more than one meaning. Create an illustration with one of the words to show that you understand both meanings.

November 23rd

- National Cashew Day*
- You're Welcome Day
- First Color Photos Released *(1863)*
- Pencil Sharpener Invented *(1897)*

Birthdays
1804   Franklin Pierce, 14th U.S. President

A Little Nutty

Learn a lot about nuts today. Try to find at least ten different kinds of nuts. Create a nut parade on poster board. Draw a picture of each kind you find (or glue a sample of the nut). Add legs, arms, feet, hats, and other things to "personify" the nuts. Label each character with a nutty name.

WALLY NUTT   ALMONDA CRUNCH   HUGH CASHEW   IMA FILBERT   HORACE P. NUT   ANGELA PISTACHIO

November 24th

- What Do You Love About America Day*
- Comedy Hall of Fame Established *(1993)*
- Softball Invented *(1887)*
- National Espresso Day
- Lee Harvey Oswald Shot *(1963)*

Birthdays
1784   Zachary Taylor, 12th U.S. President

America Acrostic

On *What Do You Love About America Day,* show what you love about America. Make an acrostic with the letters of the words that name the day. Choose things you love about America that include one of the letters below. Write those to intersect with the words below. Try to find one for each letter in the phrase.

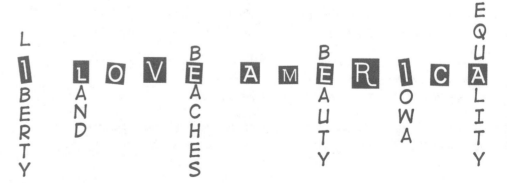

276

Peanut Butter Parfait

A *parfait* is a layered dessert that is usually served in a tall, narrow glass. Ice cream or some other frozen delight is a part of most parfaits. Sometimes everything is layered together before the dessert is frozen. In honor of Peanut Butter Lovers Month, try this parfait today. If you don't like peanut butter, choose any ingredients you like, but include some whipped cream or ice cream.

Peanut Butter Parfait

Layers:
　　vanilla ice cream
　　3 T chocolate syrup
　　crushed peanuts
　　$\frac{1}{3}$ C peanut butter

Repeat the layers.

Top with whipped cream and more crushed peanuts.

November 25th

• National Parfait Day*
• U.S. Department of Homeland Security Formed

Birthdays
1835　Andrew Carnegie
1914　Joe DiMaggio

Did you know a baseball autographed by Joe DiMaggio can sell for $1,000?

If You Live with a Lion . . .
and other proverbs

There is an African proverb that says this:
If you live with a lion, wear the skin of a crocodile.

There are thousands of fascinating proverbs from around the world. Have fun finishing these proverbs about lions and other creatures.

Even the lion must defend itself against _____

Better to be eaten by a lion than _____

A porcupine will not mind _____

A dead goat does not fear _____

Don't _____ while the tiger is sleeping.

You can't catch two frogs with _____

He who has been bitten by a snake _____

If you meet a hippopotamus on the path, _____

To threaten an elephant, you must _____

When you see a monkey in a tree, _____

If a man is running from a tiger, _____

Roasted pigeons don't _____

He who lives with wolves must _____

A chicken that gets a sprained ankle _____

November 26th

• First Lion Exhibited in U.S. (1716)*
• National Cake Day
• First Holiday Proclaimed by U.S. President (*Thanksgiving, by George Washington, 1789*)

Birthdays
1922　Charles Schulz

Nothing should be done in a hurry except catching fleas...

...and eating cake.

- Pins and Needles Day*
- Freckle Pride Day*
- National Bavarian Cream Pie Day*

More Ideas

- Find out how Bavarian Cream is different from ordinary cream.
- Design a poster that shows your support of freckles and of people, animals, and things that have freckles.

On Pins & Needles

What does it mean to be "on pins and needles"? This idiom (expression) describes a situation of anticipation. Something is about to happen, or something is coming . . . and you are waiting with excitement or fear. You might know what to expect, or you might not!

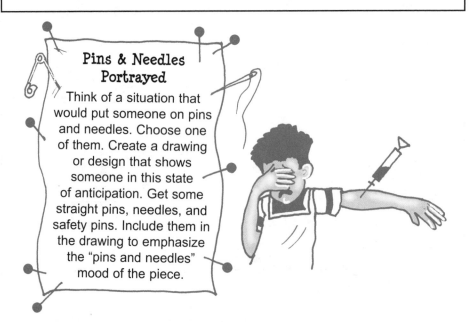

Pins & Needles Portrayed

Think of a situation that would put someone on pins and needles. Choose one of them. Create a drawing or design that shows someone in this state of anticipation. Get some straight pins, needles, and safety pins. Include them in the drawing to emphasize the "pins and needles" mood of the piece.

- Red Planet Day*
- National French Toast Day
- First American Automobile Race *(1985)*

Magnificent Mars

Red Planet Day honors Mars, the planet that appears to be red. This day celebrates the launch of *Mariner 4,* a spacecraft that was launched in 1964 on a 228-day mission to learn more about the planet. Use this day to increase your knowledge about the planet that is Earth's closest neighbor.

Find out . . .

- the number of planets between Mars and the sun
- its distance from Earth
- its distance from the sun
- the revolution time around the sun (in Earth time)
- the rotation time (in Earth time)
- the average temperature range
- the surface gravity (in comparison to Earth's)
- the number of Mar's moons
- its surface features
- its size (diameter)
- the makeup of its atmosphere

Also . . .

- Draw a Martian landscape scene.
- Draw your idea of how inhabitants of Mars would look.
- Find out how Mars got its name.
- Find a copy of Ray Bradbury's *Martian Chronicles.*
  Read some of the stories aloud with your family or your classroom.

I'm homesick.

Finish the Ads

The classified section is such an interesting part of a newspaper. It's a place where people advertise things they want to find or sell. On Newspaper Day, read several classified ads (or "want ads"). Then use your imagination to create an ad for each "need" described in these sections.

FOR SALE	WANT TO BUY	JOBS WANTED
someone selling a pair of gold-plated skates	someone wanting to buy a pet crocodile	someone seeks a job as a bear chiropractor
someone selling a collection of piggy banks	**RENTALS**	someone looking for a job as a tooth extractor
	someone looking for a tree house to rent	
someone selling a set of 3000 comic books	**JOB OFFERS**	**PETS**
someone wants to trade old videos for new DVDs	someone wanting to hire a person to take care of 15 cats	someone needs a good home for housebroken baby gorilla.

> If I want to sell my old comic books, I'd better not forget to include my price and telephone number in the ad.

November 29th

- Newspaper Day*
- National Chocolates Day
- Electronic Greetings Day
- Square Dance Day

Birthdays
1832   Louisa May Alcott
1898   C.S. Lewis

A Mousse for a Moose

Track down pairs of homonyms (such as mousse and moose). Turn them into questions. Illustrate them on mini-posters.

- Have you ever shared a mousse with a moose?
- Have you heard the tale about the gigantic tail?
- What kind of shampoo is good for a hare's hairs?
- Could you shoo a mosquito with your shoe?
- What feat can your feet perform?
- Do ants have aunts?
- Where's that barefoot bear?
- How much dough does a doe have?
- Why did that whale wail?
- Are you friends with a ewe?
- Why was the flea forced to flee?
- Might a mite be friendly?

Mousse for a Moose
(or for YOU)

Shred 3 ounces of semisweet chocolate into a bowl. Heat $\frac{1}{2}$ C heavy cream until it is quite hot—but not boiling. Pour the cream over the chocolate, and stir once. Cover the bowl. Whip a pint of heavy cream to soft peaks. Gradually whip in 8 T sugar. Stir the chocolate until it is smooth. Gently fold in the whipped cream. Put the mousse into small dishes and chill for 2–3 hours. Top this with more whipped cream, if you like!

November 30th

- National Mousse Day*
- Computer Security Day

Birthdays
1835   Mark Twain* (Samuel Clemens)
1874   Sir Winston Churchill

One More Idea

- Mark Twain, famous humorist, left behind some wonderful quotes. Find and share at least ten of them today.

> A crank is someone with a new idea—until it catches on.

> When in doubt, tell the truth.
> – Mark Twain

December

1
- Skywriting First Demonstrated*
- Rosa Parks Day
- National Pie Day
- World AIDS Awareness Day

2
- Eat a Red Apple Day*
- National Fritters Day
- Monroe Doctrine Presented
- First Man-made Atomic Chain Reaction

3
- First Successful Human Heart Transplant*
- National Roof Over Your Head Day
- International Day of Disabled Persons
- Neon Lighting First Used
  Birthdays: Illinois

4
- Santa's List Day*
- International Hug Day
- Know Your State Capital Day
- Wear Brown Shoes Day
- U.S. International Space Station Launched

5
- International Volunteer Day
- AFL-CIO Founded
- Montgomery Bus Boycott Began
- 21st Amendment to the *U.S. Constitution* Ratified
  Birthdays: Mozart, Martin Van Buren, Walt Disney*

6
- St. Nicholas Day*
- National Gazpacho Day*
- National Mitten Tree Day
- International Bad Hair Day
- 13th Amendment Ratified

7
- Hang a Wreath Day*
- Pearl Harbor Remembrance Day
- National Cotton Candy Day
  Birthdays: Delaware, Madame Tussaud

8
- Cocoa Day*
- National Brownie Day
- Winter Flowers Day
- NAFTA Signed
- Soviet Union Dissolved
- America Enters World War II
  Birthdays: Eli Whitney

9
- Computer Mouse Invented*
- First Christmas Seals Issued
- Make a Homemade Holiday Gift Day
- National Pastry Day
- Ball-Bearing Roller Skates Patented

10
- Human Rights Day
- Nobel Peace Prize Awarded Each Year
- Dewey Decimal Day
- Spanish-American War Ended
  Birthdays: Mississippi, Emily Dickinson*

11
- Make Your Own Holiday Cards Day*
- Jack Frost Day
- National Knitters Day
- Color Movies First Shown
- National Noodle Ring Day
- UNICEF Established
  Birthdays: Indiana

12
- Poinsettia Day*
- National Ding-a-Ling Day
- Bonza Bottler Day
- National Ambrosia Day
- Guadalupe Day (Mexico)
- Gingerbread House Day
- U.S. Supreme Court Ruling on 2000 Election
- Golf Tee Patented
  Birthdays: Pennsylvania, Frank Sinatra

13
- St. Lucia Day*
- Savings Bank Day
- Ice-Cream Day
- Day of the Horse
- Violins Day
- Clip-on Tie Invented

14
- Discovery of South Pole*
- Tell Someone They're Doing a Good Job Day
- Miniature Golf Began
  Birthdays: Alabama

15
- Bill of Rights Adopted*
- National Lemon Cupcake Day
- Anniversary of Death of Sitting Bull

16
- First Day of Las Posadas*
- National Chocolate-Covered Anything Day*
- Anniversary of Battle of the Bulge
- Anniversary of Boston Tea Party
  Birthdays: Ludwig van Beethoven

17
- Wright Brothers' Day*
- Cookie Cutter Day
- *A Christmas Carol* Published

18
- Reindeer Appreciation Day*
- Wear a Plunger on Your Head Day
- Bake Cookies Day
- First Broadcast from a Communications Satellite
  Birthdays: New Jersey, Stephen Spielberg

19
- Give a Homemade Holiday Gift Day*
- Oatmeal Muffin Day*
- Go Caroling Day
- Look for an Evergreen Day
- Anniversary of Christmas Greeting from Space

20
- Games Day*
- American Poet Laureate Established

For each starred* holiday, you will find one or more activities on pages 282–302.

21
- National Flashlight Day*
- National French Fried Shrimp Day
- Humbug Day
- Look at the Bright Side Day
- Forefathers Day
- Radium Discovered
- Pilgrims Landed at Plymouth, Massachusetts

22
- First Gorilla Born in Captivity*
- National Date-Nut Bread Day
- International Arbor Day
- Abilities Day
- California Kiwifruit Day
- Fahrenheit Thermometer Invented
- First Christmas Lights for Sale

23
- Metric Conversion Act Signed*
- Economists Day
- Federal Reserve System Established
- National Roots Day
- Transistor Invented

24
- Christmas Eve Day*
- National Eggnog Day*
- War of 1812 Ended by Treaty of Ghent

25
- Christmas Day*
- National Pumpkin Pie Day
- William the Conqueror Crowned King of England
- First Nativity Scenes
- Washington Crossed the Delaware River
- *"Silent Night"* First Performed
- U.S. President Andrew Johnson Grants Pardon to All Citizens Involved in Rebellion That Caused the Civil War
- "The Stars and Stripes Forever" written by John Philip Sousa
- During World War I, Christmas Truce Declared by Some British and German Troops
- *"A Christmas Carol"* Read on the Radio for the First Time
- Coronation Stone Stolen from Westminster Abbey
- Afghanistan Invaded by USSR
- First Live TV Cast of Christmas Parade
- Resignation of Mikhail Gorbachev as USSR President
  Birthdays: Clara Barton, Conrad Hilton, Humphrey Bogart, Anwar Sadat

26
- National Whiners Day*
- First Day of Kwanzaa
- Recyclable Packaging Day
- National Candy Cane Day
- Awful Tie Day
- Boxing Day
- Tsunami in Asia

27
- National Fruitcake Day*
- Visit the Zoo Day
- World's First Cat Show
- First *Howdy Doody* TV Show
- Radio City Music Hall Opened
  Birthdays: Louis Pasteur*

28
- *Poor Richard's Almanac* First Published*
- Chewing Gum Patented*
- National Chocolate Day
- *Pledge of Allegiance* First Recognized
- Card-Playing Day
  Birthdays: Iowa, Woodrow Wilson

29
- Bowling Ball Invented*
- Still Need to Do Day
- Tick Tock Day
- Anniversary of Battle at Wounded Knee
- National Chocolate Day Again
  Birthdays: Texas, Andrew Johnson

30
- Bicarbonate of Soda Day*
- USSR Established
  Birthdays: Rudyard Kipling*

31
- New Year's Eve Day*
- Make Up Your Mind Day*
- Unlucky Day
- Ellis Island Opened
  Birthdays: Henri Matisse

Month-long Celebrations

Art and Architecture Month*

Bingo Month*

Hi Neighbor Month

Made in America Month*

National Closed Caption TV Month

National Stress-Free Family Holidays Month*

National Tie Month*

Read a New Book Month*

Safe Toys and Gifts Month

Universal Human Rights Month

Write to a Friend Month

Weekly Celebrations

First Week: Cookie Cutter Week*, Christmas Tree Week, Tolerance Week

Second Week: National Hand-Washing Awareness Week*, Human Rights Week

Third Week: International Language Week*, Tell Someone They're Doing a Good Job Week

Fourth Week: It's About Time Week*

Dates That Vary: Winter Solstice*, Hanukkah*, Underdog Day, Advent, National Children's Memorial Day

December's Month-long Celebrations

National Stress Free Family Holidays Month

Holidays are so busy that all the activities often put stress on families. This month-long event is a reminder for families to slow down and take time to be together, doing things that are relaxing and enjoyable. Plan ahead to have a less stressful month with your family. Brainstorm one no-stress activity that can be done each day in December. Make a calendar with a "door" to open each day. Behind the door, write the idea. Each day, open the door, read the idea, and DO the activity (or sometimes the "non"-activity).

Bingo Month

Enjoy playing Bingo this month with your own homemade holiday Bingo cards.

Start with some holiday stickers and large index cards. Each member of the family can create his or her own BINGO card, placing stickers in 24 squares. Leave a "free" space in the center. Make an "answer key" for each card by writing each possible combination on a slip of paper. Put these strips in a jar. The "caller" can mix up the paper slips and draw them at random. Get some coins or buttons to place on the spaces as you play the game.

Note: Instead of using stickers, you may want to draw the pictures!

Made in America Month

In 1985, U.S. President Ronald Reagan issued a presidential proclamation to establish this holiday. The purpose is to celebrate and promote the excellence of American products. Use this month to learn more about products made in the USA. Visit these Web sites or find others that give information about American-made products: http:/madeinusa.org, http:/usstuff.com

- Find a USA-made brand for each of these items: toothbrush, cellphone, fishing rod, stuffed animal, athletic shoe, wristwatch, CD player, boat, camping tent, kid's bicycle, backpack.

- Examine some of your belongings or things your family owns. Look for labels and tags that show where they were made. Or, research the items to find out where they were made. How many can you find that were made in America?

Art & Architecture Month

Put your art and architectural skills to work in December with this challenge: Design and make a holiday tree using "found" materials such as wire, rolled newspaper, cardboard, plaster, food, drinking straws, aluminum cans, branches, small boxes, clay, cardboard tubes, etc. Use your imagination to build and decorate a tree.

Here are the rules:
1. You can use any safe material.
2. The end product must resemble a tree.
3. The finished tree must be able to stand up.

National Tie Month

A large percentage of the ties bought each year are purchased in the month of December—mostly for holiday gifts. Buyers can choose from literally hundreds of thousands of tie styles and designs. Have a little fun with ties during Tie Month this year. Think about the ties you would choose (or design) for certain people (or other characters). Draw a tie that you think would be fitting for five or more of these:

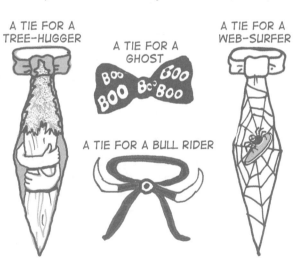

rock singer
giraffe
hairdresser
contortionist
housepainter
magician
foot doctor
children's dentist
mail delivery person
abominable snowman

ice skater
school bus driver
lion tamer
scorpion
tuba player
tree surgeon
gorilla
sausage maker
baseball umpire
bungee jumper

Read a New Book Month

Take a break from the usual. Read a new book this month—and make it something different than you would usually read. Then let the book inspire you to do something new. For example:

Read a . . .	and then . . .
book of myths	create, name, draw, and describe a mythological creature
book of science experiments	perform some of the experiments
collection of poetry	write a poem to add to the collection
play	draw one of the scenes
cookbook	write recipes for your three most favorite foods
first-aid book	prepare a lesson to teach the basics of first aid

See page 281 for other month-long holidays to celebrate in December.

Special Weeks in December

Cookie Cutter Week

This is a good week to use cookie cutters to make your favorite cookies. But, don't put those cookie cutters away! Use them to make a set of stamps that you'll use over and over during the holiday season.

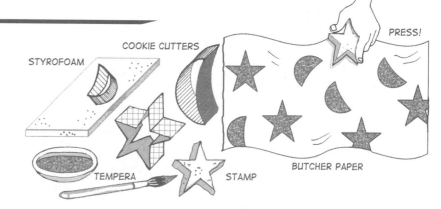

1. Press a cookie cutter firmly into a thin sheet of Styrofoam. Or, place a cookie cutter on a thin, flat sponge and draw around it. Then cut out the shape.
2. Dip your cookie cutter stamps (Styrofoam or sponge) into thick tempera paint.
3. "Stamp" holiday designs onto wrapping paper, cards, paper tablecloths, napkins, banners, or other decorations.

Second Week

National Hand-Washing Week

It's the easiest way to prevent the spread of disease, and it's simple! Wash your hands several times a day (before, during, and after handling food, after you cough or sneeze, after you use the bathroom, whenever your hands are dirty). You can even do it with your own homemade soap.

How to Wash Your Hands

1. Wet your hands. Apply soap.
2. Rub your hands together vigorously. Scrub all surfaces thoroughly. Count to 30 slowly as you continue to scrub.
3. Rinse your hands well and dry them completely.

Peppermint Soap

1. Cut a clear glycerine soap bar (such as Neutrogena soap) into 1-inch cubes.
2. Heat half the cubes in a glass measuring cup in the microwave for 15 seconds at a time. Stir gently each time you check it. Heat it JUST until it melts.
3. Pour the melted glycerine into a soap mold. (You can use a jar lid, glass custard cup, or muffin tin as a mold, too.)
4. Melt the rest of the glycerine. Stir in a few drops of red food coloring, a few drops of peppermint oil, and some glitter.
5. Pour the red glycerine on top of the other layer in the mold.
6. Swirl the two layers together with a spoon or wooden stick.
7. Cool the soap for 1 hour. Refrigerate it for 30 minutes.
8. Remove the soap from the mold. Dry it on a cookie rack.

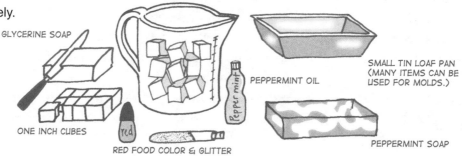

284

International Language Week

Did you know that there is an international language? It's called *Esperanto*. Dr. Ludwik Zamenhof created this language in 1887. He wanted to develop an easy language that could be spoken commonly by people all over the world to promote international understanding and peace. The goal of this holiday week is to promote awareness and use of Esperanto. Learn a few phrases. Then search the library or Internet to find more. Also, find out how many people speak Esperanto.

Some Esperanto Facts . . .
- The alphabet is similar to the English alphabet.
- All nouns end in **o**.
  tree — arbo
- To make a noun plural, add a **j**.
  trees — arboj
- All adjectives end in **a**.
  beautiful — bela
- Adding **mal** to the beginning of a word gives it the opposite meaning.
  malbela — ugly

Learn these:
saluton.................hello
bonan matenon.....good morning
bonan vesperon.....good evening
is las revido..........good-bye, see you later
Mi nomi as............My name is . . .
dankon..................thank you
pardonu min..........excuse me
Mi malsatas...........I'm hungry.
bonvolu.................please
Kie mi estas?.........Where am I?
bone.......................okay
Mi amas vin...........I love you.

It's About Time Week

It's about time! This is a familiar expression used in many situations when something happens that someone believes is long overdue. The holiday was created to encourage creative problem solving for a better world. The motto of this week is "time-to-give, time-to-live, and time-to-remember." It's a good week to think about occasions for saying, "It's about time!" Get together with friends or family members and create a list of things for which "it's about time." Make campaign-style posters for several of these occasions.

See page 281 for other weeklong holidays to celebrate in December.

The Days of December

Winter Solstice (December 21st or 22nd)

This day marks the beginning of winter in the Northern Hemisphere. The North Pole is tilted most directly away from the sun, causing the shortest day and the longest night of the year. For centuries, people have celebrated solstices with many different rituals and ceremonies. Today, research to find out about some of these celebrations. Then plan some activities for a solstice celebration of your own.

SNOW PAINTINGS

Whip up a batch of snow paint to use for painting snow scenes on paper, or to apply decorations to windowpanes.

- Beat $\frac{1}{2}$ cup Ivory Flakes detergent with $\frac{1}{2}$ cup water. (Leave the "paint" white, or color some with a few drops of food coloring.)

- Use your fingers to paint on dark-colored paper (butcher paper or shelf paper) placed on a hard surface.

- Dab the paint on windowpanes to form snowflakes or other holiday decorations.

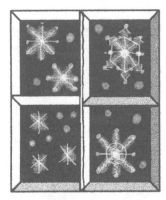

SNOW CALCULATIONS

Every snowflake has six points. Cut out a few 6-pointed snowflakes of different designs. Then make math come alive with the number SIX!

- What is the sum of 60 sixes?

- How many seconds are in six hours?

- How many toes are on six monkeys?

- How many points are on 600 snowflakes?

- How many 3-digit numbers have six in the middle?

COLD TRICKS

Get three bowls of water, one hot (not so hot that it will scald you), one cold, and one room temperature. Set the room temperature water in the middle. Don't tell your friends anything about the temperatures of the water. Have a friend put one hand in each of the outside bowls (hot and cold water). Then, ask her/him to immediately put both hands in the center bowl and decide whether it is hot or cold. Then you try it! Have fun discussing and explaining the results.

Hanukkah

Hanukkah is a major Jewish holiday—the Festival of Lights. It is celebrated for eight days, beginning in December or late November (Kislev 25 on the Jewish calendar). The holiday began to honor an important event in Jewish history when Judah the Maccabee reclaimed the temple from the Syrian King Antiochus IV. The temple was cleansed and dedicated, and the sacred Menorah (candelabra) was lit again. Hanukkah means *dedication*. To remember this event, one candle in the Menorah is lit on each of the eight days of Hanukkah. The holiday is celebrated with traditional events and rich, wonderful food. Children receive gifts and play games of *dreidel* (a special spinning top).

Do-It-Yourself Dreidel

A dreidel is a small spinning top with four sides. A different Hebrew letter is printed on each of the sides. Each letter is worth a different value. Children play the game using nuts (or some other type of counters such as marbles, pennies, candies, etc.). Any number of people can play this game.

To make the dreidel . . .

1. Copy this pattern onto sturdy paper or card stock and decorate it.

2. Fold on the lines to shape the dreidel's top. Glue each tab where it meets a square.

3. In the black dot on the fifth square, make a tiny hole to insert a pencil, point down. Push it way down.

4. Squeeze white glue around the pencil where it goes into the dreidel. Let the glue dry.

How to play the game . . .

1. Give each player 15 nuts.

2. At the beginning of each round, each player should put one nut into the center pool. If the pool gets down to 1 or 0 during the game, each player puts one nut into it again.

3. Each player takes a turn, spinning the dreidel once. When the dreidel falls, the symbol on the top will tell the player what to do.
   Nun – Do nothing.
   Gimel – Take everything in the pot.
   Hay – Take half the pool.
   Shin – Put one nut into the pool.

4. When a player has no nuts left, he/she is out of the game.

5. The game ends when one person has won all the nuts.

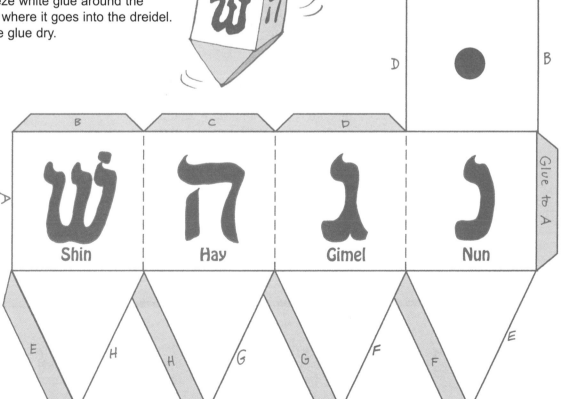

See page 281 for other dates that vary in December.

287

- Skywriting First Demonstrated (1922)*
- Rosa Parks Day
- National Pie Day
- World AIDS Awareness Day

Messages in the Sky

A small aircraft expelling a special smoke can "write" in the sky. The plane flies in patterns that create readable words. The first skywriting exhibition in the U.S. occurred over New York City. The pilot, British Air Force Captain Cyril Turner, spelled out: **Hello U.S.A. Call Vanderbilt 7200**. (147,000 people called the number after the exhibition!) You may not be able to get up in a plane today to write real messages in the sky. But, you can simulate a skywriting message. All you need is some long paper, cotton balls, glue, and a pencil.

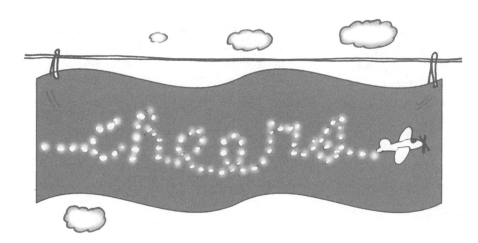

1. Get a long piece of blue mural paper, or tape together several pieces of blue construction paper to form a long strip.
2. Use your pencil to lightly write a message that you would want to write in the sky.
3. Glue small tufts of cotton at spots along the writing. Use enough cotton so that the letters will be clear to read when you hang up the message.
4. Display the "sky" strip with message along a long wall, or hang it from a clothesline.

- Eat a Red Apple Day*
- National Fritters Day
- Monroe Doctrine Presented (1823)
- First Man-made Atomic Chain reaction (*The Manhattan Project*, 1942)

It's baked apple day.

Eat a Red Apple Today

It's a good idea to eat an apple **every** day, but today is an especially fine day to do this. For a change, eat your apple stuffed and baked.

Stuffed Baked Apple

1. Cut the core out of a firm red baking apple. Make a nice "hole" in the center, but do not cut all the way through to the bottom of the apple.
2. Sprinkle brown sugar over the apple and set it in a baking dish.
3. Choose any combination of these: coconut, cinnamon candies, orange slices, pineapple chunks, raisins, banana chunks, nuts. Toss about $\frac{1}{3}$ cup of these with some brown sugar and cinnamon.
4. Stuff the center of the apple with the mixture.
5. Pour hot water into the dish to a depth of about $\frac{1}{2}$ inch.
6. Bake the apple for about 40 minutes at 400°F (until tender). Every 10 minutes, spoon some of the liquid in the dish over the apple. Let the apple cool some before you eat it (topped with whipped cream or ice cream).

Just don't call me half-baked.

For each starred* holiday on pages 288–302, you will find at least one activity.

Protect Your Heart

Surgeon Christiaan Barnard performed the first successful human heart transplant on this day in 1967 (in Cape Town, South Africa). Patients who need heart transplants all suffer from serious heart disease. On the anniversary of this historic event, take some time to learn more about taking care of your heart. One of the best ways to do this is to get regular aerobic exercise. This is the kind of exercise that increases your body's demand for oxygen, strengthening your heart and blood vessels. As you get regular aerobic exercise, your resting heart rate will get lower, and your heart rate will return to its resting rate faster after exercise.

Counting Thumps

1. Get a stopwatch or a watch with a second hand.
2. Lie down or sit very still for 15 minutes. Then take your pulse to find the number of beats per minute. (This is your resting heart rate. Write it down.)
3. Exercise for 15 minutes by jogging slowly or jumping rope. Start out slowly and speed up a little. After 15 minutes, take your pulse again to find the number of beats in a minute. (This is your exercising heart rate. Write it down.)
4. Walk around slowly for 5 minutes. Take your pulse for 1 minute. (This is your recovery heart rate. Write it down.)
5. Compare the heart rates. Keep taking your pulse every minute or so until the rate returns to your resting heart rate. How long did it take?

That's a great resting heartbeat.

December 3rd

- First Successful Human Heart Transplant *(1967)**
- National Roof Over Your Head Day
- International Day of Disabled Persons
- Neon Lighting First Used *(1910)*

Birthdays
1818   Illinois, 21st State

A Wish List

You've probably made a list of things you hope that Santa will bring to you. Even if you don't believe in Santa Claus, think about what other people need. Write a list of things you would like to see someone else get or things you wish would happen for someone else. You could make several lists for different people, or put all your wishes on one list.

Santa, please bring . . .
food for all the children in the world;
a bicycle for my little brother, Sam;
a playground for the school;
a vacation for my mother;
better health for Aunt Joyce;
some comic books for Owen; and
help for people trying to rebuild their homes.

SANTA,
PLEASE BRING A BONE AND A NEW KIBBLE DISH FOR MY DOG, SHORTY.

ALSO, HE NEEDS HIS TEETH CLEANED AND A YEAR'S SUPPLY OF FLEA POWDER.

PLEASE BRING A BIGGER YARD, AND BEST OF ALL, A NEW PUPPY FOR HIM TO PLAY WITH.

THANK YOU, SANTA.

MARIGOLD

December 4th

- Santa's List Day*
- International Hug Day
- Know Your State Capital Day
- Wear Brown Shoes Day
- U.S. International Space Station Launched *(1977)*

- International Volunteer Day
- AFL-CIO Founded *(1955)*
- Montgomery Bus Boycott Began *(1955)*
- 21st Amendment to the *U.S. Constitution* Ratified *(1933)*

Birthdays

1756 Mozart
1782 Martin Van Buren, 8th U.S. President
1901 Walt Disney*

Create a Cartoon

Walt Disney started drawing cartoons when he was very young. At age 27, he created Mickey Mouse. The inspiration for this character was a favorite mouse that kept showing up in the garbage can in his studio. Over the next ten years, he created many more famous characters, such as Donald Duck, Minnie Mouse, Goofy, and Pluto. Here are some tricks to help you become a clever cartoonist. Put these to use as you create your own original cartoon characters.

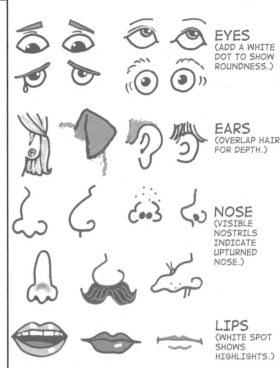

EYES
(ADD A WHITE DOT TO SHOW ROUNDNESS.)

EARS
(OVERLAP HAIR FOR DEPTH.)

NOSE
(VISIBLE NOSTRILS INDICATE UPTURNED NOSE.)

LIPS
(WHITE SPOT SHOWS HIGHLIGHTS.)

- St. Nicholas Day*
- National Gazpacho Day*
- National Mitten Tree Day
- International Bad Hair Day
- 13th Amendment to the *U.S. Constitution* Ratified *(1865)*

ST. NICHOLAS

The Secret Gift-Giver

St. Nicholas is a common name used for Saint Nicholas of Myra, a 4th century Byzantine bishop. He had a reputation for leaving money, food, or gifts in secret to help the poor, sick, or needy. His gift-giving inspired several mythical figures, including Santa Claus.

- Read some of the legends and stories about St. Nicholas.
- Find the names of other "Santa Claus" figures inspired by St. Nicholas.
- Follow St. Nick's example today. Give some gifts in secret. Leave something small or simple (an apple, nuts, a few coins, or other small gift) for someone without letting the person know that you are the giver.
- Find and listen to the St. Nicholas Suite (Cantata Op 42) by Benjamin Britten.

Easy Gazpacho

Gazpacho is a cold soup made from chopped tomatoes, cucumbers, onions, peppers, and herbs. Mix up a batch today.

Combine these in a blender or food processor until the ingredients are mixed, but still chunky:

3 C tomato juice	2 T red wine vinegar
2 C chopped tomatoes	1 t dried basil
1 clove of garlic, minced	1 t dried tarragon
1 chopped cucumber	1 T sugar
1 chopped green pepper	4 T chopped parsley
2 chopped green onions	a little salt & pepper
3 T lemon juice	

Chill the soup for 3 hours. Top it off with sour cream and tortilla chips.

A Tasty Wreath

Hang a different kind of wreath today. Use this recipe and your favorite cookie cutters to make a wreath of overlapping gingerbread cookies. (Cut out a few extra cookies to eat while you're working on the wreath.)

Making the Wreath

- Prepare a large, flat work area with a floured surface. Turn the oven to 350°F.
- Working with half the dough at once, roll the dough out to about $\frac{1}{4}$-inch thickness. Cut cookie shapes.
- Arrange the cookies in a circle on a large cookie sheet, overlapping them. Where cookies touch, press the dough together firmly.
- Bake the wreath for about 10 minutes. Let it cool a few minutes.
- Gently lift the wreath from the tin.
- When it is completely cool, weave ribbon through the spaces in the wreath. Tie a ribbon around the top to create a hanger.

December 7th

- Hang a Wreath Day*
- Pearl Harbor Remembrance Day *(1941)*
- National Cotton Candy Day

Birthdays
  1787   Delaware, 1st State
  1761   Madame Tussaud

Recipe

$\frac{1}{2}$ C soft butter

$\frac{1}{2}$ C brown sugar

$\frac{2}{3}$ C molasses

2 eggs

4 C flour

$\frac{1}{2}$ t baking soda

$\frac{1}{2}$ t salt

$\frac{1}{2}$ t of each of these ground spices: cinnamon, cloves, ginger, allspice

- Cream the first four ingredients together in a bowl with a mixer.
- Add all other ingredients to 1 C of flour.
- Combine the two mixtures.
- Gradually stir the rest of the flour in by hand. The dough will be stiff.

Winter White Cocoa

Celebrate Cocoa Day with an unusual drink—cocoa made with white chocolate instead of the usual brown chocolate. Enjoy it with a brownie or the gingerbread cookies left over from December 7th.

December 8th

- Cocoa Day*
- National Brownie Day
- Winter Flowers Day
- NAFTA Signed *(1993)*
- Soviet Union Dissolved *(1991)*
- America Entered World War II *(1941)*

Birthdays
  1765   Eli Whitney

Four servings:

Combine 2 cups of milk and 2 cups of cream (or half and half) in a pan. Set the burner to medium heat. Bring the mixture to a boil. Stir in 4 tablespoons of white sugar and $\frac{3}{4}$ cup of white chocolate chips or chunks. Lower the heat. Stir well until the chocolate melts. Stir in 1 teaspoon of vanilla extract. Serve right away. (You can top it with marshmallows, crushed candy canes, some caramel sauce, whipped cream, or dark chocolate shavings.)

December 9th

- Computer Mouse Invented (1968)*
- First Christmas Seals Issued (1907)
- Make a Homemade Holiday Gift Day
- National Pastry Day
- Ball-Bearing Roller Skates Patented (1884)

Animals in Unexpected Places

A clever inventor named Douglas Enfelbert came up with the idea for the computer mouse. There was plenty of interest in his device. It may look like a mouse, but, of course, it is not truly an animal. There are many other phrases like *computer mouse*—phrases that use an animal name, but have nothing to do with animals. Below are a few.

1. Explain what each phrase means.
2. Draw the *literal* meaning of a few phrases.
3. Think of more phrases like these.

grease monkey

SPELLING BEE

Christmas seals

I wonder what a lame duck looks like.

Pack rat

SHUTTERBUG

HOT DOGS

lame duck

bullhorn

BOOKWORM

card sharks

FIREBUG

Draw some of these phrases.

clothes horse

HUSH PUPPIES

WORMHOLE

monkey wrench

December 10th

- Human Rights Day
- Nobel Peace Prize Awarded Each Year
- Dewey Decimal Day
- Spanish-American War Ended (1898)

Birthdays

1817   Mississippi, 20th State
1830   Emily Dickinson*

What About Winter?

Emily Dickinson's poetry was not popular in her lifetime, but a great amount of it was published after her death in 1886, and she has come to be known as one of the greatest American poets. Over 1,700 of her poems have been found. Many of her poems were written about small moments and ordinary things in life. She used wonderful imagery and metaphors in numerous poems about winter. One poem begins, "The sky is low, the clouds are mean . . ." In this poem, Emily Dickinson writes about a flake of snow that debates where it will go as it travels through the air, and a winter wind that complains all day.

- Read Dickinson's winter poem.

- Collect some images about winter. Treat characteristics of winter as if they were people with feelings, thoughts, and personalities.

- Write a line about each of these: winter winds, snow, rain, sunshine, storms, temperatures, clouds, blizzard, gray sky, sleet, fog. Combine some of your lines into a winter poem.

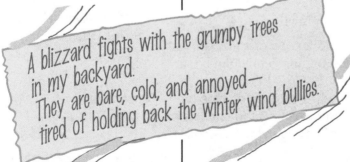

A blizzard fights with the grumpy trees in my backyard.
They are bare, cold, and annoyed—
tired of holding back the winter wind bullies.

A Holiday Pop-up Card

Save some money, stretch your creative abilities, and delight your friends with the holiday cards you make yourself. You can use any kind of paper and decorations to construct any kind of card you want. (Make your own envelopes, too.)
Since pop-up cards are such fun to receive, you might want to try to make this one (or a similar card with your own idea).

December 11th

- Make Your Own Holiday Cards Day*
- Jack Frost Day
- National Knitters Day
- Color Movies First Shown *(1909)*
- National Noodle Ring Day
- UNICEF Established *(1946)*

Birthdays
1816   Indiana, 19th State

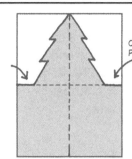
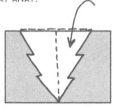

CUT THIS PART AWAY.

MAKE A SIMPLE POP-UP CARD.

TAKE A COLORED PIECE OF 8½ X 11 INCH PAPER AND FOLD ACROSS, THEN DOWN.
DRAW A SIMPLE SYMMETRICAL DESIGN, SUCH AS A CHRISTMAS TREE, ON THE UPPER HALF OF THE FOLDED PAPER AND CUT AROUND IT.
DECORATE YOUR DESIGN AND FOLD DOWN.
FOLD AGAIN TO MAKE THE CARD SHAPE. DECORATE THE FRONT.
OPEN THE CARD — YOUR DESIGN WILL POP UP!

Merry christmas, Grahma! from Kevin

- Make a poinsettia pinwheel.
- Find out how the poinsettia got its name.
- Find and read "The Legend of the Poinsettia."
- Find the answers to these questions:

  What is the native country of poinsettias?

  Are poinsettias poisonous?

  What country exports the most poinsettias?

  When did the flower come to the U.S.?

  How many varieties of poinsettias are there?

Poinsettia Pinwheel

Use Poinsettia Day to increase your poinsettia knowledge and to have fun with this easy poinsettia pinwheel.

December 12th

- Poinsettia Day*
- National Ding-a-Ling Day
- Bonza Bottler Day
- National Ambrosia Day
- Guadalupe Day (Mexico)
- Gingerbread House Day
- U.S. Supreme Court Ruling on 2000 Election *(2001)*
- Golf Tee Patented *(1899)*

Birthdays
1787   Pennsylvania, 2nd State
1915   Frank Sinatra

COPY AND ENLARGE PATTERN TO 5 IN. SQUARE. USE BRIGHT RED PAPER.

FOR EXTRA PUNCH, USE GOLD GLITTER ON THE RED LEAVES.

CUT OUT THE SHAPE BELOW AND LAY IT IN THE CENTER.

CUT AWAY THE GRAY AREAS. DO NOT CUT PAST THE SMALL DOTS ON EACH LINE. BEND THE DOTTED CORNERS TO THE CENTER AND GLUE.

HAMMER A SMALL NAIL THROUGH ALL THE LAYERS OF THE PINWHEEL AND ATTACH IT TO A DOWEL. IT SHOULD BE ABLE TO SPIN FREELY.

December 13th

- St. Lucia Day*
- Savings Bank Day
- Ice-Cream Day
- Day of the Horse
- Violins Day
- Clip-on Tie Invented *(1928)*

Lussekatter in the Morning

In Sweden, the feast day of Lucia is celebrated with a festival of lights. Early in the morning (4 A.M.), a young woman comes out of the darkness bringing steaming hot coffee and saffron buns *(lussekatter)*. She wears a white gown, a red sash, and a crown of lingonberry twigs with bright candles. Lucia symbolizes light and growth to chase away the dark of winter.

Make *lussekatter* today. These are fluffy yeast buns with the unusual taste of saffron. Search your family cookbooks, or find a recipe on the Internet. Family members often form strips of dough into figure eight or **S** shapes. Choose a shape you like for your *lussekatter*.

December 14th

- Discovery of South Pole *(1911)**
- Tell Someone They're Doing a Good Job Day
- Miniature Golf Began *(1929)*

Birthdays
  1819   Alabama, 22nd State

Race to the South Pole

Antarctica was the last unexplored continent on Earth. The South Pole was a "geographical prize" that nations wished to win by reaching it first. In the early 1900s, there was literally a race to get there. Two expeditions reached the pole within days of each other.

Find the answers to these questions:

Who was involved in the race?

What countries did they represent?

Who got there first?

How did they travel to the pole?

What happened to the people in the expedition parties?

Actually, penguins discovered the South Pole!

December 15th

- Bill of Rights Adopted *(1791)**
- National Lemon Cupcake Day
- Anniversary of Death of Sitting Bull *(1890)*

Know Your Rights

When the *Constitution* of the United States was written, the people in the new country insisted that something be added to protect and guarantee certain personal freedoms.
So, the first ten amendments to the Constitution do just that.
Together, they are called "The Bill of Rights."

I can speak or publish my opinions freely.

The government cannot require me to keep soldiers in my home.

I cannot be searched without a good cause.

I am free to practice any religion I want.

I cannot be given cruel and unusual punishment for a crime.

If I am accused of a crime, I have the right to a speedy public trial.

Which amendment guarantees each right? Get a copy of the Bill of Rights and find out.

I can publicly disagree with my government.

If the police want to search my home, they must have a warrant.

If I am accused of a crime, I have the right to a defense by a lawyer.

Sweets Fit for a Holiday

Las Posadas means *the inns* or *the shelters* in Spanish. This celebration takes place over nine days, commemorating Joseph's and Mary's search for shelter before the baby Jesus was born. It is a preparation for Christmas. The celebrations are full of music, fireworks, food, and treats. Enjoy these chocolate-dipped strawberries as you join the celebration of Las Posadas with National Chocolate-Covered Anything Day.

Chocolate-Dipped Strawberries

Wash and dry a quart of strawberries, leaving the hulls. Melt a large package of chocolate chips and 4 T of butter in the top of a double boiler. Stir in 1 t vanilla. Roll the bottom half of each berry in the chocolate. Set them on waxed paper to cool.

December 16ᵗʰ

- First Day of Las Posadas (Mexico)*
- National Chocolate-Covered Anything Day*
- Anniversary of Battle of the Bulge *(1944)*
- Anniversary of Boston Tea Party *(1773)*

Birthdays
1770   Ludwig van Beethoven

A Flyer for Fun

It was on this day in 1903 that Orville and Wilbur Wright launched a new form of transportation with the first powered airplane flight. The flight took off near Kitty Hawk, N.C., and lasted about a minute. Make this simple replica of a bi-plane like that historic plane, the *Wright Flyer*. Give it as a holiday gift to someone who will enjoy displaying it or playing with it.

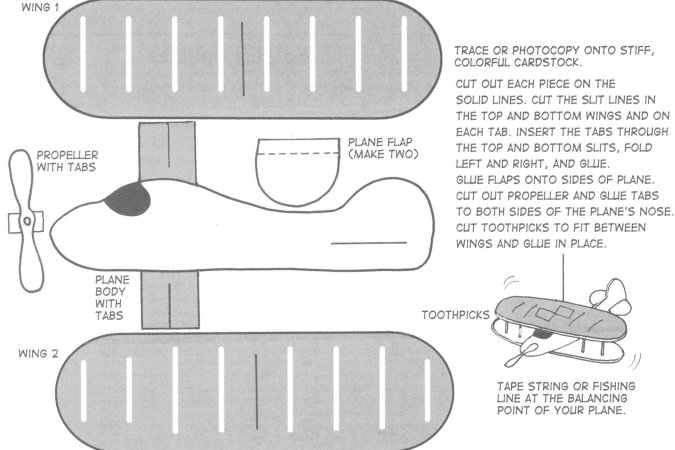

WING 1

PROPELLER WITH TABS

PLANE FLAP (MAKE TWO)

PLANE BODY WITH TABS

WING 2

TRACE OR PHOTOCOPY ONTO STIFF, COLORFUL CARDSTOCK.

CUT OUT EACH PIECE ON THE SOLID LINES. CUT THE SLIT LINES IN THE TOP AND BOTTOM WINGS AND ON EACH TAB. INSERT THE TABS THROUGH THE TOP AND BOTTOM SLITS, FOLD LEFT AND RIGHT, AND GLUE. GLUE FLAPS ONTO SIDES OF PLANE. CUT OUT PROPELLER AND GLUE TABS TO BOTH SIDES OF THE PLANE'S NOSE. CUT TOOTHPICKS TO FIT BETWEEN WINGS AND GLUE IN PLACE.

TOOTHPICKS

TAPE STRING OR FISHING LINE AT THE BALANCING POINT OF YOUR PLANE.

December 18th

- Reindeer Appreciation Day*
- Wear a Plunger on Your Head Day
- Bake Cookies Day
- First Broadcast from a Communications Satellite *(1958)*

Birthdays

1787   New Jersey, 3rd State
1947   Stephen Spielberg

Reindeer Goodies

Reindeer are a part of many holiday stories, songs, and traditions. Take some time today to learn more about reindeer than you already know. Then enjoy these fun-to-make reindeer sandwiches.

Cut a slice of wheat bread in half diagonally. "Frost" the bread with cream cheese. Give the reindeer two raisin eyes and a cinnamon candy nose. Use three small pretzel sticks to form each antler.

Leave these reindeer treats for Santa's reindeer.

December 19th

- Give a Homemade Holiday Gift Day*
- Oatmeal Muffin Day*
- Go Caroling Day
- Look for an Evergreen Day
- Anniversary of Christmas Greeting from Space *(1958)*

A Gift of Muffins

Make these easy oatmeal muffins, package them up with a ribbon, and give them as a holiday gift today.

- Mix 1 C quick oats into 1 C of milk. Let it sit for 15 min.
- Beat 1 egg and $\frac{1}{3}$ C oil together. Add the oat mixture.
- Mix together 1 C flour, 2 t baking powder, $\frac{1}{4}$ C sugar, and a pinch of salt. Stir this into the oat mixture just until all ingredients are combined.
- Spoon the batter into paper muffin cups in a muffin tin.
- Bake for 20 minutes at 425°F.

December 20th

- Games Day*
- American Poet Laureate Established *(1985)*

Holiday Spinner

Celebrate Games Day by making a spinning game for the holidays. You decide what "challenges" to put on the cards. Then gather friends or family members together and take turns spinning.

10 SECONDS 50 SECONDS 2 MINUTES 20 SECONDS 40 SECONDS 60 SECONDS 90 SECONDS 30 SECONDS

ENLARGE THE SPINNER AS DESIRED.

ATTACH THE ARROW WITH A SMALL BRAD.

TO PLAY: EACH PLAYER WRITES 10 CHALLENGES ON 1½ X 2½ INCH CARDS. SHUFFLE THE CARDS. TO TAKE A TURN, CHOOSE A CARD, THEN SPIN THE DIAL TO SEE HOW MUCH TIME YOU HAVE TO DO THE CHALLENGE. A POINT IS GIVEN FOR EACH CHALLENGE COMPLETED ON TIME. THE PLAYER WITH THE MOST POINTS AT THE END OF THE GAME WINS.

CHALLENGE IDEAS:

- SING *JINGLE BELLS*.
- NAME THE GIFTS FOR EACH OF THE 12 DAYS OF CHRISTMAS.
- MAKE UP A HOLIDAY RHYME.
- NAME 10 HOLIDAYS.
- DESCRIBE 5 GIFTS YOU HOPE YOU DON'T GET.
- LIST 10 HOLIDAY FOODS.
- GIVE AWAY SOMETHING YOU OWN AS A GIFT.

December Light Show

Celebrate the wonderful invention of the flashlight with a light show that is custom-made for this holiday month. Get the flashlights ready during the day, but plan to do the "show" after dark.

- Use black construction paper and several bright colors of cellophane.
- Gather several friends with flashlights.
- Cut circles of black paper to cover the top of each flashlight.
- Draw and cut out shapes of festive holiday items from the black circles.
- Cut circles of colored cellophane to cover the end of the flashlight.
- Place a black circle (with cut-out design) on the end of each flashlight, covered by a circle of cellophane.
- Turn out the lights and shine the flashlights on a blank wall or ceiling for a great light show.

December 21st

- National Flashlight Day*
- National French Fried Shrimp Day
- Humbug Day
- Look at the Bright Side Day
- Forefathers Day
- Radium Discovered *(Marie & Pierre Curie, 1898)*
- Pilgrims Landed at Plymouth, Massachusetts *(1620)*

Gorilla Facts

Many people are fascinated by gorillas. Learn more about gorillas on this anniversary of the first gorilla born in captivity.

- Visit www.koko.org (The Gorilla Foundation) to learn about Project Koko and the amazing research into gorilla intelligence and language. Enjoy the story of Koko and her amazing use of language.

Why did King Kong climb to the top of the Empire State Building?

What is the first thing a young gorilla learns in school?

- Explore these gorilla facts:
  - *Gorillas are the largest primates.*
  - *They walk on their feet and the knuckles of their hands.*
  - *Their arms are longer than their legs.*
  - *They look fierce, but are generally peaceful.*
  - *Some gorillas are seriously endangered.*
  - *Gorillas are very intelligent.*
  - *They sleep in nests made of leaves and branches.*
  - *A gorilla can live for 50 years.*
  - *Gorillas communicate with sounds, gestures, and postures.*
  - *Gorillas express many emotions.*
- Find or make up some gorilla jokes.
- Find out what gorillas look like. Draw your own pictures of three different kinds of gorillas.

December 22nd

- First Gorilla Born in Captivity *(1956)**
- National Date-Nut Bread Day
- International Arbor Day
- Abilities Day
- California Kiwifruit Day
- Fahrenheit Thermometer Invented *(1724)*
- First Christmas Lights for Sale *(1882)*

Read a Gorilla Book

Koko's Story
   by Francine Patterson
Koko's Kitten
   by Francine Patterson
Mountain Gorilla
   by Michael Bright
Gorilla
   by Robert McClung
The Truth About Gorillas
   by Susan Meyers
Thinking Gorillas
   by Bettyann Kelves

December 23rd

- Metric Conversion Act Signed *(1975)**
- Economists Day
- Federal Reserve System Established *(1913)*
- National Roots Day
- Transistor Invented *(1947)*

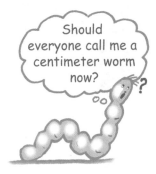

Should everyone call me a centimeter worm now?

Metrically Speaking

The U.S. Congress passed the Metric Conversion Act of 1975 to plan for increasing the use of the metric system in the United States. Another legislative act in 1988 designated the metric system as the "preferred system of weights and measures for U.S. trade and commerce." Check up on your metric skills today.

Answer these . . .

One meter is closest to one   a. quart c. foot
                                    b. yard d. mile

Five hundred kilograms is equal to _____ grams.

An inch is equal to about _____ centimeters.

Which is largest: 10 gallons, 10 liters, or 1 kiloliter?

A kilogram is a. greater than a pound
                 b. less than a pound

10,000 centimeters are equal to _____ kilometers.

Which is greater: 100 miles or 50 kilometers?

How much chocolate would you rather have: 8 grams or 10 ounces?

December 24th

- Christmas Eve Day*
- National Eggnog Day*
- War of 1812 Ended by the Treaty of Ghent *(1814)*

Plans for Christmas Eve

- Interview ten people today to find out what they do on Christmas Eve.
- Describe the plan you ordinarily follow to celebrate Christmas Eve.
- Write another description of what you **wish** you could do on this eve.
- Write a new version of an old Christmas Eve story. Start your story this way: " **'Twas the night before Christmas, when . . .**" Illustrate the story and finish it in time to share it with your family on Christmas Eve.
- Make eggnog ice cream to enjoy this evening.

WAYS OTHER PEOPLE CELEBRATE

HOW WE CELEBRATE CHRISTMAS EVE

WHAT I WISH WE COULD DO ON CHRISTMAS EVE

Let's see . . . the whole family plays word games . . . Grandpa reads "The Night Before Christmas" . . . we listen to the "Nutcracker Suite" . . . everyone opens one present . . . we put out milk and cookies for Santa . . .

What else?

EGGNOG ICE CREAM

1. Use an electric mixer to beat together 4 egg yolks, $\frac{1}{3}$ C sugar, and 1 t nutmeg until the yolks get light yellow.

2. Heat 2 C milk and 1 C cream just to a boil. Remove from heat.

3. Gradually pour the milk mixture into the egg mixture, stirring well. Return it to medium heat. Stir and cook just until it begins to boil. Do not boil.

4. Freeze in an ice-cream maker. Or, use the method on page 168 of this book.

Celebrate!

Celebrate today with these Christmas crafts and memories.

• Christmas Day*

Also on this day...

- *It is National Pumpkin Pie Day.*
- *William the Conqueror was crowned King of England (1066).*
- *St. Francis of Assisi created one of the first Nativity scenes (1223).*
- *General George Washington crossed the Delaware River to launch a surprise attack against British forces (1776).*
- *The hymn "Silent Night" was first performed (1818).*
- *U.S. President Andrew Johnson granted a pardon to all the citizens involved in the rebellion that caused the Civil War (1868).*
- *John Philip Sousa gave the title "The Stars and Stripes Forever" to one of his tunes (1896).*
- *During World War I, some British and German troops decided to call a Christmas truce and play football together (1914).*
- *Charles Dickens' story "A Christmas Carol" was read on the radio for the first time (1939).*
- *Coronation Stone was stolen from Westminster Abbey and smuggled back to Scotland (1950).*
- *The USSR invaded Afghanistan (1979).*
- *First live TV broadcast of Christmas Parade (1983).*
- *Mikhail Gorbachev resigned as USSR president (1991).*
- *Today is the birthday of Clara Barton (1821), Conrad Hilton (1887), Humphrey Bogart (1899), Anwar Sadat (1918).*

Enjoy Breakfast Fruit Faces

Put half a peach on a scoop of cottage cheese. Decorate the peach with raisin eyes, a cherry nose, pineapple lips, cookie ears, and a banana hat.
It's delicious!

Christmas Mice

Cut a raindrop shape from red felt (about four inches long). Glue on wiggly or button eyes, and add a small puffball nose. Cut a piece of green felt in the shape shown for the ears. Cut slits and insert the felt ear piece through the slits to form the ears. To make the tail, push a candy cane through a pair of slits at the tail end of the mouse and glue it on the back side.
Hang your ornament from the tree and enjoy!

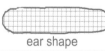

ear shape

mouse body shape

Share Holiday Memories

Get together with friends and family members and take turns sharing memories of the best or worst gift you ever got (or gave), and the funniest or happiest holiday experiences.

Make chains from leftover gift wrap.

December 26th

- National Whiners Day*
- First Day of Kwanzaa
- Recyclable Packaging Day
- National Candy Cane Day
- Awful Tie Day
- Boxing Day (Britain, Australia, New Zealand, and Canada)
- Tsunami in Asia *(2004)*

Calling All Whiners

It's National Whiners Day. Everybody whines sometimes, so this is a day that can focus on all of us. Make these lists for whiners.

People Who Should Win A National Whiners Award...
...GREAT-AUNT BERTILDA...

Things People Whine About...
...CHRISTMAS PRESENTS, WEATHER, GRADES, TESTS, HOMEWORK...

Things Worth Whining About...
...CHRISTMAS PRESENTS, BLIZZARDS, BRUSSELS SPROUTS, EMPTY BANK ACCOUNTS....

Things Not Worth Whining About...
...CHRISTMAS PRESENTS, WEATHER, YOUR HEIGHT, YOUR AGE, MISTAKES...

December 27th

- National Fruitcake Day*
- Visit the Zoo Day
- World's First Cat Show *(1871)*
- First *Howdy Doody* TV Show *(1947)*
- Radio City Music Hall Opened *(1932)*

Birthdays
1822   Louis Pasteur*

One More Idea

- Louis Pasteur was the scientist who proved that germs cause disease. Explain these terms related to germs and disease: *viruses, bacteria, white blood cells, antibodies, infection, immune system,* and *communicable disease.*

Germs can really make you sick!

Consider the Fruitcake

National Fruitcake Day celebrates this rather hard, fruit-filled, sugary holiday cake. This is a day to do one of two things: Eat some of that fruitcake or find another use for it. You need to hang onto it until January 4 (which is the day for the Great Fruitcake Toss), so you might as well make use of it! Just for fun, make a list of things you can do with an uneaten fruitcake.

WORK OUT WITH IT.

GIVE IT AWAY AS A GIFT.

USE IT AS A DOORSTOP.

USE IT AS A PILLOW.

USE IT AS A BOOSTER SEAT.

USE IT AS AN ANCHOR.

MAKE IT INTO MODERN ART.

PRACTICE FOR THE FRUITCAKE TOSS.

Unfinished Proverbs

From 1732 to 1757, Benjamin Franklin published an almanac in the American colonies. He used the pseudonym *Poor Richard* and called the publication *Poor Richard's Almanac.* The popular pamphlet was published yearly and contained weather, poetry, a calendar, and other information. It is mainly remembered for Franklin's wise sayings, or proverbs. Here are a few of his proverbs, unfinished. Think about how you would finish them (differently from the way he did).

- A bird in the hand is worth . . .
- Don't count your chickens before . . .
- A stitch in time saves . . .
- A penny saved is . . .
- Fools rush in where . . .
- He who hesitates is . . .
- A good conscience is . . .
- Don't change . . . in the middle of the stream.
- Three may keep a secret if . . .
- A rolling stone gathers no . . .
- . . . and . . . smell in three days.

Did you know there are forty million pieces of gum chewed every day?

December 28th

- *Poor Richard's Almanac* First Published *(1732)**
- Chewing Gum Patented *(1869)**
- National Chocolate Day
- *Pledge of Allegiance* First Recognized *(1945)*
- Card-Playing Day

Birthdays
1846   Iowa, 29th State
1856   Woodrow Wilson, 28th U.S. President

More Ideas
- Research the fascinating history of chewing gum.
- Find out what makes chewing gum different from bubble gum.
- Find out what U.S. city is home to Bubble Gum Alley.

Art Deco Bowling Balls

On this special day for bowling balls, hold a Best Artistic Bowling Ball Contest. Get a group of contestants together and compete by creating wonderful, exotic, unusual, and wacky papier-mâché bowling balls.

- Follow the instructions to mix wheat paste and water for papier-mâché.
- Dip strips of newspaper into the paste and wrap them around a round, sturdy balloon. Let each layer dry. Build four layers.
- When the ball is completely dry, poke a needle into it to deflate the balloon.
- Carefully cut three holes for fingers.
- Then have fun decorating the ball!

December 29th

- Bowling Ball Invented *(1862)**
- Still Need to Do Day*
- Tick Tock Day
- Anniversary of Battle at Wounded Knee *(1890)*
- National Chocolate Day Again

Birthdays
1845   Texas, 28th State
1808   Andrew Johnson, 17th U.S. President

Bill Crisman of Utah invented scented bowling balls. Would you like yours in vanilla, cherry, or mint?

Have fun inventing ways to play with your papier-mâché bowling ball—just don't try to BOWL with it.

- Bicarbonate of Soda Day*
- USSR Established *(1922)*

Birthdays
1865   Rudyard Kipling*

One More Idea

- On Rudyard Kipling's birthday, definitely read some of his great stories. Enjoy stories from one of these classic books: *The Jungle Book* or *Just So Stories*.

Soda Science Magic

Watch the powers of baking soda (bicarbonate of soda) blow up a balloon. Then see if you can find someone who will explain why it happened!

1. Cover a work area with newspaper.
2. Pour 4 T vinegar into a small bottle with a narrow neck.
3. Use a funnel to pour 2 T baking soda into a balloon. (You can make a funnel out of folded paper.)
4. Carefully stretch the balloon over the top of the bottle, but do not tip the balloon. At this point, you want to keep the soda in the bottom of the balloon.
5. Use a rubber band to seal the balloon tightly.
6. Hold the top of the bottle firmly as you wiggle the balloon so that the baking soda pours into the bottle.

Noise for the New Year

Bring in the New Year with streamers, party hats, and noisemakers you create yourself out of ordinary household "stuff."

- New Year's Eve Day*
- Make Up Your Mind Day*
- Unlucky Day
- Ellis Island Opened *(1890)*

Birthdays
1869   Henri Matisse

One More Idea

- Is there a decision you have been putting off? Write down your choices. Then quit procrastinating and **make up your mind** before the year ends.

Party Poppers
Cover toilet paper rolls with bright-colored tissue. Fill them with candies, coins, and small gifts. Tie the tissue at both ends with curly ribbon.

Paper Plate Shakers
Staple two paper plates together at the edges, leaving an opening to insert some beans or rice. Glue a craft stick in the opening before sealing. Add streamers and decorate.

Bang on pots and pans with metal spoons.

BUZZZZ

Set all the alarm clocks to ring at midnight.

Tube Horns
Poke tiny holes at several places in a cardboard paper towel roll. Cover one end with a circle of waxed paper. Secure it with a rubber band. Blow on the open end of the tube.

Noisy Bottles
Fill plastic soda bottles with a few tablespoons of large beans. Shake, rattle, and roll!

INDEX

* indicates that an activity for this holiday or event is included on the indicated page or date.

Army Day, **Apr 6**
Around the world commercial flight, first, **Jan 6**
Around-the-World in 72 Days anniversary*, **Nov 14**
Art and Architecture Month*, **Dec**, 283
Art Week, **Mar**
Arthur, Chester A., **b. Oct 5**
Ash Wednesday*, **Mar**, 68
Ashe, Arthur Jr., **b. July 10**
Asian/Pacific American Heritage Month*, **May**, 114
Ask a Stupid Question Day*, **Sep 28**
Asparagus Day, **May 24**
Asparagus Month, **May**
Astrology Day, **Mar 21**
Astronomy Day, International*, **May**, 121
Astronomy Day, **Nov 9**
Atlantic City Boardwalk opened, **June 26**
Atomic bomb dropped, first, **Aug 6**
Atomic bomb dropped, second, **Aug 9**
Atomic bomb tested, first, **July 16**
Atom split, first, **Dec 2**
Attitude Day, **June 5**
Aunt and Uncle Day, **July 26**
Aunt's Day, **Sep 9**
Australia Day*, **Jan 26**
Author's Day, **Nov 1**
Autism Awareness Month, **Apr**
Autograph-Collecting Week*, **Mar**, 66
Automobile Race, first American, **Nov 28**
Automobile speed law, first*, **May 3**
Aviation Day, **Aug 19**
Aviation History Month, **Nov**
Aviation in America Day*, **Jan 9**
Aviation Week, **Aug**
Awful Tie Day, **Dec 26**
Awkward Moments Day*, **Mar 18**
Babbling Day*, **Oct 21**
Babe Ruth Day, **Apr 27**
Baby Boomer, first*, **Jan 1**
Baby Boomer's Recognition Day*, **June 21**
Baby Month, **Mar**
Baby Safety Month, **Sep**
Bach, Johann Sebastian, b. **Mar 21**
Bachelor's Day*, **Feb 29**
Back-to-School Month*, **Aug**, 188
Backpack Safety Month, **Sep**
Backwards Day, **Jan 31**
Backyard Games Week*, **May**, 119
Bad Hair Day, **Dec 6**
Bad Poetry Day*, **Aug 18**
Baez, Joan, b. **Jan 9**
Bake Cookies Day, **Dec 18**
Bake for Family Fun Month*, **Feb**, 41
Bake Your Own Bread Day, **June 17**
Baked Bean Month, **July**

Bald Eagle Watch Month*, **Jan**, 15
Ball, Lucille, **b. Aug 6**
Ball-bearing roller skates patented, **Dec 9**
Ballet first introduced in the U.S., **Feb 7**
Balloon flight, first made by 13-year-old boy, **June 23**
Balloon flight, first round-the-world, **Mar 21**
Ballpoint pen patented, **June 10**
Banana Bread Day*, **Feb 23**
Banana Cream Pie Day, **Mar 2**
Banana Lovers Day, **Aug 27**
Banana Split Day*, **Aug 25**
Band-Aid invented, **Sep 22**
Bank in the U.S., first, **July 3**
Barbecue Month, **May**
Barbed wire patented*, **June 25**
Barbershop Quartet Day, **Apr 11**
Barbie Doll introduced, **Mar 9**
Bargain-Hunting Week, **Aug**
Barn Day*, **July**, 169
Barnum, P.T., **b. July 5**
Barton, Clara, **b. Dec 25**
Bascom, "Texas Rose", **b. Feb 25**
Baseball Fans Day, **Aug 12**
Baseball game, first World Series, **Oct 1**
Baseball game, first perfect, **May 5**
Baseball games televised, first, **Aug 26**
Baseball Hall of Fame opened, **June 12**
Baseball, no-hitter anniversary, **Aug 16**
Baseball's American League organized, **Jan 29**
Basketball Day*, **Nov 6**
Bastille Day, **July 14**
Battery Day, **Feb 18**
Battle at the Alamo, **Feb 23**
Battle at Wounded Knee, **Dec 29**
Battle of Bunker Hill began, **June 17**
Battle of Gettysburg began, **July 1**
Battle of Little Bighorn*, **June 25**
Battle of New Orleans, **Jan 8**
Battle of the Bulge, **Dec 16**
Battle of Waterloo ended, **June 18**
Bavarian Cream Pie Day*, **Nov 27**
Bay of Pigs invasion, **Apr 17**
Be an Angel Day, **Aug 22**
Be Electrific Day*, **Feb 11**
Be Humble Day, **Feb 22**
Be Kind to Animals Week, **May**
Be Kind to Humankind Week, **Aug**
Be Kind to Writers & Editors Month, **Sep**
Be Late for Something Day*, **Sep 5**
Be Nice to Jersey Week*, **July**, 166
Beach Clean-up Month, **Sep**
Bean Day, **Jan 6**
Be-Bop-a-Lula Day, **June 5**
Ludwig van Beethoven, **b. Dec 16**
Beef Month, **May**

Beef Steak Month, **June**
Bell, Alexander Graham*, **b. Mar 3**
Berlin Airlift began, **June 23**
Berlin Wall built, **Aug 13**
Berlin Wall opened, **Nov 9**
Berlin, Irving, **b. May 11**
Bernstein, Leonard, **b. Aug 25**
Better Breakfast Month, **Sep**
Better Sleep Month, **May**
Beverage Day*, **May 6**
Bicarbonate of Soda Day*, **Dec 30**
Bicycle patented*, **June 26**
Big Brothers/Sisters Week, **Feb**
Bike Safety Week, **Apr**
Bike to Work Day, **May 16**
Bike Week*, **May**, 118
Bikini debuted, **July 5**
Bill of Rights adopted*, **Dec 15**
Billiard ball patented, **Oct 10**
Bingo Month*, **Dec**, 282
Biographers Day*, **May 16**
Biosphere Day, **Sep 21**
Bird Appreciation Day, **Mar 21**
Bird Day*, **Apr 8**
Bird-Feeding Month*, **Feb**, 40
Birthday cake created, first*, **July 25**
Biscuit Month*, **Sep**, 212
Biscuits & Gravy Week, **Sep**
Bison Month*, **July**, 165
Bittersweet Chocolate With Almonds Day, **Nov 7**
Black Poetry Day*, **Oct 17**
Blackberries Day, **Sep 29**
Blackberry Month*, **July**, 163
Blackwell, Elizabeth*, **b. Feb 3**
Blah Blah Blah Day, **Apr 17**
Blah Buster Month*, **Feb**, 40
Blame Someone Else Day, **June 13**
Blizzard of 1888*, **Mar 12**
Blonde Brownie Day, **Jan 22**
Blood bank, first, **Mar 15**
Blood Type Awareness Day, **June 13**
Blossom Month, **May**
Blue Day*, **Apr 23**
Blueberry Month*, **July**, 163
Blueberry Muffin Day, **July 12**
Blueberry Pancake Day, **Jan 28**
Bluebird of Happiness Day*, **Sep 24**
Bly, Nelly, around-the-world trip, **Jan 25**
Body-Painting Arts Festival*, **May 27**
Bogart, Humphrey, **b. Dec 25**
Bologna Day, **Oct 24**
Bomb exploded at World Trade Center, **Feb 26**
Bonza Bottler Day*, **Jan 1, Feb 2, Mar 3, Apr 4, May 5, June 6, July 7, Aug 8, Sep 9, Oct 10, Nov 11, Dec 12**
Book Lovers Day, **Aug 9**

Book Month*, **Jan,** 15
Book Week, **Jan**
Boone Day, **June 7**
Boone, Daniel, **b. Nov 2**
Boost Your Brain Day*, **Oct 18**
Boost Your Self-esteem Month, **Feb**
Boss Day, **Oct 16**
Boston Fire anniversary, **Nov 9**
Boston Marathon*, **Apr,** 93
Boston Marathon, first, **Apr 19**
Boston Massacre, **Mar 5**
Boston Tea Party, **Dec 16**
Bottle cap patented*, **Feb 2**
Bowling League Day (U.S.)*, **Sep 3**
Bowling Ball invented*, **Dec 29**
Bowling Week*, **Jan,** 18
Bow Tie Day*, **Aug 28**
Boxing Day, **Dec 26**
Boy Scouts of America founded, **Feb 8**
Boy Scouts Week, **Feb**
Braille Literacy Week*, **Jan,** 18
Braille, Louis, **b. Jan 4**
Bread Machine Baking Month*, **Jan,** 13
Breathe Easy Month*, **May,** 115
Bring Your Teddy Bear to School Day,
  Oct 11
Bring Your Teddy Bear to Work Day,
  Oct 13
British Appreciation Month, **Nov**
British Columbia (Canada) Admission
  Day, **July 20**
Broadcast from a communications
  satellite, first, **Dec 18**
Bronte, Emily, **b. July 30**
Brooklyn Bridge finished, **May 24**
Brother's Day, **May 24**
Brownie Day, **Dec 8**
Brownies at Brunch Month*, **Aug,** 188
Bubble Bath Day*, **Jan 8**
Bubble Week*, **Mar,** 67
Bubble Wrap Appreciation Day*, **Jan 28**
Bubblegum Week*, **Mar,** 66
Buckle Up America Week, **May**
Buffalo Bill (William Cody), **b. Feb 26**
Bugs Bunny cartoon published, first,
  Jul 27
Build a Scarecrow Day*, **Jul 1**
Bunsen Burner Day, **Mar 31**
Burbank, Luther, **b. Mar 7**
Bureau of Indian Affairs established,
  Mar 11
Burns, George, **b. Jan 20**
Bus, first built, **Jul 4**
Bush, George W., **b. Jul 6**
Buttercrunch Day, **Jan 20**
Buttered Corn Day*, **Aug,** 193
Buttered Popcorn Day, **Aug 17**
Butterscotch Pudding Day, **Sep 19**

Button Day*, **Nov 16**
Buy Nothing Day*, **Nov,** 265
Buy a Musical Instrument Day, **May 22**
Buzzards Day, **Mar 15**
Cabin Fever Day*, **Mar 9**
Cable car first patented, **Jan 17**
Caesar salad invented, **July 4**
Caesar, Julius, **b. July 12**
Caffeine Addiction Awareness Month, **Feb**
Cake Day, **Nov 26**
Caldecott, Randolph*, **b. Mar 22**
California Admission Day, **Sep 9**
California, first European sighting of,
  Sep 28
California Kiwi Fruit Day, **Feb 2**
California Kiwifruit Day, **Dec 22**
California Salmon Month, **July**
Camcorder developed, **Jan 20**
Camera Day, **June 29**
Camp David Peace Accord, **Mar 26**
Camp Fire Girls and Boys Week, **Mar**
Camp Fire Girls Day, **Mar 11**
Campbell, Kim, **b. Mar 10**
Camping Week*, **June,** 143
Canada Day*, **July 1**
Cancer Control Month, **Apr**
Cancer Survivor's Day, **June**
Candid Camera TV show premiered*,
  Aug 10
Candlemas (Mexico)*, **Feb 2**
Candy Cane Day, **Dec 26**
Candy Corn Day, **Oct 30**
Candy Day, **Nov 4**
Candy Month, **Nov**
Canned Food Day, **Oct 23**
Canned Food Month, **Feb**
Canned Luncheon Meat Week, **July**
Canned Spam first sold*, **May 16**
Captain Kangaroo TV show first aired,
  Oct 3
Car Care Month, **Oct**
Caramel Month*, **Oct,** 238
Caraway, Hattie Wyatt, **b. Feb 1**
Card & Letter Writing Week*, **Nov,** 262
Card Playing Day, **Dec 28**
Card Reading Day, **Feb 21**
Caribbean Day, **July 5**
Carle, Eric, **b. June 25**
Carnation Day, **Jan 29**
Carnegie, Andrew, **b. Nov 25**
Carnival*, **Mar,** 68
Carousel patented, **July 25**
Carroll, Lewis, **b. Jan 27**
Carter, James Earl, **b. Oct 1**
Cartoon Appreciation Week*, **May,** 118
Cartoonists Day, **May**
Carve a Pumpkin Day*, **Oct 31**
Casey at the Bat Day, **June 3**

Cash register patented, **Nov 4**
Cash, Johnny, **b. Feb 26**
Cashew Day*, **Nov 23**
Castro, Fidel, **b. Aug 13**
Castro, Fidel, became Cuba's premier,
  Feb 16
Cat show, first, **Dec 27**
Cat Health Month, **Feb**
Cat Week*, **Nov,** 262
Catfish Month*, **Aug,** 189
Caviar Day, **July 18**
CD player debuted, **Oct 1**
Celebrate the Past Month*, **Jan,** 15
Celebrate Your Lakes Day, **Aug 9**
Celebrate Your Name Day*, **Mar,** 69
Celebrate Your Name Week, **Mar**
Celebration of Life Day, **Jan 22**
Celebration of Life Month*, **Jan,** 15
Celebration of Love Week, **Feb**
Celebration of the Senses Day, **June 24**
Cellphone Courtesy Month*, **July,** 165
Centenarians Day, **Sep 22**
Cézanne, Paul, **b. Jan 19**
Chagall, Marc, **b. July 4**
Chain store opened, first, **Feb 22**
Challenger Space Shuttle explosion,
  Jan 28
Champion Crab Races Day*, **Feb 17**
Character Counts Week, **Oct**
Chavez, Cesar, **b. Mar 31**
Check Your Batteries Day, **Apr 6**
Checkers Day, **Sep 23**
Cheer Up the Lonely Day, **July 11**
Cheerios first produced*, **May 1**
Cheeseball Day, **Apr 17**
Cheesecake Day, **July 30**
Cheese Cake Day, **August 8**
Cheese Day*, **Jan 20**
Cheese Doodle Day, **Mar 5**
Cheese Pizza Day, **Sep 5**
Chemistry Week*, **Oct,** 241
Chernobyl nuclear reactor exploded,
  Apr 26
Cherry Month, National*, **Feb,** 43
Cherry Popsicle Day, **Aug 26**
Chesapeake Turtle Derby*, **July 7**
Chess Day, **July 20, Sep 1**
Chewing Gum Day, **Sep 30**
Chewing gum patented*, **Dec 28**
Chicago Fire, Great, **Oct 8**
Chicken Month*, **Sep,** 211
Chicken Wings Day*, **July 29**
Child Abuse Prevention Month, **Apr**
Child Accident Prevention Week*,
  Sep, 216
Child Health Day, **Oct 6**
Child Health Month, **Oct**
Child Safety and Protection Month, **Nov**

306

Electric washing machine patented, **Aug 9**
Electricity Day, **June 15**
Electronic Greetings Day, **Nov 29**
Elementary School Teacher Day*, **Jan 15**
Elephant Appreciation Day, **Sep 22**
Eliot, T. S., **b**, **Sep 26**
Ellington, Duke, **b. Apr 29**
Ellis Island opened, **Dec 31**
Elvis Presley Commemoration Day,
    Aug 16
Elvis Week, **Aug**
Emancipation of 500, **Aug 1**
Emancipation Proclamation issued,
    Sep 22
Embrace Your Geekness Day, **July 13**
Embroidery Month, **Feb**
Emergency Care Month, **Sep**
Emergency Services Day*, **Sep 11**
Emerson, Ralph Waldo, **b. May 25**
Empire State Building finished, **May 1**
Encourage a Young Writer Day, **Apr 10**
End of hurricane season, **Oct 20**
Endangered Species Act, **Feb 3**
Energy Awareness Month, **Oct**
Engineering Week, **Feb**
English Toffee Day*, **Jan 8**
Epiphany Day, **Jan 6**
Erie Canal opened*, **Oct 26**
Enjoy Candy Month, **June**
Escape Day*, **Jan 30**
Escargot Day, **May 24**
Eskimo Pie Patent Day*, **Jan 24**
Espresso Day, **Nov 24**
Etch-A-Sketch invented, **July 12**
Ether, first use as anesthetic, **Sep 30**
Ethics Awareness Month, **Mar**
Ethnic Foods Month*, **Sep**, 215
Etiquette Week*, **May**, 118
Euro introduced*, **Jan 1**
European Union established, **Nov 1**
Evaluate Your Life Day, **Oct 19**
Evers, Medgar, killed, **June 12**
Everything You Do Is Right Day, **Mar 16**
Everything You Think Is Wrong Day,
    Mar 15
Expect Success Month, **Feb**
Explorer I launched, **Jan 31**
Eye Care Month*, **Jan**, 16
Eye Donor Month, **Mar**
Eye Exam Month, **July**
Eye Safety Awareness Week, **June**
Eyeglasses invented, **Aug 13**
Fahrenheit thermometer invented, **Dec 22**
Failures Day*, **Aug 15**
"Fair Deal" proposed by Pres. Truman,
    Jan 5
Fall Equinox*, **Sep**, 219
Fall Hat Month*, **Sep**, 213
Fall Hat Week, **Sep**

False teeth patented*, **Mar 9**
Family Awareness Day, **June 15**
Family Caregivers Day, **Nov**
Family Day, **Mar 24, June 5**
Family Eye Care Month, **Aug**
Family Fit Lifestyle Month, **Jan**
Family Fun Month, **Aug**
Family Health & Fitness Day, **Sep 28**
Family Health Month, **Oct**
Family History Day*, **June 14**
Family History Month*, **Oct**, 236
Family Literacy Month, **Nov**
Family Stories Month*, **Nov**, 260
Family Week, National, **June, Nov**
Family Week, Universal, **May**
Fantasy Month*, **Oct**, 239
Farm Animal Day, **Oct 2**
Farm Animals Awareness Week*,
    Sep, 217
Farm Joke Day*, **Nov 17**
Farm Week, **Nov**
Farm-City Week, **Nov**
Farmers' Day, **Mar 8**
Farrier's Week, **July**
Fast Food Day, **Nov 16**
Father-Daughter Take a Walk Together
    Day, **July 7**
Father's Day*, **June**, 145
Faulkner, William, **b. Sep 25**
FBI founded, **July 26**
FCC created, **Feb 26**
Federal Building in Oklahoma City
    bombed, **Apr 19**
Federal Reserve System established,
    Dec 23
Felt Hat Day, **Sep 15**
Female dentist, first American*, **Feb 21**
Female M.D., first in U.S., **Jan 23**
Female U.S. Supreme Court, first, **Sep 25**
Ferris Wheel Day, **Feb 14**
Ferris Wheel introduced, **June 21**
Festival of Sleep Day, **Jan 3**
Fiery Foods & Barbeque Show, **Mar 5**
Fig Newton Day, **Jan 16**
Fig Week, **Nov**
Fight Procrastination Day, **Sep**
Fillmore, Millard, **b. Jan 7**
Final Warning Day*, **Feb 13**
Find a Rainbow Day*, **Apr 3**
Fingerprint taken, first*, **July 28**
Fire Day*, **May 2**
Fire Escape Ladder Day, **May 7**
Fire Prevention Day, **Oct 8**
Fire Prevention Month, **Oct**
Fire Prevention Week, **Oct**
Firefly Season, beginning of*, **June 7**
Fireworks Month*, **July**, 162
Fireworks Safety Month*, **July**, 162
First American in space, **May**

First day of spring*, **Mar**, 69
First day of summer*, **June**, 144
First holiday proclaimed by U.S.
    President, **Nov 26**
First Hot-Air Balloon flight, **June 5**
Fishing & Hunting Day*, **Sep 25**
Fishing Week*, **June**, 142
Fitzgerald, Francis Scott, **b. Sep 24**
Flag Day (Australia), **May 22**
Flag Day (Canada), **Feb 15**
Flag Day (Mexico), **Feb 24**
Flag Day (U.S.)*, **June 14**
Flag Month, **June**
Flag Week, **June**
Flashlight Day*, **Dec 21**
Flirting Week, **Feb**
Flitch Day, **July 19**
Floral Design Day, **Feb 28**
Florida Admission Day*, **Mar 3**
Flower Basket Day, **Jan 4**
Flower Month*, **May**, 111
Fly a Kite Day, **Mar 27**
Flying saucer, first report of, **June 24**
Food Allergy Awareness Month, **Sep**
Foot Health Month*, **Mar**, 64
For Pete's Sake Day, **Feb 26**
Ford Mustang introduced, **Apr 17**
Ford, Gerald, **b. July 14**
Ford, Henry, **b. July 30**
Forefathers Day, **Dec 21**
Foreign Language Month*, **July**, 163
Foreign Language Week, **Mar**
Forest Products Day, **Oct 19**
Forest Week, **Apr**
Forget-Me-Not Day, **Nov 10**
Forgiveness Day*, **Aug**, 193
Forgiveness Week, **June**
Fork, introduced to America, **June 25**
Former POW Recognition Day, **May 9**
Fortune Cookie Day, **Sep 13**
Foster, Stephen, **b. July 4**
Frank, Anne, **b. June 12**
Franklin, Ben*, **b. Jan 17**
Franklin, Ben, proved lightning contains
    electricity, **June 15**
Frappe Day*, **Oct 7**
Freckle Pride Day*, **Nov 27**
Freedom of Information Day, **Mar 17**
Freedom of the Press Day, **June 7**
Freedom Day, **Feb 1**
Freedom Week*, **July**, 166
French and Indian War ended, **Feb 10**
French Fried Shrimp Day, **Dec 21**
French Fries Day, **July 13**
French Toast Day, **Nov 28**
Fresh Breath Day*, **Aug 6**
Fresh Fruit and Vegetable Month*,
    June, 138
Fresh Spinach Day, **July 16**

Fresh-Squeezed Juice Day*, **Jan**, 19
Fresh Veggies Day, **June 16**
Fried Chicken Day, **July 6**
Friend in Need Day, **June 15**
Friendship Day, International*, **Aug**, 192
Friendship Month*, **Feb**, 39
Friendship Week, **Feb**
Frisbee introduction, **Jan 13,** patented, **Sep 30**
Fritters Day, **Dec 2**
Frog-Jumping Day*, **May 13**
Frog Month*, **Apr**, 88
Frost, Robert*, **b. Mar 26**
Frozen Food Day, **Mar 6**
Frozen Food Month, **Mar**
Frozen Yogurt Day, **June 1**
Frozen Yogurt Month, **June**
Frugal Fun Day, **Oct 4**
Fruit Day, **Oct 20**
Fruitcake Day*, **Dec 27**
Fruitcake Toss, Great, **Jan 4**
Fudge Day, **June 16**
Fun at Work Day, **Apr 1**
Fun Facts About Names Day*, **Mar 3**
Fun With Fondue Month, **Nov**
Galileo Galilei, **Feb 15**
Game and Puzzle Week*, **Nov**, 263
Games Day*, **Dec 20**
Gandhi, Indira, **b. Nov 19**
Gandhi, Indira, became India's prime minister, **Jan 19**
Ghandi, Mahatma , **b. Oct. 2**
Garage Sale Day*, **Aug**, 193
Garden Month, **Apr**
Garden Week, **Apr**
Garfield the Cat, **b. June 19**
Garfield, James, **b. Nov 19**
Garfield, James, Assassination, **Sep 19**
Garland, Judy*, **b. June 10**
Garlic Day, **Apr 19**
Gaudy Day*, **Oct 17**
Gazpacho Day*, **Dec 6**
Gehrig, Lou, **b. June 19**
Genealogy Day*, **Mar**, 69
General Motors established, **Sep 16**
Geography Awareness Week*, **Nov**, 263
George Washington Bridge opened, **Oct 24**
George Washington elected first U.S. president, **Feb 4**
Georgia Admission Day, **Jan 2**
Georgia Pecan Month, **Nov**
German Reunification Day, **Oct 3**
German-American Day*, **Oct 6**
German-American's Day*, **Apr 5**
Gershwin, George, **b. Sep 26**
Get a Different Name Day, **Feb 13**
Get Caught Reading Day, **Mar 1**
Get Caught Reading Month*, **May**, 111

Get Organized Week, **Oct**
Get Out of the Doghouse Day*, **July**, 169
Get Over It! Month*, **Jan**, 15
Gettysburg Address delivered, **Nov 19**
Ghostbusters movie introduced*, **June 8**
Gimmicks Day*, **Jan 21**
Gingerbread Day*, **June 5**
Gingerbread House Day, **Dec 12**
Girl Scout Day, **Mar 12**
Girl Scout Week, **Mar**
National Girls & Women in Sports Day, **Feb 5**
Girls' Day (Japan)*, **Mar 3**
Give a Homemade Holiday Gift Day*, **Dec 19**
Give Someone a Dollar Today Day, **Nov 3**
Glenn, John, **b. July 18**
Go Caroling Day, **Dec 19**
Go Fishing Day, **June 18**
Go Fly a Kite Day, **June 15**
Go for a Ride Day, **Nov 22**
Go for Broke Day, **Apr 5**
Go Nuts Over Texas Peanuts Month, **Oct**
Go on a Field Trip Month, **Oct**
Go to an Art Museum Today Day*, **Nov 9**
Go West Day, **July 13**
Goat Cheese Month, **July**
"God Bless America" first performed, **Nov 11**
Gold discovered in Alaska, **June 16**
Gold discovered in California, **Jan 24**
Golden Gate Bridge opened, **May 27**
Golden Rule Week*, **Apr**, 90
Golf Day, **Oct 4**
Golf Month, **Aug**
Golf tee patented, **Dec 12**
Golf Week*, **Feb**, 45
Golfer's Day, **Apr 10**
Good Friday*, **Apr**, 92
Good-Neighbor Day*, **May**, 121; **Sep**
Good Nutrition Month, **Nov**
Good Samaritan Day, **Mar 13**
Good Stewardship Week, **May**
Goof-off Day*, **Mar 22**
Goof-off Week*, **Mar**, 67
Gorbachev, Mikhail, resigned as USSR president, **Dec 25**
Gorilla born in captivity, first*, **Dec 22**
Graham Cracker Day, **July 5**
Graham, Billy, **b. Nov 7**
Grand Canyon National Park established, **Feb 26**
Grandma Moses Day, **Sep 7**
Grandma Moses, **b. Sep 7**
Grandparents Day, **Sep 10**
Grandparents Month, **Sep**
Granola Bar Day*, **Jan 21**
Grant, Ulysses S., **b. Apr 27**
Grapefruit Month*, **Feb**, 42

Great American Meat Out Day, **Mar 19**
Great Backyard Bird Count*, **Feb**, 45
Great Barrier Reef discovered, **June 11**
Great Circus Parade Week, **July**
Great Egg Toss Day*, **Sep 6**
Great Plague began in London, **Apr 26**
Great Seal of the U.S. approved*, **Jan 28;** officially adopted, **June 20**
Greatest Show on Earth first performance, **Mar 28**
Greeley, Horace, **b. Feb 3**
Green Day*, **Apr 2**
Green Peppers Day, **Aug 5**
Gregorian Calendar created, **Feb 24**
Grey Day*, **May 26**
Greyhound bus introduced, **Aug 13**
Grilled Cheese Sandwich Month*, **Apr**, 89
Grouch Day*, **Oct 15**
Groundhog Day*, **Feb 2**
Guacamole Day, **Nov 14**
Guadalupe Day (Mexico), **Dec 12**
Guitar Month, International*, **Apr**, 87
Guitar Week, **Apr**
Gumbo Day, **Oct 12**
Gumdrop Day*, **Feb 15**
Guy Fawkes Day, **Nov 5**
Gymnastics Day, **Aug 23**
Hairball Awareness Day, **Apr 25**
Hairstyle Appreciation Day*, **Apr 30**
Haley, Alex Palmer, **b. Aug 11**
Haley, Edward, **b. Nov 8**
Halfway point of autumn, **Nov 6**
Halfway point of summer, **Aug 6**
Halfway point of the year, **July 2**
Halfway point of winter*, **Feb 3**
Halloween*, **Oct 31**
Hamburger Day, **May 28, July 28, Dec 21**
Hamburger Month*, **Mar,** 61; **May**, 117
Hamilton, Alexander, **b. Jan 11**
Hancock, John, **b. Jan 12**
Hand-Holding Day, **Aug 9**
Hand-Washing Awareness Week*, **Dec**, 284
Handel, George Frederick, **b. Feb 23**
Handwriting Day*, **Jan 23**
Hang a Wreath Day*, **Dec 7**
Hanukkah*, **Dec**, 287
"Happy Birthday to You" composed, **June 27**
Happy Goose Day*, **Sep 29**
Happy "Mew" Year for Cats Day*, **Jan 2**
Harding, Warren, **b. Nov 2**
Harrison, Benjamin, **b. Aug 20**
Harrison, William Henry, **b. Feb 9**
Harvard University founded, **Oct 28**
Hat Day, **Jan 20**
Haunted Refrigerator Night*, **Oct 30**

Have a Bad Day Day*, **Nov 19**
Have a Heart Day, **Feb 14**
Hawaii Admission Day, **Aug 21**
Hawaii annexed, **July 7**
Hawaiian Lei Day*, **May 1**
Hawking, Stephen, **b. Jan 8**
Hawthorne, Nathaniel, **b. July 4**
Haydn, Franz Joseph, **b. Mar 31**
Health Education Week, **Feb**
Health Information Week, **Nov**
Healthy Skin Month*, **Nov**, 260
Hearing and Speech Month, **May**
Heart Mania Day, **June 6**
Heart Month, American*, **Feb**, 38
Heart transplant, human, first successful*, **Dec 3**
Helicopter invented*, **June 16**
Hello Day, **Aug 15**
Hemingway, Ernest, **b, July 21**
Henie, Sonja, **b. Apr 8**
Henry, Patrick, **b. May 29**
Henson, Jim, **b. Sep 24**
Herb Week, **May**
Heritage Day (Canada)*, **Feb 16**
Hermit Week, **June**
Hero Week*, **Feb**, 44
Hershey's Chocolate founded*, **Feb 9**
Hi Neighbor Month, **Dec**
High Blood Pressure Month, **May**
Highway numbers introduced, **Mar 2**
Hilton, Conrad, **b. Dec 25**
Hispanic Heritage Month*, **Sep**, 214
Historic Preservation Week, **May**
Hitchcock, Alfred, **b. Aug 13**
Hi-Tech Month, **Jan**
Hoagie Day, **May 5**
Hobbit Day, **Jan 3**
Hobby Month*, **Jan**, 12
Hockey mask invented*, **Nov 1**
Hollerin' Contest Day, **June 16**
Holocaust Museum, U.S., opened, **Apr 26**
Holocaust Remembrance Day, **Apr 20**
Holocaust Remembrance Month*, **Apr**, 86
Holy Week*, **Apr**, 92
Homeless Animals Day, **Aug**
Homemade Bread Day, **Nov 17**
Homemade Cookies Day*, **Oct 1**
Homemade Pie Day, **Aug 1**
Homes for Birds Week*, **Feb**, 44
Homestead Act signed, **May 20**
Honesty Day, **Apr 30**
Honey Month*, **Sep**, 212
Hoodie Hoo Day, Southern Hemisphere, **Aug 22**
Hoodie Hoo Day, Northern Hemisphere*, **Feb 20**
Hooray for Imperfection Week, **Sep**
Hooray for Kids! Day, **Aug 4**
Hoover, Herbert, **b. Aug 10**

Hope, Bob, **b. May 29**
Hospital Week, **May**
Hostages, U.S. freed from Iran, **Jan 20**
Hot & Spicy Food Day, International*, **Jan 16**
Hot Breakfast Month*, **Feb**, 42
Hot Dog Birthday, **Sep 9**
Hot Dog Day, **Mar 30; July 22**
Hot Dog Month*, **July**, 164
Hot Enough for Ya Day*, **July 23**
Hot Fudge Sundae Day, **July 25**
Hot Pastrami Sandwich Day*, **Jan 14**
Hot Tea Month*, **Jan**, 14
Hotline established between U.S. and USSR, **Aug 30**
Houdini, Harry*, **b. Mar 24**
Howdy Doody TV Show, first, **Dec 27**
Hubble Space Telescope deployed*, **Apr 25**
Hubble, Edwin P., **b. Nov 20**
Hug a Friend Day, **Apr 26**
Hug a Senior Day, **Aug 2**
Hug Day, **Dec 4**
Hug Holiday, **June 11**
Hug Your Cat Day, **May 3**
Hug-a-bear Day, **Nov 7**
Hugging Day, **Jan 21**
Hughes, Langston, **b. Feb 1**
Human flight, first, **Oct 15**
Human genome mapped, **June 26**
Human Rights Day, **Dec 10**
Human Rights Month, **Dec**
Human Rights Week, **Dec**
Humanitarian Day*, **Jan 15**
Humbug Day, **Dec 21**
Humor Month*, **Apr**, 88
Humor Week, **June**
Hunger Awareness Day, **June 4**
Hunger Awareness Month, **Oct**
Hooray for Buttons Day*, **May 9**
Hurricane Awareness Week*, **May**, 119
Hurricane Hugo hit U.S. East Coast, **Sep 21**
Hurricane Rita struck U.S, **Sep 24**
Hydrogen bomb, first test explosion conducted in Pacific Ocean, **May 21**
I Am So Thankful Month, **Nov**
I Forgot Day*, **July 2**
I Love Lucy TV show premiered, **Oct. 15**
I Want Butterscotch Day, **Feb 15**
I Want You to Be Happy Day*, **Mar 3**
Ice Art Championships, World, **Mar 14**
Ice-Cream cone introduced, **July 23**
Ice-Cream Day*, **July**, 168, **Dec 13**
Ice cream first sold, **June 8**
Ice-Cream Month, **July**
Ice-Cream Sandwich Day*, **Aug 2**
Ice-Cream Sandwich Month, **Sep**
Ice-Cream Soda Day, **June 20**
Ice-Cream Sundae created, **July 8**
Ice-Skating Month, **Nov**

Iced Tea Month, **June**
Idaho Admission Day, **July 3**
Idaho Spud Day, **Sep**
Ides of March, **Mar 15**
Iditarod*, **Mar**, 69
Iguana Awareness Day, **Sep 6**
Illinois Admission Day, **Dec 3**
I'm Not Going to Take It Anymore Day*, **Jan 7**
Immunization Awareness Month, **Aug**
Inane Answering Message Day*, **Jan 30**
Indian Pudding Day, **Nov 13**
Indiana Admission Day, **Dec 11**
Indianapolis 500 Car Race, first held*, **May 30**
Indianapolis 500 Speedway constructed, **Aug 19**
Ingalls Wilder, Laura, **b. Feb 7**
Inspire Your Heart with Art Day*, **Jan 31**
Instant coffee invented, **July 24**
International Language Week*, **Dec**, 285
International Space Station launched, **Dec 4**
Internet Day *, **Oct 29**
Introduction of the VCR, **June 7**
Inventors Day*, **Feb 11**
Inventors Month*, **Aug**, 186
Iowa Admission Day, **Dec 28**
Iran Hostage Crisis began, **Nov 5**
Iran Hostages freed, **Jan 20**
Irish-American Month, **Mar**
"Iron Curtain" speech, **Mar 5**
Iron Horse transcontinental railroad began, **Sep 18**
Irving, Washington, **b. Apr 3**
Israel declared an independent nation, **May 14**
Italian Heritage Month*, **June**, 141
Itch Day*, **June 3**
It's About Time Week*, **Dec**, 285
It's OK to Be Different Month*, **Jan**, 17
Jack Frost Day, **Dec 11**
Jackie Robinson Day, **Apr 11**
Jackson, Andrew, **b. Mar 15**
Jackson, Jesse, **b. Oct 8**
Jackson, Thomas "Stonewall," **b. Jan 21**
Jamestown settlement established, **May 14**
Japanese Culture Day, **Nov 3**
Jazz Month, **Sep**
Jazz Music Day, **May 29**
Jefferson, Thomas, **b. Apr 13**
Jellybean Day*, **Apr 22**
Jewish Heritage Week, **Apr**
Jigsaw Day*, **May 11**
Joan of Arc, **b. Jan 6**
Joe Day, **Mar 27**
John Glenn Day, **Feb 20**
John Philip Sousa titled "The Stars and Stripes Forever," **Dec 25**
Johnny Appleseed Day, **Mar 11**

Lowe, Juliette, **b. Oct 31**
Loyalty Day, **May 1**
Lumpy Rug Day*, **May 3**
Luna 9, **Jan 31**
Luna I launch, **Jan 2**
Lung Cancer Awareness Month, **Nov**
Lusitania sank, **May 7**
Luther, Martin, **b. Nov 10**
Luther, Martin, posted *95 Theses*, **Oct 31**
Lyme Disease Awareness Week, **July**
Macaroni Day, **July 7**
Macaroon Day, **May 31**
MacDonald, John A., **b. Jan 11**
MacDonald's, first, opened, **Apr 15**
Machine Day, **June 12**
Machu Picchu discovered, **July 23**
MacKenzie, Alexander, **b. Jan 28**
Made in America Month*, **Dec**, 282
Madison, James, **b. Mar 16**
Magazine Day, **Nov 7**
Magazine, first published in America, **Feb 13**
Magellan began his voyage around the world*, **Sep 20**
Magic Day, **June 12**
Magna Carta Day, **June 15**
Mail order catalog published, first, **Aug 18**
Maine Admission Day, **Mar 15**
Maintenance Day, **Jan 18**
Make a Difference Day, **Oct 27**
Make a Friend Day, **Feb 11**
Make a Homemade Holiday Gift Day, **Dec 9**
Make Up Your Mind Day*, **Dec 31**
Make Up Your Own Holiday Day*, **Mar 26**
Make Your Bed Day, **Sep 11**
Make Your Dreams Come True Day*, **Jan 13**
Make Your Own Holiday Cards Day*, **Dec 11**
Make Your Own Luck Day, **Aug 26**
Mandela, Nelson, **b. July 18**
Mandela, Nelson, released from prison, **Feb 11**
Manet, Edouard, **b. Jan 23**
Manitoba Admission Day (Canada), **July 15**
Mantle, Mickey*, **b. Oct 20**
Map of the U.S. first patented*, **Mar 31**
Maple Syrup Day, **Mar**
March 4 Yourself Day, **Mar 4**
March of Dimes Birth Defects Prevention Month, **Jan**
March of Dimes formed, **Jan 3**
March on Washington anniversary, **Aug 28**
Mardi Gras*, **Mar**, 68

Margarine Patented, **July 15**
Marie Antoinette, **b. Nov 2**
Mario Day, **Mar 10**
Maritime Day*, **May 22**
Martin, Paul J., **b. Aug 26**
Marx, Groucho, **b. Oct. 2**
"Mary Had a Little Lamb" published*, **Sep 1**
Maryland Admission Day, **Apr 28**
Marzipan Day, **Jan 12**
Masking tape patented, **May 27**
Massachusetts Admission Day, **Feb 6**
Matanzas Mule Day*, **Apr 27**
Mathematics Education Month*, **Apr**, 88
Matisse, Henri, **b. Dec 31**
Maundy Thursday*, **Apr**, 92
May Day*, **May 1**
Mayflower Compact signed, **Nov 21**
Mayflower Day, **Sep 16**
Mayflower docked at Cape Cod, Massachusetts, **Nov 19**
McAuliffe, Christa, **b. Sep 2**
McAuliffe, Christa, Day, **Jan 28**
McCloskey, Robert, **b. Sep 15**
McCormick, Cyrus, **b. Feb 15**
McKinley, William, **b. Jan 29**
Measure Your Feet Day*, **Jan 23**
Meat Week*, **Jan**, 19
Medicare Program established, **July 1**
Mellow Yellow Day, **Nov 12**
Memo Day*, **May 21**
Memorial Day*, **May**, 120
Memory Day*, **Mar 21**
Men's Month, **June**
Mental Health Month, **May**
Mentoring Month, **Jan**
Merry-Go-Round Birthday, **May 17**
Messiah composed, **Sep 14**
Meteor Day, **June 30**
Metric Conversion Act signed*, **Dec 23**
Metric Week*, **Oct**, 240
Mexican Independence Day, **Sep 16**
Mexican War declared, **May 13**
Michelangelo*, **b. Mar 6**
Michigan Admission Day, **Jan 26**
Mickey Mouse debuted, **Nov 18**
Middle Children's Day, **Aug 8**
Middle East Peace Accord signed, **Sep 13**
Middle Name Pride Day, **Mar 7**
Milk Chocolate Day, **July 28**
Milk Day, **Jan 11**
Milne, A. A., **b. Jan 18**
Miniature golf began, **Dec 14**
Miniature Golf Day*, **Sep 21**
Minnesota Admission Day, **May 11**
Mir Space Station abandoned, **Mar 23**
Mir Space Station launched*, **Feb 19**
Mirth Month*, **Mar**, 65
Mirthday, **June 22**

Mississippi Admission Day, **Dec 10**
Missouri Admission Day, **Aug 10**
Missouri Compromise introduced*, **Mar 3**
Mitten Tree Day, **Dec 6**
Model Railroad Month, **Nov**
Model T introduced by Henry Ford, **Oct 1**
Modern Dance Month, **May**
Moldy Cheese Day, **Oct 9**
Moment of Frustration Scream Day, International, **Oct 12**
Moment of Laughter Day*, **Apr 29**
Mom's and Dad's Day, **Nov 13**
Moms Are Marvelous Month, **May**
Mona Lisa painting stolen from The Louvre, Paris, **Aug 22**
Monet, Claude, **b. Nov 14**
Monopoly patented, **Mar 7**
Monroe Doctrine presented, **Dec 2**
Monroe, James, **b. Apr 28**
Montague, John, Earl of Sandwich*, **b. Nov 3**
Montana Admission Day, **Nov 8**
Montgomery Bus Boycott began, **Dec 5**
Month of the Young Child, **Apr**
Moon landing, first, **July 16**
Moon walk, first, **July 20**
Moose Droppings Festival, **July 10**
More Herbs, Less Salt Day, **Aug 29**
Morse Code first used, **May 24**
Morse Code signal "SOS" adopted, **Nov 22**
Morse, Samuel, **b. Apr 27**
Mosquito-Control Awareness Weekend*, **Aug**, 190
Mosquito Day*, **July 23**
Mother Goose Day, **May 1**
Mother Goose Parade, **Nov 18**
Mother Teresa*, **b. Aug 27**
Mother's Day proclaimed, **May 9**
Mother's Day*, **May**, 120
Motorcycle Day, **May 14**
Motorcycle patented*, **Aug 29**
Motorcycle Safety Month, **May**
Motorist Consideration Day, **Aug 27**
Mott, Lucretia Coffin, **b. Jan 3**
Mourning, National Day of (Canada), **Apr 28**
Mousse Day*, **Nov 30**
Mozart Week*, **Jan**, 19
Mozart, **b. Dec 5**
Mozart, Wolfgang, **b. Jan 27**
Mr. Roger's Neighborhood debuted*, **Feb 19**
Mt. Rushmore completed, **Oct 31**
Mt. St. Helens erupted*, **May 18**
Mt. Everest summit reached for first time*, **May 29**
Mt. Vesuvius erupted, **Aug 24**

Parents' Day, **July**

Parfait Day*, **Nov 25**

Paris liberated in WWII, **Aug 25**

Parking meter invented*, **July 16**

Parks, Rosa, **b. Feb 4**

Particularly Preposterous Packaging Day, **Aug 6**

Passover*, **Apr**, 93

Pasta Day, World, **Oct 25**

Pasta Days, **Mar 15**

Pasta Month*, **Oct**, 237

Paste Up Day, **May 7**

Pasteur, Louis*, **Dec 27**

Pastry Day, **Dec 9**

Patriot Day*, **Sep 11**

Patriots Day*, **Apr 19**

Patriots Month, **June**

Paul Bunyan Day*, **June 28**

Paul Revere's Ride*, **Apr 19**

Pay a Compliment Day, **Feb 6**

Peace Corps established, **Mar 1**

Peace Day, **Aug 6, Sep 16, Nov 17, Dec 21**

Peace, Friendship and Goodwill Week, **Oct**

Peace Officer Memorial Day, **May 15**

Peach Blossom Day*, **Mar 3**

Peach Cobbler Day, **Apr 13**

Peach Ice-Cream Day, **July 17**

Peach Month, **July**

Peach Pie Day, **Aug 24**

Peanut Brittle Day, **Jan 26**

Peanut Butter and Jelly Day, **Apr 2**

Peanut Butter Day*, **Jan 24**

Peanut Butter Fudge Day, **Nov 20**

Peanut Butter Lovers Day, **Mar 1**

Peanut Butter Lover's Month*, **Nov**, 261

Peanut Day, **Sep 13**

Peanut Month, **Mar**

"Peanuts" comic strip first published*, **Oct. 2**

Pearl Harbor Remembrance Day, **Dec 7**

Pearson, Lester B., **b. Apr 23**

Pecan Day*, **Mar 25**

Pecan Month, **Apr**

Pecan Pie Day, **July 12**

Peculiar People Day*, **Jan 10**

Pediculosis (Lice) Month*, **Sep**, 213

Pele, **b. Oct 23**

Pencil Day*, **Aug 17**

Pencil sharpener invented, **Nov 23**

Pencil with eraser patented*, **Mar 30**

Penguin Awareness Day, **Jan 19**

Penn, William, **b. Oct 14**

Pennsylvania Admission Day, **Dec 12**

Penny Day*, **May 23**

Pentagon completed, **Jan 15**

People Skills Month, **June**

Pepper Month, **Nov**

Pepsi Cola first sold, **June 16**

Perrault, Charles*, **b. Jan 12**

Perry & Henson reached the North Pole, **Apr 6**

Persian Gulf War, **Jan 16**

Personal Self-Defense Month*, **Jan**, 17

Personality Day*, **Mar 5**

Pest Control Month, **June**

Pet Appreciation Week (PAW), **June**

Pet Memorial Day, **Sep 14**

Pet Owner's Day, **Apr 18**

Pet Peeve Week, **Oct**

Pet Week, **May**

Peter Pan Day, **May 9**

Peter Rabbit, introduction of, **Sep 4**

Pets are Wonderful Month, **Apr**

Phonograph patented, **Feb 18**

Photo Month*, **May**, 115

Photography Day, **Mar 27**

Physical Fitness Month*, **May**, 116

Piano Month, **Sep**

Picasso, Pablo*, **b. Oct 25**

Pick Blueberries Day, **July 14**

Pick Up Some Litter Day*, **June**, 144

Pickle Appreciation Day, **Nov 14**

Pickle Time Week, **Feb**

Pickle Week*, **May**, 119

Pickled Pepper Month, **Oct**

Pickled Pepper Week*, **Oct**, 240

Picnic Day*, **June 18**

Picnic Month, **July**

Picture of Earth taken from space, first, **Aug 6**

Picture postcard, first*, **July 6**

Pie Day, **Dec 1, Jan 23**

Pierce Your Ears Day, **Sep 2**

Pierce, Franklin, **b. Nov 23**

Pig Day*, **Jan 17**

Pigs in a Blanket Day*, **Apr 24**

Pilgrims landed at Plymouth, Massachusetts, **Dec 21**

Pilgrims sailed for America, **Sep 6**

Pineapple Upside-down Cake Day, **Apr 20**

Pink Cadillac Day*, **Sep 1**

Pink Day*, **June 23**

Pink Flamingo Month*, **Sep**, 213

Pins and Needles Day*, **Nov 27**

Pioneer Day, **July 24**

Pistachio Day*, **Feb 26**

Pizza Month*, **Oct**, 239

Pizza Week*, **Jan**, 18

Pizza with the Works Except Anchovies Day, **Nov 12**

Plain Yogurt Day*, **June 20**

Planetarium, first in U.S., **May 10**

Plant a Flower Day*, **Mar 8**

Plant the Seeds of Greatness Month, **Feb**

Plastic surgery operation, first, **Oct 23**

Play in the Sand Day*, **Aug 11**

Play the Recorder Month, **Mar**

Play Dough Day*, **Sep 18**

Playground Safety Day, **Apr 27**

Playground Safety Week, **Apr**

"Pledge of Allegiance" first recognized, **Dec 28**

"Pledge of Allegiance" written, **Oct 10**

Plum Pudding Day, **Feb 12**

Plush Animal Lover's Day, **Oct 28**

Pluto discovered, **Feb 18**

Poe, Edgar Allan*, **b. Jan 19**

Poetry Day*, **Oct 15**

Poetry Month*, **Apr**, 86

Poetry Reading Day*, **Apr 28**

Poets' Day*, **Aug 21**

Poinsettia Day*, **Dec 12**

Poison Prevention Month, **Mar**

Poison Prevention Week, **Mar**

Poitier, Sidney, **b. Feb 20**

Polar Bear Day*, **Feb 27**

Polar Bear Swim Day*, **Jan 1**

Police Week, **May**

Policewoman Day, **Sep 12**

Polio vaccine invented, **Mar 26**

Polish American Heritage Month, **Oct**

Polk, James, **b. Nov 2**

Pony Express service began*, **Apr 3**

Pooh Day, **Jan 18**

Poor Richard's Almanac first published, **Dec 28**

Popcorn Day*, **Jan 31**

Popcorn first introduced to American colonists, **Feb 21**

Popcorn-Popping Month, **Oct**

Pop Goes the Weasel Day, **June 14**

Pop Music Chart, first, **Jan 4**

Pork Month, **Oct**

Positive Thinking Day, **Sep 13**

Postcard Week, **May**

Potato Chip Day, **Mar 14**

Potato Day*, **Aug 19**

Potato Lover's Month*, **Feb**, 43

Potato Month, **Sep**

Potter, Beatrix, **b. July 28**

Poultry Day*, **Mar 19**

Pound Cake Day, **Mar 4**

Poverty in America Awareness Month*, **Jan**, 17

POW/MIA Recognition Day, **Sep 19**

Prayer, National Day of, **May**

Preschoolers Day, **Mar 14**

Presidential debate, first aired on TV, **Sep 26**

Presidential TV broadcast from the White House, first, **Oct 5**

Presidential Joke Day, **Aug 11**

Presidential pardon, Andrew Johnson, Civil War, **Dec 25**

Salad Week, **July**

Salem Witch Hunt, first arrests, **Feb 29**

Salk, Jonas, **b. Oct 28**

Salsa Month, **May**

San Francisco Cable Car Day*, **Aug 1**

San Francisco earthquake and fire, historical*, **Apr 18**

San Francisco earthquake, **Oct 17**

San Jacinto Day, **Apr 21**

Sandburg, Carl, **b. Jan 6**

Sandwich Day*, **Nov 3**

Sandwich Month*, **Aug**, 186

Santa's List Day*, **Dec 4**

Sarcastic Month, **Oct**

Saskatchewan Admission Day (Canada), **Sep 1**

Sauntering Day*, **June 19**

Sausage Pizza Day, **Oct 11**

Save a Spider Day, **Mar 28**

Save the Rhino Day, **May 1**

Save the Tiger Month*, **Sep**, 215

Save Your Vision Month, **Mar**

Savings Bank Day, **Dec 13**

Saxophone Day, **Nov 6**

Scarry, Richard, **b. June 5**

Scavenger Hunt Day*, **May 24**

School Breakfast Week, **Mar**

School Bus Safety Week, **Sep**

School Celebration, **Oct 12**

School Crossing Guard Week*, **Jan**, 18

School Internet Safety Week, **Sep**

School Librarian's Day, **Apr 4**

School Lunch Week, **Oct**

School Nurses Day, **May 12**

School Principals Day*, **Mar 3**

School Success Month*, **Sep**, 211

Schulz, Charles, **b. Nov 26**

Science Youth Day*, **Feb 11**

Scouting Month, **Feb, Oct**

Scrabble Day*, **Apr 13**

Scrapbook Day, **May 3**

Scrapbooking Month*, **May**, 116

Scrapple Day*, **Nov 9**

Sea Monkey Day, **Feb 15**

Sea Serpent Day, **Aug 6**

Seafood Month*, **June, Oct**, 238

Sears Tower opened*, **May 3**

Second atomic bomb dropped, **Aug 9**

Secret Pal Day*, **Jan 11**

Secretaries Day, **Apr**

Secretary Week, **Apr**

Self-Improvement Month, **Sep**

Self-Awareness Month, **Sep**

Send a Card to a Friend Day, **Feb 7**

Senior Citizens Day, **Aug 14**

Sense of Smell Day*, **Apr 26**

Serpent Day, **Feb 1**

Sesame Street TV show premiered, **Nov 10**

Seton, Elizabeth, **b. Jan 4**

Sewing machine invented, **Aug 12**

Sewing Machine patented, **Sep 10**

Sewing Month*, **Sep**, 211

Shakespeare, William, **b. Apr 23**

Shamu (the whale) introduced*, **Sep 26**

Share a Smile Day, **Mar 1**

Shark Awareness Day, **July 19**

Shavuot*, **May**, 120

Sherlock Holmes Birthday*, **Jan 6**

Shoe Week*, **May**, 119

Shopping cart introduced, **June 4**

Shortbread Day, **Jan 6**

Shovel Race Championships, **Feb 8**

Show and Tell Day at Work, **Jan 8**

Shredded Wheat introduced, **July 31**

Shrimp Scampi Day, **Apr 29**

Shrove Tuesday*, **Mar**, 68

Sibling Appreciation Day, **May 2**

Sibling Day, **Apr 10**

Sidewalk Egg-Frying Day, **July 4**

Siege of the Alamo ended, **Mar 5**

Sierra Club organized*, **May 28**

Sign Up for Camp Month, **Feb**

"Silent Night" first performed, **Dec 25**

Silly Putty debuted, **Mar 1**

Silverstein, Shel, **b. Sep 25**

Simplify Your Life Week, **Aug**

Sinatra, Frank, **b. Dec 12**

Singing telegram, first, **Feb 10**

Sing Out Day, International, **Apr 23**

Sisters Day, **Aug**

Sitting Bull, death anniversary of, **Dec 15**

Skeptics Day, **June 13**

Skin Cancer Awareness Month, **May**

Skyscraper Day, **Sep 3**

Skywriting first demonstrated*, **Dec 1**

Slavery abolished in U.S., **Apr 16**

Sleep Comfort Month, **Nov**

Sleep Day, **Apr 2**

Slow Down Day, **May 5**

Smallpox epidemic, **May 26**

Smallpox vaccine discovered*, **May 14**

Smile Day*, **Oct 5**

Smile Month, **Apr**

Smile Power Day, **July 10**

Smile Week*, **Mar**, 67

Smith Day*, **Jan 6**

Smith, Jedediah, **b. Jan 6**

Smith, Captain John, **b. Jan 6**

Smithsonian Institute founded, **Aug 10**

Smokey Bear*, **b. Aug 9**

S'mores Day*, **Aug 10**

Snack Food Month*, **Feb**, 42

Sneak Some Zucchini onto Your Neighbor's Porch Night, **Aug 8**

Sneaker Day, **Apr 23**

Snowman Burning Day, **Mar 20**

Social Security check, first, **Jan 31**

Socrates, **b. June 5**

Soft Pretzel Month*, **Apr**, 87

Softball invented, **Nov 24**

Someday We'll Laugh About This Week*, **Jan**, 18

Something Day*, **May 25**

Something on a Stick Day*, **Mar 28**

S.O.S. signal first used, **Aug 11**

Sound barrier broken, **Oct 14**

Soup Month*, **Jan**, 13

Sourest Day*, **Oct 25**

Sousa, John Phillip, **b. Nov 6**

South Carolina Admission Day, **May 23**

South Dakota Admission Day, **Nov 2**

Soviet Union dissolved, **Dec 8**

Soyfoods Month, **Apr**

Soyuz 4 launched, **Jan 14**

Space Day*, **May 4**

Space Shuttle *Columbia*, first launched*, **Apr 12**

Space Week*, **July**, 167

Space Week, World, **Oct**

Spaghetti Day, **Jan 4**

Spanish-American War began, **Apr 25**

Spanish-American War ended, **Dec 10**

Spay Day USA, **Feb 25**

Spay or Neuter Your Pet Month, **Feb**

Special Olympics Day, **July 20**

Spiderman first seen in publication, **Aug 1**

Spielberg, Stephen, **b. Dec 18**

Spinach Festival Day*, **Mar 26**

Split Pea Soup Week, **Nov**

Splurge Day, **June 18**

Spoil Your Dog Day, **Aug 10**

Spongecake Day*, **Aug 23**

Spooner's Day*, **July 22**

Sports Trivia Week, **Mar**

Spring Fever Week, **Mar**

Spruce Goose flight anniversary, **Nov 2**

Spumoni Day*, **Aug 21**

Sputnik 5 carried first living organisms into space, **Aug 19**

Sputnik first launched, **Oct 4**

Square Dance Day, **Nov 29**

Squirrel Appreciation Day*, **Jan 21**

St. Crispin's Day, **Oct 25**

St. Jude's Day, **Oct 28**

St. Laurent, Louis, **b. Feb 1**

St. Lucia Day*, **Dec 13**

St. Nicholas Day*, **Dec 6**

St. Patrick's Day*, **Mar 17**

St. Patrick's Day Parade, world's smallest*, **Mar 17**

Stamp-Collecting Month, **Oct**

Stamp collection, first*, **May 7**

Stand for Children Day, **June 1**

Stanley, Henry, found David Livingstone, **Nov 10**

Stanton, Elizabeth Cady, **b. Nov 12**

Tortilla Chip Day*, **Feb 24**
Totally Chipotle Day, **May 5**
Tourist, first, launched in space, **Apr 28**
Tournament of Roses Parade & Rose
  Bowl Game, **Jan**
Traffic light invented*, **Aug 5**
Trail Mix Day, **Aug 31**
Trails Day, National, **June 7**
Train robbery, first in the U.S.*, **Oct 6**
Transatlantic phoning, first*, **Jan 7**
Transcontinental flight, first, **Jan 25**
Transcontinental railroad (U.S.)
  completed*, **May 10**
Transistor invented, **Dec 23**
Transportation Month, **May**
Transportation Week, **May**
Traveled in space, first person*, **Apr 12**
Treaty of Paris ended the Revolutionary
  War, **Sep 3**
Treaty of Versailles signed ending WWI,
  June 28
Trivia Day*, **Jan 4**
Truck Driver Day, **Aug 12**
Trudeau, Pierre, **b. Oct 18**
Truman, Bess, **b. Feb 13**
Truman, Harry S., **b. May 8**
Trust Your Intuition Day, **May 10**
Tsunami in Asia, **Dec 26**
Tuba Day, **May 7**
Tuberculosis Day, World, **Mar 24**
Tubman, Harriet, **b. Mar 10**
Tuchman, Barbara, **b. Jan 30**
Tug of War Tournament Day*, **July 21**
Tulip Day, **May 13**
Turkey Lovers Month, **June**
Turner, John N., **b. June 7**
Turner, Nat, **b. Oct 2**
Turtle Day, **May 23**
Madame Tussaud, **b. Dec 7**
Tuxedos worn, first, **Oct 10**
TV broadcast, first, **July 1**
TV for children, first aired, **Aug 19**
TV-Turnoff Week*, **Apr**, 91
Twain, Mark, (Samuel Clemens),
  b. Nov 30
Tweed Day, **Apr 3**
Twelfth Night, **Jan 5**
Twinkies™ introduced, **Apr 6**
Twin-O-Rama*, **July**, 169
Typewriter Day*, **Jan 7**
Typewriter, first, patented*, **June 23**
UFO Day*, **June 24**
UFO Days, **July**
Ugly Truck Contest Day*, **July 20**
Umbrella Day*, **Feb 10**
Umbrella Month, **Mar**
UN Charter signed, **June 26**
UN Day for the Elimination of Racial
  Discrimination, **Mar 21**

UN General Assembly, first meeting of,
  Jan 10
UN International Youth Day, **Aug 12**
UN World Population Day*, **July 11**
Uncle Sam cartoon, first published,
  Mar 13
Uncle Sam legend created, **Sep 3**
Underdog Day, **Dec**
UNICEF Day, **Oct 31**
UNICEF established, **Dec 11**
UNICEF Month, **Oct**
Unique Names Day, **Mar 4**
United Nations Day, **Oct 24**
United Nations established, **Oct 24**
"United States of America" name adopted,
  Sep 9
Unlucky Day, **Dec 31**
Uno card game debuted, **Sep 25**
Upsy Daisy Day, **June 8**
Uranus (planet) discovered, **Mar 13**
U.S. Air Force Academy established,
  Mar 31
U.S. Air Force established, **Aug 1**
U.S. Army established, **June 14**
U.S. Census, first*, **Mar 1**
U.S. Coast Guard established, **Aug 4**
U.S. Congress, first meeting, **Mar 4**
U.S. Constitution final draft signed,
  Sep 17
U.S. Constitution went into effect*, **Mar 4**
U.S. Copyright law went into effect,
  May 31
U.S. Department of Homeland Security
  formed, **Nov 25**
U.S. income tax enacted, **Aug 2**
U.S. Independence Day*, **July 4**
U.S. Interstate Highway System instituted,
  June 29
U.S. Marine Corps Day, **Nov 10**
U.S. military created, **Sep 29**
U.S. Mint created*, **Apr 2**
U.S. Navy established, **Oct 13**
U.S. paper money, first*, **Mar 10**
U.S. passport issued, first, **July 8**
U.S. Patent Office established, **July 31**
U.S. Post Office established, **Sep 22**
U.S. Postage stamps first issued, **July 1**
U.S. Postal Service began, **July 26**
U.S. Presidential Inauguration Day*,
  Jan 20
U.S. presidential photograph, first, **Feb 14**
U.S. Stock Market crashed, **Oct 29**
U.S. Supreme Court ruling on 2000
  election, **Dec 12**
U.S. Treasury Department established*,
  Sep 2
USO formed, **Feb 4**
USS Constitution launched*, **Oct 21**
USS Princeton exploded, **Feb 28**

USSR established, **Dec 30**
USSR invaded Afghanistan, **Dec 25**
Utah Admission Day, **Jan 4**
Vacation Month*, **Aug**, 189
Vaccine for polio developed, **Apr 12**
Valentine's Day*, **Feb 14**
Value Friendship Day, **Feb 13**
Van Buren, Martin, **b. Dec 5**
Van Gogh, Vincent, **b. Mar 30**
Vanilla Cupcake Day, **Nov 11**
Vanilla Ice-Cream Day, **July 23**
Vanilla Milkshake Day, **Jan 20**
VCR, introduction of, **June 7**
Vegetarian Food Day, **July 11**
Vegetarian Month*, **Oct**, 239
Verne, Jules*, **b. Feb 8**
Verranzano Day, **Apr 17**
Vespucci, Amerigo, **b. Mar 9**
Veterans Day, **Nov 11**
Veterinary Week, **Aug**
Victoria Day (Canada)*, **May 22**
Video Game Week, **Aug**
Video Games day, **Sep 12**
Video recording on magnetic tape, first,
  Sep 6
Vietnam Peace Agreement, **Jan 27**
Vietnam Peace Treaty, **Mar 1**
Vietnam Veteran's Day, **Mar 29**
Vietnam Veteran's Memorial unveiled,
  Nov 9
Vinegar Day*, **Aug 16**
Violins Day, **Dec 13**
Virginia Admission Day, **June 25**
Viking I landed on Mars, **July 20**
Virus Appreciation day, **Oct 3**
Visit the Zoo Day, **Dec 27**
Visit Your Relatives Day, **May 18**
Vitamin C discovered*, **Mar 16**
V-J Day, **Sep 2**
Volunteer Blood Donor Month*, **Jan**, 16
Volunteer Day, **Dec 5**
Volunteer Fireman's Day, **Jan 10**
Volunteer Recognition Day, **Apr 20**
Volunteer Week*, **Apr**, 91
Volunteers of America Week, **Mar**
Voting age lowered to 18, **June 22**
Waffle Day*, **Mar 25**
Waffle iron patented, **Aug 24**
Waffle Week*, **Aug**, 191
Wagon train, first to reach California,
  Nov 4
Waitresses/Waiters Day, **May 21**
Walk Around Things Day*, **Apr 4**
Walk Day*, **Apr 30**
Walk in space, first, **Mar 18**
Walt Disney TV show premiered*, **Oct 27**
War of 1812 began, **June 18**
War of 1812 ended by the Treaty of
  Ghent, **Dec 24**

318